RELIGION AND PUBLIC MEMORY

CHRISTIAN LEE NOVETZKE

RELIGION AND PUBLIC MEMORY

A Cultural History of Saint Namdev in India

COLUMBIA UNIVERSITY PRESS   NEW YORK

Columbia University Press
Publishers Since 1893
New York Chichester, West Sussex
Copyright © 2008 Columbia University Press

Library of Congress Cataloging-in-Publication Data

Novetzke, Christian Lee, 1969–
  Religion and public memory : a cultural history of Saint Namdev in India /
Christian Lee Novetzke.
      p. cm.
  Includes bibliographical references and index.
  ISBN 978-0-231-14184-0 (cloth : alk. paper)—ISBN 978-0-231-51256-5 (e-book)
  1. Namadeva, 1270–1350—Influence.   2. Hinduism and culture—India—
Maharashtra.   3. Bhakti.   I. Title.

PK2418.N23Z764   2008
691.46'11—dc22

                                                    2008007050

Columbia University Press books are printed on permanent
and durable acid-free paper.
This book is printed on paper with recycled content.
Printed in the United States of America
c 10 9 8 7 6 5 4 3 2 1

For S, S, and S

and

In Memory of Vithal Parashuram "Tatya" Paranjape
(1919–2007)

CONTENTS

ILLUSTRATIONS

PREFACE: THE SHAPE OF THE BOOK

THIS BOOK is about how a religious figure of fourteenth-century India has been remembered over seven centuries, through multiple media, including performance, writing, and film. The figure is Namdev, a *sant* important to Hindus and Sikhs in central, western, and northern India. The book focuses primarily on the cultural history of Namdev's legacy in the area coterminous with modern-day Maharashtra. The theoretical rubrics used to understand this long tradition of recollection through multiple media are encompassed by the term "public memory" and are derived from both the study of "publics" of various kinds and the study of memory, particularly in ways similar to what Jan Assmann has call "mnemo-history" or the "history of cultural memory."[1] In the book I argue that the ubiquitous religiosocial category of *bhakti*, or "devotion," in India that surrounds Namdev is best understood neither as a "*bhakti* movement" nor "personal devotion" but, rather, as an ongoing effort to construct publics of belief, maintained through intricate systems of memory. The book endeavors to uncover both the practices of memory that surround Namdev and the publics that maintain, and are sustained by, that memory.

I have divided the book into two parts that address different but interconnected aspects of Namdev's Marathi public memory. The first three chapters are organized primarily around issues of practice, while the remaining four chapters endeavor to understand Namdev's Maharashtrian legacy in historical terms by asking questions about the kinds of publics that would have engaged with Namdev's memory. Throughout I invoke the major theme of how public memory is constructed as an explicit component of *bhakti*. Several secondary themes also recur, such as questions surrounding the nature of authorship in various practices and times. The book is designed to ask and answer questions about how Namdev's legacy in the history of the Marathi-speaking region maintains itself over centuries, what issues it takes up or discards, and why we find a link between the devotional sentiments of *bhakti* and the public realm of memory.

Chapter 1 begins by observing the search for the "historical" Namdev and how this figure appears in modern Marathi scholarship. This gives the reader a sense of how Namdev is received in the modern period as a real character from the past, and how his character is presented to various publics, those of scholarship and those of belief (which often overlap). I also hope to show the spaces where a social scientific concern for evidence meets the archive of religious materials. Like the historical search for the identities of saints and prophets the world over, this is an important academic endeavor, but in many ways remains a minor aspect of the lived tradition that surrounds Namdev in Maharashtra just as the search for the "historical" Jesus is not of concern to most Christians. Far more central to how Namdev is remembered is hagiography, the sacred biography of a miraculous life. As a guide through our survey of this public memory in this chapter we call on the work of the doyen of Marathi hagiography, the eighteenth-century *kirtan* performer and author Mahipati, who had largely set the definitive narratives for the lives of the Marathi *sants*. His principal work, the *Bhaktavijay* (Victory of the Bhaktas), not only details Namdev's life, and that of his contemporaries, but significantly relies on work attributed to Namdev in order to tell the lives of the early *sants*. Mahipati's position as the most authoritative source for Marathi hagiography, and in particular of the Varkari *sants*, makes him an ideal escort through the broad public remembrance of Namdev in Marathi. The practice highlighted here is thus of hagiographical structure and the ways in which the character of a *sant* is tied to stories of his or her life. However, I also point out what Mahipati omits: stories that were current in his time but judiciously excised from his accounts. Thus we observe the larger process of presenting a *sant* in a particular way, reflecting the desires of an audience and the proclivities of an individual storyteller to address, and perhaps craft, his or her public of reception.

In chapter 2, I depart from the usual format for studying devotional figures in South Asia, especially those with a legacy of songs or compositions surrounding their names. Rather than move immediately to textual sources, I approach, through ethnography and a close reading of particular songs, the performance tradition that lies at the heart of the Namdev tradition in Marathi, the *kirtan*. From chapter 1, the reader might observe how Namdev's miraculous biography is shot through with references to the power of *kirtan*, yet is conspicuously silent on the role of writing. Chapter 2 engages this apparent lacuna by demonstrating first the importance of *kirtan* in songs attributed to Namdev and in his hagiography and second the primary position of Namdev in the genealogy of the practice of *kirtan* from the fourteenth century to this day. I also show how literacy and writing are demoted to a lesser form of remembrance. Through an explanation of the parts that make up a *kirtan* performance, and the relationship of performance to its genealogical sources of songs, stories, and practices, I present a notion of "corporate authorship" whereby authorship is never a solitary site for authority, but rather involves several participants, especially the live performer, the purported author of the songs used in performance, and the *sant* who originated the particular performance art itself, Namdev.

With this notion of the centrality of performance within Namdev's remembrance, and the corporate character of authorship as it functions there, in chapter 3 I look to the literary remnant of the Marathi Namdev tradition. In this chapter, I demonstrate how *kirtan*, along with Namdev's public memory, conditions the uses of writing within manuscripts that contain his songs. We see stark contrasts in how Namdev's verses are recorded when set against those of other *sant*s, such as Jnandev and Tukaram. This provides an opportunity to construct a more nuanced view of how writing functions in the Namdev Marathi tradition, supplying a kind of ethno-history of textuality within the *sant*'s legacy. Despite the avowed nonliterate character of the Namdev Marathi tradition, writing remains our principal key to historical questions, which makes it all the more imperative to understand how a nonliterate *sant* and the songs associated with him are portrayed within a host of written records. Thus the practices of performance and writing, of orality and literacy, are observed together as they interact over centuries to form the textual record of this Marathi *sant*. Chapters 2 and 3 are therefore interrelated, parts of one another, in the pursuit of how public memory is sustained at the juncture of writing and oral performance, but in a tradition that privileges the oral-performative over the written.

In chapter 4 I turn the emphasis of the book toward the historical study of the possible publics to which Namdev was vital. This chapter takes on a perennial problem in the study of devotional figures, the apparent plethora of later composers who amend the attributed corpus of an earlier *sant*. The bane of text critics, this accretion over time of songs and stories associated with a *sant* is often considered a kind of historical detritus that must be removed from the core legacy of songs of the "original author." In the case of Namdev's Maharashtrian legacy, we see three or more figures appear, beginning in the sixteenth century, who use a portion of Namdev's ideography or *bhaṇita*, the title "Nama," to sign songs of their own composition. These songs seem to have been purposefully composed to enter in the stream of the earlier Namdev's public memory: the songs take up themes and subjects associated with the first Namdev, and mimic points of style and reference; and the ideographs chosen by these later authors invoke aspects of the former Namdev's remembrance, borrowing key phrases from his songs or aspects of his received biography into their own ideographs. I describe this process as a kind of authorial anamnesis, a mnemonic system based on repetition, imitation, and similarity. However, we also see how these later authors distinguish themselves from the first Namdev, primarily through an assertion of their own sovereign authorship surrounding other texts. Given this interplay between mimesis and distinction, chapter 4 endeavors to understand how these later "Namas" deliberately contributed to Namdev's public memory in a way that further agitates a normative notion of the sole author, and how this is a project of historical memory, on the one hand, and encoded maintenance, on the other.

Chapter 5 recalls a story from certain, sometimes marginal, Marathi biographical sources that tell us Namdev was a robber and a murderer in his youth, a story many of his Marathi followers consider apocryphal. I do not argue for the historical veracity of this narrative (and have found no historical evidence to support the claim that Namdev was a robber or murderer) but, rather, observe how, when, and to whom it was told—circumscribing the shape of the story's likely public—and speculate on why it held particular currency in the eighteenth century in the Marathi Deccan region. Building on the characterization of Namdev as a "social bandit," to borrow Hobsbawm's term, I survey how a similar story arises in which Namdev is set in confrontation with a figure of temporal authority, usually a sultan.[2] In these encounters, he betters his political superiors through his religious devotion, and in one case, with violent resistance as well. Continuing an argument set out by David Lorenzen on the uses of the "good demon" Prahlad in northern Indian devotionalism, I suggest that both stories—Namdev as robber and as interlocutor with a sultan—spoke to publics in the eighteenth century who had suffered war, famine, and economic oppression under various feudal and dynastic reigns.[3] I connect these stories with pilgrimage networks and cycles of military conscription to suggest that the performance of the narratives would have held the attention of audiences who could relate to the situations into which Namdev had been projected. Therefore, I argue the narratives serve historiographic purposes in that they purport to tell true stories of the past, interpreted and made relevant in the language of the historical present—the eighteenth century, in this case—and consumed primarily by a subaltern public.

Chapter 6 begins by observing how the legend of Namdev as a robber, current (though disputed) in eighteenth-century Marathi circles, became a liability to the efforts of some of Namdev's followers to write him into the proto-history of the Indian nation. We witness attempts to recuperate an image of a Maharashtrian Namdev who was not a robber or murderer, but was a figure who challenged temporal political might in the name of "humanism" and secularism. In the public spheres of Hindi, Marathi, and English in the late nineteenth- and twentieth-centuries, Namdev is considered a progenitor of the Indian nation, a case made with resort to a number of biographical details. In these nationalist narratives, his confrontations with sultans and Brahmins account for his rejection of prejudice based on class, religion, or caste. His peregrinations through the subcontinent, evident in biography, in his presence in multiple traditions, and in sites of memory scattered throughout India, are said to attest to his early circumscription of the yet-to-be-formed Indian nation, tapping the imagination of *the* Indian public as a geographically, linguistically, and religiously diverse region that nonetheless is a social unity. The broad linguistic range of the songs attributed to him, and in particular the notion of a Hindi speaker whose mother-tongue is not Hindi, are said to represent his desire for cultural cohesion. The chapter concludes with a reflection on the interaction of nations and religions, and in particular the way Namdev comes to mark a post-Nehruvian "Hindu secularism," which nevertheless still stands in opposition to the religious nationalism of the Hindu Right.

In chapter 7 I recall two films that commemorate Namdev's public memory, both entitled simply *Sant Namdev*. By engaging these two films in the context of the long history detailed in the preceding chapters, the reader has an opportunity to observe how centuries of public memory are presented in this modern medium, and how a new set of social and economic circumstances are addressed by marshalling this public memory. The first film was made in Marathi in 1949 by Keshav Talpade and was shot in black and white. Although produced on the heels of independence, the film concerns itself almost entirely with Namdev's Marathi public legacy, giving only brief reference to Namdev's pan-Indian influence, the sphere one might expect a "postcolonial" film to engage. The film also emphasizes the association between Namdev's *bhakti,* his public memory, and the experience of economic and caste-based oppression. I position this film in the context of the anti-Brahmin sentiment that developed in the late nineteenth century and reached a zenith in Maharashtra following the assassination of M. K. Gandhi in January 1948.

The second film, shot in 1991 in color, was made by Yeshwant Pethkar. The film uses both Marathi and Hindi in its dialogue, though it is properly considered a "Marathi" film. This *Sant Namdev* was made in a way that was meant to encapsulate the broad reach of Namdev, yet hit upon the specific features of his legacy that have endured through the centuries. Financed by Namdev devotees throughout India, the film adjudicates his roles in Maharashtrian and in North Indian religious life, providing a logical narrative to connect the various elements of his hagiography, and even seeking to grapple substantially, through suggestion, with the legend of Namdev's robber days. Throughout the film the viewer is made to understand that Namdev was a performer of *kirtan,* a *bhakta* of Vitthal, and a unifier of Indian religious and cultural life. The film also attests to the vivacious legacy of Namdev's public memory, so rich in content that there appears a never-ceasing demand that his remembrance be articulated anew. Unlike its predecessor, this film makes explicit connections between Namdev and a clear national imagination.

The book concludes by rehearsing some of its major themes and situating these themes within possible future avenues of study. The conclusion reinforces the way the shape of the book tracks Namdev's memory in Maharashtra, first highlighting practices then historical episodes crucial in this process of remembrance. I also reflect on the much larger project of understanding the relationship between history and religion within ever widening circles, from Namdev's spheres of public memory, to postcolonial India, to modernity at large.

In an effort to make this book more accessible to nonspecialists, while maintaining linguistic exactitude for the specialist, I provide diacritical marks only for the first instance of a non-English word of Indian origin. All subsequent appearances of a word occur without diacritical marks. For instance, the first appearance of a word would appear as *kīrtan* and thereafter as *kirtan.* In some cases, the first letters of the word change, as in the first appearance of the word *śiṁpī* and subsequent appearances as *shimpi.* I have maintained this convention for common nouns and proper nouns denoting religious or other communities, however, I have retained the diacritics throughout for the titles of texts. I have not used diacriticals for the names of individuals, languages, places, or other words of non-English origin that have a commonly accepted English spelling. A glossary appears at the end of the book that provides definitions for all commonly used nouns as well as the nouns' diacritical notations. In some cases in the text, I have given original text in Marathi and Hindi with diacritics. In these cases, because they are singular instances, I have not provided glossary definitions as the word or phrase is defined in relation to the preceding translation.

Finally, a statement must be made about the content of this book. The violence, litigation, and censorship that followed the release of James Laine's book *Shivaji: Hindu King in Islamic India* in 2003 has occasioned an atmosphere of academic and public anxiety in Maharashtra (and elsewhere) over any work about any revered figure in Maharashtrian cultural or political life. I want to state clearly my position on several issues that are important to those who revere Namdev. Let me affirm emphatically that I do not assert any belief that Namdev was a thief or murderer at any point during his life. I reference the tale, which is widely known, and refer readers to excellent work, which I have cited in this book, that refutes all such claims about Namdev's life. My work engages the ways in which Namdev has been remembered in Maharashtra, and this story is part of this remembrance. In addition, I discuss the idea that many figures composed in Namdev's name over the years, an idea expressed in at least a century of scholarship in Marathi. But I do not make any claim about which songs are attributed to which figure, nor do I state the belief that any single song attributed to Namdev is not composed by Namdev of the fourteenth century. I cite scholarship and offer conjecture, but make no truth claims whatsoever on this issue.

Should anyone, for whatever reason, find in this book anything insulting to the memory of Namdev, or anyone else, it will have been contrary to my intentions. I have profound respect for the legacy of this extraordinary figure and for Namdev's followers throughout India. I have benefited from their generosity, openness, and warmth during my research. Whatever the historical and biographical arguments that surround Namdev, there can be no doubt that a charismatic figure lived in the early part of the second millennium, and this figure's legacy is richly, and deservedly, remembered today. Everything in this book that is not cited or explicitly marked out is my opinion alone. No one other than me should be held accountable for any statements in this book and any reactions, political or otherwise, arising from its publication.

ACKNOWLEDGMENTS

The author is the principle of thrift in the proliferation of meaning.
—MICHEL FOUCAULT

FOUCAULT POINTED out in 1969 that authors are just the tip of the iceberg. The name of a book's composer obscures the countless individuals, institutions, and processes that accumulate in the cultural product marked by an author's name as his or her "work." I attempt here to acknowledge and thank all the individuals and institutions that have helped this book see the light of day, but I will certainly fail to account for them all. Ultimately, I am simply thankful for the privilege of my role as a principle of thrift.

I have benefited from the generosity of several granting agencies, including the Jacob K. Javits Program at the Department of Education, the Social Science Research Council, and the American Institute of Indian Studies. At the University of Pennsylvania, this work was supported by funds from the University Research Foundation and the Penn Humanities Forum.

I would like to thank several journals and organizations for permission to use material here. For permission to use images, I thank Oxford University Press (UK); M. G. Dhadphale and the Bhandarkar Oriental Research Institute; S. K. Sasidharan and the National Film Archives of India; the Indian Department of Posts; and Anna Schultz. For permission to reprint my previously published materials, I thank the University of Chicago Press and the editors of the *History of Religions* for permission to reprint portions of "Divining an Author: The Idea of Authorship in an Indian Religious

Tradition," *History of Religions* 42:3 (February 2003):213–242; Routledge Press at the Taylor and Francis Group for permission to use portions from "Memory," in G. Thursby and S. Mitthal, ed., *Studying Hinduism: Key Concepts and Methods*(New York: Routledge, 2007); and Springer (NY) for permission to use portions of "Bhakti and Its Public," forthcoming in the *International Journal of Hindu Studies.*

Winand Callewaert provided vital manuscript materials to me, including his own research on Namdev's Marathi legacy. The staff of the American Institute of Indian Studies, in the US, Delhi, and Pune, and especially Madhav Bhandare and Purnima Mehta, have always shown great generosity and kindness. I have also valued the help and friendship of Prashant Kothadia, Uttara Jadhav, and Pravin Kasote. I have appreciated access to materials granted by the Bhandarkar Oriental Research Institute, Deccan College, and Pune University. I have presented aspects of this work in a number of venues, such as the Religious Studies Colloquium, the South Asia Graduate Colloquium, and a conference on Indian Cinema at the University of Pennsylvania; the annual meetings of the American Academy of Religion, the Association for Asian Studies, the South Asia Conference at the University of Wisconsin, Madison, and the Maharashtra Studies Group; and the International Conference on Indic Religions in Delhi, the conference "On Knowledge and Its Objects in South Asia" at Columbia University, and a conference on the life and work of Sane Guruji in Pune in 2003. In all cases I received helpful feedback from fellow panelists and engaged audience members. Jack Hawley assigned a draft of this book to his seminar at Columbia University in November 2006 and I am thankful to him and his students for their excellent criticism. I have also had the great fortune to teach outstanding graduate and undergraduate students during my four and a half years teaching at the University of Pennsylvania; I thank them for many cooperative learning opportunities. My colleagues at the University of Pennsylvania, and the vibrant intellectual environment they have sustained there, served as a constant benchmark for my work and source of academic and personal sustenance; I offer them all my fond appreciation.

In the United States, India, and Europe, many individuals have heard or read portions of this book, and have offered generous criticism and advice, including (in alphabetical order): Janaki Bakhale, Aditya Behl, Maxine Berntsen, Graham Bond, Jeff Brackett, Winand Callewaert, John Carman, Elizabeth Castelli, Gayatri Chatterjee, Indrani Chatterjee, Whitney Cox, Steve Dunning, Dusan Deak, Madhuri Deshmukh, Prachi Deshpande, Purnima Dhavan, Wendy Doniger, Diana Eck, William Elison, Philip Engblom, Jason

Fuller, Surendra Gambhir, Vijay Gambhir, Pranoti Gangulee, Sumit Ganguly, Sumit Guha, Kathryn Hansen, Linda Hess, Dan Jasper, Priya Joshi, Devesh Kapur, Suvir Kaul, Jon Keune, Elizabeth Kolsky, Meera Kosambi, Hariharan Krishnan, Omar Kutty, Jim Laine, Spencer Leonard, Wendy Steiner, Steven Lindquist, Ania Loomba, David Lorenzen, Tim Lubin, David Ludden, Philip Lutgendorf, Gurinder Singh Mann, Ann Matter, William Mazzarella, Rachel McDermott, Mary McGee, Michael Meister, Allyn Miner, Farina Mir, Lisa Mitchell, Ann Murphy, David Nelson, John Nemec, Gail Omvedt, Lisa Owen, Laurie Patton, Heidi Pauwels, Kelly Pemberton, Indira Peterson, Vijay Pinch, Andrea Pinkney, Shelly Pollock, Susan Prill, Fran Pritchett, Teena Purohit, Eliot Ratzman, Ramnarayan Rawat, Uzma Rizvi, Andy Rotman, Adheesh Sathaye, Lee Schlesinger, Anna Schultz, Martha Selby, Shana Sippy, Svati Shah, Gordon Stewart, Gary Tubb, Ananya Vajpeyi, Guy Welbon, Eleanor Zelliot, and Angela Zito.

I would like to single out Anne Feldhaus, who has buoyed my scholarship through unwavering support and precise criticism at important junctures, and who has provided scholarly exemplars to me through her own unparalleled work on Maharashtra; and Nicholas Dirks, who first inspired my interest in ethnohistory and in critical questions about the relationship between history and religion, and who has always remained supportive. And I want to direct particular acknowledgment to Jack Hawley for his encouragement of my work over the years as a teacher, advisor, mentor, and friend. For me he is a model scholar, who skillfully intertwines ethnography, literary criticism, and history, and remains a deeply humane and inspiring intellectual.

Some names are intentionally absent from the list above, primarily friends and colleagues in Maharashtra. Many of these unnamed people provided the most crucial assistance and guidance I received as I worked on this project. As the end of the preface to this book suggests, the recent political troubles, and personal suffering, caused by the reprehensible reactions surrounding the release of James Laine's book in India in 2003 have elicited understandable wariness among my friends and colleagues about being mentioned in connection with scholarship on Maharashtrian figures. For this reason, some of my friends and colleagues have explicitly requested that their names be withheld. I have also omitted the names of those I was unable to contact before publication, in order to err on the side of caution. It is a great sadness that I cannot see the names of people I have depended upon so extensively be properly honored here in print. I look forward to the pleasure of conveying my deep appreciation to each of them in person.

My thanks to Wendy Lochner for unflagging editorial support, to Christine Mortlock for her patience and guidance, to Debra E. Soled for excellent editorial advice, and to the four anonymous reviewers who read my manuscript for Columbia University Press. I also want to thank Rivka Israel for her editorial acumen and keen critical eye. For cover design suggestions, I thank my old friend Martin Curley of Solvent Design.

My friends, both in and outside the academy, have provided a foundation of happiness and stability through years of peregrinations through Minneapolis, Cambridge, New York, Berkeley, Austin, Philadelphia, Pune, Bombay, Madras, and Delhi. I am fortunate to have them in my life. My family has grown over the years, from Sioux Falls and Cincinnati to Pune and Mumbai, and all have supported this project and shown enthusiasm for the work. I am deeply thankful for my good fortune to be sustained by them. I express, in a most understated way, my thanks to my partner, Sunila Kale, who cared for me and this book, even while writing her own, and who has made life immeasurably more fulfilling than I had imagined it could be. And my children, Sahil and Siyona, the sum of all good things, I thank for simply existing.

Philadelphia, Pennsylvania

RELIGION AND PUBLIC MEMORY

Introduction

NAMDEV IS believed to have been born into a low-caste, impoverished family of tailors in the Marathi-speaking region of the Deccan in the latter part of the thirteenth century. He is said to have lived the life of an ardent devotee, a religious composer, and singer of great wisdom, therefore attaining, perhaps in his lifetime, the designation of a *sant*.[1] Sant Namdev, sometimes referred to as Nama, is regarded as having grown up near the preeminent Maharashtrian pilgrimage center Pandharpur, the geographical and spiritual center of the Varkari theistic community. The Varkaris are *vaiṣṇava*, Hindu worshippers of Vishnu or Krishna, who venerate the deity Vitthal (Viṭhṭhal). Namdev is considered a foundational figure of the Varkari religious sect, which forms the largest religious tradition in the immediate region, as well as one of the oldest. This book is a cultural history of Namdev's public memory, imagined over the past seven hundred years by his devotees, admirers, detractors, and others who applied his memory in the service of some social goal.

Namdev's influence spread well beyond the linguistic provinces of present-day Maharashtra.[2] He is a key figure in Maharashtra as well as central, western, and northern India, and virtually ubiquitous in the Hindu and Sikh religious-literary traditions of these regions from the fifteenth century to the present, a period spanning Sultanate, Mughal, Maratha, and British rule, as well as postindependence India. His songs are remembered in literary sources and in primarily oral performance traditions in the regions of present-day Maharashtra, Rajasthan, Gujarat, and throughout central and northern India, especially in Punjab. He is one of the first non-Sikh figures canonized in the *Guru Granth Sahib,* the devotional-textual core of Sikhism. Namdev is central to the hagiographical traditions of the Varkaris, Nāthas, Dādū Panthīs, Kabīr Panthīs, and Sikhs. In all these religious and literary fields, his songs are prevalent. In the modern period, Namdev is a regular character in the public spheres of Marathi and Hindi, and in India at large, where his identity exists in a state of flux between his regional associations in places like Maharashtra and Punjab, and his pan-Indian profile, preserved in popular writing about the protohistory of the Indian nation. Maharashtrian and Indian, provincial and cosmopolitan, Namdev spans realms of imagined communities and has become integral to the very process of imagining those realms into existence. In this book, however, the pan-Indian view of Namdev must sit in the background of formulations in Maharashtra of Namdev's remembrance from the seventeenth century onward; this latter period frames the last three chapters, particularly the penultimate chapter, on nationalism, and the final chapter, on film. Therefore, in order to supply the reader with a manageable historical context and to approximate the very "Maharashtrianness" of Namdev as he has been received for centuries in India, I confine this study to Namdev as a feature of Maharashtrian public memory.

Given his wide reach in India, and his deep influence particularly in Maharashtra, Namdev's legacy in Maharashtra can be approached as a lens through which to view religion and public memory within one important linguistic and cultural region in India and thus stand as an empirical example of the pan-Indian phenomenon of regionalized religious practice and history. The locus of this regional cultural memory is the idea of *bhakti,* which I discuss in more detail below, but which might be temporarily defined as "devotionalism" formed in social contexts. Through an in-depth study of Namdev's Maharashtrian public remembrance, I argue that *bhakti* in this context can be viewed as a form of public memory, the preservation of a past full of sentiment and historical sense maintained by religious communities. Whereas other studies of *bhakti* figures have highlighted the productions of practice—literature, biography, performance, and festivals, for example—I focus on the process by which *bhakti* both historicizes moments and itself becomes historicized and inserted into historical contexts. I do this by investigating literary traces, biographical sources, performance arts, and modes of remembrance. My intention is to see how these activities constitute a practice that creates a dialogue between the past and the present and how this dialogue in turn constructs publics of reception in time. A study of how *bhakti* traditions reconstitute the past is missing in the larger body of literature that investigates this subject, yet a consciousness of the past and its portrayal is as much a part of *bhakti* in South Asia as is its "theology," its possibilities for understanding divinity, the sacred self, and the cosmos. While other studies may have explored the latter, I turn to the former, to the historical sense of this particular religious tradition, in the hope that in its specifics this study of Namdev's Maharashtrian legacy might point to possibilities in Indian religious and cultural history more generally.

The key ideas that make up this book deserve specific attention at the outset. These interlocking aspects are examined in turn: *bhakti,* public, and memory. But let me begin with the figure at the intersection of these three cultural forms, the *sant* Namdev.

NAMDEV

In almost all studies of Namdev, we find the common, and likely, assumption that we are talking about someone who lived at some point in history and who composed songs. This is important to recall: Namdev's tradition is a living one in Maharashtra and outside this linguistic region, and it invokes a once-living, certainly historical being at its social and literary center. Opinions differ about the details of Namdev's life, but I have yet to encounter a work in Marathi, English, or Hindi that suggests Namdev is a purely fictional character, the product of social forces and fantasies and nothing more. Indeed Namdev is so regularly treated as one treats a modern author, as a historical figure whose desires and biography influenced his literary production, that we find a paucity of studies exploring what happened after the attributed years of his life. How has Namdev's remembrance been maintained over centuries? What issues along the way have shaped or guided the reception of Namdev in our present, or any other historical moment? This study then is not about uncovering the historical Namdev; I am inclined to believe that such a man did exist and that the aura of his charisma remains the fulcrum of his public memory. Instead, this book examines how Namdev's life and literary production have been incorporated into the way people collectively remember this great figure of Marathi and north Indian regional religious and literary history. In this study, "Namdev" marks an idea as well as a historical person, but my subject is nonetheless the *idea* of Namdev and the historical maintenance of his memory.

At least by the sixteenth century, and probably earlier, a general image of Namdev began to form in the songs and biographies of the many traditions in India that remember him. Thus Namdev is usually remembered as having been from among the lowest strata of *varṇa*-caste society, that of the *śūdra*, though many scholars and devotees insist that Namdev's *varna* was *kṣatriya*, or "warrior," as seen below and in chapter 5. His *jāti*-caste title was *śimpī*, meaning "tailor," and about his *jati* there is no dispute. Eschewing the traditional occupation of a tailor, he is said to have chosen the life of a singer, traveler, and performer. In songs attributed to him and in hagiography, Namdev is represented as having rejected caste hierarchies, being of a low caste himself. Like many other devotional figures of India, Namdev was someone positioned outside societal norms, who repudiated the quotidian political economy of everyday life in favor of an all-consuming engagement with his deity. His presumed struggle against caste prejudice, as his followers recall, set him at odds with Brahminical orthodoxy, as well as the temporal authority of kings and sultans.

Though Namdev is believed to have been born in Maharashtra, and to have spoken Marathi as his mother-tongue, thousands of songs in several north Indian languages are attributed to him, and he is a significant fixture in the *bhakti* public memory of northern India. Popular culture recalls Namdev's cosmopolitan appeal through the legend of his pan-Indian travels. According to Sikh historiography, for example, Namdev lived a majority of his life in Punjab, in the village of Ghuman, where Namdev figures prominently in local memory, both textual and architectural. A parallel remembrance in Punjab, centered in the area of Bassi Pathana, notes that Namdev visited Punjab only briefly and spent most of his life in, and indeed died in, Pandharpur, Maharashtra. Thus even in one linguistic region of India, Punjab, Namdev presents an indeterminate diversity. Likewise, memorials and temples are dedicated to Namdev throughout central, western, and northern India, and none conform to any unified historical consensus. In a sense, the figure of Namdev has served as a biographical device of translation, a means of crossing linguistic and culture boundaries, as he is remembered in biography and as his songs attest in a variety of early "Hindi" dialects. Although Namdev is recalled primarily as a historical figure, he can provide in a secondary capacity a mode of articulation between different cultural and linguistic spheres. His biography and his songs link many cultures, languages, literatures, and histories. During several years of fieldwork on this project in India, both in and outside Maharashtra (as well as in the United States), it seemed as if every Indian (Sikh, Hindu, or Muslim) to whom I disclosed the nature of my work knew about Namdev and, moreover, knew a story about him that they could tell with confidence. Many people knew of famous recordings of Namdev's songs by Marathi singers, such as Bhimsen Joshi or Lata Mangeshkar, but almost all could tell a story from Namdev's received biography. Namdev's life, perhaps even more than his attributed verses, served to form the widest base for his public memory and appeared to enforce, almost dogmatically, a heterogeneity.

Despite this diversity, there is some core to "Namdev" as an idea, at least as a biographical subject. Namdev's pan-Indian cosmopolitan biography, and multilingual corpus of songs, presents a deeply encoded Maharashtrian ethnicity attributed to the *sant*. The songs ascribed to him throughout India and the biographies that remember him outside Maharashtra all mark his regional identity; it is vital that Namdev be a native Marathi speaker, a son of Maharashtrian soil, and this especially so outside Maharashtrian contexts. His songs in the *Guru Granth Sahib* contain some of the vocabulary and grammar of Marathi, though they are clearly preserved in a dialect of Hindi. Similarly, in the *Guru Granth Sahib* and in other north Indian sources, Namdev's deity is often referred to as Vitthal or a derivation of that name (Bitthula, for example), and his home is Pandharpur. One gets the sense that Namdev's being of Marathi-speaking origin is essential to his pan-Indian remembrance. Furthermore, in Marathi hagiography and popular culture, Namdev as an itinerant links the Varkari tradition to figures like Kabir and Surdas (sixteenth century), especially in the work of Mahipati in the eighteenth century. Namdev's presence outside Marathi contexts is a means of inserting Maharashtra into larger, and eventually national, contexts, and similarly his Maharashtrian character in non-Maharashtrian contexts recalls his received biography.

Given Namdev's broad reach, it is perhaps a surprise that there is no designation for the multiple legacies that surround his name in Maharashtrian environments or anywhere else in India. Terms in English and Indian languages have been used at various times to refer to "Namdev followers," such as by caste (*jati*, that is, *shimpi* in Marathi or *chīpī* in Hindi), class/tribe (*kula*), practice (*dharma*), sect (*panth*), society (*samāj*), and faith (*bhāv*), yet none of these designations carries with it a sense of a cohesive long-term social community oriented around Namdev; rather, they supply one identification among others for individuals. In other words, a Namdev follower may identify primarily as a Dadu Panthi, Kabir Panthi, Varkari, Sikh, or simply a "Hindu," but not as a "Nāmdev Panthī"—an association with Namdev is almost never offered in response to queries that plot identity. Namdev is inserted into categories that have their own wide reach, such as the designation of pan-Indian Vishnu worship (*bhāgavata dharma*), the classification of nondualist religious singers (*sant paramparā*), devotionalism in the second millennium (*bhakti mārg*), as well as figures who served as precursors to the Indian nation (*rāṣṭrīya sant*) and models of humanism (*mānavatāvādī sant*), or as a figure of Indian cinema's "devotional" genre of film.

Adrift in a virtual sea of saintly figures, Namdev is ever-present yet regularly set in relief. He is a secondary or tertiary figure within the pageant of *bhakti* on the subcontinent, an actor in a supporting role. In Marathi hagiography, he often plays second-fiddle to his more famous colleague, Jnandev, more popularly known as Jnaneshwar or Dnyaneshwar of the thirteenth century. In Hindi, he is overshadowed by the giant figure of Kabir, and this holds true for Namdev's secondary status vis-à-vis Kabir in the roster of Sikh *bhagat*s. Although this general second-rank position may never amount to a single religious tradition or *sampradāy* in his name, it highlights the way multiple traditions are linked through his legacy and suggests his ability to articulate times, places, and ideas together. Namdev can embody cosmopolitanism, marked by a regional affiliation with Marathi, but never defined by that affiliation, because of this second-rank status. Indeed, Namdev's premier characteristic outside the Marathi milieu is his transregional appeal; within the Marathi milieu, this property of his remembrance is shared in importance with his central position within the genealogy of the performance art of *kirtan*, the subject of chapter 2.

Even though those who revere Namdev span the socioeconomic field in contemporary India, and beyond, the legacy of Namdev is one situated within the ontology of the demotic and "subaltern," as a figure who represents the powerless, disenfranchised, and excluded, epitomized in his low-caste status as a *shudra*. Little early Orientalist history or ethnography discusses the followers of Namdev in terms of socioeconomic position. William Crooke mentioned Namdev in *The Tribes and Castes of the North-Western Provinces and Oudh* (1896) as a "tribal saint" of the "Dhuniyas," a caste of both Muslims and Hindus, but certainly of low social status in the traditional hierarchy.[3] Namdev does not appear in any of the "history from below" or "people's history" that studies South Asia, such as the work of the Subaltern Studies Collective or the long tradition of Marxist and social historiography in India. Yet, as shown throughout this book, Namdev's low social status is a vital element of his high religious capital in the multiple traditions that remember him. His experience of social suffering is a key feature of his position in narratives of affliction and redemption, as well as his designation as a humanist in the twentieth century.

Like so many other *bhakti* figures, Namdev is established in public memory as a performer and a singer. However, he has not been remembered as a writer, nor do his songs or biographies claim the skill of literacy. Although this is common among north Indian *sants* like Surdas and Kabir, within Marathi circles literacy was the norm, as with fellow Varkari *sants* Jnandev, Eknath (sixteenth century), and Tukaram (seventeenth century). In contradistinction, Namdev is remembered as an oral performer of songs of devotion to God, especially in the Marathi form of *kirtan,* which is different from other kinds of *kirtan* found in India, as chapter 2 shows. A purposeful distance from literacy is marked in the Maharashtrian public memory of Namdev, and this feature of his remembrance receives special attention here. The deliberate disavowal of literacy helps form the Maharashtrian tradition around an epicenter of performance and allows Namdev's pan-Indian fame a modal function: with few set texts and no tradition of textual corroboration of fixed composition, Namdev's renown, his songs, and his biography traveled freely. Thus, though Namdev was in all likelihood a real person who lived some time before the end of the fifteenth century, Namdev is also a feature of public memory, a character positioned on a broad stage, one among many actors in the story of *bhakti,* regional literatures, and performing arts of the second millennium of the Common Era in India. It is to this public memory in which *bhakti* is sustained that the discussion turns its attention.

BHAKTI

It is a commonly cited conceit that no indigenous Indian language has a single word that correlates to the English word "religion." This is a partial truth. As in any act of translation, a direct transfer of a word's meaning is impossible; indeed, the linguistic turn of contemporary critical theory proposes that even the same word in the same language is subject to a variety of interpretations. For example, Saussure's assertion made in 1910 that "in language there are only differences" suggests that varieties in meaning and interpretation are the very life-blood of language, and the pleasure, not the bane, of the language user.[4] There are certain words in all languages that defy even heuristic definition, much less an exact and lasting one, and the words "religion" in English and *bhakti* in Indian languages are two of these enigmatic terms.[5] I have observed these two words, "religion" and *bhakti,* as interchangeable in the context of Namdev's legacy in Maharashtra. Often in interviews in Marathi and Hindi, my interlocutors would use the English word "religion" in place of *bhakti* (while speaking in Marathi or Hindi), and in English *bhakti*, likewise, would often come to stand in the spot where one would expect the word "religion." When matters turned away from Namdev specifically and toward generalities about religious practice, and in particular Sanskritic, Vedic, or Brahminical practice, people would use the word *dharma* and never the word *bhakti*. *Dharma* in colloquial speech often also pointed to something transcendent, applicable to all people, whether Hindu or simply human, whereas *bhakti* invoked in the context of Namdev meant something specific, yet open-ended, but centered on Namdev, or more precisely, on vicariously experiencing Namdev's direct relationship with his deity, Vitthal.

The many attempts by anthropologists, psychologists, historians, textualists, and religionists to define the word "religion" need not be rehearsed here. I would suggest, however, that my own use of the term is quite far from the realm of the "personal" as William James formulated religious experience in the early part of the twentieth century. In the context of this book, and perhaps in India as whole, the word "religion" suggests both the public and the private—spheres of community and cultural capital that extend well beyond "personal devotion" to a deity. Indeed, as scholarship of secularism in India, and the long history of religion and politics on the subcontinent, bears out, the "religious" in India is a highly public phenomenon. In contrast to American secularism, which appears to suggest an individual freedom *from* religion, Indian secularism presents freedom to publicly practice your religion, that is, freedom *to be publicly* religious, one of the few protected freedoms of the late colonial period in India. A simple example might be found in the Indian flag: the two colors of saffron and green are signs for the religions of Hinduism and Islam, respectively; and in the center one finds an explicit religious symbol, the Ashokan Buddhist "Wheel of Life," which invokes the central principle of *saṃsāra* (metempsychosis), shared by Buddhists, Hindus, and Jains. The American flag, in contrast, displays no religious characteristics whatsoever; it signals the state's excision of religion from its imagination of its public. By contrast, the Indian flag makes the imagination of Hindu-Muslim (and some say Christian, symbolized by the interposed white strip) unity a secularist mandate.[6]

The semantic range of the word *bhakti* always requires much more contextualization in the field of the study of religion. A student of Hinduism at an American university or college is likely to encounter the word *bhakti* first in the context of a set of poetic translations of songs composed by an Indian "saint" (e.g., *sant, bhakta, bhagat, āḷvār, nāyaṇmār*) from the sixth century to the present. Here *bhakti* is often referred to as "personal devotion to a deity" and set against Vedic or post-Vedic Brahminical ritual excess, dogmatic canonical adherence, caste discrimination, and gender inequity. Imagined this way, one might receive *bhakti* as a literary challenge to a prosaic religious orthodoxy, often couched in the lyric of passionate love and painful separation. A further pursuit of *bhakti* might reveal it to have been a confrontation with the hegemony of caste in social contexts, a sentiment supported, for the most part, by *bhakti*'s literary traces. A student might be taught that *bhakti* appeared to colonial Orientalist scholars as the social cognate of the European Protestant Reformation and re-emerged as a significant area of study for the regional and literary characteristics of religion in India. There are still more possibilities. We might find *bhakti* presented in its performative contexts, in yearly rituals of theater, pilgrimage, and personal vow. Or we might see it invested in the history of Indian nationalism configured through its "saints" as progenitors of the nation and through its very sentiment as "devotion to the land" or *deśbhakti.* One can track the career of the term *bhakti* through a staggering number of venues, from the earliest oral narratives to the latest Bollywood films, from individual engagements with a deity in a moment of visual contact (*darshan*) to the imagination of a unified yet heterogeneous nation.

Bhakti has appeared in texts and practices for over two millennia and has attracted two centuries of Western scholarly scrutiny, yet retains its essential ambiguity.[7] However, we can chart the term's contours to some degree. The word appears in a number of South Asian religions, but particularly in Hinduism, in which it signals a host of meanings related to its Sanskritic verbal root, *bhaj* ("to share, to proportion," and hence most commonly comes to indicate "love, sharing, worship, devotion"). However, the associations with the verbal root are vast. They include sentiments such as to divide, distribute, allot, or apportion; to share with; to grant, bestow, furnish, or supply; to obtain as one's share, receive as, partake of, enjoy (also carnally), possess, or have; to turn or resort to, engage in, assume (as a form), put on (garments), experience, incur, undergo, feel go or fall into, including falling into a feeling of terror or awe; to pursue, practice, cultivate; to prefer, choose; to serve, honor, revere, and adore.[8] Given this semantic range, we find that a *bhakta* is a person (or in some cases a thing) in whom some qualities of *bhakti* inhere. Thus a *bhakta* is someone who is devoted, who serves, who is associated with a community, is faithful and loyal, and who displays his or her status to others, who "shares" it with others.

A common scholarly convention interprets *bhakti* to mean "personal devotion" or a sentiment of intimacy with a deity, but the term is also used in highly abstract contexts where the "personal" is not present. In some cases, *bhakti* denotes a "movement" of social protest against caste, class, religious, or gender inequities, but a coherent social movement does not form around the term except in small, discrete periods and places. Although the primary association with *bhakti* in scholarly work correlates literary practices with the rise of devotional sentiment (often also marking the first or second literary traces of regional literatures),[9] many nonliterary practices are also described as *bhakti,* including pilgrimage, daily worship, and the repetition of a deity's name or names. In terms of practice, *bhakti* resists confinement to any particular action or utterance.

The literary genealogy of *bhakti* is equally broad. Traces exist as early as the *Ṛg Veda*, approximately 1200 B.C.E., where we find the variations of the verbal root *bhaj* appear in the context of entreaties to particular deities, such as Saraswati, or, as in the "Gayatri hymn," a call to the deity Varuna to protect a supplicant. The first uses of the term come in a very early Buddhist text. In the *Theragāthā*, probably composed in the fourth century B.C.E., *bhakti* appears to indicate devotion to the way or *dharma/dhamma*—another term that resists definition—of the Buddha. Around this period, the word also appears in the *Aṣṭhadyāyi* of Panini, the preeminent Sanskrit grammarian, indicating "devotion" to something, but not necessarily a deity. A general scholarly consensus sees the first full articulations of *bhakti* as the term is used today in the *Bhagavad Gītā*, expanded from an episode of the epic *Mahābhārata*, probably around the beginning of the Common Era; in the *Bhagavata Purāṇa,* a collection of stories detailing the incarnations of Vishnu (primarily Krishna), and probably composed around the ninth century C.E.; and in the *Bhakti Sūtras,* attributed to mythical sages Shandilya and Narada (who is discussed in subsequent chapters), probably composed around the tenth century C.E. However, the first regional languages to express sentiments associated with *bhakti* appear in south India, perhaps as early as the fifth century. The next 1,200 years see a long efflorescence of regional literatures throughout the subcontinent, within which the expression of *bhakti* appears a consistent and prominent feature. The Marathi regional literary tradition enters this efflorescence in the thirteenth century with the work of Namdev and his contemporaries, as well as the Mahānubhāvs, a Krishna sect, as seen in chapter 1.

Alongside the literary production of *bhakti,* we can see a turn toward "devotion" of a personal nature in other contexts. Within India's "Golden

Age" of the Gupta empire (320–647) and in the reign of the Pallavas and the Pandyas in south India (fourth to tenth centuries), we see temple construction, the creation of "homes" for deities and loci for public, if personal, worship. This is perhaps one possible origin for the practices associated with *bhakti,* such as the process of making visual contact with a deity, or *darshan,* and the offering of goods to a deity's image, or *pūjā.* These acts were replicated in homes—there is good reason to believe that these acts *originated* in the domestic sphere—and the transformations of the public economy of worship bear some significant relationship to the development of regional literatures that take up the ethos of *bhakti.* Perhaps in the midst of the cross-currents of regional literary developments and the opening of public economies of devotion, we find the rudiments of public performative expressions—the plays, dances, theatrics, and songs that have come to stand for *bhakti* in modern scholarly discourse. It is out of this milieu that Namdev's public memory emerges as a *bhakta* and an exemplary practitioner of *kirtan,* a performance art that mixes music, dance, songs attributed to *sant*s, and sacred biography with moral exposition and social commentary.

In songs attributed to Namdev, *bhakti* appears constantly in several ways, all of which inform the content of this study. We find the word in compounds with the names of Vitthal, including Krishna, Hari, Vithoba, and Panduranga, indicating the worship of this deity. We also find the word in compound with, or in proximity to, the word *prem,* or "love" devoid of sexual overtones. The two, at times, become interchangeable, indicating an equation in Namdev's songs between love and devotion. One often finds *bhakti* summoned to explain the devotion of family members, especially sons and daughters for their parents. *Bhakti* is invoked as a sentiment that soothes troubled souls, as the recourse a devotee can take to escape from worldly suffering. It also indicates a community in Namdev's songs, likewise a refuge from the world. *Bhakti* is linked in compounds with the word *bhava,* translatable as "faith," as well as "state of mind" or "intention," usually indicating the combination of devotion and trust in one's deity. When Namdev or others perform *kirtan*s, we hear of *bhakti-rasa,* or the flavor (*rasa*) of *bhakti,* the result of a good performance; one thus also "feels" (*lāgīṁ*) the *bhakti* of a performance.

We find *bhakti* contrasted with other options within the sphere of religious action and sentiment, especially between *bhakti* and technical or scholastic modes of approaching God. In one particularly famous episode from Namdev's life, he is asked by Jnandev, his learned *yogi* companion, to describe his *bhakti* because, as Jnandev says to Namdev, "you are a thorough *bhakta;* you have no longing for the vast world of knowledge."[10] Namdev gives this reply:

> Hearing Jnandev say this, a great love [*prem*] wells up within Namdev.
> He says, "Listen to the story of my experience.
> Action [*karma*], laws of religion [*dharma*], and the rest, they're all extraneous.
> It's too tiring to learn these things.
> Those who achieve detachment from worldly things are filled with love,
> And because of this good fortune, they meet the *sant*s.
> Where spiritual power serves mercy and faith serves compassion,
> There the sense of otherness diminishes.
> Singing songs [*bhajan*] to God tastes sweet to me;
> it is labor without reason.
> I see no sin in bowing to the soft, blissful inner light.
> Learn to recognize the fraudulence in that illusion we call reality [*māyāvī*].
> In life, I put no faith in reality.
> Vithoba [Vitthal] has made me see that in my world,
> Unfaltering meditation on His Name is a good thing.
> I endlessly remember him in my heart:
> Those beautiful feet together on the brick. . . .
> We divide and categorize everything,
> But Vitthal *bhakti* is simply the art of love in a state of bliss.[11]

Jnandev is convinced. He replies:

> I've heard many *bhakta*s of Vishnu.
> Many have gone, and many more will come.
> But there's been nothing like Nama's speech [*bolaṇeṁ*]; it is poetic [*kavitva*].
> His words are essential, fantastic, and unparalleled.[12]

The vision of *bhakti* attributed to Namdev here is couched in orality—he commands Jnandev to listen and describes his practice as "singing songs"—and in experience rather than knowledge or reason. Namdev's *bhakti* in Maharashtrian public memory is explicitly attached to Vitthal and his image in Pandharpur, invoked in this passage by reference to Vitthal's feet on a brick, an image long associated with Vitthal, and perhaps adopted from the practice in early Buddhist iconography of representing the Buddha only by absence, by his footprints, for example. However, in the context of Vitthal worship the feet of the deity represent presence and a specific location rather than a reminder of absence—they recall Vitthal standing on a brick in Pandharpur awaiting his devotees. In this way Namdev's Marathi *bhakti* is *saguṇa*, *bhakti* that focuses on the physical and emotional characteristics (*guṇa*) of a deity. Yet Namdev also claims to put no faith in reality, to accept the notion of illusion, or *māyā*, suggesting an affinity with *nirguṇa*, or "character-less" *bhakti*. Despite these variances, what we find in this passage is a vision of *bhakti* that is all-consuming, and publicly enacted, setting a *bhakta* outside the usual economic and cultural spheres, but solidly within a socially shared space of devotion.

Perhaps most important for this study is the fact that Namdev's *bhakti* is social and expressive, encapsulated in "speech" and "poetry" and in interaction with other figures, with the opportunity to "meet the *sants*," to form communities with like-minded people. The song above is a dialogue, the snapshot of a social interaction between two famous figures of Marathi devotional memory. We, as listeners, form an audience, and this song has had a long career in the biographical legacy of Namdev (and Jnandev) in Marathi, repeated for many like-minded audiences over the centuries. This episode, as many if not most from Namdev's pool of textual and biographical materials, relies on publicity, on being publicly displayed, for its rhetorical impact. *Bhakti*, in this context, is always a matter of demonstration, or specifically, of performance. The desire for a company of *bhaktas* is apparent in this song and throughout Namdev's legacy in Marathi; Namdev's *bhakti* appears inherently to draw out and call on various publics, forming audiences of listeners over the centuries.

PUBLIC

Unifying the myriad forms that *bhakti* has historically taken and continues to take is the idea of a public, which I think of as a social unit created through shared cultural phenomena, and reinforced by demonstrations in public of these shared cultural phenomena. Publics are not exclusive—indeed they are hardly able to be regulated at all. The idea of a (or "the") public has a long history in Western theoretical writing and political life, ranging from Kant's ideas about reason among a reading public,[13] John Dewey's ideas of public political deliberation,[14] and Habermas's influential theory of "the public sphere,"[15] to the attribution of all kinds of opinions to the "public" by politicians, and the metrics of public opinion employed by pollsters around the world. One regularly finds the word "public" in scholarship, as noun or adjective, as a designation for the state. For example, the historiographic genre of "public history" tends to focus on state-controlled historical discourse and education, whereas "public memory" is more traditionally associated with the ways the state seeks to form or maintain a state-centered memory, as in the erection of public memorial, or the enactment of public holidays of remembrance.[16] In this book, however, I do not use the term "public" to indicate a state-centered activity in any way; rather, as I mark out in detail below, a mode of social cohesion, temporally bounded, and united in its aim toward affective display.

My understanding of "public" owes a debt to several concepts. When the word "public" appears in this book, it draws in particular from the excellent literatures on public culture[17] and the public sphere[18] in India, which are theoretically in line with my subject but tend to take modernity as a prerequisite for the existence of publics. The idea of public culture and the public sphere as it appears in these works has a more explicit place in the final chapter on Namdev and the national imagination. However, I use neither of these terms exclusively in order to avoid stretching the idea of *bhakti* too far to meet concepts more explicitly situated within urban-global contexts[19] or in relation to Western modernity.[20] Instead, I hope to use the word "public" in a way that does not go beyond serving as a description of the project of *bhakti* among those who remember Namdev in Maharashtra. In other words, I use the idea of a public in this book without allegiance to any reigning theoretical formulation of the term but, rather, in whatever way it might heuristically serve to draw a clearer picture of the cultural history of Namdev's memory in Maharashtra.

As shown throughout this book, much of Namdev's remembered life is a public affair. Significant episodes take place that require observers, such as miracles occurring before audiences, who later report the sight to others. The need for observers and participants is perhaps most apparent when Namdev enacts any kind of performance, primarily *kirtan*, which he does with regularity both in songs attributed to him and his received biography. Throughout Namdev's songs, one finds the invocation of something like "the public," which is how I read the Indic word *loka*, a noun in Marathi that almost always indicates the plural and primarily indicates the receptive public at large. The *loka* are often the addressees of Namdev's verses, and within songs he calls on them to listen or witness. This is not a theorized social entity but, rather, a surrounding social force with which Namdev's songs and biography interact and take shape; it is his audience, both immediate and in historical transmission. Namdev's audience becomes transformed into the *loka,* the public that receives his legacy long after he is said to have died. The second meaning of *loka* in Marathi indicates "the world," but a human world, not a physical one. This second meaning of *loka* depends on the first to impart its sense of a human field of reception and interaction, and one unmarked by caste, class, or gender. What makes a *loka* in Namdev's verses is the human world alert to its own inward, referential gaze. The word *loka* designates either the first person plural, as in "*We people* do this," or in the third person plural, "That is the practice of *those people.*" The public as expressed through this term creates both self and other. The *loka* form the audience of *bhakti,* both in Namdev's songs and in Marathi scholarship about Namdev; without this audience, Namdev's *bhakti* would remain silent, unrecalled, and lost to time.

This nexus of public and *bhakti* is not unique to Namdev. Norman Cutler, in his brilliant work, *Songs of Experience,* which largely involved Tamil literary examples, understood "gods," "poets," and "audience" in a triangular relationship with one another, a relationship Cutler referred to as the "verbal event" (following Roman Jakobson) of *bhakti.*[21] By invoking the idea of a "public" I do not wish to isolate any one of these three nodes—though that of "audience" might seem the most appropriate. Instead, I want to point to the tripartite structure itself, to the ways *bhakti* relies on the flow of sentiment and information, and the visibility of that flow. We can see this visually in the modern medium of film and its attendant idioms. As in all the great *bhakta* films of Indian cinema—such as the Damle and Fattelal films about Tukaram (1936) or Jnaneshwar (1940)—we are the observers of a *bhakti* public, always represented as an activity performed before people, which is in turn projected on a screen and performed for a film-viewing audience. In other words, as viewers of these films, we are watching Cutler's triangle in its entire form: we see the *sant,* we hear his or her songs to God, and we observe the audience observing, and subsequently remembering, him or her as a *bhakta.* In a sense, *bhakti* is this very *mise en scène,* the composition in its entirety made up of layers of reception. This *mise en scène* is essential to centuries of hagiography as well, where the reception of the *sant*—the host of miracles and places that take the shape of a biography—is given to us already supplied with audiences who adore, or persecute, the *sant* in question. The highly personal "memoir," I would suggest, is never found in hagiography. The story of a *sant*'s life is always also a story of a context for that life and is always coded with the reception of that life in its context. I describe the transmission of this notion of *bhakti* from the past to a present, receptive public as an act of memory.

The identification of publics in scholarship on South Asia is now a richly textured decades-long project. The fields of political studies and historical anthropology have provided the most salient treatments of the functioning of publics. For example, the many studies by Paul Brass in political science have long engaged the formation of publics, as has more recent work, such as studies by Ashutosh Varshney on civil society.[22] In historical anthropology, the work of Bernard Cohn pioneered a new genre of the study of publics and the colonial state,[23] carried on in the work of scholars such as Nicholas Dirks and Arjun Appadurai,[24] as well as more recent work by Douglas Haynes, Anne Hardgrove, and Sandria Freitag.[25] We have the excellent work of Francesca Orsini on the Hindi public sphere in India; similarly, within this context Milind Wakankar has shown how figures of *bhakti* appear prominently, such as Kabir.[26] In this public sphere, *bhakti* can be integrated into ideas of what it is to be "Indian," that is, into a discourse of nationalism, of *deshbhakti,* both a devotion to the nation and a commitment to the public that comprises the imagined nation.

When "publics" are introduced in the context of South Asia, it is usually as a description of some formulation of the public sphere or of public culture. In both cases, the publics scrutinized tend to be set firmly with a designated modern period (usually the nineteenth century to the present). Given the intimate association between the rise of mass media, printing, and the nation that tend to characterize scholarship on the public sphere, the association with modernity makes sense. The case of public culture is somewhat different. Like subaltern studies, the study of public culture entered mainstream academia at the hands of South Asianist scholars. Although the term "public culture" predates the usage of it by the influential work of Arjun Appadurai and Carol Breckenridge, under their stewardship through publications and journals,[27] South Asia has remained a key area for the study of public culture in general.[28] However, these studies tend to remain within modernity, expressing the relationship between modern forms of the state (colonial or democratic) and publics, or within modern cultural formations, like the public sphere. For this reason, though these excellent studies make lucid use of ideas about the public in modern contexts, they cannot provide a model for understanding *bhakti* in its broadest, historically richest manifestations.

In formulating a broader usable outline of the idea of a public, I have relied on Michael Warner's work on queer publics in America, in which he provides a description of a public like the one I use here in the context of *bhakti:* "a public enables a reflexivity in the circulation of texts among strangers who become, by virtue of their reflexively circulating discourse, a social entity."[29] The circularity of this heuristic definition is purposeful and recalls the kind of circularity that was used by Clifford Geertz to describe religion as a self-reinforced system of symbols,[30] or a socially repetitive system, as in Peter Berger's work,[31] or as a principle of the "reflexive sociology" of the cultural field, as Bourdieu has described it.[32] Importantly, however, Warner makes plain what at least Geertz implies: the object of the belief, in this case of a public, is a fiction, a narrative form whose basis in fact is not necessary for its acceptance.[33] It is not a physically demonstrable thing, like a state, village, township, or other polity; nor does it exist in a carefully constructed discourse, like a judiciary, a set of laws, or a dogma. A public relies as much on the imagination of each individual as on a collective agreement as to its existence. People must believe they are part of a public: this gives it both its strength and its ephemeral quality.

The word "public" often also marks places where the common good is situated. Unlike a term like "popular," which makes a utilitarian appeal to a majority, or the word "communal," where the individual is subordinated to the whole, the idea of a public points to the resistance of homogenous social entities implying the erasure of the individual. Note that I distinguish here between "a public" and "the public." The latter designation of "the public" implies homogeneity, often enforced or primarily influenced by the state or generated from the magic of statistics or surveys. This is the public measured by pollsters and appealed to by politicians. It is also the public invoked by scholars of phenomena such as "the public sphere" and "public opinion." This notion of the public is also usually associated almost exclusively with modernity.[34] In contrast, "a public" implies a much greater flexibility of social organization. Warner outlines a handful of characteristics that help us identify "a public" when not qualified by its state-centered, hegemonic sense as "the public." Warner conditions a public with these principles: publics (1) are self-organized; (2) exhibit a "relation among strangers"; (3) are both personal and impersonal in their address to an audience; (4) require "mere attention"; (5) construct a "social space . . . by the reflexive circulation of discourse"; (6) "act historically," which is to say they address the issues of their time—they historicize themselves; and (7) enact a project of "poetic world-making," which is to say, publics give character to themselves and their participants, a character that is often then embodied in signs of dress and bodily display that recall the poetics of a public.[35]

Warner is useful in identifying the heuristic value of the theoretical category of the public, but it comes with its limitations. Warner and most scholars of publics, even scholars of South Asia mentioned above, tend to understand publics to be modern phenomena exclusively. I depart here from Warner and others in that I understand the explanatory value of the idea of a public to be both geographically and temporally modular. The central operation of a public is its inward circularity, its internal system of self-reference, and thereby its ability to compose its ephemeral body in time by means of the chimera of discourse. A public is substanceless but, like any social formation, still powerful. It is not, therefore, confined to any of its highly scrutinized forms, most of which have been explicated in the context of modernity. In other words, there is no prerequisite for a public that makes it germane to modernity—not literacy or print; not rationality or transglobal cultural flows; not even a shared verbal language. Publics form by reference and reinforcement, whether visual, oral, aural, or literary, and are not measured by their size or influence as some objective quality; rather, they are the product of their actors, of their circle of attention. For this reason modernity is no more suitable than any other epochal epistemology to host a discernable public. I also depart from Warner and others in my understanding that publics are more than phantom social forms that dissipate in the flow of time, but they contain within themselves a chronography, a way to both record time and engage it critically. I discuss this general notion further below, but I would argue that publics, by their nature, remember and are constituted by a shared memory. Indeed, to append Warner's list above, publics are systems of memory.

The *bhakti* public associated with Namdev is centered on the circulation of a common stock of memory and mnemonic practices and participation in the publics that surround Namdev are ruled neither by dogma nor coercion, but made cohesive by a kind of social agreement that has a precedent in the genealogy of *bhakti*. We can see that historically and textually *bhakti* indicates a practice of sharing, equal distribution, and mutual enjoyment, what Karen Prentiss calls "participation," an interaction that suggests the "embodiment" of *bhakti* as a prerequisite for its practice, and the body, we know from several generations of feminist scholarship, is the pre-eminent public text.[36] Likewise, the Latin origins of the term "public" are rooted in the body, that is, in the condition of being an "adult man" (*pubes, publicus*) in reference to both sex and age. The term's deployment in Western academic and social discourse assumes that a public is made up of embodied viable participants in social political life. Hence we have the rather more common association of the "public" with the identification, by the state, of its constituency.

In the context of *bhakti*, this concern with responsibility and constituency can be transposed to an understanding of what forms the social environment of *bhakti*. Images of *bhakti* are associated with acts of sharing through religious performances (*kirtan, bhajan, rāslīlā*) and communities of pilgrimage. Although little studied by historians or anthropologists of religion, the sharing of food constitutes another significant form of *bhakti.* We see it in the breaking of the taboos of caste commensality during pilgrimage, for example, or the act of exchanging an item, often food, with a deity, called *prasād,* which is then redistributed to friends and family. In this way *bhakti* shows a parallel with older Sanskritic uses of the word in the context of the preparation and distribution of food, which is one of the key anthropological markers of a community, in addition to marriage.[37] As early as the *Ṛg Veda,* the verbal root *bhaj* and its nouns, such as *bhakti* and *bhakta,* indicated the sharing, serving, and distributing of something, whereas in the *Manusmṛti* and *Mahābhārata,* the noun *bhakta* indicated prepared or cooked food.[38] Panini uses the word *bhaktakaṁsa* to indicate "a dish of food," and many other compound words formed around *bhakta* relate to food preparation and distribution.[39] Indeed, *bhakti* can be translated as "commensality," the sharing of comestibles by a community as a way of marking their kinship. In this way, *bhakti* becomes metaphorical when applied to religious contexts. It takes on the meaning of sharing food, as a symbol, with both deity and fellow devotees and, by extension, the sharing of a visible, interactive community, a public.

The sharing and handling of food appears significantly within *bhakti* hagiography, especially in the stories of Namdev's life within Maharashtrian public memory, as seen in chapter 1. In such cases, we have caste critique as well as models for public association centered on commensality as a practice of *bhakti.* The idea of *bhakti* points toward a religious, social, and theological position that entails a mutually shared space and purpose, the division and public distribution of the bounty of a religious experience. We might think of *bhakti,* then, as inherently directing the creation of a socioreligious public through the metaphorical sharing of a common object, the object of devotional fervor.

Bhakti traditions reflect the social ethics of the public. We see this through the notion of sharing food, places, and time together in religiously defined collectivities (such as performative moments, on pilgrimage, during the exchange of *prasad* or the act of *puja*). We also find a social impetus toward the creation of public spaces, especially temples, something resonant with the common (though not at all ubiquitous) sentiment of *bhakti* that sites of exclusive, elite religious practices are to be revolutionized. There is, of course, the opposite tendency to close temples to other religious or caste communities—the creation of publics is also always a creation of some difference between various publics, some discrimination of inclusion. This division is commonly expressed in the bifurcations of certain communities, Hindu and Muslim, or *vaishnava* and *śaiva*. Perhaps the most pernicious of these divisive uses of public occurs within and around the Namdev tradition in terms of Brahmin and non-Brahmin alliances. As seen at various moments in the history and literary remnant of the Namdev tradition in Marathi, a clear anti-Brahmin sentiment arises, parallel to periods of caste discrimination, such as one sees in the many centuries in which the Vitthal temple in Pandharpur, under the management of a particular Brahmin community, refused entry to the lowest castes. Publics in the context of *bhakti* are therefore both created and opposed: within them, certain things circulate freely, but without are the usual features of social chauvinisms, the exclusions, repressions, and discourse of alterity that mark all cultures. Nevertheless, the theoretical sentiment of *bhakti*, based on a principle of apportionment, appears to more positively define publics as inclusive, especially when one views this notion against the primary antagonists one finds in *bhakti* literature and performance throughout India—caste and class.

In reference to the idea of caste as occupation and class as socio-economic status, the notion of the public designates a world outside the home, a place of labor and interaction with social powers (such as the law and the state), and this is rich field for the metaphorical stock of *bhakti* cultural production. Indeed, many hagiographical accounts of *bhakti* figures take place outside the home, or suggest the violation of the home, and use the materials of public differences—Hindu vs. Muslim, male vs. female, and high caste vs. low caste. The hagiography of Mirabai, for example, tells us of her repudiation of the normative private life of marriage, her refusal to marry a human man, and her choice of the peripatetic and public display of her private love for Krishna, the purported source of her famous songs. The story of Kabir's death, a well-rehearsed metaphor for religious pluralism, is likewise focused on a public moment—the *sant*'s funeral procession—when his body, fought over by both Hindus and Muslims, dissolves into flowers. In Namdev's hagiography, multiple examples set in public a hagiographical scene that mediates the dialectics mentioned above, most often that of caste difference.

Publics are also the places where our social economies obtain, the sphere of markets and exchange, where capital, whether cultural or economic, is accumulated and spent. As discussed in chapters 2 and 3, the "market" that sustains Namdev's songs, and perhaps the bulk of *bhakti* compositions in general, is the market of performance, the traveling circuit of the performers who have been the human "archive" of *bhakti* in

South Asia over the centuries. These markets circulate conterminously with pilgrimage circuits as well as trade circuits. Like the proverbial actor who must take a day job waiting tables to make ends meet, we must imagine that the performance of devotional songs was a viable occupation for few, whether today or five hundred years ago. Most performers of devotional songs had to respond to the demands of publics of reception. As my research into the literary remnant of Namdev's songs shows, we know from the notebooks carried by performers from the sixteenth century to the present that they had to be versed in multiple genres of entertainment, many of which were unrelated to *bhakti* as a genre or a motif. Thus *bhakti* as occupation, one might say, as the heart of one's performative repertoire, was also deeply invested in the nature of a public, responding to the very question of "public-ness" and hence crafting the narratives that come to us today as the poetry and life stories of the world of *bhakti.*

My association of *bhakti* with publics may appear to come at the expense of what is certainly one of the central explanatory devices of *bhakti* and is perhaps its root practice, the sense in which *bhakti* is a private affair, between God and devotee, a "personal devotion" as the term is so often glossed. While I would not argue that *bhakti* never describes a private affair of devotion, the sense in which *bhakti* enters the history of India is not through the private realm but through the same social world of caste, labor, and markets outside the home and the heart of an individual. There are no doubt many highly internalized theological and philosophical reflections on *bhakti* that stress an internal, individual, sentiment. The most famous of these is perhaps the five-stage understanding of *bhakti* discussed by the mid-eighth-century philosopher-theologian Shankaracharya in his *Śivānandalahirī.* But this is the realm of theology or of textual hermeneutics, not of history or culture. Similarly, as discussed below, we might view memory. The domain of the individual's memory is a subject for psychology, neurology, and psychotherapy, but only when one views memory as a social function does it become possible to discuss the way memory works in culture. Thus, in this book, I am asking questions of *bhakti* that are, like such questions of memory, presupposing its social existence and importance. Many subjects contain this dual mode of investigation. Perhaps the most famous is religion itself, in which the timeless investigation of the internal character of religious sentiment is accompanied by the historical, social, and anthropological understanding of what constitutes religion in the world of human interaction. One cannot understand the "personal" as a historical formation without first understanding it as social and public. *Bhakti,* as a subject for cultural history, must be taken in its social forms and not theorized solely within the sphere of an individual's consciousness if we are to understand *bhakti* in terms cultural and historical.

Conversely, when scholars do seek to understand *bhakti* socially, one still finds *bhakti* described in terms of a "movement," suggesting a single associated community of people who over time have propagated a unified vision of *bhakti* as a social principle. Although there appears to be no sociological or historical reason to accept that *bhakti* ever formed a solitary movement in the history of South Asia, the fact that this designation retains purchase in academic and public culture, in India and the rest of the world, indicates the inherently social aspect of *bhakti*, which I have implied by use of the term "public." The issue of identifying *bhakti* as a single social project throughout South Asian history is not a new problem,[40] though the term "*bhakti* movement" still seems to hold credibility in academic and nonacademic settings. However, few studies, other than those that seek to introduce Hinduism to undergraduate students, ever take "the *bhakti* movement" as a meaningful social category. Most studies, in other words, use the "*bhakti* movement" as a very general, and hence very imprecise, gloss for numerous discrete movements and moments, or they address one particular historically and textually bounded example of *bhakti*, such as that which surrounds Mirabai, Kabir, or Surdas, and their set of textually preserved songs, or studies explore the ritual or social enactment of *bhakti*, such as pilgrimage. No studies, to my knowledge, defend explicitly the idea that a unified social movement existed in Indian history under the sign of *bhakti*, though many deploy the term "*bhakti* movement" as shorthand for the heterogeneous cultural and literary products that have been formed around the term.

This work attempts to chart a course between these two extremes—of *bhakti* as personal devotion and as a social movement. I propose that we use the idea of a public to describe the vast area between these poles where a complex interchange exists that presupposes the individual as the essential node of creation and transmission, but understands that until ideas, materials, and memories circulate among individuals, and indeed among individuals in diachronic measure, there is no *bhakti* outside the mysterious confines of the human soul in solitude. For the purposes of this study—and, I would argue, of any study of *bhakti* that is not essentially theological or didactic—*bhakti* must always be a social or, I would say, public subject. This does not mean I believe that the only way to understand *bhakti*, or Namdev's legacy, is as a public, but it is a useful way, and a way that maps on to many of the presuppositions of *bhakti*, and the partic-

ular character of Namdev, as I hope to have hinted at above and to demonstrate throughout the book.

MEMORY

Implied in the broad array of literature that takes a "public" as a significant
theoretical category—whether public culture or the public sphere—is the
imperative for publics to possess some system of historical memory. Such
memories may be formalized histories or less logically structured modes
of recollection; they might center on a site or an object, or a shared imagination, and the perpetuation of memory might be restricted to, or combine
with, orality, literacy, visuality, ritual, and so on. But publics must record
themselves in order to be sustained even for the shortest duration—they
must remember.

A study of how the *bhakti* publics that surround Namdev through time
recall the past and rectify it with the present must also provide some theoretical understanding of this process. One might choose among several
theoretical approaches to the study of indigenous, localized notions of
time and historiography forms. The field of historical anthropology, or
ethnohistory, possesses a subfield (sometimes called "ethno-ethnohistory")
devoted to understanding how a given "ethnos" or specific cultural system
recalls the past, that is, the anthropological study of indigenous historiography. However, this is a comparatively minor strand within the larger field
of historical anthropology, though it is nonetheless a vibrant strand.[41] One
more commonly finds studies that combine the approaches of Western
historiography and anthropology to produce histories of a particular time
and place rather than the "anthropology of time."[42] Excellent examples
abound of the historiography of anthropology itself, such as Nicholas B.
Dirks's study *Castes of Mind*, which explores the colonial reification of
caste through what he calls the "ethnographic state" enacted by colonial
ethnologists and administrators through sociological devices such as the
census.

A second example regularly accessed by South Asianists is the field of
Subaltern Studies. In what one might call its "second phase" epitomized
by the work of Gyan Prakash and Dipesh Chakrabarty, Subaltern Studies has sought to "provincialize Europe" in the field of modern historiography[43] that is, to de-center Europe from its nodal place in the writing of
history, or to explore the possibilities of "postfoundational" histories
that search for historiographic fundamentals not decreed by Western

historical forms.[44] However, the challenges posed by the second phase of Subaltern Studies have largely remained in the form of critique and not prescription, which is itself valuable but leaves little in terms of a "blueprint" with which to proceed in a study of culturally relative memory systems. Furthermore, in both the case of historical anthropology and the second phase of Subaltern Studies, the exploration of South Asian pasts is bedeviled by the cross-currents of the centuries-old debate about the "people without history," inaugurated in large part by Hegel in the early nineteenth century.[45] The field of historical anthropology must still grapple with the force of gravity at its center, its disciplinary core that makes certain requirements on historiography (rationality, the reliable archive, literacy, historical self-awareness, etc.) obtain even in non-Western contexts, a force that Jan Vansina tried to unsettle in 1960 in his study of the Bakuba of the Democratic Republic of Congo: "history in illiterate societies is not different from the pursuit of the past in literate ones ... and there is therefore no need to coin a special term, such as ethnohistory just for this reason."[46] Subaltern Studies, likewise, must always return to representing the "historical consciousness" of the subaltern insurgent rather than allowing the shape of that consciousness, often cast in religious terms and symbols, to stand on its own.[47] It seems, even in a postcolonial, postmodern world, we still ask whether Indians (and the rest of the formerly colonized or otherwise "developing" world) ever had a sense of "history" before modern Europe entered their cultural fields.[48] But asking this question is much different from asking whether the vast nonmodern world has now, or has had in the past, complex systems of memory. Regarding this latter statement, there is very little dissent. In other words, everyone can have memory, but only a select few civilizations can maintain history.

So we arrive at a third option for understanding how cultures remember their past: the social study of memory. This is a field of study that developed in the 1920s in Europe and, though not as old as "historical anthropology" (once considered the comparative study of the "races" of mankind in history)[49] or ethnohistory (founded in the early twentieth century among American anthropologists studying Native Americans), predates the Subaltern Studies Collective and indeed the theoretical interventions of postcolonialism and postmodernism. At the same time, it challenges some of the same modern forms and mentalities. It is to the concept of social memory that this book turns for its explanatory framework in understanding the cultural history of Namdev's public memory. This approach has several advantages. First, its foundations are in sociology, not history, and it is thus less burdened by the pressures exerted by the field of modern history on its theoretical and practical deployment, yet it also regularly engages a productive dialectic between "memory" and "history." We might also note that the panglobal trace of queries about memory—as an art of recollection, as a system of "traditional" maintenance, as a means of education, or as a social prerequisite—has a far deeper and, over the *longue durée* of millennia, a far richer representation in human thought than does history.[50] This is not to say that history is not, nor should not be, our pre-eminent mode of accurately recalling the past (one thinks of the recent intersections of history and false memory in the condemnation of Holocaust deniers working as "historians," such as David Irving), but only to point out what historians would readily, and indeed necessarily, admit: that history as a professionalized discipline is only some two or three hundred years old, whereas the arts of memory are far older.[51] Second, memory studies is cognizant of literate and nonliterate memory forms, and though the "oral" is often glorified in modern memory studies, this is by no means the norm. When approaching a cultural field largely defined by a performance art that exists at the nexus of writing and orality—such as Namdev's legacy—memory studies can offer novel insights. Third, memory studies has regularly been associated with the study of religious phenomena, and though this comes with its own problematic reductive tendencies (as in, all orality is definitive of the primitive and the religious, and so on), it by no means creates the kind of overt antagonisms that professional historiography has maintained with institutionalized religious forms of history (the debate on the "historical" Jesus is emblematic of this confrontation). Finally, memory studies, grounded in sociology, tenaciously hews to the conviction that all memory is social or, as I presume in this book, public. From within the broad array of articulations of what the social function or condition of memory might be—that is, social, cultural, ethnic, etc.—I find most useful the term used by Jan Assmann, who described memory as "connective," as functioning in an articulative way, not a definitional one; it is instead something that is "bonding" that "makes communities possible."[52] For Assmann, connective memory is also fundamentally moral, in the sense that its memorial function recalls those aspects of public memory that form moral orders, and here the emphasis on *bhakti* should be clear. Although I disagree in this book with Assmann's understanding of the relationship between literacy and memory (see chapters 2 and 3), I concur with the idea that memories form publics, and that those publics see themselves in moral terms, and these ideas will help us understand why the concept of *bhakti,* with its own moral, as well as theological, impetus, is a key locus for both memory and public formations.

The social and cultural study of memory, like human memory itself, is vast and amorphous. Since the early twentieth century, memory has appeared as a key term utilized by anthropologists, sociologists, literary critics, folklorists, and religionists, and in all cases one finds a heterogeneity of opinion and use. The academic literature on "memory" is vast and comprehensive, emerging over the past century within sociology,[53] history,[54] and religious studies.[55] Particularly since the 1980s, memory has enjoyed a bonanza of appearances in theoretical and critical scholarship, most notably as part of the postmodern critique of modern metatheories, especially of nineteenth-century trends in professional historiography tied to the nation-state, ideas of historical and social progress, and in scientific reasoning about adjudicating past events. At least one scholar has described this girth of literature as "the memory industry."[56] Understandably, historians have an ambivalent relationship with the notion of memory, many seeing it more as an enemy at the gates than a guest at the table. Scholars across disciplines outfitted their studies of memory with different adjectival designations that added to the complex character of the general field of memory research. Thus we have "collective memory,"[57] "cultural memory,"[58] "social memory,"[59] "community memory,"[60] and "popular memory,"[61] as well as "mimetic memory," "material memory," and "communicative memory,"[62] all terms suggesting that memory is essentially a social phenomenon. The social situation of memory follows the seminal work of the Durkheimian sociologist Maurice Halbwachs (1877–1945), who first proposed that memory is always a social and collective endeavor, thus opposing the view of Freud and others that memory is an individual, psychological affair. Contained in this social critique of memory is the inherent assumption that in modernity memory comes into sometimes contentious relationship with other social forms, especially coercive and hegemonic ones, such as the nation-state and its official memories. This particular deployment of memory describes the work that surround "counter-memory"[63] and the opposition between memory and history.[64] In concert, scholars of memory assert that no individual remembers without the aid, consciously or unconsciously, of a social milieu. Just as Prentiss suggests we think of *bhakti* as "participation," we might also think of memory as participation, as predicated on social cooperation. Where the two worlds intersect, *bhakti* and memory, is the space where publics are created.

Memory in Euro-American cultural and social theory is almost always construed as collective and related to "identity" formations of many sorts. Memories are regularly considered localized and tied to specific places, particularly situated within the physical spaces of civic and public culture. Memory and history are often dialectically discussed, where memory has served the critiques of history mounted by cultural anthropologists and contained within the various forms of historical anthropology (or ethnohistory). History, on the other hand, tends to receive its power from the ubiquitous locales of the state and is often the domain of the archive, the repository of historical memory. In chapter 1, I discuss this dialectic between memory and history more deeply as it pertains to scholarship, primarily within India, that seeks to recover a "historical" Namdev. But here I wish to point out one significant influence on this work at the intersection of memory and history. While I engage Namdev's public memory primarily, I call this book a "cultural history" of that memory in order to point out the methodological principles of the study, which are perhaps more exactly between ethnohistory and literary-performance studies. My claim to present a cultural history of Namdev's public memory returns us to Jan Assmann and in particular his methodological idea of "mnemo-history." Assmann describes mnemo-history as the investigation of "the history of cultural memory," the primary method for historically engaging the way cultures, or in this case publics, remember.[65] Mnemo-historical work aims not to settle historical facts but to trace, often in genealogical fashion, the connections of memory that inform the construction of cultures. The "facts" of mnemo-history are the articulations of memory focused on a particular subject, often an individual—in Jan Assmann's case, for example, the subject is the cultural memory of Moses and his relationship to Egypt played out in the fields of cultural citation from antiquity to Freud. I have not replicated Assmann's theoretical approach here, but have borrowed from him, and others, the idea that the public construction of memory forms its own archive for cultural history and indeed, one might argue, its own "indigenous" historiography. Assmann's work seeks to understand memory as a historical project, and I too undertake that endeavor in this study of Namdev's fascinating public memory in Maharashtra.

Many scholars who engage in this large-scale debate about modernity's hegemonic forms come to see memory as inherently tied to modern ideas, such as the nation,[66] and the modern configuration of religion;[67] still other scholars see memory mediate between the nation and religion.[68] Given the expansive range of memory as a field of study, one finds excellent historical investigations of memory as a practice and an idea.[69] Such "histories of memory" go a long way toward explaining what differentiates memory from history and for what phenomena memory remains a sign.

Memory also evinces a strong association with religion. For example, as a student of Durkheim, it is no surprise to see in Halbwachs a preoccupation with religion.[70] He wrote about Catholicism, Christianity, Judaism, Buddhism, and Greek religion, granting "religious collective memory" a rubric all its own, alongside "social classes," family, and locations. He chose as his first subject for the application of his ideas about collective memory the early Christian religion and the ways in which memory, and especially what he called its "localization," provided crucial social coherence. Halbwachs argued that early pilgrims and other Christian travelers set in collective memory the locales of the Gospels, wedding memory and place in a shared remembrance of the sacred geography attached to the life of Jesus.[71] Halbwachs does not argue that religion is the exclusive domain of memory, nor that memory is the only mode of recalling the past available to religion (indeed, he makes the point that formalized rational adjudication of events and ideas has always been part of Christian thought), but his choice of subjects presages the deep connections between memory and religion that would be a standard feature in the theoretical work of the 1980s and later.

While sociologists, particularly those following Durkheim, continued their work on the social character of memory, historians became increasingly interested in memory as a subset of inquiry, particularly after the Holocaust, which demolished any Western hubris to historical superiority or progress in what Hegel had termed the "Spirit" of history. A later intervention also arose within the larger context of the challenges of postmodernism and the linguistic turn of the 1980s. Pierre Nora is emblematic of this second renegotiation of Halbwachs's legacy between historiography and the challenge to metanarratives.[72] As such, Nora investigates one of the greatest of the modern metanarratives, the nation, through an expansive study of what he called "sites of memory" (*lieux de mémoire*) throughout France, which he defined as "any significant entity, whether material or non-material in nature, which by dint of human will or the work of time has become a symbolic element of the memorial heritage of any community."[73] Nora had in mind not just obvious sites, such as memorials, archives, and museums, but also ritual moments of commemoration, linguistic formulae of recollection (mottos, clichés, etc.), and visual cultural artifacts, such as books, logos, and motifs. Even archives, the exemplary source of history, are sites of memory for Nora because of their symbolic power as the inchoate repository of historical memory.

In theorizing his ideas about *lieux de mémoire*, Nora follows a pattern of associating memory with religion when he observes a deep fissure between historical and memorial recollection characterized by religious sentiment: "History, because it is an intellectual and secular production, calls for analysis and criticism. Memory installs remembrance within the sacred; history, always prosaic, releases it again."[74] Nora seems to brood over the contradictions of a society that obsessively, even "religiously," documents itself through archives and technologies of data storage, yet transforms this information into the historiography that lays waste to practices of memory.[75] Nora's sympathies for "traditional memory" are apparent and contain a kind of postmodern nostalgia for the thought worlds of the premodern. He refers to "peasant culture" as "that quintessential repository of collective memory," and clearly understands this cultural field—itself preserved as a feature of public memory and consumption—to be deeply marked by religious sentiment woven through collective memory.[76] This dichotomy of the modern and its antithesis, set along a dialectic between history as modern and memory as nonmodern, are discussed in chapter 1.

Memory studies tends to absorb another key dialectic of the anthropology of modernity, which is the idea of oral and literate societies and their differentiation.[77] In these studies, memory tends to be aligned with orality and history with literacy.[78] Yet because these studies are also sympathetic to, or within, the larger postmodern critique of metatheories, we often find the oral and mnemonic valorized as essential to understanding the meaning of literate phenomena—an argument that echoes Derrida's expansion of the idea that all verbal communication, whether written or oral, depends on the dynamics of orality, or rather the uncertainties of language use generally.[79] Scholars in this mode argue that writing, and historiography, distance the past from the present, whereas memory, and orality, make the present and the past coexist. Memory is, furthermore, the universal and public mode of recollection, whereas history is restricted to highly literate societies, and is the preserve of the elite. While such reasoning may drastically overemphasize the nonliterate mode of memory—think, for example, of the literate memoir, or the engraving on statues, memorials, or other edifices of memory—their goal is often less a matter of documenting traces of memory than theorizing critiques of history and the supremacy of literacy.[80] Yet the central idea that history requires literacy whereas memory does not is both reasonable and self-evident to most historians whose craft of historiography, like an ethnography to an anthropologist, is both the means and the ultimate end of their endeavors.

Throughout the book, these themes will recur. Chapters 2, 3, and 4 all endeavor to understand what happens in a "nonliterate" tradition, that is, in a system of memory that has access to writing, and even well-developed literary practices, yet eschews literacy and writing in favor of an oral-performative mode of address to the past and present. The book as whole stands as an engagement, in most cases in a passive voice, to the dialectic of memory and history in modernity by demonstrating a social mnemonic system at work over centuries and in multiple media. However, the key to this investigation is not the memory/history dialectic because this dialectic is not central to Namdev's memory as his admirers and followers have maintained it over centuries. What is far more important is social construction, the creation of publics under the sign of *bhakti*. For this reason, in light of Halbwachs's work, I view memory and society as intertwined in the notion of "public memory." Memory is also situated within the structures of religion, construed primarily as an antipode to modernity, as Nora finds memory in contemporary France. However, I do not view memory (or religion) as archaic or necessarily overrun by history, as Nora tends to do. Memory is certainly invested with trauma at times, following the insights of Wyschogrod, Yerushalmi, and LaCapra, but the necessity of memory to stand as a witness against the fading or purposeful deletions of history is not an acute problem with regard to the Namdev tradition in Maharashtra. Memory of trauma and suffering parallel memories of victory, contentment, and happiness. In many cases, suffering and happiness define a memory in equal parts, as when we find songs attributed to Namdev that eulogize his contemporaries, especially Jnandev.

This book, therefore, is a cultural history of the character of Namdev within Maharashtrian public memory, in which he appears as a significant exponent of *bhakti*. Within the scope of memory studies, it occupies a place similar to that of "reputation" studies, but endeavors to go beyond an emphasis on the biography of its central figure, Namdev, and extend its analysis to the cultural fields in which Namdev's legacy has long been at play.[81] Although at times I see the ideas of *bhakti*, public, and memory as distinct, the book as a whole suggests that the three notions work together in forming what scholars consider the phenomenon of *bhakti* in South Asia, both as historical subject and anthropological practice. Indeed, the theoretical nexus I propose here is a symbiotic interaction of these three ideas: *bhakti* is a form of public memory. A handful of recent, good studies have engaged the notion of "public memory,"[82] but few have been concerned with religion, and none have sought to observe the ways in which public memory sustains and even comes to define the notion of *bhakti*. Lastly, no book in English has approached Namdev's Maharashtrian legacy, though there are several excellent studies on Namdev's Hindi legacy.[83] This text is a small effort at understanding the vast, complex, and rich cultural field in Marathi that surrounds Namdev.

PART I

◈ PRACTICES OF MEMORY ◈

{ 1 }

A SANT BETWEEN MEMORY AND HISTORY

Memory installs remembrance within the sacred; history,
always prosaic, releases it again.
—PIERRE NORA

THE STORIES of the lives of *sant*s are tales of the supernatural, of a fantastic realm of experiences, summoned into the mundane world. This is why we mark off these areas of remembrance as "sacred biography" or use the more skeptical term "hagiography"—skeptical because we understand hagiography to bear no direct and intentional relation to fact but, rather, to "truth," forged in theology. These narratives are not history in the professional-academic sense, but they can serve as an archive for history. The search for history through religious compositions, and especially through hagiography, is a well-trod path in the context of European history. Following the innovations of Caroline Walker Bynum, a host of studies have used hagiographical materials as historical archives, and in some cases, scholars have argued that hagiographies are to be read as contextualized histories.[1] These studies strategically interpret stories of the miraculous to find encoded social history, often revealing the life-worlds of those people who stand outside the pale of "Universal History," such as women and subalterns.

Whether or not hagiography is historiography, the will to remember undeniably motivates sacred biography. Memory, here, serves to draw us back into the worlds of religious exemplars and to connect devotees of the present to the past. Unlike historical narratives, there is no sense of the mastery of epochs, eras, and events in these narratives of remembrance—indeed, a great store of hagiography tells us of the lives of martyrs, those who sacrifice their worldly being for some moral or spiritual ideal, a sacrifice often facilitated by the lords of worldly power, kings and the like. Yet both historiography and hagiography often seek teleologies that explain a certain development, a core trait of biography, whether of a nation or an individual, in general. Hagiographies in India often undertake the lives of Hindu saints as series of vignettes, consumed as a whole, and connected by an assumed spiritual progression, and thus track a teleology of development, similar to the most common narrative conceit of modern historiography, the tracking of a progression of events toward some end, the realization of "Spirit" as Hegel argued. In the case of modern historiography, this end is epitomized by the narrative of the modern nation; in Indian hagiography, this end is the perfection of the sacred figure, here understood to be the *sant*. It is no surprise that many of these Hindu hagiographies are described as "A Necklace of *Bhaktas*," or *Bhaktamāla*, as Nabhadas called his work, suggesting a "chain of memory" as Danièle Hervieu-Léger has used the term,[2] or "The Nectar of the Play of the Sants," or *Santalīlāmṛta*, as Mahipati called one of his major compositions, suggesting a composition of "textures" coalescing into a whole. These are splendidly circular compositions, like a necklace, a chain of events that oscillate between "argument" and "mystery," intended to impart an emotion, to give a listener (or reader) a "taste" or a sense of the *sant*'s life on Earth. History, however, follows rules and conventions of adjudicating the past, and these rules are very much modern, secular, and scientific as they are enacted and reinforced by historians. History as a discipline is intended to ward off the nonrational, replicative, and mimetic, in order to propose a rational adjudication of the past based on evidence rather than emotion, with all the caveats toward narrative and form that can be traced to the work of scholars such as Hayden White. The difference between memory and history is important not just as a scholarly theoretical debate but because it marks a distinction in the way Namdev has been studied and remembered for many centuries in India. As this chapter shows, there are two distinctly different ways of recalling Namdev's life and his influence, and though the key terms deployed in Marathi and Hindi before the modern period are not usually "memory" and "history" (roughly *smṛti* or *smaraṇa* and *itihāsa*) there is a viable distinction to be maintained between the two practices of remembrance.

Let me provide a metaphorical sketch of how I understand this difference between memory and history. Two recessed scars in the middle of my left forearm are sites of memory for me, or *lieux de mémoire*, as Pierre Nora has coined the term. Through these two scars, I recall a compound fracture I suffered as a nine-year-old child. The memory of that injury contains still more memories, immediately related, like the day my cast came off, and distantly related, like the first time, during a rainy fall day in southern Ireland, that I realized the bones ached in the wet chill. To this site of memory is also attached an archive of official documentation: records of doctor's visits; bills and financial transactions; schedules of treatments and medication prescriptions. This data cannot recreate the emotional or physical sensations of my childhood, but I can pinpoint dates, places, and times; procedures and expenses; and the names of people involved. These are the materials of the historian and, in some crude way, form a history themselves, a narrative that is sketched by medical professionals in all my subsequent medical interventions and read as a "medical history" by medical practitioners. I am never asked to remember that time, but to *document* it—that is, these traces represent the documentary history of my broken arm, not its memory. The memories of these events, however, exclude these official interlocutors and their documentation. They exist in the social nexus between me, the sites (the scars), and the people to whom I relate my memories. Thus there are two records of these broken bones, but one is memorial, while the other is historical.

Such a dialectic of memory and history remains the most basic point of contention in Western memory theory. Although late eighteenth- and nineteenth-century philosophers of history did not systematically use the term "memory" in an oppositional or conditional way with regard to "history," we can see as early as Hegel the silhouette of this later debate. In *The Philosophy of History,* Hegel is broadly concerned with the alignment of the progress of reason and of "Spirit" in the course of human self-awareness and those areas of the world (that is, *most* areas of the world in Hegel's opinion, especially India) that have not progressed, while they possess a past and a recollection of that past, their intelligence is only "half-awakened," preserved in "[l]egends, Ballad-stories, Traditions" all of which "must be excluded from . . . history."[3] As for India in Hegel's thought, he finds that "Hindoos . . . are incapable of writing History . . . all that happens is dissipated in their minds into confused dreams . . . what we call historical truth and veracity—intelligent, thoughtful comprehension of events, and fidelity in representing them—nothing of this sort can be looked for among the Hindoos."[4] One can read throughout Hegel's work the word "dream" as a synonym for "memory" used to characterize the non-Western, nonmodern practices of recollection.[5]

By the time we arrive at the work of Western philosophers of history like Benedetto Croce, Wilhelm Dilthey, and R. G. Collingwood in the first half of the twentieth century, memory is clearly understood as history's opposite in the field of recollection.[6] As Collingwood said in his lectures on the philosophy of history in 1926, "history and memory are wholly different things . . . memory [is] *subjective* [and] *immediate* . . . history on the other hand is *objective* [and] *mediate*," by which he meant that memory stands regardless of proof or rationale, while history must always rest on some ground of evidence, proof, and rationality.[7] The shape of this dialectic would largely remain intact, but the key characters would switch positions in the postmodern mode, where subjectivity and reflexivity would be lauded as method and where memory would become the protagonist of a story that opposed the metatheories of "objective, mediate" history and, in some cases, as in the living testimony to the Holocaust, would become the very "objective" corrective set against the activities of Holocaust deniers operating under the guise of "historians."

Yet many contemporary scholars of memory and history concur with the idea that these are distinct and mutually exclusive modes of recalling the past. Jan Assmann, for instance, describes the "major difference between history and memory" that "the distinction between fact and fiction is of no importance" in the context of memory.[8] Jacques le Goff states plainly that "there is no such thing as history without *scholarship*," while memory does not require the structures of professionalize scholarly fields.[9] For le Goff memory is "the raw material of history," its archive and source of substance, but memory cannot replace its rational, adjudicatory charge.[10] But le Goff, like Michel de Certeau, understands that this difference between memory and history does not excuse history from its position as a social practice; like memory, it is a social effect.[11]

In the emergent study of memory, challenges to history were less common. Halbwachs does not directly oppose memory and history, and his sociological concerns tend more toward social reasons for organizing memory in particular contexts, a kind of sociological historicism. Aby Warburg's work on art, archetypes, and social memory was well within the nascent field of cultural history in the first quarter of the twentieth century. These two streams—of an uncomplicated relationship between memory and history in the philosophy of history, and an emerging field of memory studies from both sociology and within the history of art and culture—did not merge until the "linguistic turn" of the 1980s, when together they came to embody a critique of modern historiography and modernity itself.

The specific "problem" of history in the study of South Asia, deeply embedded as it is in colonial prejudice and postcolonial "third world-ism," is well known, and I will not attempt to replicate those arguments here. A recent work by three scholars of South India suggests we examine history in premodern India as a "texture" set within other genres of composition, and I largely agree with this point.[12] If we accept this premise, a position held by others as well,[13] that history as we know it in the modern West is present, to a certain degree, in premodern India, but in traces, fragments, and "textures," then we might also understand that some notion of what is not history was also present. In this case, I argue that within Namdev's public remembrance in Maharashtra the miraculous is meant to serve as a counterpoint to regal or economic histories bound to some sort of "proof" within the narrow public cultures of royal courts, dynastic genealogies, land grant or tax records, or other records of financial transaction—all of which are narratives supported by evidence and archive, and ultimately buttressed by clear economic relationships to power. Memory, like anything else, may succumb to powerful forces (economic, colonial, social, etc.), but, unlike history, it does not depend on these powerful forces to sustain itself. Its archive is public sentiment and its text is human memorial interaction.

My aim is not to challenge the Western normative use of "history" as both discipline and narrative form but, rather, to use history as a counterpoint to memory. Thus memory, as opposed to history, does not follow standard rules of adjudication and procedure—it is not, in this way, artificial, though it is certainly constructed. Memory presupposes at least a latent social knowledge, whereas history assumes a rational reader. Memory involves sensual and physical interaction, as well as intellectual understanding; history relies only on the latter. This is important in the context of Namdev's public memory, which travels through time in the media of performance, meant to stimulate and elicit emotional responses from audiences. Although Hayden White demonstrated the aesthetic formulae of historiography, the effect of history is not an emotional recollection but a correct, conscientious representation of past events.[14] I argue that the distinction between memory and history, as I have outlined these concepts, is clearly understood within Namdev's Maharashtrian legacy at an early stage, even if the boundaries between these practices became blurred. Hence, I reserve a fuller explanation of the differences within the Maharashtrian Namdev tradition between memory and history for the remainder of the book.

I propose a heuristic division between history and memory, useful only insofar as it assists us in understanding two "textures" of remembrance: one tied to rectifiable or certifiable time, and the other to self-supporting recollection. History, here, is marked by the logic of time and place, set in the language of proof and fact. Memory makes connections freely, dips into shared pools of legend, and forms associations that are inherently social. The sense of history in the subjects surveyed in this chapter are nonsocial, that is, not dependent on a collective acceptance of the past, but appeal to a rational adjudication of evidence, locked up in systems of knowledge, such as astrology, on the one hand, or literary historicism, on the other. Recall that Halbwachs famously suggested all memory (other than dreams) is collective and social.[15] Later theorists, such as Pierre Nora, Cathy Caruth, and Elizabeth Castelli, have largely agreed. I concur with Halbwachs and others here in suggesting that the mode that dominates the recollection of the past in the Maharashtrian legacy of Namdev is a social one, tied most tightly to memory rather than to history. To many readers, this distinction may seem too academic, too wedded to social, cultural, or historiographic theory that seeks workable, if ineffable, typologies. But as V. N. Rao et al. have recently demonstrated, if we look widely in the available literatures and performance traditions of South Asia, we see different textures of narrative serving different goals of historical recollection.

In this chapter, as a means of more fully introducing Namdev, I first survey the historical engagement with Namdev's legacy that seeks to portray an image of Namdev as a figure of history. Scholars who endeavor to accomplish this task do so through textual sources, corroborating evidence in contemporary documents, and other kinds of physical evidence. One particularly vibrant aspect of the search for the historical Namdev—and I use "historical" while knowing many historians might protest—is the use of star charts, based on birth or death information given in songs or other sources. The same diagrams that foretell future events have been employed to pinpoint dates of birth, matching them with the supposedly indubitable history of the celestial sky. Rather than the future, these scholars seek to tell a story about the past. This historical search is concerned primarily with hard details of existence, of when a person was born, or when he or she died; where he or she lived; and where he or she traveled. The shape of the soul, as it were, is outside this purview. This latter space is reserved for the explorations of memory and hagiography.

We move on to this much vaster realm of memorialization through Namdev's received biography. Our guide through this survey is the pre-eminent hagiographer of the Maharashtrian *sant*s, Mahipati, an eighteenth-century Brahmin scribe and former accountant. Mahipati is the ideal adviser for this venture because he is also within Namdev's religious and literary genealogy:

he is both a biographer who relies on Namdev's own biographical work for the lives of Namdev and his contemporaries, and a performer of *kirtan* whose written corpus reflects what must have been a masterful show in the eighteenth century. Our investigation of Mahipati's Namdev, largely received as the definitive portrait of the *sant,* is also our thorough introduction to Namdev in Maharashtrian public memory in general. As a visual guide to the narrative images Mahipati left behind, this chapter includes illustrations taken from the earliest printed version of Mahipati's hagiography, published in 1890 in Pune.

NAMDEV IN HISTORY

The textual materials attributed to Namdev are diverse. Fifteen anthologies printed over 120 years exist to present Namdev's songs today, and the largest printed anthology of Namdev's work, the *Sakala Santa Gāthā,* records more than 2,400 songs of varying lengths and has been available within the Marathi public sphere for almost a hundred years.[16] Manuscripts that record Namdev's songs, though rare, are as old as 1581, though most of them date from the seventeenth and eighteenth centuries. The largest manuscript to contain songs attributed to Namdev, dated to the mid-seventeenth century, holds more than 1,800 compositions ascribed to the *sant.* Within this corpus, there are numerous subsets of songs, probably created by editors of the sixteenth century and later, in the philological mode of the great Maharashtrian saint-scholar Eknath of the sixteenth century.

The philological work of collating, dating, and cross-referencing the diverse collection of manuscripts that contain Namdev's songs appears today an almost impossible task. No single archive contains all, or even a small majority, of the texts, and several have not circulated since they were used by the Government of Maharashtra's editorial committee in the compilation of the *Śrī Nāmdev Gāthā* in 1970. My own work with archived manuscripts has taken place among far less prestigious collections, the small compendiums of songs called "notebooks" or *bāḍa*s that are the subject of chapter 2, documents carried by performers of songs for centuries. In this chapter, I rely on the general notes provided by the *Śrī Nāmdev Gāthā* editorial committee. Manuscripts without colophons are generally dated according to their contents and orthography, and for this information I depend on the adjudications made by the committee and printed in their introduction to the edited edition of Namdev's songs.

Three collections of songs in particular have emerged from the numerous manuscript sources as cohesive units. These are all biographical works whose subject is Namdev's purported contemporary and friend, the yogi-saint Jnandev. The *Ādi*, or "Beginning," tells the story of Jnandev's life, starting with his grandparents and ending with the trials he and his siblings are said to have endured in Paithan in order to have their caste reinstated, required because their father was a Brahmin who had elected to renounce or take *saṁnyās*.[17] This text is usually coupled with another that is said to tell the story of Jnandev's voluntary entombment, or *samādhi*. This narrative is called simply *Samādhi*, in reference to the deep state of meditation that Jnandev is believed still to maintain in his tomb in Alandi. Situated in narrative time between these two stories about Jnandev is a composition called the *Tīrthāvaḷī*.

There are two very different versions *Tīrthāvaḷī*. The best known of the two versions of the *Tīrthāvaḷī* is represented in manuscripts from the mid-seventeenth century. This version begins with the story of Jnandev and Namdev traveling throughout northern India, hence the name, a "Garland of Pilgrimage Places." However, a major part of the story actually takes place within the confines of Pandharpur for reasons that will become clear when we discuss Namdev's sacred biography below. Though ostensibly about Namdev's journey to pilgrimage sites all over India, it is really only about Pandharpur and its greatness. I call this version the biographical *Tīrthāvaḷī* because it is written in the third person and involves Namdev as one character among several. The second version of this story, and the older one in terms of representation in manuscripts, shares the same name but almost none of the same characteristics. This is a story in which Namdev alone travels the length and breadth of India, north to south and east to west, visiting almost every major site of the worship of Shiva and Vishnu in all their forms. Although the refrain of this poetic narrative constantly recalls the figure of Vitthal in Pandharpur, it is a true travelogue, rather than a disguised argument for the supremacy of Pandharpur. For reasons I speculate on below, this second version of the travel story is obscure and has been printed only twice, even though it is the oldest attested work attributed to Namdev in any manuscript in Marathi, contained in a text completed in 1581 C.E. I refer to this version of the story as the autobiographical *Tīrthāvaḷī* because it is composed in the first person and attributed to Namdev. I engage these two *Tīrthāvaḷī*s in greater detail in chapter 4. Early references to Namdev are found in the compositions of his family (*kuṭumba*), such as those of Rajai, his wife; Vitha, his son; and Gonai, his mother, and also in the compositions of his close associates (*sant-parivār, -melā, -saṅga*, etc.), including those of Gora Kumbhar, a pot-ter; Visoba Khecar, Namdev's Natha *shaiva* guru; Cokhamela, a friend and a member of the *mahar* "untouchable" caste; and Janabai (Jani), a low-caste woman remembered to be Namdev's closest disciple (*dāsī*). Although Jnandev and his siblings—Nivritti, Sopan, and Muktabai—are also remem-bered as companions of Namdev, Jnandev's songs appear rarely, if ever, to mention Namdev.[18] This does not mean that Jnandev did not know Nam-dev but, rather, that Jnandev's songs generally did not concern biography or autobiography; the historical truth of their friendship is beyond my ken to determine and has remained an unsettled subject in Marathi scholar-ship for over a century.[19]

No trace of Namdev is found in any court records or inscriptions attrib-uted to the local ruling family that would have existed in Namdev's pur-ported lifespan, the Yadavas, though some legends suggest that Hemadri, the great Yadava minister under Ramchandra's rule (c. 1271), had an inter-est in the *sant*. The earliest written record not contained within the Var-kari ambit is attributed to the Mahānubhāv tradition. The Mahanubhavs arose in the thirteenth century around the figure of Cakradhar, remem-bered as a native of Gujarat who came to Maharashtra in his youth.[20] The Mahanubhavs are essentially *vaishnava,* or rather, Krishnaite; their theo-logical nucleus is formed by the *pañcakṛṣṇa* or "five Krishnas," a lineage of five reincarnations of Krishna, of which the last was Cakradhar.[21] Among the several biographies produced by Mahanubhav devotees, the account of the life of Cakradhar, the *Līlācaritra,* attributed to Mhaibhata (a contem-porary of Cakradhar) is probably the most famous, and almost certainly the first biography in Marathi as it is said to have been composed in 1278.[22] Many parallels exist between the prose and plot of the autobiographical *Tīrthāvalī* and the *Līlācaritra.* The protagonists of the two narratives share a simple style of language, attention to geographical details, and an em-phasis on the minutiae of experience and feeling. Like Namdev, Cakradhar was a traveler and a preacher of sorts, around whom legends recall a trou-bled early life—a gambling problem, so the story goes—followed by a change of heart.[23] In Namdev's case, as seen in the last three chapters of the book, there are some biographical traces that allege Namdev was a robber. Where Namdev is remembered in northern India as having immi-grated to Punjab for much of his adult life—and by Sikh accounts, to have died there in Ghuman—Cakradhar, legends assert, came to Nagpur in Maharashtra from Gujarat in search of the perfect land in which to live a life of penance and communal solidarity.[24] The similarities in accounts, coupled with the historical proximity of the figures, suggest that the advent of the stories of these two figures in Marathi contexts occurred close in time to one another.

The relationship between the Mahanubhavs and the Varkaris involved more than a shared interest in biography. By many accounts, the two religious groups were bitter rivals, disparaging each other in their narratives, though the lion's share of lampooning came from the Mahanubhavs, directed at the Varkaris.[25] For example, the *Līlācaritra* attributes the origins of the Varkari religion and the deity Vitthal to a clumsy attempt at stealing cattle.[26] Far from being an incarnation of Krishna or Vishnu, Vitthal is portrayed as a common cattle thief who traveled the countryside terrorizing villagers, flanked in his exploits by two assistants, "Nemdev" and Mhaya. When one particular attack went wrong near Pandharpur, the three would-be thieves were killed. Cakradhar, according to Mhaibata's account, recalled that the residents of Pandharpur erected a "hero stone" to the leader of the thieves, Vitthal. The story seems an unlikely explanation for the origins of Vitthal, but functioning as something like religious slander, it perhaps does tie Namdev (or "Nemdev") to Vitthal as a servant in the achievement of the latter's aims. If there is any metaphorical value in the tale, it might be to point out that Namdev traveled the countryside with Vitthal as his "leader" and gathered the attention of villagers with his verses. Of historical import to Marathi scholars is the apparent need for the Mahanubhavs to grapple with the rise of the Vitthal cult and with one of its apparently prominent figures, Namdev. Although the *Līlācaritra* is attributed to a period that coincides with Namdev's floruit (though if one follows traditional dates for Namdev, he would have been at most only eight years old), the earliest manuscripts of the *Līlācaritra* date from the early seventeenth century.[27] The text thus provides historical corroboration for the existence of a figure ("Nemdev" but possibly Namdev), associated with Vitthal, but only insofar as one accepts its purported period of composition.

To my knowledge, no other mention of Namdev—if this *is* a mention of Namdev—appears in Mahanubhav compositions until the *Smṛtisthaḷa*.[28] Tradition places the composition of the text in the first decade of the fourteenth century and assigns the work to Nagadev, otherwise known as Bhatobasa.[29] The *Smṛtisthaḷa* purports to record the discourses of Cakradhar. Nagadev was supposedly handpicked by Cakradhar to succeed him as the sect's leader (*ācārya*) after Cakradhar's death. In the biographical tradition, Nagadev's work retains the character of firsthand experience and assiduous attention to detail. This proximity to Cakradhar, proven through the text (even as the text is "proven" through the proximity), probably lent to Nagadev the authority necessary to be the leader of the Mahanubhavs in his day. Nagadev reports a debate between "Vishnudas Nama" and the Mahanubhav, Damodar Pandit (fourteenth century), in which the Mahanubhav philosopher bettered the simpleton Namdev.[30] The debate or *saṃvād* is a very common narrative frame in which to set the meeting of figures who stand as exemplars of particular cultural fields (the *samvad* is used in very early speculative or philosophical debates in the Upanishads and similar literature of around the sixth century B.C.E., for example). The most common form of the *samvad* in *bhakti* hagiography seems to involve an encounter with competing traditions or with representatives from the generalized field of power, that is, kings, sultans, Brahmins, Muslim "judges" (*qāzī*), and the like.

At least one modern scholar of Namdev, S. B. Kulkarni of Nagpur University, who is one of the most prominent voices in the historical study of Maharashtrian *sant* figures, has suggested that this reference to a "Namdev" is not to the Namdev of the fourteenth century (actually, Kulkarni believes even *that* Namdev lived much earlier, in the late twelfth and early thirteenth centuries).[31] Instead, Kulkarni believes this is a reference to a sixteenth-century Namdev, Vishnudas Nama, discussed in chapter 4. Although Kulkarni does not adequately account for the interaction between this sixteenth-century Namdev and the fourteenth-century Damodar Pandit, the rhetorical device of *samvad* has often been employed to put into conversation figures who lived centuries apart. For example, in my own research, I have found at least one *samvad* staged between Namdev and Kabir, between whom at least a century existed by most scholarly accounts, if not more. What is clear from the *samvad* and other references is that someone named Namdev was significant enough to garner the literary attention of Mahanubhav leaders in two chief textual productions attributed to the thirteenth and fourteenth centuries, roughly coterminous with *sant* Namdev's traditional dates of life.

The legend of Namdev meeting the challenge of a sultan in debate occurs in a small portion of the *Mahikāvatīcī Bakhar*, with a figure who is unnamed for reasons indicated in chapter 5 but who appears to be Giyasuddin Balban (1200–1287), who came to power in the Slave Dynasty of the Delhi Sultanate in 1266. This text is perhaps the oldest representative of a long tradition of Marathi prose chronicles called *bakhar*.[32] The composition of the portion of the *Mahikāvatīcī Bakhar* that contains the story about Namdev was finished, according to its colophon, in 1538; the entire *bakhar* was edited in the seventeenth century.[33] The story in this *bakhar* constitutes the next major document in the search for the historical

Namdev as well as a rare, if not single, source associated with royal or dynastic chronicles that can be used as an archive in reconstructing a historical view of Namdev in Maharashtra.[34] The Marathi *bakhar* form is considered a royal prose history, akin to the more poetic and more recent Marathi chronicle genre, the *povāḍā*. The *bakhar* form is also similar to the romantic/erotic poetic genre, the *lāvaṇī*. Poet-performers called *śāhirs* often composed within these three poetic forms—*bakhar, povada,* and *lavani*—that were popular in courts and in public performances during the Maratha period (1600–1818), particularly so in the court of Shivaji and in Thanjavur.

This reference to Namdev in this historical text appears to Maharashtrian scholars to corroborate the existence of *a* Namdev in the vicinity of Delhi in the late thirteenth century. In Namdev's received biography, it is believed he traveled to northern India with Jnandev in his youth, then again alone in the latter half of his life. Yet his years of life as generally accepted by scholars and believers are from 1270 to 1350 C.E. S. B. Kulkarni, noting that Jnandev is not mentioned in the *bakhar* and finding it improbable that someone could have accomplished two such extensive journeys before the age of seventeen, concludes that Namdev's dates must be much earlier than those usually given.[35] He suggests the dates 1207 to 1287 C.E., thus allowing for the scenario portrayed in the *bakhar*. Chapter 5 offers an extended analysis of Namdev's appearance in the *Mahikāvaticī Bakhar,* and related narratives from other sources.

There have been perennial debates about when Namdev lived, and debates about dates of life and death are the cornerstone for biographical historiography. A key topic of these debates is the evidence of family genealogies (*vaṁśāvaḷīs*). By tracing lines of kinship back to Namdev, an estimate is made about his years of life. Many such genealogies can be found for Namdev, and, naturally, they conflict.[36] Arguments were also based on evidence internal to Namdev's purported corpus of songs. Of these songs, one appears with the most regularity as it seems to make a statement of biographical fact for the benefit of posterity—in essence, it "archives" itself. It reads:

Listen as I draw out the story
Of how my star chart [*janmapatra*] was written by the Brahmin Babaji.
According to his calculations, [Namdev's birth] was at the count of
    twenty-nine years,
[When] the sun was in the east over the star Rohiṇī,

And it was Sunday, the eleventh day of the dark half of the month
  Kārttik,
In the first [*prabhāva*] year within the Śālivāhan calendar,
When my mother gave birth to me.[37]
That day is written on [people's] tongues by God.
[The Brahmin] read the signs and saw
That [the child] would promise to compose a million songs.
The chart is proof that in a lifetime of eighty years
The Name [of God would] grew [through the practice of] *kirtan*.[38]

This song is attested in a manuscript probably from the late seventeenth
century from Pandharpur, according to the editors of the *Śrī Nāmdev
Gāthā* and is exceptional within the corpus of Namdev songs.[39] No other
song appears so exact in its relation to time or as concerned with "proof"
(*pramāna*). I would argue, following the work of N. Rao et al., that we see
the "texture" of history in this composition, an appeal to evidence outside
the subject, in this case, to the celestial archive, the testimony of the moon,
sun, and stars. The references made in the song are to the lunar calendar
attributed to a king, Shalivahan, the grandson of the king Vikramaditya,
who established his calendar in 78 C.E. This calendar, like others, is ultimately founded on the more general notion of dating contained within the
idea of the four ages, or *yūga*s, of which most calendars take the final one,
the Dark Age, the Kali Yuga, also called the Bhakti Yuga, as the starting
point for the enumeration of days. Dating is accomplished by reconstructing the Śālivāhan calendar to find what date corresponds to the first year
in a cycle of sixty in which Sunday (*ravivār*) was the eleventh day of the
dark fortnight of the month of Kārttik.

The science (*śāstra*) of creating star charts based on the birth of a child,
as a predictive tool for life, is an old practice, one not confined to a special-
ized elite. As shown in the discussion below on the notebooks carried by
performers through centuries, there is often an association between the
craft of the traveling *kirtan* performer and the *jyotiṣthar*, or "fortune teller,"
the person who conducts a mathematical analysis based on Hindu astrology. These charts are not only predictive of the future, based on the influences of planets and stars during the course of a subject's life, but they are
also diagnostic of personality. Hence, any attempt by a historian to recon-
struct Namdev's *janmapatra* (astrological chart) based on evidence given
in a song must also yield the portrait of Namdev as he is received in
hagiography—a circle is formed between historical adjudication based on

numbers and celestial facts and the character of a *sant*. This balance of fact
and character has long held a place in the modern Western practice of historical biography. There is a rich tradition of using such exact references of
the birth of famous figures, and especially of kings and saints, to "explain"
their lives through science. In 1940, S. Vyas wrote a book in Marathi in
which he gives *janmapatra*s for the key Maharashtrian *sants*.[40] So an astrological chart, like the one that appears in the Government of Maharashtra's edition of Namdev's songs, is read to indicate reasons that Namdev
had the characteristics he is said to have exhibited, such as a desire to write
songs, a simple-minded nature, and propensity for travel.[41]

Here we have a confluence of history and memory. A historical desire to
rectify facts, dates, and events with the aid of corroborating evidence is
clear, but conclusions are also drawn to justify the nature of a personality,
the stuff of sacred biography. Given that the earliest record of this song is
in a manuscript from the late seventeenth century, and that it is unique
within Namdev's corpus of songs, one might be tempted, perhaps correctly, to assume that it was composed as part of the tradition of constructing star charts rather than as a record of Namdev's time, that is, as a
later addition to Namdev's corpus in the late seventeenth century. If this is
so, it says something interesting about the role of rationality or indigenous
science in determining the past. It would indicate an impetus to discuss
the past in a way different from the mere statement of fact that rests on the
assumed authority or even divinity of an author, something we might consider more akin to hagiography. We would have to suppose here that in the
late seventeenth century someone within the sphere of Namdev's devotional world believed that it was necessary to invoke the science of the
stars to "prove" the dates of Namdev's life, to offer a historically sound argument, a science applicable to all people, king to peasant to *sant*. This
would appear very much as a "texture" of history within the field of
memory.

Based on this song and the science of reading the stars, we have a number
of arguments from important Maharashtrian and non-Maharashtrian
scholars of the nineteenth and twentieth centuries. Scholars like R. G.
Bhandarkar, R. D. Ranade, T. H. Avate, and M. A. Macauliffe all accepted
the date of Namdev's birth as determined by this song. R. Bharadvaj, writing in 1898, read the word *pramoda*, or fourth, rather than *prabhāva*, or
first, in a manuscript in his care. Based on this difference, Bharadvaj argues
for different lifespan dates for Namdev, from 1309 to 1372, finding the last
two lines of the poem cited above to have been added later, thus not confin-
ing his age to eighty as those lines suggest. Given these dates, Bharadvaj

suggests that Namdev and Jnandev were not contemporaries; Namdev lived later and wrote his biographies of Jnandev based on the testimony of others.[42] Given that a slight change in a word can shift the *sant*'s life by decades, we see a proliferation of possible dates supported by astrological and other evidence. Of course, this leads to several conjectures about Namdev's date of death.[43]

Connected with the latter is another historical problem for scholars of Namdev. Given that Namdev is remembered to have been a traveler, and a figure significant in the *Guru Granth Sahib*, we see centuries of debate about where Namdev died, with biographers and scholars selecting one of three: in Pandharpur, on the second step (*pāyrī*) of the old entrance to the Vitthal temple (Ill. 1.1); in Ghuman, in Punjab; or in Narsi Bahmani (near Pandharpur), where he is said to have been born. All three places have memorials (*samādhi, smrtisthaḷa*), temples (*mandir*), and other physical sites attesting to his final rest.[44] While these conjectures are based on the evidence of Namdev's songs, they are reinforced by an appeal to physical sites. The evidence for this "history" is a "site of memory," a *lieu de mémoire*, as described by Pierre Nora (1989).

Another common site of memory is encompassed by visuality, by depictions of people or metonymic representations of events, the function of the memorial and the portrait. In the case of Namdev, there is very little visual record in terms of portraiture before the modern advent of devotional poster art and printing press folios. Some visual representations of Namdev

ILLUSTRATION 1.1 Namdev *payri*, or "step," at the Vitthal Temple in Pandharpur.

SOURCE: AUTHOR'S PHOTO.

ILLUSTRATION 1.2 "Group of Indian Saints" depicting Namdev, third from left.

SOURCE: REPRODUCED FROM L. BINYON, *THE COURT PAINTERS OF THE GRAND MOGULS* (LONDON: OXFORD UNIVERSITY PRESS, 1921), PLATE 19. USED BY PERMISSION.

are presented below and in subsequent chapters, but here we might note what I believe is the first visual representation of Namdev. A small portrait of Namdev appears in what is probably an early eighteenth-century Mughal miniature painting.

The illustration provided is only the left half of a predella that features twelve various Hindu *sants* and Sufi *pīrs* (Ill. 1.2).[45] The painting was likely composed during the reign of Shah Jahan (r. 1627–1658) or possibly even during the reign of Aurangzeb (1658–1707). Namdev is drawn with the *sants/bhagats* Raidas (early fifteenth century) and Pipa (fifteenth century) to his right, and Sain (latter fourteenth century?), Kamal (early sixteenth century?), an Aughar *shaiva* ascetic, and Kabir (fifteenth century) to his left. Kabir and Namdev are depicted as the eldest, with Raidas and the Aughar ascetic depicted in an age between Kabir and Namdev, on the one hand, and Sain, Pipa, and Kamal as the most youthful, on the other. The *sants* all face in different directions, though Pipa and Sain appear to be gazing at one another.

However, the figures depicted on the right half of the predella are all gazing over at their counterparts on the left (their right); they are: Pir

Muchhandar and Gorakhnath (both remembered as contemporaries of Kabir); a figure named "Jivarupa" which appears to be a conflation of Rupa Goswami and Jiva Goswami, both sixteenth-century Gauḍīya Vaiṣnava disciples of Caitanya (late fifteenth to early sixteenth centuries); a figure labeled "Lal Swami," which may be a depiction of Lal Sahib Fakir, a contemporary of Jahangir (r. 1605–1627); and a figure labeled as a *pir panth swami,* which I take to mean a "holy man of the Sufis." Above the predella Sufis are displayed dancing and swooning. The painting as a whole describes a religious syncretism between Islam and Hinduism, and between *shaiva* and *vaishnava,* and may reveal a predisposition toward the northern *santmat,* or the *nirguna* and nondual (*advaita*) theological-poetic traditions of *bhakti.* The figures on the left, with the exception of the Aughar ascetic, are all *bhagat*s canonized within the *Guru Granth Sahib,* though Nanak is conspicuously missing from this montage. In any case, Namdev's inclusion here makes plain his importance in the devotional worlds of central, western, and northern India as remembered visually in this image, and it suggests a visual historical record produced in the Mughal court, a kind of visual ethnography akin to what the British would accomplish through photography and their nineteenth-century obsession with caste and racial difference (see chapter 5). There are many more ways in which modes of record—visual, textual, corroborative, and localized—help to form a historical vision of Namdev's past, but this vision is, like so many others associated with "saints" of all sorts, a matter of constant contention. Of course, this is the mode of science, a field of play that is always "advancing" in knowledge, thus inherently incomplete. In contrast to this world of history, we can see one of memory, where the past is received not uncritically, but with a different set of referents and a differing agenda, and always in retreat from a position of completeness, for the moment remembered.

At the very earliest period of Marathi sacred biography, and in historical records from Shivaji's court of the seventeenth century, Namdev appears in various ways, not all flattering. Yet even at such an early stage, Namdev's legacy demonstrates its broad appeal and its ability to interconnect various fields. Namdev was important enough to warrant attention by detractors as well as at least one court historian, as attested to in texts both germane to the Namdev Maharashtrian tradition and outside it, such as the Mahanubhav work and the early *bakhar* literature. These two sources, along with the autobiographical story of Namdev's travels (dated to 1581) and the significant attention given to Namdev in one of the earliest collections of Varkari devotional songs, a manuscript from Dhule finished in 1631, indicate Namdev's star was rising in the galaxy of devotionalism in India over several centuries. Namdev can therefore be said to be a subject of historiography in Marathi-speaking circles from a period possibly coterminous with his own traditional dates of life, but certainly within the copious written sources in Marathi that date to roughly the late sixteenth and early seventeenth centuries.

I have yet to encounter any Marathi, Hindi, or English scholar who would suggest that Namdev, as a *sant* who lived some time between the thirteenth and fifteenth centuries, never existed. Scholarly debates about Namdev seek to pinpoint biographical details—dates of life and death, places of birth and death, and so on—and to determine if, and when, other figures used the name "Namdev" or a variation to compose poetry, and what songs have been confused among these later figures and the first Namdev. The historical method opens up these possibilities to scrutiny and provides a guide through details of a recreated life. But the historical method is not designed to understand the contours of belief or the emotional echoes of memory. In Marathi, as in many languages, this remains the purview of sacred biography, and it is to this field of memory that I now turn.

NAMDEV IN PUBLIC MEMORY

I refer to Namdev's biography as being "received" because, during my several years of ethnography in India among Namdev's many communities, I have found that his biographical details come from a heterogeneous pool of public knowledge rather than a definitive text, tradition, or archive; indeed it is my conviction that public memory prefigures these latter sources, as well as reabsorbs them. As I discuss Namdev's eighteenth-century biographer, Mahipati, I show that he suggests a scrupulous use of textual sources, though these sources go largely unnamed. Where they are named, if one were to follow the trail back in time one would be led not to the historical Namdev but to secondary sources, famous hagiographers blessed with the seal of authority. In Mahipati's case, the chief source within this sphere is Nabhadas, who is said to have composed hagiographies in northern India one century earlier and to have done so in a proto-Hindi dialect. I venture a guess at textual sources, but I also argue that the ephemeral archive of public religious memory, maintained primarily in performance, is the chief source for the life of Namdev and perhaps for the lives of all saints, and though it is open to historiographic scrutiny, it takes no sustenance from it, and answers none of its questions satisfactorily.

In the survey that follows, I consider the account of Mahipati in his *Bhaktavijay*, probably composed around 1762, the standard narrative, transported into the nineteenth and twentieth centuries more or less in this form. Mahipati is considered the authoritative biographer of the Varkari *sant*s and other sacred figures. He was a writer by profession, having served as scribe to a Mughal landlord and to the village of Taharabad near Nasik in what is now Maharashtra. Mahipati is characteristically self-effacing, though he is considered the preeminent biographer of the Maharashtrian *sant*s. He calls himself "dull-witted" (*mandamati*) and "unlearned" (*ajñāna*), perhaps taking his cue from Namdev whose autobiographical references are likewise often self-effacing, and claims to know neither Sanskrit nor the *purāṇa* literature, though we find a reference to the contents of the Sanskrit *Bhaviṣya Purāṇa* in his work.[46] Despite this avowed ignorance, Mahipati refers to his literary source materials, stating that he has composed this book not based on his own imagination (*mati*) but on texts of Nabhadas in the "northern country" composed in the "Gwalior" language and on the work of Uddhava Ciddhan of Mandesh.[47]

In the early seventeenth century, Nabhadas produced his *Bhaktamāla*, which may have drawn from the earlier work of another hagiographer, Anantadas.[48] Around 1588, the biographer Anantadas produced "Introductions" (*paracaī* in Marathi and Hindi; *paricaī* also in Marathi) to the lives of significant figures: Namdev, Kabir, Pipa, Dhana (late fifteenth century?), Trilochan (fourteenth century), and Ravidas. The *Nāmdev kī Paracaī* attributed to Anantadas is attested in a manuscript from 1658;[49] by comparison, the oldest attested version of the *Kābir kī Paracaī* is from 1636.[50] By Anantadas's reckoning, Namdev is the "first *bhakta* who lived in this Kali age," a significant assertion attributed to one of the first principal hagiographers in northern India.[51] Anantadas's work is the earliest full biography of Namdev in any language and securely anchors the *sant* within the pantheon of *bhakti* figures in northern India. One can therefore trace a lineage from Anantadas to Nabhadas to Mahipati. From proto-Hindi sources to the medium of Marathi, Namdev's biography appears to have traveled the same circuitous routes attributed to him in his own later life as a wandering *sant*.

One of the key socioreligious questions that arise from Namdev's Marathi hagiography is the way in which this rather cosmopolitan *sant*, whose songs are so widely sung and biography so ubiquitously retold in northern India, becomes redomesticated into a Maharashtrian milieu; how he is remembered as being Maharashtrian. This appears, in relation to Namdev, to be Mahipati's self-ascribed duty, a reconciliation of the northern remembrances of Namdev with a Maharashtrian sense of his biography. This is seen not so much in the content of the biography, where Mahipati has borrowed heavily from previous sources, including Namdev's own works, as in the organizational principles Mahipati employs in order to bring Namdev into contact with important figures, like Kabir, while maintaining a close connection with Marathi hagiographical characters, like Jnandev, Janabai, and Cokhamela.

Although Mahipati does not reference any verses attributed to Namdev himself as a source for his biography, the early narrative passages appear to correspond to one particular song found in manuscripts from Mahipati's time and anthologized in most printed editions of Namdev's verses. This song is examined more closely in a chapter 5 because it is the autobiographical source for the disputed tale of Namdev's robber days. But it also appears in important ways in debates about Namdev's dates, place of birth, and the litany of miracles that make up his standard hagiography. The song appears in the *Sakaḷa Santa Gāthā* (no. 7) in a section reserved for the "biography" (*caritra*) of Namdev.[52] The *Gāthā* is considered almost canonical in the Varkari tradition and is a regular source for scholarship and performance alike. Little information is available about the compilation of the *Gāthā* under Tryambak Hari Avate at the turn of the twentieth century, but it appears to follow closely several conventions of thematic grouping of songs present in manuscripts from the seventeenth and eighteenth centuries. Indeed, the remainder of songs contained in this edition of the *Sakaḷa Santa Gāthā* match the chronology laid out by Mahipati in the first section on Namdev in his work, as if Mahipati had referred to the same sources as Avate.[53] In addition to Mahipati's use of Namdev's autobiographical songs, it is apparent that he had copies of the *Ādi* and *Tīrthāvaḷī*. Namdev appears prominently in the latter text as one character among others, and, though he is the purported author of the text, he does not take on the sole narrative role one might expect.

Mahipati devotes four sections to Namdev's life, three sections to Namdev and Jnandev in one another's company, and three sections to Namdev in relation to other contemporary *sant*s, such as Janabai and Cokhamela. The account of Namdev's life given by Mahipati starts with an "immaculate conception" story, one found regularly for other *sant*s in India and of course, much further afield in the world of saintly literature.[54] Namdev's would-be parents, Damashet and Gonai, are quite far along in years and lack a son. At Gonai's insistence, Damashet prayed to Vitthal for a child, and, in a dream, Vitthal answered his prayers. The next morning while they bathed in the Bhima River, a shell floated downstream carrying the little *sant*. There appears here a play on the word for "shell" in Marathi (*śiṁpa*) or Hindi (*sīpa*) and the caste name for Namdev, *shimpi* (Marathi) or *ciṁpi* (Hindi).[55]

This reference to a shell in Mahipati is what could be called a judicious avoidance of what was probably then a contentious issue, Namdev's caste status. I discuss this issue throughout the book, but here reiterate that Namdev's caste or *jati* in Marathi is *shimpi*, or "tailor," while his caste in northern India is *chimpi*, or "calico-printer." This is undisputed, but what causes dispute is the position of these caste titles within the frame of Brahminical *varna* theory. Outside the caste community of *shimpi* in Maharashtra or *chimpi* in northern India, these two castes are considered *shudra*, that is, at the lowest rung, above only the so-called Untouchables. However, both in Maharashtra and in northern India the followers of Namdev who consider themselves within this caste bracket have remembered their status differently. In both cases, they understand their origins to be *kshatriya*, that is, second in the *varna* pyramid, in the position of "warriors." At the same time, Mahipati is composing this recollection of Namdev's life, a rather enigmatic and little-studied figure of Marathi literature, Dattatreya, is recalling the story of Namdev's days as a robber, a story Mahipati omits even though he was likely to be aware of the tale. In Dattatreya's context, Namdev is indeed a warrior, albeit on the wrong side of the law. Through puns and *purana*, a different story is created to demonstrate Namdev's *kshatriya* lineage. These stories are discussed later in the book, where their contexts will be clearer. Here, however, it is worthwhile to note that Mahipati may have been treading lightly regarding this issue by ascribing to Namdev a miraculous birth, one that would make any caste affiliation part of the play of such a sacred figure. The invention of biographical details like this one is a common practice. Chapter 7, for example, shows that in the hands of filmmakers, Namdev's biography is freely adapted and emended through story devices that serve to smooth over possible communal disagreements over issues like caste, Namdev's purported days as a robber, or where or when Namdev died.

To my knowledge, no earlier biography suggests this liquid origin for Namdev, though the river is important in the dispute over where Namdev was born. Mahipati, by making a reference to the Bhima River, implies that Namdev came into the world in or around Pandharpur, which lies along the Bhima River. However, Dattatreya and several modern Marathi scholars believe that Namdev was born in Narsi Bahmani or Vamani, which lies along the Krishna River in the region of Marathwada.[56] Today, both places are celebrated as the birthplace of Namdev, though Pandharpur is certainly considered his spiritual home and the location where much of Namdev's biography takes place.

A handful of miracles appear in a kind of semiotic narrative code as signs for Namdev in the hagiographies of both Maharashtrian and non-Maharashtrian origin. The story of Namdev's feeding milk to Vitthal is the second miracle that Mahipati reports, the first being Namdev's aquatic birth. The legend of Namdev's feeding milk to Vitthal features in the biographies of Hariram Vyas (sixteenth century), Anantadas, Nabhadas, Caturdas (early nineteenth century), and in the *Guru Granth Sahib* and was evidently a very popular episode in the *sant*'s life. It also appears in several autobiographical songs in the Marathi and Hindi collections and is always staged in dramatic form in performances, theatrical productions, or films that tell Namdev's life story. The tale recalls that in Namdev's early childhood he was an ardent devotee of Vitthal in Pandharpur, regularly spending his days before the austere idol of God. He would dote on the image, bathing and clothing Vitthal, performing the usual acts of *puja*, including the offering of *prasad*. Vitthal would eat this food before Namdev, but refused to do so before anyone else. When Namdev's doubtful father accompanied his son to the temple, Vitthal would not consume Namdev's offerings unless they were alone. Namdev chastised Vitthal, and God conceded by drinking milk from Namdev's hand in his father's presence.[57]

Mahipati, as in the *Sakala Santa Gāthā* series of autobiographical poems, gives us a view of the domestic hardships of a *sant*. Namdev is married, and a series of dialogues follows among Namdev, Vitthal, Namdev's mother Gonai, and his wife Rajai, among others, that all pertain to the neglect of domesticity by the exceedingly devoted Namdev. We have a story here of Vitthal appearing as a merchant who gives a bag of gold to Namdev's wife because she has complained about her state of poverty. We also have the story of Gonai visiting Vitthal to chastise him for not allowing Namdev to work for a living. Vitthal will not relinquish Namdev, so great is his love for him, so Gonai carries her complaint to Vitthal's wives, Rukmini and Satyabhama. In what may be a covert reference to the legend of Namdev's wayward ways, Gonai calls Namdev a "thief" of their everyday lives, someone who robs Rajai of the chance to have a normal, prosperous life.[58] Gonai takes Namdev back home, where Rajai has created a feast with the gold Vitthal has given, disguised as a merchant. Namdev finds the display of wealth repugnant and insists that all food be given to wandering holy men and all excess funds distributed to the Brahmins of Pandharpur. This marks the first installment of a recurring theme throughout Namdev's vast legacy in India: his refusal to participate in the world of economic and domestic gain.

This ends the first section of Mahipati's account of Namdev's life. Mahipati next discusses the life of Kabir and then presents a series of eight sections associated with Namdev. The first three sections are Namdev's biographies of Jnandev. Of these the first follows almost word for word (see chapter 4) Namdev's *Ādi* and the second and third, Namdev's "biographical" *Tīrthāvaḷī*, the first of the two mentioned earlier in this chapter. Mahipati follows the *Tīrthāvaḷī* narrative faithfully, highlighting the meeting of Jnandev and Namdev and the appeal Jnandev makes to Vitthal (Krishna) to allow his beloved *bhakta* to travel with Jnandev to northern India. However, Mahipati adds a curious portion not in Namdev's text, but present in the hagiographies of Vyas, Anantadas, Nabhadas, Priyadas (early eighteenth century), Caturdas, and the *Guru Granth Sahib*, among other sources, and mentioned above in the early *bakhar* literature. This is the story of Namdev confronting a sultan, here occurring in Hastinapur or Delhi. The sultan is given various names in the equally various accounts, a subject taken up more fully in chapter 5. In brief, Namdev is summoned by a sultan who has heard of the *sant*'s greatness as a *bhakta* (Ill. 1.3). The sultan requires that Namdev revive a dead cow or a dead Brahmin or brave being trampled by a wild elephant. Namdev survives these challenges, through the miraculous intervention of Vitthal. Given that neither version of the *Tīrthāvaḷī* narra-

ILLUSTRATION 1.3 Namdev (center, left) and the Badshah (seated, right).

SOURCE: FOLIO FROM MAHIPATI, *BHAKTAVIJAY* (BOMBAY: NIRNAYA SAGAR PRESS, 1890). AUTHOR'S COLLECTION.

tives attributed to Namdev contains reference to a confrontation with a sultan, its appearance here is odd and important to note.[59]

The interpolation of the sultan story at this point is significant because it indicates the negotiation of received biography that Mahipati undertook in his *Bhaktavijay* regarding Namdev. No other Maharashtrian *sant* had so fully entered northern devotional traditions, hence this is a unique problem with Namdev. Mahipati must insert this very popular narrative from the northern hagiographies into his own Maharashtrian milieu. He does this, astutely, in the only Marathi narrative attributed to Namdev that suggests he left home, which is the *Tīrthāvaḷī*. It is entirely an invention of Mahipati to append this incident with the sultan to the *Tīrthāvaḷī* narrative, but in so doing he appears to wish to make historical sense of the event, placing it at a moment when Namdev would have been in northern India, according to Mahipati's narrative. This process of providing chronological coherence to the memory of Namdev at the hands of authors or editors (or other creative producers) recurs, for example, in the context of the 1991 film *Sant Namdev*, discussed in chapter 7. The inclusion of the sultan story is also a key to linking Namdev's memory within northern India to his memory in Maharashtra. Influenced as he was by north Indian hagiographers of the seventeenth century, this would form an important thesis in Mahipati's work.

Mahipati presents another vignette meant to link Maharashtrian public memory to northern India. In this case, Mahipati stages a meeting between Namdev, Jnandev, and Kabir (Ill. 1.4), though it is unclear whether Mahipati intends this meeting between two *sants* who probably lived a century apart. The meeting is relatively uneventful. Namdev hears of Kabir and persuades Jnandev, while on their visit north, to make a stop at Kabir's home. Kabir welcomes them, and in conversation, Jnandev reminds Namdev that Namdev is an incarnation of Uddhav and Kabir is an avatār of Shukadeva, the son of the sage Vyasa, purported author of the epic *Mahābhārata*. Both figures, Uddhav and Shukadeva, are messengers and storytellers, thus implying an earthly role for these two new avatārs. Jnandev informs them that they were both born in shells and that they both have come to earth to restore *bhakti*. Jnandev then describes Pandharpur and secures a promise from Kabir that he will one day visit Vitthal's town. Mahipati was no doubt taking an opportunity to further link Kabir and Namdev by presenting the legend, common to both figures, of a miraculous birth in a shell floating down a river. Mahipati does not imply that this makes Kabir a *shimpi*, however; it appears simply as a means of marking similarity and creating a common stock of hagiographical capital shared by the two figures.

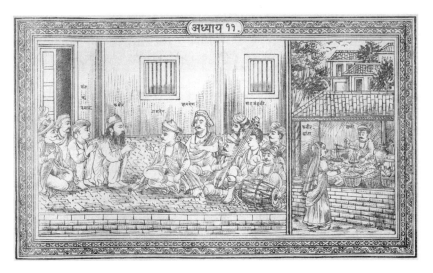

ILLUSTRATION 1.4 In the left frame Namdev (center, right) and Kabir (center, left).

SOURCE: FOLIO FROM MAHIPATI, *BHAKTAVIJAY* (BOMBAY: NIRNAYA SAGAR PRESS, 1890). AUTHOR'S COLLECTION.

The recollection that Namdev and Kabir met is uncommon, and nearly all hagiographers, biographers, and scholars agree that while Kabir's exact lifespan dates are hard to determine, it is not likely that they coincide with those of Namdev of the fourteenth century or with those of Jnandev of the late thirteenth century. To my knowledge, only Mahipati makes the assertion that Namdev and Kabir ever met. In most other hagiographies, and implied in songs attributed to Kabir, Namdev is clearly a historical and intellectual predecessor to Kabir, not a contemporary.

Yet the connection between Kabir and Namdev is very significant in northern India, and this is doubtless why Mahipati arranges for this meeting. In the context of the work attributed to Kabir, Namdev emerges as what David Lorenzen has called a "transitional figure" from the highly descriptive and iconographic songs of *saguna* (a theology of poetics that ascribes "qualities," or *guna*, to a deity) to one strand of the developing religioliterary traditions of northern India, emphasizing the physically abstract, iconoclastic, and highly philosophical, "unqualified" theology of the *nirguna* tradition.[60] Kabir recalls several stories from Namdev's life, including the miraculous drinking of milk from Namdev's hand and the repair of Namdev's roof.[61] Kabir recollects Namdev's devotion to his guru, Visoba Khecar, and his low-caste status from birth (the first mention of

Namdev's caste outside Marathi sources). Charlotte Vaudeville notes that Kabir is attributed references to Namdev's "crazy" devotional antics, a description of Namdev common in biographical and autobiographical sources in Marathi.[62]

Kabir's literary legacy grew into three major streams: the Eastern tradition, composed in areas of present-day Bihar and Uttar Pradesh, is preserved in the *Bījak* and represents a collection of verses sacred to the Kabir Panthis; the Sikh tradition records verses attributed to Kabir in the *Guru Granth Sahib,* themselves culled from older manuscripts, especially the *Goindvāl Pothīs*; and the Western or Rajasthani tradition, where Kabir is one of the Dadu Panthi's luminaries, remembered in the *Pañcavāṇi* and *Sarvāñgi* collections.[63] In all three contexts, Namdev appears either in Kabir's songs, as, for example, when Kabir lists sacred figures and their stories important to his own development, or alongside Kabir in the songs of others and especially of biographers.[64] Kabir and Namdev have an intertwined public memory that remains strong throughout several centuries of north Indian regional literature and is apparent today in multiple scholarly works in the Marathi and Hindi public spheres that discuss religion and literature in central and northern India. This bond was clearly present in Mahipati's day and required attention in his work.

In addition to Kabir's hagiographical association with Namdev, the two sacred figures share many biographical elements. Common to both are miracles of reviving a dead cow, causing a Brahmin to rise from the dead, and provoking the welling up of water in a river or pond/well, a common trope in mystical Natha literature and a story discussed below.[65] Their labor-associated caste is also characteristic of both; in Kabir's case, it is the occupation of a weaver and in Namdev's case in northern India, that of a printer of cloth (unlike his Marathi biography, which remembers him as a tailor). They both exhibit a nonattachment to family that becomes a source of contention and difficulty in their biographies, as when they find themselves admonished by their mothers, or, in Kabir's case, when he finds that his mother is conspiring to end his life. The two figures share confrontations with Muslim rulers; trickery by God to prove devotion; and, as would be almost dogmatic in the *santmat* and *nirguna* trends of devotion, the espoused need for a guru.[66] Namdev and Kabir become almost inseparable through many biographies, as the songs of Raidas/Ravidas reveal.[67] Songs attributed to Ravidas in the *Guru Granth Sahib*—the creation of which is dated to 1603–4—present lineages of *sant*s. Three of them link Namdev and Kabir.[68] Both figures share the biographical motif of a confrontation with temporal authority.[69] The connection between the two *sants* continues into the eighteenth century, when Mahipati stages meetings with Namdev and Kabir in his biographical work, and into the late nineteenth and early twentieth centuries, when the two share the designation of "national integrator" and "saint of the nation" (*rashtriya sant*), along with others.[70] Linked with Kabir, Namdev became one of the first figures—if not *the* first figure—in the general *sant parampara* or "tradition" of northern India.[71]

The importance of this meeting of the two *sants* in the *Bhaktavijay* is apparent. By positioning Jnandev at this meeting, Mahipati is reinforcing his position that it is the Namdev of the fourteenth century, friend to Jnandev, who met Kabir, and not a later Namdev (see chapter 4). Mahipati is also tying together hagiographical worlds: Namdev must be present in northern India, but must also remain essentially Maharashtrian. Furthermore, Jnandev's invitation to Kabir reminds us of Namdev's *saguna* Maharashtrian character. Jnandev recalls that Vitthal took a human form in Pandharpur and that he stands on a brick. He invites Kabir to "see" with his own eyes the figure of Vitthal. And when Kabir promises to come to Pandharpur, he is extracting a vow to link two historical figures in terms both geographical and ideological. The divide between *nirguna* and *saguna bhakti* has often been overemphasized by scholars, both Indian and non-Indian.[72] In Maharashtra, as indeed the case may be throughout Kabir's own corpus of literature, this division of *guṇa*s marks tendencies in expression, not battle-lines of debate. Thus this meeting is more than association, but rather is polemical as well, arguing that the *guṇa*s of *bhakti* represent ends of a continuum, that they are not separate. The promise made by Kabir, through the genius perhaps of Mahipati, is also nativistic in intent; it draws Kabir to Pandharpur and reinforces the importance of Maharashtrian culture within the larger public memory of central, western, and northern Indian *bhakti*. If a Maharashtrian Namdev can become part of north Indian devotion, then a north Indian Kabir can join the Maharashtrian welkin of *bhakti* luminaries.

Mahipati rejoins the *Tīrthāvaḷī* in the third section with a story that is meant to contrast the mode of Sanskritic knowledge, which is Jnandev's route through the spiritual world, with the path of devotion (*bhakti marg*), which is Namdev's mode.[73] In the preceding section, during the duo's travels, they conduct a debate of sorts that contrasts these two modes, articulated, along with the ways of *karma* and *jnana yoga*, in the *Bhagavad Gītā*. During this exchange, Jnandev tries to convince Namdev of the merits of *advaita*, of nondualism, in order to assuage his anxiety over being far from

Vitthal in Pandharpur. Namdev responds by expressing his deep and personal love for Vitthal. The narrative, meanwhile, switches back to Pandharpur, where Vitthal is indeed pining away for his beloved *bhakta.* This scene appears to exist in order to emphasize the truth of dualism and the need for *saguna bhakti,* and to demonstrate that dualism cuts both ways, causing the suffering of separation in the deity as well. Thus the overarching narrative has already foreclosed Jnandev's philosophical stance and has provided a metaphor that brings the debate to its dénouement. The text of Namdev's *Tīrthāvaḷī* that Mahipati follows so faithfully is also filled with these omniscient, third-person narratives, as if Namdev is a character in the story rather than its author.

The third section begins as the two find themselves in an arid land and suffering intense thirst. This is an opportunity for a miracle that has become a hallmark of Namdev's devotional life and a pan-Indian mystical trope. The two find a well, but the water is too deep to be retrieved. Jnandev states that his yogic powers, a byproduct of his practice of *jnana* and Natha *yoga,* will allow him to fly down the well and drink his fill, which might be a reference to the motif of the upside-down well in Natha devotional songs.[74] Returning to the top of the well, he offers to bring water for Namdev, but the *bhakta* refuses. Instead, Namdev calls out to Vitthal, who, the narrative reports, hears his cries. Vitthal causes the well to overflow with water, thus supplying Namdev, Jnandev, and the drought-stricken village with water. Seeing this, Jnandev admits the superiority of *bhakti,* or "devotion," over *jnana,* or "knowledge."

This story carries a number of valences significant in working out how *bhakti* imagines a public figure like Namdev into being. One valence is through a comparison of other paths of spiritual life. Jnandev's yogic powers serve only him; though he might perform a service for someone else, he commands this power. This is not a social power. However, in Namdev's case, his plea for help transcends individual ability, and the result, likewise, extends far beyond his own needs.

Two other vignettes make up the remainder of the third section, both of which depart from Namdev's *Tīrthāvaḷī* text. The first appears to be a condensation and insertion of the second of the two versions of the *Tīrthāvaḷī,* the one described here as both older and truer to the form. It is certainly possible that Mahipati would have had both versions of the travel story, and we have already seen that the biographer makes efforts to integrate almost all available materials into a cohesive narrative. Although the older of the two *Tīrthāvaḷī* stories does not mention Jnandev, Mahipati uses the third person plural pronoun in this section, implying that Jnandev too traveled to these places. No direct correlation can be drawn between this section and any other text I have encountered, so I offer this explanation as conjecture.

The second episode involves another signature miracle associated with Namdev, one recalled in various sources: by Vyas in the sixteenth century; in a song attributed to Kabir; in a song attributed to Namdev in the Fatehpur manuscript of the sixteenth century; in the *Guru Granth Sahib* and other Sikh hagiographical sources; and in the biographical accounts of Anantadas and Nabhadas. This is the story of Namdev's causing a temple to turn by means of the performance of his *kirtan*. The story suggests that the two *sant*s reached the town of Aundhya, where a temple to Naganath, "The Lord of Serpents," or Shiva, was to be found. Namdev began to perform a *kirtan* before the temple's entrance, and this attracted the temple's patrons who awaited the morning arrival of the temple's Brahmin priests. When the Brahmins arrived and found a lowly *shimpi* playing hand-cymbals and singing, they demanded that he remove himself. He obliged, shifting behind the temple to carry on his performance. The priests went inside the temple and conducted their rituals. But when they emerged, they found Namdev again in front of the main gate. At first angry, they later became puzzled: "The sun appears to have come up in the west."[75] Their bathing place likewise had been transposed. After some calculations, they realized that the temple itself had rotated as they were inside to face Namdev. Begging forgiveness, they prostrated themselves before the powerful *bhakta*.

The fourth chapter concludes the *Tīrthāvaḷī* in the same way as the text attributed to Namdev does. This section, like the former story of the Brahmins and the temple, contains a critique of Brahminical myopia that uses Namdev as its foil. Upon Namdev's return to Pandharpur, Vitthal elects to celebrate the conclusion of the pilgrimage and the return of his *bhakta* with a feast for all the Brahmins of the town. In this gathering, Vitthal appears as the chief host, taking human form. The Brahmins observe Vitthal in this form and marvel at his beauty and perfection. They judge such a perfected person necessarily to be a Brahmin. The comedy of the situation is, of course, that they are not able to see Vitthal for what he is—God—because they consider themselves gods. When Namdev sits down to join the meal, they all protest to their host, demanding to know why they must sit in such low-caste company, and why someone so obviously pure, as Vitthal appears, would deign to do so himself. Vitthal then shows his real form to the Brahmins, who realize that he is God. They repent and enjoy their meal, God, lowly *bhakta*, and all.

At the end of this chapter, Mahipati tells the story of Gora the Potter, or Gora Kumbhar. In a series of tragic events, Gora—who, like Namdev, is consumed with devotion—kills his infant daughter by mistake. While Gora is dancing with devotional joy in the rain, his daughter crawls out to her father, but he does not notice the infant, and she is trampled under his dancing feet. His two wives, though furious, wish to have another child, but he refuses to touch them. One night, they each place one of his hands on one of their breasts, hoping that this will arouse him. Instead, he awakens disgusted and, in a way not clearly explained in the text, manages to sever both of his hands. The potter is thus left bereft of the tools of his trade. Shortly thereafter, Gora hears that the famous Namdev will be performing one of his *kirtan*s nearby and hurries to attend. He finds the *kirtan* under way and the audience clapping with delight to the beat of Namdev's rapturous songs. Sitting among the ecstatic, Gora feels compelled to clap, to participate in this public celebration, but, of course, he is not able to do so. He cries out to God for the return of his hands so that he can clap along with Namdev. God hears him and restores the lost limbs. The metaphorical juxtaposition of the tools of the trade with those of devotion is made clear. Gora's elder wife observes the miracle and begs for one of her own: the return of their infant daughter. A baby girl comes crawling out from the throng of devotees, the prayer answered.

The triumph of *bhakti* over personal and domestic hardship mirrors the previous two episodes, from Jnandev's acceptance of Namdev's superior *bhakti* to the display of Brahminical myopia. Yet the resolution here is not directly clear. The baby girl is resurrected and Gora continues his life as an oblivious *bhakta,* which has now been sanctioned by this miracle. As in Namdev's autobiographical accounts of domestic struggle, issues about contestations in the domestic sphere are never addressed, just delayed, as if *bhakti* were by its nature a disruption of the domestic sphere. Every solution to domestic strife is temporary and conditional and is played out in public.

The fifth section on Namdev begins with a story about Gora in which their roles are reversed. In this story, Namdev becomes the subject of the vignette, and Gora the agent of the story's dénouement. This is also a tale richly alive in Maharashtrian public memory, re-enacted in performance and film, to the delight of audiences because of its comedy, placing the *sant* in the position of the sympathetic buffoon. The story begins with Jnandev and his siblings, at the initiative of their sister Muktabai, seated in a line next to Namdev. Gora, our myopic potter, is asked to test the five *sant*s to see if they are fully "baked," if they are finished pots. Gora takes a spoon and proceeds to hit each saint on the head, listening for the reverberations of the strike that will tell the potter if the pots are solid or unfinished. Each "pot" returns a solid echo, indicating it is "done." However, when Gora reaches Namdev, the *sant* lets out a yell as spoon meets skull, and the *sant*s laugh at Namdev. Gora declares this particular vessel to be unprepared to hold spiritual substance. Namdev, humiliated, turns to Vitthal, who tells him that he needs a guru in order to complete his spiritual training.

At this point in Mahipati's narrative, we find one of the key hagiographical moments in Namdev's legacy, his encounter with Visoba Khecar, a Natha and hence *shaiva* yogi, who becomes Namdev's guru (Ill. 1.5). This is one of two associations with the worship of Shiva encountered in Namdev's Maharashtrian remembrance. The second association is discussed below and lies outside Mahipati's narrative, as it relates to Namdev's "robber" days. Here, however, Namdev comes to Khecar innocent of religious instruction. And in the entirety of Namdev's hagiography, this is the only lesson recorded that Khecar imparts to his "half-baked" student.

Namdev is directed to a *shaiva* temple, where he finds Khecar in the guise of a ragamuffin renunciant asleep on the floor with his feet propped up on Shiva's *linga*, his aniconic, phallic representation. Appalled, Namdev

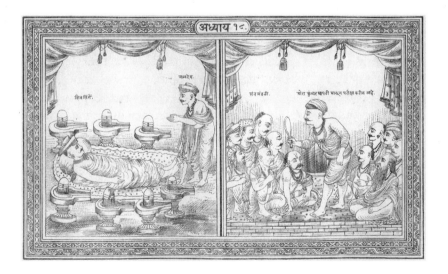

ILLUSTRATION 1.5 Namdev and Visoba (left frame); and Gora (right frame).

SOURCE: FOLIO FROM MAHIPATI, *BHAKTAVIJAY* (BOMBAY: NIRNAYA SAGAR PRESS, 1890). AUTHOR'S COLLECTION.

demands that the holy man wake up and move his feet. Khecar tells Namdev that he is welcome to move his feet to any place where Shiva's *linga* is not resting. But as Namdev lifts Khecar's feet and attempts to place them elsewhere, he finds the temple filled with *linga*s. Things and people all take on the form of Shiva's *linga*, including Namdev's own body. The point is well made, and Namdev learns the lesson of nonduality. Mahipati makes no effort to resolve what might appear to be a contradiction here. In the miracle of the well that appears in the story of the *Tīrthāvaḷī*, Namdev's argument for duality, for a difference between Vitthal and *bhakta*, is victorious. Here, however, the theology of nondualism that Jnandev argues unsuccessfully in the *Tīrthāvaḷī* is demonstrated as superior to the simple devotional dualism Namdev normally practices. How should this apparent contradiction be read?

As mentioned above, by the time Mahipati sets down his stories of Namdev's life in the *Bhaktavijay*, he is in discursive conversation with Namdev's significant north Indian legacy, represented by figures like Hariram Vyas, Nabhadas, and Anantadas, as well as Namdev's placement in the *Guru Granth Sahib*. In this context, Namdev is a *nirguna bhakta*, like Visoba Khecar, who does not valorize the image of God but, instead, finds through a nondual philosophy an abstract notion of the deity, a figure "without qualities" or *nirguna*. Yet Namdev in Maharashtra has always been a *saguna* figure, someone who worships an anthropomorphized deity, a God "with qualities." In this episode, as in all Mahipati's stories, he appears to draw from specific songs within Namdev's corpus. Here Mahipati follows a series of songs that record a conversation between Namdev and Vitthal about the need for a guru.[76] These songs do not appear in the oldest manuscripts available, but have some currency in several different sources contemporaneous with Mahipati, and with Mahipati's probable reference to them here, constituting an amalgamation of Namdev's pan-Indian and local Maharashtrian legacies. There is much Mahipati elects to omit from this pan-Indian reception; his inclusion of this story, however, points to an affinity with Namdev's position in northern traditions that portray him as a figure who straddles the ideas of *nirguna* and *saguna*.

The next story appears to be unique to Namdev's Maharashtrian memory, not repeated in northern sources and suggests many of the same themes found with Namdev's confrontation with the Brahmin dinner guests at the end of the journey with Jnandev. This is the story of pebbles turned into touchstones, that is, stones that turn other objects into gold. The tale involves a poor Brahmin, Parisa Bhagavat, who wished to perform his worship of Vitthal's primary wife, Rukmini, without the interruptions of work and labor. Rukmini gave him a touchstone to relieve this burden. However, this led instead to a duplicitous life: the family maintained the outward appearance of poverty and hence of indifference to wealth, but hoarded gold in their cellar and ate the finest foods in private. Parisa's wife, Kamalaja, was entrusted with the stone, and she confessed to Namdev's wife, Rajai, of its possession. She lent the stone to Rajai, who had complained that her husband, Namdev, did nothing for their worldly upkeep. By the time Namdev returned home, Rajai had a storehouse full of gold and fine food ready to serve. Namdev asked innocently about the secret to this wealth, and Rajai told him, showing him the stone. Namdev grabbed it and threw it into the river. When Kamalaja and Parisa came to retrieve the stone from Rajai, they heard what Namdev had done and cursed him. With villagers gathered around, Namdev and Parisa had a showdown. Parisa insisted that Namdev himself coveted the stone and had stolen it from him and his wife. Namdev replied that Parisa only affected the veneer of indifference, but in truth was greedy. He reached into the water and pulled out a handful of stones, all of which now became touchstones. Thus Namdev demonstrated true detachment from worldly wealth, having at his disposal the infinite capacity to make gold, but never using it. Parisa was contrite and recognized Namdev's superior spiritual status.

This story contains several common themes, immediately apparent to the listener attuned to a *bhakti* public. There is the juxtaposition of worldly desire and detachment; the power of *bhakti* to cause miracles, which teach a lesson; and the Brahmin as the figure who requires this lesson. In addition, the public is present as a witness to the dénouement of the story. This story foregrounds the religious "debates" (*samvad*) attributed to Namdev and Parisa, and reprinted in several editions of Namdev's songs, as well as songs in praise of Namdev attributed to Parisa. These songs take up issues of caste difference, but make no reference to Parisa's poverty. Parisa plays a significant role in the 1991 film *Sant Namdev,* examined in chapter 7. Such hagiographical encounters with figures mentioned in Namdev's songs, or who mention Namdev in songs attributed to them, help knit together the Maharashtrian Varkari networks of memory that see communities and "families" of *sant*s form in time.[77]

The next two episodes Mahipati relates are two of the best-known stories associated with Namdev. The first has appeared in the hagiographies of Namdev attributed to Hariram Vyas and Anantadas and in other important works, such as the songs of Narsi Mehta in the fifteenth century.[78] The story recalls when Vitthal resolved to test Namdev's conviction that God resides in all creatures. Vitthal takes the form of a dog and begins to steal food from various pilgrims in Pandharpur or sit near people, especially Brahmins, and beg for food, to no avail. Finding Namdev eating, Vitthal in his canine disguise steals some bread and starts to run away. Namdev pursues the dog with butter in his hand, insisting that the dog take some butter with his bread. Mahipati's version, however, adds a twist to the tale. In versions from northern India, this story expresses Namdev's devotion to all creatures, but here Namdev claims to have "recognized" Vitthal in the dog through signs taught to him by Visoba Khecar. Thus Namdev is both compassionate and wise.

The second story has been told by Anantadas, where it appears as one of two principal tales recalled by the sixteenth-century hagiographer. Mahipati relates how Namdev vows to fast on the *ekādaśi*, or eleventh day of the bright half of the lunar month. Vitthal visits Namdev and complains that no one keeps the vow to fast on this day any longer. Namdev claims that he will keep his vow to fast, come what may. Vitthal decides again to test his *bhakta* and assumes the form of an emaciated Brahmin who comes to Namdev's house begging for cooked food. The fast of *ekadashi* allows no cooked food to be consumed, but uncooked food is acceptable. However, when Namdev offers this alternative to the Brahmin, the guest refuses and claims that if he is not fed cooked food he will die. If the Brahmin dies, the guilt of his death and the sin of killing a Brahmin will rest with Namdev. Still Namdev refuses to cook food, asserting that he is someone free from the karmic rules of life and hence beyond the touch of such sin. Following Namdev's claim to incorruptible status, the Brahmin promptly drops dead. Villagers gather and accuse Namdev of "Brahminicide," a grave sin. Namdev takes the body of the Brahmin to the bank of the Bhima River, where he places it on a funeral pyre, lights the pyre, and lies down beside the deceased Brahmin as the flames engulf them both. Namdev's resolve tested, Vitthal reveals himself, saving his devotee from immolation. In this case, involving food, and in two previous stories—of the dog and the bread, and of the feast for Brahmins after Jnandev and Namdev return to Pandharpur—the sharing of food is indicative of some aspect of *bhakti*, hence of social interaction.

This effectively marks the end of the stories that are principally about Namdev. Here Mahipati proceeds to tell the biography of Janabai, recounting several miraculous episodes from her life, all finding their origin in songs attributed to Namdev, Janabai, or a purported contemporary. Mahipati does this by interweaving vignettes of miracles from Namdev's life with those of Janabai, as if to emphasize not only their connected biographies but also the similarity of their miraculous experiences. The story tells of how Janabai, on a visit to Pandharpur with her parents as a little girl, refused to leave the city. Her parents agreed to let her stay, and she was adopted by Namdev (in other stories, she is adopted by Namdev's father and thus is a sort of sibling of Namdev). Mahipati makes explicit here that Janabai's role in the family was as a domestic servant. However, in the songs on which Mahipati's accounts are based, those attributed to Namdev, we know of Janabai as a "slave," or *dasi*, signaling here her dependence on Namdev as a spiritual teacher, but not necessarily implying the further connection of domestic labor. However, as a woman, she is often depicted as engaged in domestic labor. One of the most common visual representations of Janabai shows her grinding flour with the help of Vitthal. Yet the notion of Janabai as a domestic servant, rather than a woman upon whom domestic work is incumbent, appears to be a later assumption of the hagiographical tradition.

The way in which Namdev's memory is intertwined with that of Janabai is apparent in this portion of Mahipati's *Bhaktavijay*. After introducing Janabai as Namdev's adopted "servant," Mahipati tells us the story of how on a stormy, rainy night, when the roof of Namdev's hut blew off, Vitthal came to repair it with his own hands. Though simple, the story is widely retold in northern sources, by Surdas, Hariram Vyas, Anantadas, and Nabhadas, and appears in a similar form in a song attributed to Namdev in the *Guru Granth Sahib*, in *rāg sorāth*. In this latter appearance, Namdev is questioned by a neighbor about the carpenter who constructed his beautiful house; she offers to pay the carpenter double his wages to build a new house for her. The song then uses the metaphor of the house and the carpenter to comment on the relationship of *bhakti* between a deity and devotee. There is here no mention of a storm or a reason given as to why Vitthal (or Ram, in the *Guru Granth Sahib* version) would literally build a hut for Namdev. Mahipati's retelling includes what may be an oblique reference to the story as it is told in the *Guru Granth Sahib* and elsewhere. Mahipati presupposes a listener's question, who might wonder why, if Vitthal is rebuilding Namdev's hut, he does not improve it as well, make it palatial, if not perfect. Mahipati suggests that Vitthal does not do this because he does not encourage attachment to material goods. Although Mahipati regularly inserts verses that expound and elaborate on images or moments that are otherwise drawn from other sources, here he performs more as an exegete than as an embellisher. He imparts a moral lesson, as if correcting the alternative story, represented by the verse in the *Guru Granth Sahib*, for example, of which his listeners might be aware.

The repair of the hut provides Mahipati with a chance to connect a story about Janabai with that of Namdev. Mahipati, departing significantly from previous hagiography, has Vitthal stick around for dinner. When Vitthal does not sit next to Janabai, she protests and pouts outside. Vitthal leaves some of his food on his plate, which he eats later in Janabai's hut, thus demonstrating his disregard for caste commensality, and further explicitly associating *bhakti* with the sharing of food. Interestingly, Mahipati is careful to point out that Janabai's access to Vitthal comes as a result of her association with Namdev.[79] This allows Mahipati to tell several more famous stories about Janabai: how Vitthal helped her turn her grinding wheel, a miraculous moment regularly depicted in film and iconography; and how Vitthal saved Janabai from execution on suspicion of thievery. In Mahipati's narration, Vitthal then calls on Namdev at his house and requests to see Janabai. All the other *sant*s had gathered as well (including, oddly, Kabir),[80] and Jnandev reports having witnessed Vitthal writing down Janabai's songs. To this, Vitthal states that these are glorious songs, the sound of which summons his presence and removes sin. With such an endorsement, Janabai is accepted into the company of the *sant*s. Janabai, under questioning from Jnandev, reveals that she has come to serve Vitthal as Krishna, through each of her *avatār*s, just as Namdev has appeared in his earlier *avatār*s. Mahipati's final passage, in which Vitthal assigns a scribe to each *sant* (except Namdev), is a word-for-word reiteration of a song attributed to Janabai and examined in chapter 2.[81] With this doling out of scribal duties, Mahipati's treatment of Namdev's public memory comes to an end. And the scenic backdrop of this end is important. Mahipati wraps up Namdev's public memory in Namdev's own home, in the domestic sphere, which is populated by *sant*s, even Kabir—the internal turned outward. The metaphor of the *sant*s all inhabiting the same domicile suggests something of the play of "public" and "private" in *bhakti* and its attendant tropes.

Mahipati's copious hagiography exhaustively encompasses most stories about Namdev current in Maharashtra and in northern India, but he does omit a few stories present within Namdev's northern reception. Anantadas, for example, mentions a handful of miracles not enumerated by Mahipati, including the story of Namdev summoning a bed, miraculously dry, from a river and making a stone image speak. One of the two most important stories in Anantadas's work on Namdev is also neglected. It recalls how a merchant tried to match the weight of a Tulsi leaf, with the character *rā* or half the name of Ram written on it, with the weight of his personal wealth. Naturally, the scales fell to favor the leaf, and a lesson was imparted about wealth, hubris, and the simple power of reciting the name of God.[82]

Yet the most conspicuous absence from Mahipati's roster of miraculous events in the Maharashtrian public memory of Namdev's life is the story (likely apocryphal) of Namdev's days as a robber, his encounter with a widow, and his repentance at a *shaiva* temple in Aundhya in Maharashtra. The song attributed to Namdev that records his days as a robber is likely present in the oldest layer of written records of Namdev's songs in Marathi.[83] However, the story does not appear in any north Indian hagiographies, though it is known in public memory there, at least in the contemporary period, as it was told to me by informants during my research in Delhi. Importantly, the story appears in the only other significant Marathi biography available for Namdev, also from the eighteenth century, attributed to a figure named Dattatreya in 1723; by comparison, Mahipati is said to have completed the *Bhaktavijay* in 1762. Given Mahipati's concern with sources, it is conceivable that when he composed his own biography of Namdev set within the larger work of the *Bhaktavijay*, he had access to Dattatreya's materials, or at least knowledge of the work, as well as the song attributed to Namdev that recounts his waywardness.

Like Mahipati, Dattatreya attributes to Namdev a miraculous birth and recounts familiar episodes, such as Vitthal drinking milk from Namdev's hand, the meeting with Visoba Khecar, Namdev's travels with Jnandev throughout India, and their discussions of the nature of *bhakti*, without such a clear resolution, in this case. Dattatreya's biography describes complaints by Namdev's wife about his neglect of the duties of home, a story of riches given to Rajai, Namdev's wife, but disposed of by Namdev—a general focus on the struggle between economic prosperity and the life of a complete devotee. Dattatreya's biography is filled with confrontations and debates, battles not only violent (as in the robber story) but domestic, theological, and political. There is also the story of a confrontation with the sultan, who kills a cow and its calf in this version. In addition, there is an interesting internal recollection, a story of Jnandev's *samadhi*, and the locations of the *samadhi*s of his siblings.

Another story told by Dattatreya that is not told by Mahipati, recalls the debates about the historical Namdev, in particular, regarding where he took *samadhi*, where he eventually died. Dattatreya recounts a version of Namdev's death that is rarely told, but still known by some, in which Namdev's entire family commits ritual suicide by drowning in the Bhima River in Pandharpur. Unable to bear the absence of Jnandev and his siblings, they throw themselves into the water's current: father, mother, Namdev, his wife, and their four children. This recalls the ritual suicide of Jnandev's parents. Thus Dattatreya's biography more completely frames Namdev's life, but presents it within contexts of hardship, struggle, and contention. Mahipati may have refrained from providing an end to Namdev's life story, thus avoiding comment on where among the many locales (especially in Pandharpur and Punjab) associated with his final *samadhi* the actual Namdev of history might rest. Dattatreya experiences no such compunction and indeed invokes a rather unpopular conclusion to the *sant*'s life, the mass suicide of his family in Pandharpur's sacred river. Dattatreya's account denies both the northern tradition and the dominant Varkari tradition their public memories of Namdev's final place of death, hence, of his memorialization through the location of his *samadhi*. The act of suicide by drowning (*jalasamādhi*) offers something of a resolution by washing away in the current of the Bhima River one of the abiding debates about the historical Namdev.

An Indian *sant*, perhaps like any famous figure, is situated somewhere between history and memory, pulled from the past by scholars who adjudicate facts and corroborating data and summoned by devotees who remember the *sant* for the emotional and cultural value of poetry and life stories. This survey of Namdev's position in both contexts has been intended primarily to show what shapes these two kinds of recollection have taken and to support my contention that something like the modern distinction between history and memory is active in Namdev's legacy outlined here. Moreover, this chapter presents a review of Namdev's public memory as a *bhakti* figure in Maharashtra, painting a portrait of the received *sant*. Namdev's public memory in Marathi is shaped by the interaction of history and sacred biography and the eliding of the distinction between the two. I have also tried to show how Namdev's public memory, like the historiography that takes up his life as its subject, seeks conversation with other discourses. In the case of Namdev's sacred biography, the Marathi tradition converses with traditions of northern India, quite explicitly in Mahipati's case. The interaction of voices over centuries implies a broadening of public memory in ever-widening spheres throughout the centuries that lead up to Mahipati's final iteration of Namdev's life. The increasing circumference of memory is perhaps what leads scholars in the nineteenth century to perceive a "*bhakti* movement" where what we have indisputably is a thriving *bhakti* public memory, localized, but connected to other locales.

The figure of Namdev in public memory remains, in many ways, indeterminate, whether framed in the language of historiographic exploration or in the more common mode of performative hagiography. Invention and emendation within the public recollection of Namdev's life continues into the present, transferred from live performance and literature to the "big screen." The contours of a *sant*'s life are responsive to historical contexts. The next chapters turn to the practices, especially performances, that have allowed for elasticity and continuity within the Maharashtrian Namdev tradition and have crafted a public remembrance of this famous Maharashtrian *sant*.

I maintain in this book that history "takes time" in two sense: it takes a while for the "historical" to crystallize into a purportedly accurate view of the past, and it appropriates time itself as the material under its control, as the thing it mediates between an event and an observer. Memory, by contrast, gives time back; it restores the connection severed by the lapse of time and returns the observer to the immediacy of an event. Memory is the site of continuity with the historical subject, whereas history is the source of disassociation from the past through its scientific, factual mastery. Although history, in this way, is an important tool to Maharashtrian followers of Namdev in the nineteenth and twentieth centuries, memory, and its public performative forms, holds a much more consistent and central place.

{ 2 }

PUBLIC PERFORMANCE AND
CORPORATE AUTHORSHIP

"Come now Lord
And bless me with your presence.
So vigilant I've been for days
That I've rid myself of future lives.
My good deeds lie in a heap
And I rest at your feet."
The disciple Jani was enraptured,
Listening to these words of Namdev.
—ATTRIBUTED TO JANABAI

AMID THE host of miracles associated with Namdev are several instances of the miraculous and efficacious nature of *kirtan*. Namdev turns a temple with his *kirtan,* and through *kirtan* he restores
to the potter Gora Kumbhar his hands, as well as the life of his daughter. In
this chapter, I observe, through the lenses of ethnography and textual
analysis, the shape and practice of public remembrance that takes place
within the performance of *kirtan*. The history of this performance art is
deeply entwined with Namdev's Maharashtrian tradition, and Namdev's
name has been preserved in relation to this art. To understand this connection between Namdev's public memory and the practice of *kirtan* is to
reach the heart of the tradition in Maharashtra that surrounds his name.

Namdev has been richly remembered in a variety of Marathi media over
the past century and a half. From printed anthologies, scholarly studies, and
written biographies, to theater, television, radio, and film, Namdev has entered the public memory of Marathi speakers, as well as those who revere
and recall Namdev throughout India, thinking of him as a Maharashtrian
sant with a cosmopolitan ethos. It is well understood that the strength of
this public remembrance rests with Namdev's appeal as a foundational figure of central, western, and northern Indian *bhakti,* but the activity that lies
at the core of this remembrance is less well comprehended. What practices
have transmitted the Namdev tradition in Maharashtra over time? How
have human agents interceded in the perpetuation of tradition?

The Marathi song above, attributed to Janabai, provides the hint of an answer to these questions. The soulful vigilance of Namdev's faith is voiced, and Janabai registers this voice by telling us she has *listened* to Namdev speak these words, and they have induced in her a state of rapture. Janabai's biography is rife with the motif of reception as she sits by Namdev, listening to him perform his songs and stories. While Namdev is construed as the eyes and ears of *sant* history in early Marathi literature, recording the lives and deaths of famous figures, Janabai becomes Namdev's biographer, a doting, devoted "servant" or *dasi,* a disciple of Namdev, the master performer. Whatever the historical truth of their relationship, the discursive certitude of their connection through performance is a foundational construction in Namdev's legacy.

Janabai may be the best example of this relationship between live performer and audience, oral production and reception of religious discourse, but she is not the only one to mark this continuity in verse. Nor is *bhakti* verse the sole repository for the performative, oral legacy in Namdev's name. What are the means of producing and maintaining the narratives at the core of the Namdev tradition in Marathi? In this case, this process is carried out through a performance art called *kirtan. Kirtan* in its many structures is a performance art thoroughly associated with Namdev's public memory in Maharashtra, where he is considered the first and archetypical *kirtan* performer, or *kirtankar.* I discuss what makes Marathi *kirtan* unique from other forms by detailing its practice and its function as a means of accessing and sustaining public memory. In the process, I observe how authorship functions within the context of mixed composition and fluid narratives. This brings us into the sphere of oral performance, which is often construed as antagonistic to the project of literacy. At least one premier philologist of South Asian texts and language, S. M. Katre, expressed the sentiment of many of his philological colleagues when he referred to the realm of the "oral" in the context of writing as the "pathology of the text," by which he meant that orality appears as a systemic illness that distorts the body of a text over time.[1] Yet, at least in the Namdev tradition in Maharashtra, this "pathology" seems to be doctrine.

ORALITY AND LITERACY IN NAMDEV'S MARATHI LEGACY

The Marathi Varkari tradition has a close relationship to writing and literacy. The most famous of the Varkari *sant*s could write, except Namdev.

Jnandev (also called Jñāneśvar) is said to have written down his own compositions, most famously the eponymous *Jñāneśvarī*. The sixteenth-century *sant,* Eknath—a Brahmin whose guru, Janardan, some believe was a member of the Sufi order Sijrā-i-kādrī[2]—not only wrote but also edited, collated, and anthologized the work of earlier *sants.* The seventeenth-century, low-caste *sant* Tukaram is remembered to have written down his own verses, an anthology of songs that he was supposedly compelled by jealous Brahmins to immerse in the local river in his hometown of Dehu. The book resurfaced miraculously thirteen days later and is today on display in a glass case in Dehu. Tukaram even had a companion travel with him, the *sant* Jaganade (Jagaṇāḍe), whose position in the hagiographical ensemble is entirely due to his ability to write down Tukaram's songs, creating a kind of "back-up copy" of Tukaram's work. What is said to be Jaganade's original manuscript is extant, with a colophon placing it in the *shaka* year 1653, or 1731 C.E. Mahipati, as we have seen, was a writer by profession, having served as the scribe to a Mughal landlord and to the village of Taharabad near Nasik. Visually, Namdev is almost never depicted in film, poster art, or other media as writing or seated before a text, whereas Tukaram, Eknath, and Jnandev, in particular, are almost always presented before the texts with which they are associated. These postage stamps issued to commemorate the lives of these four famous Maharashtrian *sants* clearly indicate the visualization of this difference (Ill. 2.1).

Despite this impressive literacy rate among the Maharashtrian *sants,* neither Namdev's autobiographical songs nor the songs attributed to his companions describes him as writing anything. When the verb "to write" appears in songs attributed to Namdev, it usually refers to the "writing of fate," the life divinely prescribed for a person.[3] Rather than writing, what is far more common in the songs of Namdev and his compeers is speaking and listening to the speech of others. As for books, Namdev has nothing kind to say.[4] He states in a Hindi song contained in the Marathi textual corpus:

> I don't know scripture or lore.
> I've ignored paper and books.
> Without verses like pearl-white clouds
> I have only the spotless gem of the mind.[5]

A Marathi song attributed to Janabai ("Jani" in the song) gives a description of the power of Namdev's speech:

ILLUSTRATION 2.1 Indian saint stamps. Indian Five Rupee Stamp, 1997, depicting Sant Jnandev. Indian Four Rupee Stamp, 2002, depicting Sant Tukaram. Indian Five Rupee Stamp, 2003, depicting Sant Eknath. Indian Twenty Rupee Stamp, 2000, depicting Sant Namdev.

SOURCE: USED BY PERMISSION OF THE INDIAN DEPARTMENT OF POSTS.

How many *sant*s of the past
Could speak the way Namdev does?
Nama went to the temple
And God spoke to him excitedly.

Just to tell you about this miracle,
Jani the disciple [of Namdev] writes [*lihiṇe*][6] this verse [*pad*]. [7]

In another song attributed to Janabai, many of the companions of Namdev and Janabai explicitly mentioned in scribal partnerships are featured. It is this verse that Mahipati uses to conclude the section of his *Bhaktavijay* that details Namdev's life, as discussed near the end of chapter 1. In this roster of poets and scribes Namdev is conspicuously absent:

Cidananda Baba wrote down the words
Of the verses Jnandev spoke.
Sopan wrote the words of Nivritti,
And Jnandev wrote the sayings of Muktai.[8]
The one who wrote for Canga was Sham the blacksmith,
And Khecar would write the words of Paramananda.
What Purnananda said, Paramananda wrote.
He found God when he happily met Ramananda.
The one to write for Savata the Gardener
Was Kashiba Gurav.
Vasudev was the scribe [*kāīt*] of Kurma.
Ananta Bhatt was a scribe for Cokhamela's songs,
And at last Pandurang became the scribe
For Nama's Jani. [9]

This may contain an argument in silence, as Janabai enumerates poets and their scribes. Why would Janabai, a figure so intimately associated with Namdev in hagiography, not include Namdev in her roster of authors and scribes? The implication is that Namdev remains absent because he does not need a scribe. Namdev eschews the medium of writing, but his songs endure because he initiated the medium of *kirtan*. Because of the way Jani identifies herself at the end of the song as the disciple of Namdev, any listener would likely note the lacuna and understand its implied message.

Another poem attributed to Namdev cleverly critiques literacy by employing a secondary meaning of the verb "to write," *lihiṇe,* which can indicate "to draw" or "to sketch" an image:

Artists have sketched bouquets of flowers,
But their lovely perfume can't be expressed.
The moon, the sun—even their reflections:

One can learn to illustrate all this.
But the light they give can't be drawn.[10]

The song implies the monochrome of life replicated on inert paper, the restriction of the senses from multiple to singular. There is also the suggestion that essences evaporate on the page and experience is diminished. The song is about illustration, not literacy, but the relationship between something alive and in context and something recreated on paper implies a critique of literacy. Like a drawing, the written page is a lifeless art compared to the "real thing," for example, compared to performance. The song almost prognosticates the ideas of Walter Benjamin on the "aura" of art lost in an age of mechanical reproduction.[11] The aura lost in the song is the light of the celestial bodies that cannot be captured on paper. If the logic of Namdev's song is applied to literacy, the performance of *kirtan* is the ideal form for the expression of the tradition, and the medium most suited to its ends is the human body employed in performance.

In a different song by Janabai Namdev and his companion, Nivritti (the brother of Jnandev), are attributed different modes of religious expression: "Nivritti wrote the words that Vitthal placed on his tongue . . . and Namdev expounded the practice of *nāmsaṃkirtan*."[12] Whereas Nivritti writes down his songs, Namdev sings and performs his verses in the musical and theatrical tradition of *kirtan* and in the process expands a particular kind of performance where the name of God is chanted (like *namasamkirtan*).

It is here, in speech and performance, not in literate practices, that Namdev's songs endure. Namdev was renowned for his oral performance of *kirtan*, whereas Jnandev, Nivritti, Muktabai, Cokhamela, Janabai, and the other *sant*s within the Varkari tradition were equally famous or more famous for their other accomplishments and motivations, and many—such as Jnandev, Eknath, and Tukaram—were associated with actual, physical writing.[13] Thus, even among explicitly literate fellow *sant*s, many of whom also performed *kirtan*, the preservation of Namdev's legacy through *kirtan*, through oral performance outside available written resources, is acknowledged and celebrated as a singularly important detail.[14] This consistent attribution of a commitment to oral performance in Namdev's legacy is all the more striking when one considers the possibility that many singers have composed over the centuries in Namdev's name. In this scenario, it appears as if oral performance becomes an orthopraxis distinguishing Namdev from other figures, upheld for generations.

While the technology of writing is absent in auto/biographical references to Namdev as an author, Namdev's position in relation to literacy has guided the practices of performance and preservation within the Namdev tradition in Maharashtra. How can a tradition be preserved over hundreds of years without an explicit reliance on some static form of preservation, such as literacy? How can a process of authority and authenticity be established without the aid of a single author, accountable for his or her assertions? What is the role of human intervention in an oral/performative chain of transmission?

THE MARATHI *KIRTAN* TRADITION, CORPORATE AUTHORSHIP, AND NAMDEV'S PUBLIC MEMORY

The practice and logic of *kirtan,* conducted by a *kirtankar,* has preserved the Namdev tradition and its public memory in Maharashtra for centuries. A full treatment of the sparse but important literate practice of transcribing songs into notebooks carried by performers for the past three hundred years is reserved for chapter 3. These notebooks were, and still are, a resource for *kirtankar*s, who use them to record songs and many other things. Namdev's legacy has existed in the space created between the performance of *kirtan* and the physical transcription of his songs by *kirtan* performers. However, the preeminent site of innovation and propagation in Marathi environments remains the *kirtan.*

There are at least three distinct categories of authorship in Marathi *kirtan* within the Namdev tradition: first, Namdev appears as an author through his compositions; second, particular performers become authors of their specific performances, even though they use the songs of Namdev and other famous figures; and, third, the performance form itself is attributed to an eponymous author or originator. These three elements intermix in the Namdev tradition and allow it to weather time, linguistic difference, geography, and the intrusion of various knowledge-systems over the past seven hundred years in India.

The term *kirtan* describes a variety of performance in India. From *saṃkirtan,* "collective performance," and *nāmakirtan,* "performing the Name [of God]," in northern India to *harikathā,* "stories about Hari," and *kalākṣepam,* "performance art" in southern India, *kirtan* and similar genres form a heterogeneous practice.[15] Dance, music, theater, oration, audience participation, and moral narration mix to varying degrees in the different kinds of *kirtan* in India. *Kirtan* is vital to Sikh religious practice, for example, where the songs of the Gurus are sung with precision and reverence, accompanied by melody (*rāg*).[16] However, the overlay of discourses amid the songs, extraneous musical embellishment, or any kind of dance is discouraged. In Kannada, *kirtan* is simply a devotional song but is often surrounded by other elements of performance and audience participation. Performances of *kirtan* like *namasamkirtan*, "collectively performing the Name [of God]" or *akhaṇḍa kirtan,* "endless performance," can last for days, led by a series of *kirtankar*s in relay. Sufi *qawwālī* bears a relationship to *kirtan,* mixing religious songs, adept musical performance, improvisation, and dance. *Kirtan* inevitably has been incorporated into the new generation of hybrid spirituality available at yoga studios and meditation centers in the United States, Europe, and elsewhere.

Kirtan in Maharashtra is different from that found in the rest of India, with the possible exception of Bengal, and is more complex in terms of narrative, musical, and theatrical elements than most other practices referred to as *kirtan.* A *kirtan* performance in Marathi involves a lead performer, a *kirtankar,* who invokes one or two famous songs or stories and gives a narrative philosophical interpretation of the selected texts. This is combined with music, dance, theatrical flourishes, and often a call and response with the audience. In the parlance of performance theory, *kirtan* resembles music/text/dance theater, akin to Japanese kabuki, Iranian *ta'ziyeh,* or the Turkish *orta-oyunu.* The content might be classified as a mixed form, where some material is scripted or prepared and some is improvised within the performance. The Javanese form of puppet theater, *wayang kulit,* is an example of this genre. This mix of formula and improvisation suggests the kind of "oral theory" proposed by Milman Parry and Albert Lord in the early twentieth century to explain the oral origins of Homeric verse.[17]

The *kirtan* involves the audience both as participant—a key feature of ritual, according to performance theory[18]—and as evaluator, where the material presented is well known to the audience, who would look for virtuosity and novelty amid the familiar, the remembered. The involvement of the audience, often through call and response—and at the end of the performance, through donations of money and gifts—also invokes reception theory, a means of literary criticism that approaches a text from the reader's or, in this case, the listener's point of view.[19]

In songs attributed to Namdev, *kirtan* performance has many names: *harikatha, harikirtan, namakirtan,* and *kirtan* are the most common. One also finds *viṣṇukirtan, kṛṣṇakirtan, kṛṣṇakathā,* and other variations. Although in Namdev's songs *kirtan* invariably refers to performance, in twelfth- and thirteenth-century Marathi preserved in stone inscriptions—dated from 1146 to 1289—*kirtan* (often written *kīrttan*) meant "temple" or "home" without the connotation of performance; literally, the meaning was probably "a glorious place/thing."[20] This simply might be a case of one word with two distinct meanings, but the connection between temples and performances is an appealing one. Bruno Dagens has shown how Hindu temples replicate a basic human form, or rather a divine anthropomorphic form, in their architectural design.[21] This may indicate that the practice of performing *kirtan* in or around temples was an old one—perhaps *kirtan* provided a surrogate "temple" for those positioned too low in the hierarchy of Brahminical caste orthodoxy to have access to Brahmin-controlled temples.[22] But by the thirteenth century, *kirtan* certainly indicated a ritual religious performance art, and by the sixteenth century—and probably sooner—*kirtan* in Marathi came to indicate a multifarious practice, interweaving narratives, songs, stories, lectures, anecdotes, current events, ethics, or politics; it did not, however, indicate a temple any longer. In modern Marathi too the word *kirtan* is no longer used to refer to temple.[23]

A Marathi *kirtan* can take a number of forms, from a line of devotees dancing and singing a song under the direction of a *kirtankar* to an intricate scholarly treatise, a social commentary, or a philosophical/linguistic exposition. In general, *kirtan* emphasizes narration, allegory, humor, virtuosity, erudition, and entertainment, all brought together to assess the *raṅga,* or "beauty," of the *kirtan.* Therefore, the aesthetic of presentation, and the musical mastery of a performer, are of central importance to the success of a *kirtan.*

Traditionally, the mythic sage Narada is considered the first *kirtankar* based on a reference to a verse from the *Padmapurāṇa* that describes a musical get-together with other mythic figures like Prahlad and Uddhav; it is interesting to note that Mahipati calls Namdev an incarnation of both Prahlad and Uddhav.[24] Narada is a musician and storyteller, a witness of events, and a traveler who carries news from other parts. He appears when something important happens, so that he can sing about it later. Although in general discourse about *kirtan,* Narada is often considered the earliest *kirtankar,* in Marathi, he shares the spotlight with Namdev, who is also associated with the advent of *kirtan* and, in particular, of the Marathi variation. For example, Namdev is the only figure depicted as a performer in the illustrations accompanying the 1890 publication of the *Bhaktavijay* (Ill. 2.2). Thus Namdev is usually called the first Marathi *kirtankar* and was certainly the first to present explicit descriptions of *kirtan* in his own songs and through his biography, as shown below. Stories in Namdev's biography assert the centrality of *kirtan* to his legacy, as well as the effect a

ILLUSTRATION 2.2 Namdev (center) performing *kirtan*.

SOURCE: FOLIO FROM MAHIPATI, *BHAKTAVIJAY* (BOMBAY: NIRNAYA
SAGAR PRESS, 1890). AUTHOR'S COLLECTION.

Namdev *kirtan* could have on its listeners. Namdev constantly sings about performing *kirtan*s and listening to the *kirtan*s of others, and his companions reiterate his association with *kirtan*. Like Narada, Namdev is described as a traveler, a paradigm for the *kirtankar* whose show is always on the road. Namdev is even said to have observed during his famous travels around the subcontinent the difference between Marathi *kirtan* and the *kirtan* practices of other traditions. In one of the earliest written accounts of any collection of songs attributed to Namdev—the autobiographical version of the *Tīrthāvaḷī* dated to 1581—he recalls hearing *karikatha* in south India, but not the commentarial *kirtan* that he and his companions practiced.[25]

The most common references to *kirtan* in Namdev's songs appear in his accounts of the deaths and burials of his friends and fellow authors (*parivar*) from the fourteenth century. These threnodies or *samadhi* songs eulogize Jnandev, Muktabai, Sopan, Nivritti, Cokhamela, and Cangadev, among others. Here, the actual death of a fellow author provided an opportunity to celebrate the vivacity of authorship between Namdev and his contemporaries. The threnodies are ritually performed during the public death memorials for these figures, especially during the *samadhi* celebration for Jnandev in Alandi in the month of Kartik (usually November), when Namdev's palanquin (*pālkhī*) travels to Alandi from Pandharpur. As Namdev's songs tell it, Namdev and his group, with almost Gaelic zeal, engaged in a kind of before-and-after wake surrounding the deaths of their friends, mixing sorrow and celebration, combining joyous, raucous, intoxicating *kirtan*s with grief and remembrance. The report comes to us through Namdev's voice that the *kirtan*s have gone on for so long into the night that Namdev fears Jnandev will be too tired to carry out his own demise:[26]

> They ate until the late afternoon.
> When the meal was finished, the *kirtan* started up.
> The vibrant performance enthralled Govinda,
> Yet he worried, "It's time for Jnandev's *samadhi*."
> Nama says,
> "Dear Lord, if this goes on much longer,
> Jnandev will be too fainthearted to leave us."

The *samadhi* series of songs is filled with moments of solemnity, as when Namdev sings, "I cannot utter another word; my best friend is leaving me."[27] However, *kirtan* is often associated with curative powers, both physical and spiritual. In Namdev's songs, *kirtan* is called a "remedy" for affliction (*tapatraya*) and the drudgery of life (*saṃsāra*), where the prescription is simple: "let the *kirtan* pour into your ears and you will be cooled inside."[28] Even death has a cure, because "*harinamakirtan* . . . can save everyone . . . [can] break the yoke of death . . . and cut the rope of the body."[29] Against temporality, Namdev sings that *kirtan* can "banish the ravages of time"[30] and, in the performance, "time and death are trampled under the rhythm of the dancing feet, stamped out in the ringing of the ankle bells,"[31] an illustration that conjures up an image of Shiva as the Dancing Lord, Nataraja, crushing under foot the demon of ignorance, an ally to the phenomenal world and suffering.[32] The *kirtan* is configured as a cure for every author's twin archrivals: time and death.

That the ethnographic view of *kirtan* finds a correlation in songs about *kirtan* attributed to Namdev and his companions should come as no surprise. The detailed narratives recalling that famous *kirtan*s performed at significant moments, such as on a *sant*'s death, serve not just to remember the *sant* but also to supply a model for practice. As practice, there are at least two significantly different genres of *kirtan* in Marathi: Nāradiyā, which looks to both the sage Narada and Namdev as points of origin and style; and Varkari, which takes as its subject songs from the five primary *sant*s of the Varkari religion: Namdev, Jnandev, Eknath, Tukaram, and Niloba (eighteenth century). Varkari *kirtan* also uses Namdev's performative innovations as a source of its practice. As seen below, the two types of *kirtan* are significantly different in terms of style and content. They also exhibit divergent sociocultural convictions. However, there are many points of concurrence, and the two categories are sometimes elided in practice, where *kirtan* performers use whatever means are at their disposal to construct a good performance.

NARADIYA *KIRTAN*

A Naradiya *kirtan* usually begins with the *kirtankar* offering praise (*naman*) to the deity of the temple or home, depending on the venue; to Saraswati and Ganesh, the deities of learning and the arts; to the *kirtankar*'s own family deity (*kuladevatā*); and to his/her guru (Ill. 2.3). Often there is also an image of Narada that receives the performer's reverence.[33] The audience gathers around, in two groups segregated by gender, seated opposite each other with a thin aisle in between. At one end of the aisle is the *kirtankar*, who faces the temple's deity at the other end. The performance begins with short songs of praise (*jayajayakār*) that are usually followed by various epithets for God (*bhajan*).

The Naradiya *kirtan* is then divided into two parts, the "initial discourse" (*pūrvaraṅga*) and the "key discourse" (*uttararaṅga*). In the initial

ILLUSTRATION 2.3 Vasudev Burse *kirtan*.

SOURCE: ANNA SCHULTZ. USED BY PERMISSION.

discourse, the performer presents the *kirtan*'s theme by singing a particular song attributed to a famous singer, like Namdev.[34] The song is sung in full, with extensive musical accompaniment by percussion, harmonium, and other singers; often the audience also joins in. The performer then turns to an explanation (*nirūpaṇ*) of the song's meaning through references to other kinds of compositions: the epics, popular literature, songs of other *sants*, current events, or any other cleverly utilized allusion. Often, a Naradiya *kirtankar* demonstrates his or her erudition by quoting from Sanskrit sources, especially from philosophical and ethical texts.

The singing of more praises and epithets for God separates the first and second parts. Again, the audience often joins the *kirtankar* and *kirtan* musicians in singing these songs. This is also a time when the *kirtankar* is formally honored and garlanded by a member of the audience, whom the *kirtankar* garlands in return. *Kirtankars* often demonstrate their musical prowess during this interlude between the two parts of the *kirtan*, taking up a particular song for vocal-musical elaboration.

In the remainder of the "key discourse," the performer tells a story (*kathā*) that sheds light on the song chosen for the initial discourse and that extracts from this song its essential ethical or philosophical elements. The theatrical and musical energy put into this part of the performance is emphasized by the *kirtankar* when he or she ties any loose portion of the *dhotī* or *sari* (*sāḍī*) to his or her waist, as if the action to come requires that everything be well-secured. This segment of the *kirtan* is aptly called "the famous story" (*ākhyān*) because in it the *kirtankar* retells stories that are assumed to be well within the realm of public memory. And it is here that the performance is judged a success or not. All the performer's energy is poured into this section of the *kirtan*, and thus the *kirtankar*'s own fame is or is not made. If the initial discourse highlighted the performer's erudition, the "key discourse" is a theatrical rejoinder. A Naradiya *kirtan* is almost entirely dependent on the learning and performative virtuosity of its *kirtankar*.

The *kirtan* ends with the performer leading the audience in a final round of singing epithets and praises to a deity. A tray is usually passed around to collect donations for the performer, or donations are made after the entire performance ends. The *kirtankar*'s final act is to solemnly pay homage to the temple's or home's deity by prostrating him- or herself on the ground before the image. An important moment should be highlighted here, as it happens at the end of the Naradiya *kirtan*. Before the performance officially concludes, the *kirtankar* receives audience members who honor (*darshan*) him or her as the one who occupies the "seat of the sage

Narada."[35] Throughout the *kirtan*, the *kirtankar* has dressed like and, in some sense, acted the part of the sage Narada. The performer is thus engaged in mimesis of the great sage but is also required to be original and spontaneous in the performance; a balance is struck between the familiar, on the one hand, and the novel and surprising, on the other.

From a sociocultural perspective, the performers of Naradiya *kirtan* are almost always Brahmins and usually male. However, it is not uncommon—and is becoming more common—for Brahmin women to perform *kirtan*. The audience of a Naradiya *kirtan* is usually composed of a variety of castes and an equal number of men and women, though I had begun to notice more women than men attending performances during my research in Pune from 1998 to 2001. Audience members can frequently be seen taking notes on the discourses. In the summer of 2000, after observing a *kirtan* in Pune, I inquired about the note taking and was told that many of the audience members—more women than men—were themselves studying to perform *kirtan*s.

VARKARI *KIRTAN*

Varkari *kirtan* takes its name from the Varkari religious community of the Marathi-speaking region. This performance of *kirtan* is more narrowly circumscribed in narrative and polemical scope, as well as musical and theatrical range, than a Naradiya *kirtan*. Furthermore, a Varkari *kirtan* relies on more communal, interactive participation with an audience than does Naradiya *kirtan*. A Varkari *kirtankar* uses only the songs of the five principal *sant*s of the Varkari tradition. As in a Naradiya *kirtan*, a Varkari *kirtankar* first gives a discourse on a chosen song, but this discourse is purposefully simple and brief. Instead of highlighting musical and scholarly virtuosity, a Varkari *kirtan* accents religious ecstasy and dance, accompanied by cymbals (*tāl*), drums, and clapping. The second phase of the Varkari *kirtan* also involves the further explication of the selected song, but with more unambiguous ethical and religious content, rather than materials meant to entertain. Although there is one lead *kirtankar*, he or she is accompanied by many other *kirtankar*s, often standing in a line (*raṅgaṇ*) and dancing in synchronicity. All the *kirtan* members and the audience join in the refrain (*dhṛpad*) in the song.

A Varkari *kirtan* is less a stage for a skillful *kirtankar* than a social gathering, a point made explicitly in the songs of Namdev and other Varkari *sant*s. It is a place for the "orphaned" (*anāth*), "uneducated" (*ajñān*), and "powerless" (aśakta), as Namdev's songs often assert. One important social difference between the two forms involves caste. A Varkari kirtankar can be from any caste and is often of a middle or Maratha (Marāṭhā) caste or a low caste, reflecting the social teachings of most Varkari sants, whatever their caste. One Namdev song puts it bluntly:

> Ritual baths and chanting mantras
> While hoarding gifts and ignoring
> Hari's stories [harikatha]:
> You should know that one who does this is evil,
> A terrible, wicked sinner.
> Give up Brahminical pride [brāhmaṇapaṇ]
> And give up practicing caste [śūdrarīti].
> The suffering these things cause
> Can only result in calamity.[36]

This kind of explicit critique of caste in the performance of a Varkari kirtan would be uncommon in a Naradiya kirtan, for the clear sociocultural reasons mentioned. Inherent in this critique is a devaluation of individual fame and an emphasis on communal solidarity.[37] It is important to note that all performers of Varkari kirtan are themselves Varkari adherents. However, Varkari adherents—especially Brahmin ones—also perform Naradiya kirtan. The two kinds of kirtan are not mutually exclusive, and popular kirtankars are often adept at both forms. However, this caste-critical aspect of a Varkari kirtan reveals particular facets of authorship. Although a Varkari kirtan has a lead kirtankar, the community symbolically grants him temporary authorial status when the vīṇā player hands him the vina—a stringed instrument that appears regularly in accounts of kirtans in Namdev's songs and is a common symbol of Narada. There is also some symbolic association between the kirtankar and Vitthal at the beginning of the kirtan. A Varkari kirtan starts with songs that describe Vitthal's physical form (rūpāce abhaṅga), most famously as standing on a brick with his arms crooked at his sides. The series of descriptive songs ends with the line: "Fix your attention on the beautiful one who stands on the brick." At that point, the kirtankar rises to accept the vina and to officiate over the kirtan. At the conclusion of the kirtan, the kirtankar returns the vina to the vina player, which signals the end of his or her authorial moment. The conditions of this state of authorship, at least symbolically temporary, can be seen as in accordance with the consistent sociocultural message in Varkari religious sentiment that abhors caste discrimination. With that sentiment comes a critique of other hierarchies, such as the one represented in Naradiya *kirtan* in the person of the *kirtankar.*

A distinction may also be evident in Namdev's songs between Naradiya and Varkari *kirtan,* though the words "Naradiya" and "Varkari" are not used to distinguish the two forms. In Namdev's verses, when Narada appears, an audience gathers, usually under an awning (*mandapa*) and is seated (*baisale*) before Narada to listen to his *kirtan.*[38] Just as in a contemporary Naradiya *kirtan,* the audience is portrayed in these songs as by and large physically passive during the *kirtan*'s performance—they listen and respond verbally, but do not rise up to dance and join the *kirtankar* in the *kirtan.* This might be a description of the archetypical Naradiya *kirtan,* and it appears to be the form of *kirtan* that Namdev is depicted as performing in Ill. 2.2, which is also the form of *kirtan* Mahipati probably would have performed in his time.

When Namdev or others perform *kirtan* in Namdev's songs—as opposed to Narada performing the *kirtan*—it is usually amid many fellow *bhaktas,* and both audience and performers dance and sing together.[39] No one sits still. This is a form of *kirtan* that more aptly reflects the practice of Varkari performers and audiences than of Naradiya *kirtan.* However, both styles of *kirtan* as we know them today probably took on their present forms and distinctions over a long period. Naradiya *kirtan,* for example, was most likely the form of *kirtan* Eknath and Ramdas (seventeenth century) practiced in their time, though they too do not use the terms "Naradiya" or "Varkari" to specify what sort of *kirtan* they practiced, much less "Eknāthī" or "Rāmdāsī"; they are merely performing *kirtan.* Varkari *kirtan,* by contrast, probably developed as an explicitly different style in the mid-nineteenth century under the guidance of famous *kirtankar*s like Bhausaheb Katkar (1813–78 C.E.) and Vishnu Jog (1867–1920 C.E.) and represents a kind of "reformation" of the performance art to more accurately replicate the perceived social ethos of the Pandharpur pilgrimage and the verses of the *sants.*[40] The few notebooks (*bada*) that house the written archive of songs used in *kirtan* are mostly from the late seventeenth and early eighteenth centuries. Different types of *kirtan* are not plainly enumerated in any notebooks or *bada*s that I have examined; they contain only hints and inference, without a direct statement about types of *kirtan.* Thus the fact that *kirtan* performers themselves draw these distinctions but tend to do so in particular contexts, coupled with the evidence that notebooks used by *kirtan* performers for centuries do not demarcate distinct genres of *kirtan,* all suggests that the various types of *kirtan* exist in a fluid relationship to one another, drawn on, in most cases, as the needs of a public are addressed.

THE AUTHOR INCORPORATED

If we examine the Marathi *kirtan* inspired by Namdev in general, we can see layers of authorship emerging in performance. Immediately manifest in a performance is the famous *sant* whose song is to be performed and elaborated on in the *kirtan*. In a performance, when a *kirtankar* invokes the songs, lines, or legends of a famous figure—a *sant* or character from history—the authority of that figure lends legitimacy to the *kirtan* and establishes the authenticity of the performance. A Marathi *kirtan* would not be a *kirtan* without that central song or story to which the performance's meaning is anchored and with which the performer plays with language, music, and narration. A *kirtan* could be said to be an exploration of the intentions of the principal song's author. Certainly, at the center of the performance is the famous author. At this level, authorship is based on the work of a single, famous singer, a kind of genealogical authorship. Varkari *kirtan* in particular follows a strict genealogy as songs are chosen from only one of the five most revered *sants* of the Varkari tradition. Naradiya *kirtan*, however, is freer to respond to the desires and expectations of a particular audience—urban, rural, southern, eastern, and so on; yet here, too, there is a genealogy of fame and popularity where Namdev is still considered the doyen of the *kirtan* form and Tukaram is remembered as the most popular of the *sant* poets.[41] This type of authorship taps the expectations and collective sentiment of a broad Marathi-speaking *bhakti* public, the desires of which influence the selection of songs, and hence the valorization of a particular *sant* and his/her compositions.

At a second level, we have seen that an adept *kirtankar*, especially a Naradiya one, must mix popular, expected material—such as stories from myth or the lives of famous figures—with spontaneous, extemporary oratory and verse. Here, the genius of an individual as the originator of a text is represented in the authorial, creative status of the *kirtankar* in the performance of *kirtan*. The *kirtankar* becomes the *kirtan*'s composer or author, quoting from various sources, creatively altering and melding narratives, engaging the material with his or her unique artistic abilities, and stamping the performance as an original composition. However, this aspect of authorship ends with the conclusion of the *kirtan* and needs to be re-established repeatedly through performance. This kind of author is like what Pierre Bourdieu has referred to as "the apparent producer," who sees to the connection between production and consumption and who presents and represents the work.[42] In this case, authorship is transient because the *kirtankar* is the author only of that particular performance, for that particular period of time. The receptive public here is likewise transient, but vital; they form the most immediate *bhakti* public that we can identify, shaped around the charismatic figure of the *kirtankar*.

A third level of authorship involves the origins of the *kirtan* performance art itself within Maharashtrian public memory. In most cases, this is an authoritative seal attached to the name of Narada, the eponymous originator of Naradiya *kirtan*; likewise, Eknath and Ramdas are at the root of Eknathi and Ramdasi *kirtan*, respectively. As with the use of songs and invocation of famous names, the moniker "Narada" authorizes the *kirtan*'s form, tracing the invention of the style to the famous sage. This connection is made explicit in Naradiya *kirtan* through mimesis when the performer assumed the role—the garb and "seat"—of Narada. In the case of *kirtan* in Maharashtra in general, Namdev shares some of Narada's glory, as Namdev is said to have popularized *kirtan* in the Marathi-speaking world. At this level, authorship is eponymous: the particular kind of *kirtan* being practiced takes the name of its originator (Narada) or its constituency (Varkari).

What links these three aspects of authorship is the location of agency within human lives, especially in the moment of performance when the *kirtankar* embodies all three aspects of authorship in him- or herself. I think of this embodiment of transmission as the use of "human media" at the corporeal site of corporate authorship, that is, in the body itself.[43] This notion of locating agency within human performers is the core of the idea of authorship exhibited in the practices and songs of the Maharashtrian Namdev tradition. Furthermore, human media provide an inexhaustible archive as well as a stable stage for performance. Vasudha Narayanan, discussing Bharata Nātyam ("classical" Indian dance), writes, "Through the dance, many worldviews and concepts are transmitted synchronically to the viewers and diachronically through the generations."[44] Similarly, the performing body conducts both emotional energy and public memory as the very site of affect and hence of authorship. Corporate authorship is a possibility only when tied intimately to human media as a means of transmission. Jan Assmann, in discussing memory in "nonwritten" contexts says that memory relies for its successful transmission "on the amount . . . of tradition . . . [one] is able to embody and present in visible and oral form."[45]

However, as discussed below, textual scholarship (as opposed to oral orthopraxy) and ideas of authorship, while obsessively focused on the historical truth and intentions of an author, prefer authors to be inert after their literary production enters the world, not living and continually animated, or reanimated, over time. The interference of later redactors is often construed as a blight on the purity of the original text in the case of much scholarship on authorship. The Namdev tradition of *kirtan* in Marathi allows the historical author to be reinvented ever anew, an idea that does not sit well with the modern notion of authorship.

OLD COPPER AND NEW GOLD

The particular nature of authorship in the Namdev tradition can be described with reference to various ideas within the ongoing, interactive history of the idea of the author in both Euro-American and Indian contexts. As many contemporary social critics have amply demonstrated, modern knowledge about the world may be fragmentary but is nonetheless conjoined in mutually descriptive cultural fields, areas marked as "social," "artistic," "religious," or "political," that theorize the role of "agents" and "consumers." The subject of authorship enters these multiple fields.

The genealogy of the author as a concept in Western critical theory forms a circle. Presaging Barthes's morbid perspective on the death of the author, a twelfth-century Welsh scholar and satirist, Walter Map (c. 1140–1210 C.E.), wrote of his authorial status and the condition of editing, "My only fault is that I am alive. . . . I have no intention, however, of correcting this fault."[46] Living, Walter Map still asserted control over his work, but he knew that in death, critics and editors would emend his writing, or, as he put it, "every defect in [my writing] will be remedied by my decease."[47] A fourteenth-century English grammarian, William of Wheteley (fl. 1309–16 C.E.), wrote lectures on the standard mode of critical theory in medieval scholarship, a form of exegesis in which the author was the first or "efficient" cause of a text, but not necessarily the key to understanding it.[48] The identity of the author gave some indication of the category of the text and its genealogical environment, but not much more; instead, a composition moved in streams of discourse, amid other texts set adrift by authors and prodded downstream by critics and scholars. Walter Map took some ironic solace in knowing that, with the passage of time, his work, cut from its author by mortality, would grow in value because "then, as now, old copper will be preferred to new gold."[49]

Studies that point out the nature of scribal transmission in early European literature, before the advent of the printing press, compound the problems of modern authorship in Europe. Scribal transmission involved "manuscripture"—the physical creation of manuscripts—as an iconographic tradition, where scribes became coauthors, adding their voices and artistry to the accretion of a text, as well as to the beauty of its physical presentation.[50] This idea of manuscripture implies the importance of performance where the physical manuscript itself is the result of an artistic act, an illustrated, calligraphic work of art. The mix of performance in the construction of texts also emerges in musicology and discussions about the editing of musical scores from all periods. The performer of a musical score becomes an interpreter and transitory author between the composer and the audience, introducing a third axis and breaking the binary of author and audience, an idea similar to the corporate authorship proposed here. If the composer and the performer are not the same person, then is there any one person who can be considered a work's sole author?[51]

The unsettled situation of the author in European history was mirrored in India. In the context of Sanskrit literature in premodern India, Gerard Colas has demonstrated how text editing proceeded along the lines of purifying texts, not according to an author's intentions, but with regard to the logic of arguments and semantics.[52] Sheldon Pollock has likewise presented a perspective on theorizing in Sanskrit before the modern period that was largely nontemporal and unconcerned with the intentions of particular authors, but rooted in correctly perceiving or remembering universal truths.[53] Discourse centered on arguments outside the context of historical situations. There was no need to credit an individual argument to so-and-so, barring exceptional circumstances. In this way, debate continued across generations.

Among European Orientalists, William Jones (1746–94 C.E.) inaugurated a century of text editing and philology. The *Ordinances of Menu* is a prime example of Jones's endeavors, completed while the translator was on his deathbed in Calcutta.[54] Among Indian Orientalists, classical philology provided a blueprint for the purification of ancient texts. S. M. Katre, in his *Introduction to Indian Textual Criticism,* provides a principal statement on the modern text-editing practice in India.[55] He describes the work of editing as "the skilled and methodical exercise of the human intellect on the settlement of a text with the sole object of restoring it . . . to its original form . . . [and] by 'original form' we understand the form intended by the author."[56] A modern editor has to use reason and probability to abrogate obvious scribal mistakes. The last step in the editing process involves tendering the restored text of the author unto higher criticism, an exploration of the author's relationship to the text that Barthes laments as "tyrannically centered on the author, his person, his life."[57] The author becomes the solution to the miasma of multiple texts, the chief arbiter of meaning and verification.[58]

In late modernity, the author is part and parcel of this miasma and its attendant interpretations, reflecting a return to something like a medieval European or Indian perspective on the author. In postmodernism, the author has either been effaced from the text (Barthes), has given up his or her proper name as a commodity or metaphor (Derrida), or has been dispersed into innumerable demand-driven functions (Foucault). Bruno Latour and Brian Trainor have both pointed out this recycling of premodern ideas in the context of postmodernism, what the latter calls a "post-modern medievalism."[59] Traces of William of Wheteley's theory of the author resurface in Foucault's pithy statement of the author's function, "The author is the principle of thrift in the proliferation of meaning."[60]

John Stratton Hawley addresses the function of authorship in the context of songs attributed to the sixteenth-century figures Surdas and Ravidas. He concludes, "the meaning of authorship in devotional India . . . is not what we have come to expect in Europe and America since the Renaissance."[61] The character of the author in this other-than-modern context dovetails with some late modern ideas, like Foucault's author function. As Hawley argues, a song attributed to the author Ravidas or Surdas gives context and genealogy to a verse and ties the verse to a historical figure, but does not necessarily imply that the verse—in part or in whole—originated with that figure. Social, religious, political, and literary forces engulf an essentialist conception of the author and produce around the author's name and "signature" a kind of corporate authorship.[62] In the case of Surdas (sixteenth century), authorship in practice engendered a body of literature called the "Sūr Sāgar," or the Ocean of Sur, a metaphor that captures the vast, porous, and shifting concept of the author associated with figures like Surdas, for whom no distinct text exists to transmit his intentions. Instead of writing, the dominant mode of transmitting Surdas songs involved performance, where the songs of Surdas were intermingled with the creative inclinations of performers and the demands of an audience.

The last *kirtan* of Gadge Maharaj, a famous *kirtankar* of the twentieth century, offers a portrait of corporate authorship and human media, as it may have existed for centuries, at work in a performance in the modern period. And it also portrays well the vitality of a *bhakti* public. Gadge Maharaj, named Deboo at birth, was born in 1876 into a mostly illiterate and impoverished caste of clothes-washers, or *parit* in the Amravati district of preindependence Maharashtra, then known as the Bombay Presidency. He became a professional *kirtankar* in 1905, taking a new name with his new vocation. As a symbol of his renunciation and dedication to the itinerant life of a *kirtankar,* Deboo is said to have carried with him an empty clay pot (*gaḍgā/gaḍge*), which as a symbol of asceticism, of the body as an empty vessel and of the unfinished nature of human beings, became the inspiration for his new given name—the ultimate symbol of the flexible nature of human media.[63] He became famous for his *kirtan*s, including nationalist ones, and his advocacy of education, as well as for his frank diatribes against gluttony, sloth, and the allure of modern European culture.

Only a few months before his death in 1956, Gadge Maharaj found himself surrounded by police from the Bandra Railway Police Station in Bombay. They had learned that he was staying nearby and had come to plead with him to perform a *kirtan* in front of their offices. Although he was gravely ill, Gadge acceded to their request. Since Independence, Gadge's *kirtan*s had prescribed that one should live an ethical, balanced existence as a contribution to the nascent Indian state. In this particular *kirtan,* the last of his life, delivered before a demanding and adoring public, Gadge Maharaj invoked the verses of Tukaram, interspersed with his own comments and moral prescriptions; he also recalled songs by Jnandev and Kabir and quoted Gandhi. Furthermore, Gagde Maharaj's style—like that of many Varkari *kirtankar*s, of which he was one—involved eliciting responses from the audience in the call-and-response mode reminiscent of a Baptist preacher. In this particular *kirtan,* recorded by a member of the audience, transcribed and reprinted in 1976 by G. N. Dandekar and translated by Eleanor Zelliot and Maxine Berntsen in 1988, Gadge Maharaj did not disappoint.[64] He artfully interwove Tukaram's verses with his own eloquent words and drew out the voice of the audience, often eliciting a simple cry of "yes!" or "no!"

Imagine that this *kirtan,* rather than being fifty years old, were 250 years old. Its contents might have been recorded (but in writing, of course), and the name of the scribe and date of writing might have been noted in a colophon. How would we parse from its text a single author? We have Tukaram and other figures, whose names and verses appear throughout the transcript. We have Gadge Maharaj, who brings the words to life and surrounds them with his own narration at the behest of an insistent cadre of police. We have a recorder of the *kirtan,* a transcriber, an interactive public, and, eventually, a printer, a publisher, an editor, and a translator into English, presenting Gadge's performance to an entirely new audience, the modern Indian public sphere. We have the *kirtan* tradition itself, its form and function within a history stretched over seven hundred years behind Gadge Maharaj. Without the collective authorship of all these players, this *kirtan* of Gadge Maharaj before the Bandra Railway Police Station in 1956 would never have reached the present year in its current multiple forms. Gadge as an author, and as an authority, has been immortalized because of the corporate nature of authorship, captured in a moment of spontaneous, human performance.

The Namdev tradition can be historically, ethnographically, and even textually described as harboring at its very core an oral performance in the service of public memory. The Janabai poem translated and quoted at the beginning of this chapter relies on the device of a performance within a performance, a play within a play. The poem is a song. If we imagine a historical Janabai, who is said to have also been adept at *kirtan*—having learned from one of the best, Namdev—we might picture her singing this song to an audience in memory of her teacher.[65] Janabai the performer, in this scenario, is presenting a song about a performance that she experienced aurally, a fact highlighted by her choice of verb, *aikaṇe*, "to hear." Yet the song is not *about* performance as such; rather, it assumes the centrality of performance in its very structure. What Janabai has heard is an *abhang* performed by Namdev, that is, a *kirtan*. Although the song is attributed to Janabai, a majority of the content is attributed to Namdev. Who is the author of the song? Who is its agent?

The context of reception and the demands of audiences exert a substantial force on the performance context where reaction and interaction with the consumers of narratives is immediate, as Philip Lutgendorf has demonstrated with regard to the "life" of the *Rāmcaritmanas*.[66] In J. S. Hawley's ethnoliterary study of *raslila* performance, he noted the reception of the performance by the audience in general: "One question that outsiders immediately ask—who wrote these plays?—does not occur to anyone in Braj. These are not individual compositions, but a collective forum in which Krishna makes himself available to those who love him."[67] The *bhakti* public of Braj has formulated a system of authorship that transcends any individual in the context of the *raslila*.

Although Hawley is not discussing a body of work attributed to a single author, as in the case of Surdas, he is invoking a general sentiment that surrounds "folk" performative practices and commenting on the reaction of the nonspecialist member of the audience. Some narratives are freely available in public culture, with no copyright or attributed authorship. In this work, the "text" is constituted from a series of four oral performances, transcribed and translated. While we have no "author" in a modern sense, we do have agents of narration within the plays, and agents of production, the two *rāsdhārī*s who together produced the plays Hawley recorded. And, of course, we have Hawley's transcription, translation, and commentary—a function of scholarly authority that produces a kind of author not alien to the Marathi Namdev tradition or that of the Braj public that Hawley studies.

I suggest here that authorship functions in a tripartite way that ensures a lively connection between memory and performance in public spaces. In one way, authorship within *kirtan* rests with the authority of the *sant* whose verses are invoked and elaborated on in performance. We might consider this genealogical authorship. In a second way, authorship functions eponymously, relating its authority to the art form itself and thus to the originator of that art form, to its genealogy of practice.[68] This we might call eponymous authorship. Finally, authorship resides within the moment of the *kirtan* and inhering in the prowess of the *kirtankar* him- or herself. This is what we can call performative authorship. The three exist—genealogical authorship, eponymous authorship, and performative authorship—only within a Maharashtrian *bhakti* public. Outside this field, the function of authorship must be reassessed; that is, authorship here is *public specific.*

Karen Prentiss makes a similar point when she locates within the bio-histories of famous *bhakta*s the very "embodiment" of devotionalism, the physical sign to a devoted public of a "good" person, a *sant.*[69] This "embodiment" translated easily into a broad field of literary production received by a public, which still held at its core a notion of the body and voice of the *bhakta* as the premier site of devotional experience. In the Janabai song, two levels of this corporate authorship and public memory are readily apparent: the first author is perhaps the performer, an instance of performative authorship, and a function served by Janabai here; and a second level of authorship, what I call genealogical, referring to the famous poet whose name and voice through song is invoked by the performer and hence connected to the performer genealogically. Namdev holds this position in the Janabai song. The third aspect of corporate authorship, which I refer to as eponymous, is implied by Janabai's physical description of how the song affected her, how it made her enraptured, evinced by the way she would "sway" (*ḍolaṇe*) in response to the performance. In Marathi *kirtan*, this would signal to a receptive public that a kind of performance was taking place that would aptly (though anachronistically) be called Varkari. As we have seen, Varkari *kirtan* in Namdev's songs invites ecstatic engagement; it is meant to elicit a physical and emotional response from its audience—to make them sway and swoon to the music and words, or to sing and dance along with the *kirtankar.* The song, therefore, must be received and experienced; its ultimate goal is not the emotional-devotional state of Janabai alone but, through her experience, of all listeners. A contemporary performance of this song would draw a line from Namdev's live performance, to Janabai's live recollection, to the live performance of the contemporary *kirtankar:* a chain of public memory incorporating authorship in multiple ways.[70]

[3]

ORALITY AND LITERACY/PERFORMANCE
AND PERMANENCE

The tongue makes a good book.
—ATTRIBUTED TO NAMDEV

JONATHAN Z. SMITH hypothesized that if an alien were to pilot its flying saucer to Earth, presumably landing in the courtyard of the Divinity School in Chicago, and observe scholars of the history of religions at work, the extraterrestrial would deduce that these scholars were philologists. Girded by texts and having completed years of language study in graduate school, the alien's subjects would evince a conviction that through reading the writing of religious traditions, a story of the past of particular religions can be told.[1] Smith locates the foundation of the historical study of religions in philology—the study of "dead languages"—which has brought about a condition in the discipline whereby language study and philological work are paramount.[2] Thus the modern study of religions, even of "nonmodern" ones, is regularly a study of their textual remains. Indeed, the idea that history is preserved best in writing, and that literacy not only leaves a record for historians but allows for the very ability to think historiographically, is almost canonical for historians, religionists, and frequently anthropologists.[3]

While the historical study of religions may be ruled by texts, the public memory of the Namdev tradition in Maharashtra is not. I argue in chapter 2 that Namdev typifies a practice of performance that uses nonliterate methods, primarily *kirtan,* to maintain its remembrance over time. We have seen that hagiography and songs attributed to Namdev reveal a purposeful distance from literacy. Namdev is remembered as someone who sings and performs his songs, and because generations of *kirtankar*s have done the same, his legacy endures and enters the world of the public. Indeed, performance surrounding Namdev has been engineered to create public spaces where the ideals of *bhakti* can be expressed.

Although the Maharashtrian Namdev tradition has remembered the preeminence of performance, it has simultaneously produced a written corpus of his work, a by-product perhaps of the central performance tradition of *kirtan*. Furthermore, the accumulative written economy of Namdev's songs has organized, managed, and reorganized his literary corpus through a constant interaction of the performance tradition with various written traditions and the sociopolitical landscapes through which Namdev's memory has traveled, whether in courts, at the periphery of colonialism, or in the contemporary period. What do we do with the literate legacy of this nonliterate tailor who disregarded writing and books? How do we read the literary remains of a tradition that disavowed literacy from a theological and perhaps social point of view?

Namdev's nonliterate ethos, and the practice of *kirtan,* are encoded in the written remnant of the Maharashtrian Namdev tradition, but not subjected to them. Although the preeminent literate archive of the tradition, the *bada,* or "notebook," has been carried by performers for centuries, it is primarily a device of memory, not its source. I argue that the contents of these notebooks show that they were produced in the service of performance and are not considered records superior to human memory. This is an important point to assert, as the creation of a public within a largely illiterate sphere requires the transcendence of literacy through orality. I also investigate two examples of ways in which the logic of the *kirtan* is encoded in writing, revealing a hybrid interaction of orality and literacy in the late eighteenth century. I contend that the modern dialectic of orality and literacy does not capture the intentions of writing put forth by Namdev's Maharashtrian tradition. Instead, a different set of objectives is at work that shifts between an investment in oral performance and a desire for an enduring public memory, a dialectic between two intentions that I label "performance" and "permanence."

Before the nineteenth century, at a time when Namdev's songs were handwritten, this writing took two distinct forms: the *bada,* a simple notebook used by performers to record songs, make notes on performance, and record a variety of other information; and the *pothī,* a well-constructed type of manuscript intended to preserve texts, often for ritual religious practices. *Pothi* is a common term for a manuscript or "book" in northern traditions—such as Sikhism—as well as in Marathi.[4] In Marathi, *pothi* generally refers to a well-fashioned and carefully preserved document. Usually the word designates a Sanskrit manuscript, though in the case of Sikhism, as Gurinder Singh Mann has explained, *pothi*s that contain songs in Punjabi and other north Indian languages form the earliest layer of Sikh scripture.[5] In some cases in Marathi, the word *pothi* is used to describe a particularly important text, without regard to the language in which the text is written. This is the case with the translation and commentary on the *Bhagavad Gītā* attributed to Jnandev, called the *Bhavarthadīpika*, or eponymously titled the *Jñāneśvarī*. Manuscript versions of this text are called *pothi*s and receive the kind of pride of place afforded Sanskrit and other manuscripts usually of a "classical" nature. However, Jnandev's name is also attached to thousands of song-narratives, or *abhang*s. When these songs are collected and written down, they are not contained in a compendium called a *pothi*, though they are attributed to an author whose other works are preserved in *pothi*s; instead, Jnandev's songs, like Namdev's, are recorded in the decidedly less high-class form of the *bada*.[6]

This difference in terminology is significant, as indeed are the differences between the cultural status of Jnandev's *Jñāneśvarī* and his *abhang*s. The *pothi* marks a text with superior cultural capital in the world of "higher learning" in Marathi or what we might call, perhaps anachronistically (and with apologies to Habermas), the premodern Marathi public sphere. There is only one composition in Namdev's extensive literary corpus that is preserved in the form of a *pothi*. This composition is the autobiographical version of the *Tīrthāvaḷī*, discussed in chapter 2, an exceedingly rare narrative with only two extant copies, to my knowledge. I briefly discuss this text and its possible route of transmission toward the end of this chapter. A comparison of the *pothi* and *bada* helps in highlighting how the *pothi* serves what we might call "private" or elite memory, the literate, perhaps courtly archive, as against public memory, an open, lightly mediated, and often nonliterate archive—the domain of the *bada*. The *bada* is the far more common storehouse for the few written records of Namdev's songs, and I turn to this first. How has the *bada* been used as a tool? How are its contents structured and what does this structure indicate about those who have carried and used these notebooks from the sixteenth century to the present? In asking these questions, I examine the interplay of *kirtan* and text in a few specific cases in order to realize the full interaction of performance and literacy in the Maharashtrian Namdev tradition and the *kirtan* tradition more generally.

NOTEBOOKS AND PERFORMANCE: THE *BADA*

In Namdev's songs, the word *bada* does not appear, which may be explained by the etymology of the word. The word *bada* in Marathi refers to a stack of pages (*tāṃcaṇācī vahī*) that has been stitched at some median place to form a spine over which the pages of the notebook can be folded (Ill. 3.1).[7] The word *bada* may be related to a word for "line," of Persian origin, corresponding to the lines often drawn in notebooks to help with transcription or maybe suggesting the stitch sewn to make a spine. The word suggests a cognate with the English word "bard," particularly through the connection with poetry, singing, and traveling. Although this is a tempting route, I think a more likely connection (if there is one at all) to English comes through the Arabic word *al-bada'ah,* a saddle bag used on a mule or horse, which gives us the second, less common, definition of the word "bard" in English, protective armor for the flanks of a warhorse. This sense of the word does not make its way into Marathi, Urdu, or any other language in India, except for Persian, as far as I know. The former meaning, however—*al-bada'ah* as a bag used for travel on a horse—may have some association with the pockets or bags the notebooks were kept in or with the very construction of the *bada,* bound in leather and serving as a kind of "pocket" for the recording of performances. There also may be some association with travel in general, an occupational necessity for *kirtankar*s. If this is the etymology of the word *bada,* it would seem to have come into use after Namdev's traditional floruit, in the seventeenth century at the earliest.

ILLUSTRATION 3.1 Typical *bada*s.

Despite its late entry into Marathi, and thus its absence from any verse attributed to Namdev, the word *bada* is the one most commonly used in modern Marathi to refer to the notebooks that hold the bulk of Namdev's written corpus and contain many of the songs of other Maharashtrian *sant*s as well. The word *vahi,* however, is reserved in modern Marathi for notebooks carried by schoolchildren or so it seems to this observer.[8] However, in Namdev's verses, *vahi* does appear once, in a single song, to describe a notebook:

"Resolve has arisen from compassion,"
Said the Teacher, Lord of Gods, Panduranga.
Hari [spoke] to Saraswati, along the riverbank
Of the Bhima, [saying,] "Sit on Nama's tongue.
This darling lad Nama, he's my little baby.
Without me, whom does he have?
I am deeply in his debt [*ṛṇa*],
By such small installments, I will repay [*uttīrṇa*] him."
Nama says, "Panduranga sits down to write,
Stitching the notebooks [*vahyā*] with his own hands."[9]

This is the only appearance of the word *vahi* in the Government of Maharashtra's edition of Namdev's songs, the *Śrī Nāmdev Gāthā.* Yet here ostensibly is a narrative instance of Namdev's words being written down by Panduranga/Vitthal, which apparently contradicts what I stated in chapter 2 about the indifference to writing in Namdev's songs and in songs about Namdev by other *sant*s. Here, it seems as if Panduranga, often described as "indebted" to Namdev, attempts to repay his debt by writing down Namdev's verses in much the same way as he did for Janabai in an earlier poem. In this case, Namdev becomes a conduit, literally a "human medium," through which Saraswati directs verses "sit[ing] on Namdev's tongue," Namdev pronounces them, and Panduranga writes them down. The "small installments" toward the repayment of a debt indicate such verses attributed to Namdev, inspired by Saraswati, and transcribed by God.

In the oldest version of this song, present in a collection from Pandharpur, dated to around the late seventeenth or early eighteenth century by the editors of the *Śrī Nāmdev Gāthā,* we are told of one more verse inserted after the second verse where Saraswati is asked to sit on Namdev's tongue. This verse later disappears from the song, but in the early eighteenth century, it was part of the composition in at least one version. The line goes:

Hearing these words [of Panduranga, Nama] says, "Panduranga,
Tell me, who will write this all down?"

The words Namdev hears are Panduranga's instructions to Saraswati to
inspire Namdev's speech. The poem appears to mark an anxiety in Namdev over how to handle such exalted inspiration coming as it does from the
goddess of learning, of Vedic recitation, and of the arts; she is often depicted holding a written text of Vedas in her lower right hand. The need for
writing is at Namdev's insistence, but it is occasioned by an uncommon
charge—to relay the words of higher learning rather than those of mundane life. Indeed, the presence in this song of Saraswati is uncommon—the
goddess appears almost nowhere else in Namdev's Marathi corpus. The
coincidence of this rare appearance and the only instance of Namdev being positively associated with writing in any songs attributed to him is
highly suggestive. Of?

Saraswati is a goddess of ancient lineage, appearing as Vac, the goddess
of orality and the recitation of sacred text, as early as the *Rig Veda*. She de-
velops in later centuries into a goddess of learning in general, in particular
as a deity of the arts. Within Saraswati is a melding of literacy and orality,
mediated by performance. This poem transfers these functions to Namdev,
who becomes a medium for recording verses inspired by Saraswati and
committed to the written page by Panduranga. In this way, the song does
not disrupt the thesis that Namdev is considered nonliterate. Instead perhaps it serves to explain why a nonliterate *sant*'s verses would find their way
into literate archives. Although Namdev remains at the center of literary
production in this song, he is not its agent. It is Panduranga who presumably writes down Namdev's verses. It is also Panduranga who physically creates the notebook that will hold the verses. Namdev does not even do the
stitching, an activity that one might expect from a tailor—he has abandoned this trade in favor of the life of a *bhakta*.[10] Thus Namdev remains a
nonliterate performer of songs, even in this rare but important *abhang*.
Around him, however, there exists an economy of preservation that relies
on recording oral performance, but works to create both the physical artifacts of notebooks and the words transcribed in them.

The song seems to describe the creation of a *bada*, and it is in these
notebooks that is found the vast bulk of Namdev's written legacy, preserved in an informal, largely unstructured archive, scattered throughout
Maharashtra, in which the modern printed editions of Namdev's work find
their source. The term *bada* designates a wide range of manuscripts that

share a few physical and cultural characteristics. The notebooks generally have stitched spines that allow their pages to fold and form a "book"; the text runs left to right, but the orientation of a *bada* can be either vertical or horizontal and sometimes a mix of these two in a single notebook. The text can be in either Devanagari or Modi script. The *bada*s are dressed in a thick cloth cover, usually pasted or stitched around the outermost pages. They range in size and shape from as small as 2 inches by 2 inches, to 8½ inches by 6 inches. The majority of the *bada*s I have examined open vertically like a long note pad (see Ill. 3.1).

Most notebooks are an omnium-gatherum of information far beyond the enumeration of songs attributed to famous *sant*-singers. Although some *bada*s—perhaps a tenth of the ones I examined—contain only songs, the majority are filled by an array of information, and this varying content in the *bada*s speaks volumes about the professional lives of their former owners. The *bada*s contain all kinds of seemingly mundane information: astrological charts; records of births and deaths; notes on crop prices, geography, weather conditions; surveys of general news; and even bawdy songs, similar to the Marathi *lavani* genre. These materials indicate the diverse applications of the *kirtan* profession, which required a *kirtankar* to be peripatetic, a multitasking, jack-of-all-trades, carrying information about neighboring villages or entirely different regions of the subcontinent. Although a handful of notebooks are attributed to the early seventeenth century, most extant *bada*s come from the eighteenth century onward, a period in the history of the Marathi-speaking area of relentless warring among landed families, Maratha expansionary expeditions, Mughal armies, and the southern kingdoms of Golconda and Bijapur.[11] The tradition of keeping these notebooks traverses the period of colonialism as well. Throughout these eras, *kirtankar*s kept track of births and deaths, changes in commerce, politics, and the lives of famous personalities. A *kirtankar* was part journalist, part foreign correspondent, part actor, part scholar, and part religious commentator, all in the context of the *kirtan* performance. Records of royal patronage to *kirtankar*s make clear that monetary rewards reflected the entertainment value of a performance; the *kirtankar* had to sing for his supper.[12] However, the regular terrain of the *kirtankar* was not the Maratha courts, Mughal courts, or colonial metropoles, but mundane village centers, pilgrimage networks, and holy sites. In these locations they performed the sacred stories, biographies, and songs of those figures that had ascended from ordinary life to hagiographical stardom.

Everything about *bada*s reveals a utility and an economic status far removed from the carefully copied manuscripts of medieval Europe or of Sanskrit and Pali literature, different especially from the *pothi* mentioned above. The manner in which these notebooks are preserved today in archives is very different from the careful attention given to other manuscripts, as different in accommodation as the five-star Taj Hotel is from the Bombay YWCA just down the street. *Pothi*s are preserved in glass cases, in teakwood cabinets, carefully arranged and catalogued; *bada*s are piled in closets or stacked in storage spaces. The different valuation of the two kinds of manuscripts is also apparent when *bada*s and *pothi*s are referred to in English: a *pothi* is always rendered with the English word "manuscript," which carries a weighted importance among types of documents, whereas a *bada* is designated with the English word "notebook," a second-class citizen in the world of paper records.

The oldest *bada*s that have been used in compiling editions of Namdev's work contain colophons that give the date 1631 or later, but *bada*s were probably compiled and carried by *kirtankar*s from the beginning of the practice. Collections of these notebooks are scattered throughout Maharashtra in private and temple archives in Dehu, Paithan, Alandi, Pandharpur, Nagpur, Pune, and elsewhere; a few libraries, such as the Bhandarkar Oriental Research Institute and the Thanjavur Saraswati Mahal Library in Tamil Nadu and the Deccan College Library in Pune also store notebooks. Few if any *bada*s have been either catalogued or preserved under the auspices of colonial-sponsored archives, indicative of general British colonial indifference to the practices of the Maharashtrian Namdev tradition and its literary remnant. For example, I have been unable to find *bada*s in the India Office Library in London or any mention of old Marathi notebooks in any scholarship in English from any period.

The notebooks probably bypassed inspection by European scholars for a host of reasons: they were the occupational materials of a group of performers who held no obvious position of power in the political economy of the Deccan; they did not contain information, such as land grant transactions, or obvious historical records, and hence they would be useless to the exercise of colonial power and the gathering of intelligence. Furthermore, these *bada*s were not intended to be visually pleasing pieces that preserved textual traditions. They were neither examples of careful calligraphy set amid wondrous illustrations nor bound in materials meant to weather the ages. Instead, they were designed to hold for a short time the notes and jottings of *kirtankar*s—at most for a generation or two.

Other work on similar manuscripts, especially in western and northern India, has revealed a comparable relationship between text and performance. Winand Callewaert and Mukund Lath (1989), in their important work on Namdev's textual legacy in Rajasthan and northern India, found that the songs in manuscripts were frequently organized according to the *rag* system of Hindustani classical music. For example, the contents of the *Guru Granth Sahib*, including the songs attributed to Namdev, are arranged primarily by *rag* and secondarily by author, first Guru, then *bhagat*. A similar system is followed in many collections of other *sant* figures and sacred traditions, such as those that surround the figures of Dadu, Kabir, Raidas, and Haridas, as Callewaert and Op de Beek have shown.[13] In contrast, the songs in the old notebooks within the Namdev Marathi tradition do not exhibit this kind of musical association with *rag*, nor is there any other primary logical association, except in the instance of particularly famous compositions, which I note below. When there is some discernable order, it is by purported author, not by *rag*. The mere fact that *rag* is an organizational principle of a manuscript's contents does not unequivocally establish that the manuscript itself was used in performance. Organization by *rag* may indicate a common source for songs grouped together—and this form of organization may have served performance—but the manuscripts themselves were likely to be meant as static archives.[14] We might imagine that the *rag*-based codification of *sant* songs in manuscripts in northern India—the subject of Callewaert's several excellent textual studies—was an attempt to deal with the kinds of unclassified, diverse records also seen to the south in the Marathi *bada* tradition. In other words, *rag* may have become the organizational key to orderly preservation that north Indian editors of the late sixteenth and seventeenth centuries used to sort out the morass of detail in even earlier manuscripts, which might have more closely resembled the *bada*s and *vahi*s of Maharashtrian *kirtankar*s. Callewaert and Lath imply as much when they assert that it was "musicians" who classified songs by *rag*, but it was "scribes" (I assert that they were "editors," that is, scribes with agency) who "kept the *rag* tag of each song" in the creation of manuscripts.[15]

Another feature of the notebooks that suggests their role in performance is their uniqueness: the *bada*s are each distinct. As mentioned above, there appears to be no tradition of copying entire *bada*s as discrete literary pieces, as there is with other sorts of manuscripts, especially Sanskrit manuscripts, or with the autobiographical *Tīrthāvaḷī*, preserved in the *pothi* form. While it is quite plausible that early *kirtankar*s compared notebooks and shared verses, this is not part of a "scribal" tradition but, rather, indicates the circulation, through writing and performance, of particular songs and compositions; in other words, I believe that this is more indicative of the social interaction of performers than the commissioned, formalized scribal process of copying manuscripts.[16] Individual songs do appear in multiple notebooks, often word for word, which might indicate that individual verses were copied from one notebook to another or that an oral performance, perhaps aided by a notebook, was transcribed by another performer. We observe an economy of texts that reveals a network of performance traditions throughout the Maharashtrian Deccan. This is far different from a scribal tradition of the sort text editors often encounter that copies entire narratives or manuscripts with the aim of faithful representation and physical preservation.

Although there is no evidence of a tradition of copying individual manuscripts, there are numerous examples that particular songs have been copied into multiple notebooks. We find recorded in notebooks Namdev's two principal biographies/autobiographies about Jnandev: the *Ādi* biography of Jnandev's short life and the biographical *Tīrthāvaḷī*. The *Samādhi*, Jnandev's threnody, is copied in its entirety less frequently. These three compositions appear in eight of the thirty *bada*s consulted by the government-sponsored *Śrī Nāmdev Gāthā* editorial committee, for example. The committee described those eight *bada*s as the "chief texts" (*pramukha prat*), which might indicate that the committee believed certain manuscripts were resources for others.[17]

Old collections of handwritten songs are stored in Pandharpur at the Namdev Mandir, as well as in the private collections of *kirtan* performers throughout Maharashtra. Dhule has been a vital center for Maharashtrian culture and religion for centuries, as well as the administrative headquarters of the West Khandesh district of the Bombay Presidency during the late colonial period, an interesting alignment of colonial and noncolonial concerns. Dhule is home to two important archives and research institutes that have preserved *bada*s for research: the Samartha Vagdevata Mandir and the Rajvade Samshodhan Mandal.

A Pandharpur manuscript collection, in particular, has served as the largest source for the Government of Maharashtra's anthology of Namdev's songs; and a single voluminous manuscript housed in Dhule, with a date of 1631, provides the oldest stratum of extant Namdev songs in Marathi outside the fixed compositions of the *Ādi*, *Tīrthāvaḷī*, and *Samādhi* triptych.[18] On a recent visit to Pandharpur, however, I found the flow of information also ran in the opposite direction. Interviewing P. D. Nikte, the director of the Namdev Sevak Mandir in Pandharpur and an educator in Namdev Studies, I asked about the manuscripts that he kept. He mentioned the Pandharpur manuscript collection and informed me, "When we hear a new song, or a new version of a [Namdev] song, we write it down in the book."[19] This seems always to have been the practice, providing a link between writing and performance—a stockpiling of songs, selected from time to time by individual *kirtankar*s for performance. There is no sense in which the collection now on hand has been frozen or restricted to the past or that Namdev songs do not themselves travel, change, and return anew.

Rather than a story about professional scribes, the legacy of the *bada* tells us about *kirtankar*s who traveled regular tour routes throughout the Deccan, met in various venues and exchanged information. In large pilgrimage places or centers of culture—such as Pandharpur—particular archives of materials were kept. From these stationary collections, traveling *kirtankar*s may have found and copied into their notebooks more material; in exchange, they may have also supplied the keepers of these collections with song material not yet archived.

We hear echoes of some aspects of the practice of recording songs in old notebooks in the activities of contemporary *kirtankar*s, for whom the notebook is an ever-present prop. It is important to note that *kirtankar*s often will not read from a notebook in an actual performance but, rather, use the notebook as a way to prepare for the performance. Of course, contemporary *kirtankar*s also have at their disposal the large printed anthologies of the works of Varkari *sant*s, such as the *Sakaḷa Santa Gāthā* or the various state-funded critical editions. Yet the genealogies of these anthologies are rooted in the notebooks of earlier *kirtankar*s, hence these modern printed editions are the products of premodern performance traditions. Very little attempt has been made by the various organizers of printed anthologies to mediate between the old manuscripts and the printed form. Instead, with a few notable exceptions, a compiler would include as many songs attributed to Namdev as possible, a practice highly "uncritical" from the perspective of modern text editing.

The relationship between performance and the compilation of songs is not merely a premodern phenomenon. A celebrated Varkari *kirtankar*, V. Jog (1867–1920 C.E.), produced one of the first and most influential anthologies of Namdev's verses, called *Nāmdevācā Gāthā*, published posthumously in 1925 by Chitrashala Press. He is one of several well-established *kirtankar*s who edited the works of Maharashtrian *sant*s. In important ways, the modern printed edition inherits the tradition of the handwritten notebooks kept by *kirtankar*s, and, as such, these printed tomes transport the structure of oral, live performance into modern media through the replication of the contents of old notebooks.

THE LITERARY FOSSILS OF PERFORMANCE?

The preeminence of live performance over the commitment of text to the written page in the Namdev tradition notwithstanding, the *bada*s carried by *kirtankar*s reflect a clear utilization and dependence on writing, and this dependence perhaps grew as more written materials, and later printed collections, became widely available to performers. How has the performance of *kirtan* itself—as opposed to the use of literacy to aid *kirtan*—moved in to the realm of writing? To answer this question, I examine two manuscripts. The first is a *bada* likely from the early eighteenth century that, I argue, includes a record of the live performance of a *kirtan.* The second is a portion of the *Bhaktavijay*, which served as a guide to the shape of Namdev's publicly received biography in Marathi, and was preserved before print in the *pothi* form (because it was a fixed, single-author, composition, and composed by a high-caste, influential individual). In exploring the interaction of performance and writing, I also borrow a theme from chapter 2 and examine how the concept of authorship in these various contexts functions as a principle of organization, a focus of historical and cultural remembrance conditioned by orality.

An Early *Kirtan* Primer?

A manuscript in the collection of the Bhandarkar Oriental Research, *bada* number 52, is one of the largest notebooks I have examined in terms of physical size (Ill. 3.2) and is likely from the mid-eighteenth century. It measures 8½ by 6 inches and consists of eighty-five folded pages, with writing on both sides. The *bada* displays an elegant, professional orthography, particularly throughout the second half of the notebook. The *bada* contains no colophon or other datable information. However, the orthography and grammar of the *bada* are similar to those of other texts of the eighteenth century, and this is the probable timeframe in which the *bada* was finished.

The contents of the first portion of the *bada* are varied, but generally include songs organized by author. Especially frequent are songs marked with explicit reference to the purported author. For example, one finds *sūrdāsapada* or "songs by Surdas," referring to the famous sixteenth-century

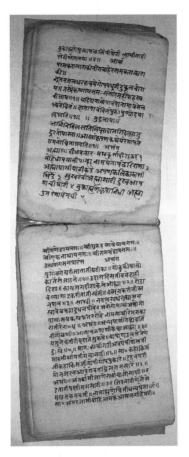

ILLUSTRATION 3.2 BORI *bada* number 52, first page [bottom] and facing
page of special section.

singer from Braj, or a section marked *Narsīkṛta,* or "[compositions] by
Narsi [Mehta]," referring to the works of the famous fifteenth-century Gujarati *sant.* It has divisions by verse form as well—by *ārya, śloka, sākhī,
dohrā,* and *abhang*—as well as the prose ballad called *kaṭāv.* Other sections invoke particular stories from the Hindu epics, retold in brief Marathi verse, such as the "Ayodhya Āgaman" or "[The] Story of the Arrival in
Ayodhya," from the *Rāmāyaṇa.* This *bada* has songs attributed to Mad-
havnath (sixteenth century), whose Guru was Eknath (sixteenth century);
Ranganathaswami (seventeenth century) of the Ananda Sampraday;

Amritarao, a balladeer from the late seventeenth–early eighteenth century; as well as the usual fare for a Marathi *bada,* such as songs attributed to Tukaram (seventeenth century) and, less common in *bada*s with Namdev verses, ones attributed to the poet and figure of political intrigue during Shivaji's period Ramdas (seventeenth century), contained under the rubric *rāmdās kṛta.* Despite these organizational rubrics, in sections where Namdev's songs appear, one finds no heading devoted to Namdev. His songs appear throughout the notebooks, in a particular sequence—as shown below—and interspersed among the songs of all the figures mentioned above, but they are interwoven without any explicit rubric as with other authors/*sants* or even other types of verse. It is as if Namdev needs no introduction or he is not treated as an author in the same way as these other *sant*s. Indeed, not only are his songs not demarcated in a clear fashion, but his songs are dissected with selections of verse attributed to Namdev in Hindi and to other *sant*s; his words are interlaced with the words of other songs in a fashion wholly unprecedented with regard to any other *sant.* The very nature of this interlocking display of songs, I argue, is at the core of the oral remnant that inhabits these written texts.

The *bada* in question does not follow a logical theme that connects the various works it contains—in other words, it has no discernible overarching thesis that has warranted the sequence of songs and compositions, except to say that the songs in the *bada* are *Bhāgavata* in nature, that is, concerned with the worship of Ram, Krishna, and Vishnu. The *bada* itself does not make this connection—the songs are merely given without explanation. However, fourteen pages of text toward the end of the *bada* indicate a dramatic shift from the stockpiling of songs in the previous pages to an apparently systematic formulation. What changes in those fourteen pages is the way in which the songs are organized and handled as text. In the bulk of the *bada* is the usual accumulation of materials meant to serve performance, perhaps to be drawn on in order to recall or alter songs within a *kirtan.* In the peculiar fourteen pages, by contrast, I consider the transcript of a *kirtan* or, at least, the outline or "strategy" for one, with the overall subject being stories about Krishna's childhood pranks (*bālkrīḍā*). The plan of these fourteen pages is demonstrated in the layout of the verses and in the position and use of the songs, phenomena not seen in any other *bada,* but indicative, nonetheless, of the use to which *bada*s have been put for centuries. This unique piece of writing deserves careful attention.

A switch occurs in the handwriting from the preceding pages to a much more disciplined orthography, suggesting that the contents of the fourteen pages are not the work of the same writer/editor who compiled the preceding, or the following, sections (Ill. 3.2, compare top and bottom folios). The section begins with a salutation to Ganesh, "Guru Dattatreya," Eknath, and "Ramchandra." The salutations are followed by the statement "the [story of] the arrival of Uddhav begins [here],"[20] and then the word *abhang*, indicating that the next song will be an *abhang* on a common theme, the popular story of Uddhav (*utdhava* in the text), Krishna's messenger who comes to console the forlorn *gopīs* in Krishna's absence.[21] The song is one of the first in the *balkrida* series, which is the first editorial collection to be made of Namdev's songs in *bada*s beginning in the eighteenth century and represented in old notebooks, and is the single most utilized section of Namdev's work in contemporary *kirtan* performances.[22] Every song that follows this one in the fourteen pages—whether by Namdev or another singer—is likewise about Krishna's childhood.

The section immediately following the salutation opens with the first six lines of an eight-line song attributed to Namdev that has been recorded in other manuscripts—as early as 1631 from Dhule.[23] After the sixth line of this particular *balkrida* song is an unattributed *sakhi*, or "witness" song, in Hindi that I assume to be attributed to Namdev. The subject of the *sakhi* (in the form of a *pad*) and the *abhang* into which it is inserted are the same, that is, they are both about the birth of Krishna. Following the *sakhi* are the last two lines of the Namdev *abhang*. Then there is another *sakhi*, then the first three-quarters of an *abhang* by Namdev—which is the second song in the order of the *balkrida* series as it is represented in every printed anthology and in a handwritten manuscript by that title composed in the eighteenth century.[24] This pattern continues for several pages, with a portion of an *abhang* given first, then a *sakhi*, an *arya*, a *shloka*, or a *pad* interjected, but on the same theme as the *abhang;* and finally the conclusion of the *abhang* is given on the fourteenth page. The section ends with the last line of the eighth song in Namdev's *balkrida* sequence about the arrival of Uddhav. At this point, the handwriting again changes—perhaps indicating that another writer has begun a different section or the earlier writer has resumed transcribing. Indeed, the story of Uddhav ends, as a new series of songs begins—a ballad or *katav*, then several songs by Tukaram and Namdev. However, the songs are not broken up by other material, as in the preceding section, but presented uninterrupted, returning to the form more common in *kirtankar* notebooks in Marathi.

To return to the substance of the story containing in the fourteen pages of interwoven verse, we have the narrative of the birth of Krishna, who is feared by the king of the Mathura region. The king, Kamsa, is told that the eighth son born to his sister Devaki will kill him and end his reign. Kamsa has his sister imprisoned, along with her husband, Vasudev, and kills their children. After the eighth child is born, a son, Vasudev manages to smuggle him out of Kamsa's palace and give him to Yashoda, a woman in the village of Gokul, taking her newborn daughter back to the palace with him. Kamsa hears of the child's birth and comes to kill the baby, who taunts him (she is a goddesses herself), saying that Devaki's son is alive somewhere in the kingdom. Kamsa has all the male children of the kingdom killed, but Yashoda manages to hide Devaki's son. He is thus raised in secrecy, in the forest of Gokul, near the Yamuna River, all within the region called Braj. The series of songs in the fourteen pages outlined above describe the moment when Krishna, now a man, has been summoned to face Kamsa in Mathura, and the outcome of the battle is unknown to the citizens of Gokul. They recount the laments of the people of Gokul as they await news of whether or not Krishna, also known as Gopal, has survived the night. Krishna's friend, Uddhav, is deputized to reassure them of his well-being, but also bears the news that he will never return to Gokul even though he is victorious. Here is the translated text, which is written alternately in Marathi and Hindi, and arranged in a way that reflects its sequence on the handwritten page with corresponding line numbers (or lack of them) given in the original text:

The Beginning of [the story of] Uddhav's Arrival

ABHANG [MARATHI]

Age after age the bell rings
[And Krishna] thus comes to the people of Gokul ||1||
Sadness was everywhere around in the forest
[People cried,] "Why, Oh Lord of the Land, have you done this to us?" ||2||
Distressed, the cows become gaunt; the calves do not nurse ||3||

SAKHI [HINDI]

Nine hundred thousand cows will not eat the grass
[Their] calves will not drink milk ||
"Oh Gopal, Oh Gopal! The stars are like stones to us now," they were crying
Nama [says], "Companions, do not lose heart." Refrain

ABHANG [MARATHI]

The cow-maidens rejected food and water ||
"Now from where will Cakrapani (Krishna) [come] to us?" ||4||
The trees along the Yamuna have dried up ||
Rocks split in half because of sadness ||5||

In the morning all the companions were conversing [about their grief]

[But] the Lord had not died. ||6||

SAKHI [HINDI]

"Where? Who? Where? Who?," the cowboys and cowgirls cried out. ||

The sight [of Krishna] did not appear in the town, as all the people of Braj
wept ||2||

ABHANG [MARATHI]

[Gopal said,] "All those dear people who witnessed [this] ||

Were crying like birds for me." ||7||

Like a fish out of water, under duress ||

Nama says, the blessing of love is in the heart. ||8||

SAKHI [HINDI]

Those dear people, they kept their hope in life [even before] death ||

In each eye a tear fell, as the flute, Murari, softly played. ||3||

ABHANG [MARATHI]

Seeing this love, just then ||

Govinda was overcome by their tears ||1||

Repeating [his] names, defeating sin ||

None of the cow-maidens lost their concentration ||2||

The very soul of faith [Krishna] felt no sadness ||

But was overcome by the love of *bhakti* ||3||

The thought entered Rishikeshi's [Krishna's] mind ||

Who shall I send to Gokul?" ||4||

At that very moment he appeared before Utdhav ||

And spoke to him just then ||5||

Nama says, "Now will come a very private moment ||

Remember to stay alert!" ||6||

ABHANG [MARATHI]

The parrots and other [birds] who sing the praises [of Krishna] ||

They all cried out to Utdhav ||1||

SAKHI [HINDI]

In a loud, bellowing [voice Krishna] said,

"Udho, listen to my victory!

Go tell the cow-maidens [that]

You, with your own [eyes], have seen [me] incarnate." ||4||

ABHANG [MARATHI][25]

The text continues this way, dividing Marathi *abhang*s with Hindi
*sakhi*s, most attributed to Namdev, for the remainder of the fourteen
pages, at which point the orthography again changes perceptibly (Ill. 3.3).

ILLUSTRATION 3.3 BORI *bada* number 52, last page [top] and facing page
of the end of special section.

SOURCE: USED BY PERMISSION OF THE BHANDARKAR
ORIENTAL RESEARCH INSTITUTE.

Although the notebook as a whole appears quite ordinary, the phenomenon observed in this particular portion of the notebook is entirely unique in *badas*. The portion contains a highly systematized arrangement of texts with an obvious intent. Furthermore, nothing in the text marks these particular fourteen pages as anomalous or unique. Whoever kept the notebook seems not to have found this layout of songs and their verses incongruous with the other, more common way of recording information in the notebook.

My early attempts to understand what was going on in this particular notebook were fruitless. This changed on a visit to Pandharpur during the large annual pilgrimage in the summer of 2000. Among the many religious wares and paraphernalia for sale around the Vitthal temple in Pandharpur during the pilgrimage one finds book stalls selling everything from texts of Sanskrit verse, anthologies of the songs of the *sants*, and books for pleasure reading, to picture books of Vitthal and Pandharpur, and guides for pilgrims regarding safety and proper behavior. Amid this plethora of publications are numerous works that deal with *kirtan*. I picked up several booklets that serve as primers for students of *kirtan*. These texts reveal the same layout as in the fourteen pages of the eighteenth-century notebook.

One of the most popular of these modern *kirtan* manuals, the *Kirtan Mārgadarśikā* (*Exposition on the Kirtan Tradition*), is a series produced by Krishnadas Lohiya, trustee of the Maheshvari Dharmashala organization, which has branches in Pandharpur, Alandi, Tryambakeshwar, and Tirupati.[26] Although the book is not about the same set of songs (*balkrida*) as in the *bada* mentioned above, a comparison of the general shape of Lohiya's text and that of the *bada* is instructive. Lohiya's book opens to a brief introduction, followed by several pages of images found in this order: Vitthal, Jnandev, Lohiya himself, Eknath, Namdev, Bankatswami—Lohiya's *kirtan* guru, with Lohiya seated at his feet, Tukaram, and finally another picture of Lohiya, garlanded, with a book open on his lap and a halo surrounding his head, the iconographic pose of a *sant*. These opening images are important for what they suggest about orality, literacy, and authorship. All the *sants* pictured are seated before their texts with the exception of Namdev and—until the end—Lohiya and his guru, Bankat. However, the last image of Lohiya shows him in a pose more reminiscent of Jnandev than Namdev, seated in the lotus position, with a book on his lap. These images are meant to invest the text in the reader's hand with some degree of sanctity and auspiciousness. Lohiya's tradition is *kirtan,* not textual or written scholarship; yet he has produced a text of *kirtan*s, and the images that precede the text give the reader an orientation, a visual key to this transition between orality and literacy, from Lohiya as performer to Lohiya as textual scholar. The images also serve to root the text in the visual, in *darshan* or the sight of the guru, the *sant,* and the *kirtankar,* who, as shown in chapter 2, sits in "the seat of Narada" in Naradiya *kirtan*. Therefore, the images help to reinforce the continuum of orality, literacy, and visuality (specifically visual performativity) inherent in the *kirtan* form, but literally disembodied in the printed one where no human exists to mediate the information received.

They indicate a clear expression of a lineage of authorship: Lohiya's own authorial position is bound up in the genealogy of the preceding *sants* and his own guru. However, the ascription of authorship, so common for the printed text, goes to Lohiya alone. Lohiya tries to obviate the connotation of sole authorship, which seems inherent in the modern printed book form,[27] by making clear his reliance on his guru, Bankat, in the introduction, the dedication, and in the images that lead into the text, the entirety of which is "offered at the feet" of Bankat, in common guru-student fashion.

The transcription of the first *kirtan* in Lohiya's text begins with an opening chant, or *jayjaykār*, and a *rūpācā abhang*, as is normal with Naradiya *kirtan*. Thereafter follows the *kīrtanācā abhang*, or "song for the *kirtan*," which is usually attributed to Tukaram, Eknath, or Jnandev. After the introduction of this song is enlarged boldface text that provides songs by other authors—*pad, abhang, sakhi, shloka*, etc.—interspersed with commentary on the first *abhang*, set in smaller, nonbold type, all meant to serve the elucidation of the *kirtan*'s first *abhang*. The *kirtan* ends with a single line from Namdev on the importance of the name of God in worship.

If one were to delete the interjected commentary throughout Lohiya's text, which presumably would be supplied spontaneously in the act of performance, as is normal in a *kirtan*, the remaining structure would be identical to the fourteen pages of the eighteenth-century manuscript discussed above.[28] One finds a portion of the song that is the main presentation of the *kirtan*; the song is given in parts, interrupted by other songs that elucidate the thesis of the theme song. Songs are set within songs as a practice of exegesis in live *kirtan*, replicated in this printed manual. The similarities between Lohiya's text and the fourteen pages of the eighteenth-century manuscript suggest that the manuscript, like the printed manual, is a transcription of a *kirtan* performance, lacking only the spontaneous commentary that is scripted and present in Lohiya's text. The content of this interweaving of songs is also indicative of Namdev's position in Maharashtrian public memory. Although this particular manuscript contains both Hindi and Marathi songs, no *sant* represented in this text other than Namdev is remembered to have sung in both languages, and thus no *sant*'s songs are interspersed in this way that reveals so fluid a relationship between languages, regions, and poetic styles. The correlation of themes—two sets of songs about the same subject—should stand in some metaphorical relationship to Namdev's own remembrance. In the story recounted in the songs, both Hindi and Marathi, Uddhav is Krishna's messenger, who brings with him proof of the authenticity of his message. That proof is a flute, an instrument of performance, of exciting the desire of the *gopi*s, but also symbolizing the object of their affection. The sound of the flute, *murārī*, triggers memories in the *gopi*s throughout devotional literature in India, and it becomes a sign for Krishna himself, as it does in this series of songs. Uddhav carries the message that Krishna will forever be absent. Bereft of their beloved, the people of Gokul enact practices of remembrance: they retell the stories of Krishna's childhood (*raslila*, *kṛṣṇalīlā*, *harikatha*). One might see here the implication that Namdev does the same, that he becomes the "messenger" for the memories of *bhakti* delivered to God's adoring public. Although here we have the memories of Krishna, Namdev is also the biographer of the *sant*s of his age, the messenger of those lives and memories. By Mahipati's time in the late eighteenth century, this vague connection between Namdev and Uddhav is made explicit: Mahipati claims that Namdev is none other than Uddhav's incarnation, Krishna's messenger to his people in a new era, with a new voice in a new language.[29]

Yet, I still wish to ask, why is it only with Namdev that this interlocution of verses takes place? I think the reason must go beyond the mere fact that Namdev is unique in his association with a substantial bilingual corpus of songs and instead points directly to the performative nature of his remembrance. The composer of these fourteen pages understood that the performance, or the blueprint of one, should be presented in the voice and form of Namdev. As the ideal *kirtan* performer in Marathi, Namdev makes the perfect exemplar. The section brings together, in the shadow of the performance for which it was designed in the eighteenth century, an elegant integration of Namdev's biographical transregional appeal and his local, Marathi character as an ideal performer of *kirtan*. The literary medium here gestures toward its inherent oral function and, furthermore, to a receptive public of memory that would have understood the virtuosity of the section in biographical, religious, and literary terms.

The fourteen pages of this eighteenth-century notebook are a direct indication that *bada*s served performance. Furthermore, this *bada* fulfilled a dual purpose for its owner: a majority of the notebook provided source materials for *kirtan*, whereas the fourteen pages gave the structure of what appears to be at least half a *kirtan* performance. The continuity between what this eighteenth-century text records and Lohiya's *kirtan* primer published in 1997 suggests a similar continuity in the teaching and practice of *kirtan*.

The Logic of *Kirtan* in the Writing of Hagiography

A second setting for the intermixing of oral performance and text is in the work of Mahipati, an exceptional personality in Marathi literature.[30] Remembered as the premier compiler and commentator on the lives of the Maharashtrian *sants*, as well as of figures like Kabir, Mahipati wrote more than twenty-five separate biographical compendia in his lifetime, comprising some 35,000 verses. One of his most famous is the *Bhaktavijay*, said to have been composed in 1762.[31] Much of his hagiographical material on the early *sants*—Jnandev, Namdev, Janabai, Cokhamela, etc.—is drawn from biographical songs attributed to Namdev. The very practice of sacred biography was initiated in the Varkari tradition by songs carrying Namdev's name. Namdev is an "author" on whom much of the first portion of the *Bhaktavijay*'s "authority" relies. A survey of this text makes clear the genealogical interrelationship of literacy, biography, and performance.

Mahipati was a stickler for sources, as mentioned earlier. He claims to have composed nothing from his own imagination, but depended solely on written texts set before him.[32] We know that he had access to the *Ādi* and biographical *Tīrthāvaḷī* as in old manuscripts; Mahipati's inclusion of these stories in his own work follows these early compositions almost word for word. He reiterates that he did not fabricate any part of his biographies, but faithfully followed standard texts, that is, transcribed them and incorporated them into his own work without intervention. In the *Santalīlāmṛta*, Mahipati preempts his critics when he writes, "You will raise this doubt in your mind and say: You have drawn on your own imagination. This is not so."[33] And in the *Bhaktavijay*, he asserts, "You will say I have compiled this book on my own authority. This indeed is not so. Hold no doubts in your minds."[34] As discussed in chapter 1, Mahipati uses several key hagiographies from northern India in his work, which he references. Interestingly, though songs attributed to Namdev make up a significant portion of the *Bhaktavijay*, Mahipati nowhere cites Namdev as a source.

Mahipati may have been faithful to his sources, but he was far more than a mere scribe. He was famous in his lifetime as a skillful *kirtankar*, and this fame no doubt led to the distribution and preservation of the works attributed to him. He also seemed to have been a student of sorts of Namdev, borrowing from him and mimicking some of his poetic style. A reading of Mahipati's mid-eighteenth-century account of Jnandev's life side by side with the account ascribed to Namdev reveals an almost exact transcription of Namdev's composition—first articulated in notebooks from 1631—interpolated with a kind of poetic commentary by Mahipati in

1762. He creatively interwove stories, songs, and a narrative reminiscent of a *kirtan* into a text already well established a century before his lifetime, as *bada*s attest.[35] All around and throughout the extended quotations of authoritative biographical sources, Mahipati has placed his own embellishments and explanations, much like Lohiya's text above and the fourteen peculiar pages of the *bada*.

Mahipati's *Bhaktavijay* appears to be a kind of written *kirtan,* a textual commentary that emerges from the performance tradition of elaboration on the verses of a famous *sant.* Between the lines of older texts, Mahipati inserts his own superfluities and flourishes, exactly as a *kirtankar* would in a live performance. That is, he does not tamper at all with the texts that he used as sources—he keeps his word to his readers. Instead, he applies his own genius in the creation of a hybrid text, consisting of exact quotations from earlier sources and novel creations all his own. Mahipati bridges a gap between oral performance and literacy with what appears to be a transcribed *kirtan,* word for word.

At the conclusion of the *Bhaktavijay,* Mahipati makes his connection to performance explicit in his text. He first reinforces his position as a "scribe," but one who copies and creates from a source of inspiration and devotion:

> I have written every single letter in this book
> Just as Rukmini's husband has commanded.
> Like the puff of breath blown by a musician,
> I am the wind that sounds the flute.[36]

Mahipati tells us here that he is the instrument for expression, not the genius of the music itself. The metaphor is clearly meant to invoke a performance, not the preservation of literacy (he is not the ink of the pen, for example), yet he is explicit that he has "written every single letter" just as each note of an instrument is sounded. Mahipati concludes his *Bhaktavijay* this way:

> To some you have given knowledge of the soul.
> Some have begged to dwell in the union of self and universe.
>> My heart's desire is that I will sing [*varṇīn*][37]
>> About the character [*guna*] of Hari.
> Some sit on beds of nails,
> Some sit with Vishnu in heaven.
> For me, in the *kirtan* of your servants
> I have become lost in supreme love.[38]

Mahipati is both producer and consumer of the *kirtan* of the *sant*s and closes what is probably his most famous hagiography by invoking the oral context of performance, set down on the written page. The last verse addresses his audience: "Listening to this, the Lord of the World is gratified. Listen all you faithful, loving *bhaktas*."[39] Indeed, each of the fifty-seven chapters ends with an order to Mahipati's audience to "listen" to these stories of the lives of the *sant*s. A written text that concludes by asking its audience to "listen" is one that has not divided orality and literacy but understood the text as inherently performative and oral.

Mahipati lived in a transitional period, when oral literatures were increasingly written down and many were slowly finding themselves replicated in blocks on printing presses, responding to the interest of colonial personages and the access to print technology and the printing machines they brought with them. In addition, during this period *kirtan* performance had reached a high point of appeal and patronage (with *kirtankar*s regularly serving in courts in Thanjavur and the Maharashtrian Deccan), and the feudal political landscape of India was coalescing under the expansion of British power. Mahipati's occupation as a scribe and his religious vocation as a *kirtankar* melded—to the benefit of historians—in his compositions. As argued above, his chief composition, the *Bhaktavijay,* is composed in the style of a *kirtan;* indeed, it may actually be a transcript of a *kirtan* performance, as well as an archive of biography and history. This text can be read like a fossilization of bones that occurs in an epoch of drastic climatic change, a fossil that records a negotiation of orality and literacy. Within fifty years of his death in 1790, his *Bhaktavijay* would enter the discourse of modern printed scholarship on India in European and Indian languages, reflecting the changes modernity augurs and find new media, such as print and later film, in which to continue Namdev's Maharashtrian legacy.[40]

PUBLIC MEMORY AMID LITERACY AND PERFORMANCE

What do we make of literacy when it is produced within a cultural field, in this case Namdev's Maharashtrian public memory, that disavows writing? This chapter builds on the previous one in demonstrating how performance, specifically oral performance, is the primary means of communicating Namdev's Maharashtrian memory into any given present moment. Amid a highly literate world of *sant*s and hagiographers, it appears as if the authentic recollection of Namdev involves not only retelling stories or performing songs attributed to him but couching these cultural productions in discursive realms appropriate to Namdev's character. This chapter investigates writing to see how the quandary of a nonliterate *sant* represented in literary media can be addressed. In the case of *bada*s, the medium of recollection serves performance. Literacy is a tool to assist the practice of *kirtan*. It is not until the advent of print that Namdev comes to exist as a *sant* whose legacy is contained in writing. For all the performative power of a public reading of the *Jñāneśvarī*, it is still a text, genealogically connected to Jnandev's own hand. And for all the ways that Tukaram has entered into performative places—in *kirtan*, in music, in film—there are still hagiography and physical artifacts that tell us Tukaram's work is contained in a book that he wrote with his own hand as well. The literacy of figures like Eknath and Mahipati becomes part of their very character as *sant*s: Eknath as a text editor and literary conduit for the epics into Marathi, and Mahipati as collator of hagiography and writer of books. There is no figure amid Namdev's fellow *sant*s who stands in such stark contrast to literacy.

The reason for this contrast is that Namdev is remembered first and foremost as a *kirtankar,* a practice he is said to have developed in order to reach the widest possible swath of humanity. The interweaving of Hindi and Marathi in the manuscript examined in this chapter indicates this well, suggesting that an essence is communicated through various performances. A story is retold, slightly or significantly, but in a way appropriate to the context and time. In this case, the story was of Uddhav delivering his message to the *gopi*s of Gokul told in two languages (Hindi and Marathi) and attributed to one person (Namdev). The arrangement of the verses in the two languages hinged on these points of connection, on the suffering of the cows and calves, for instance, or the crying of the birds. These pivot points tell us something about the structure of Namdev's remembrance. It comes to a devotee through impressions that often cannot be captured in a single, authoritative version of a song. The songs have a character that attests to their authenticity, rather than a reference to a previous textual source, and this character is performative. A memory of who Namdev was, in which languages he composed, what subjects he undertook to explore, and in what performative ways he explored them—this memory moves throughout the text examined above.

Likewise, this memory is revealed in the use of the *bada*s. Those *kirtankar*s who took Namdev as their exemplar were not compelled to commit their work to the written page. This is not the case with Tukaram, for example, where not only the manuscript attributed to Tukaram under glass in Dehu remains, but also the work of his scribe, Jaganade, whose seventeenth-century manuscript is one of the largest compendiums of Tukaram's verses other than the Dehu *pothi*. The finer of the written records of Namdev's songs are frequently appended to a collection of songs by Tukaram, as if Namdev received the literary largess that surrounded Tukaram. This fact should lead to the conclusion that literary recording of songs, unlike the recording of long compositions like the *Jñāneśvarī*, began in earnest in Tukaram's period, invested with the desire to preserve in writing his songs, as he is said to have done himself. If the transportation of Tukaram's verses into the future became a concern of literacy, it might have pulled within its orbit Namdev's memory, which was otherwise not concerned with writing for the sake of preservation.

It should be clear at this point that the Maharashtrian Namdev tradition requires a different dialectic from that of "orality" or "literacy" to account for its practices of remembrance. Before suggesting what this different dialectic might look like, it may be worthwhile to understand how the dialogue of orality and literacy privileges the latter over the former in modern historical and anthropological research.

In the highly influential and diverse work of figures like Jack Goody, Ian Watt, Walter Ong, and Marshall McLuhan, society in general is described as flowing from orality/illiteracy to visuality/literacy, which tracks a similar course from premodern and prescientific thought to modern, rational thought.[41] Especially in the early work of Jack Goody and Ian Watt, a culture that shifts from oral/illiterate to literate is characterized as passing from "simple" to "complex,"[42] from a society that has a sense only of the culture of the present and the capacity for "collective memory," as Halbwachs coined the term, to one that has the power of "history."[43] These seminal studies, and Goody's work in particular, all propose an essential technology of the intellect in the context of culture, which is also a teleology, a standard typology in modern social reasoning.[44] Cultural development always seems to run hand in hand with race, and George Stocking has demonstrated how literacy and orality inform early anthropological formulations of evolution among "races."[45]

Yet this dialectic did more than divide the "modern" world from the rest, it parsed levels within its own domains. Michel de Certeau, in a study on the writing of history in France from the seventeenth century to the present, argues: "Orality is displaced, as if excluded from writing. It is isolated, lost, and found again in a 'voice' which is that of nature, of the woman, of childhood, of the people."[46] Furthermore, he finds "orality" to be the purview of "religion" and "popular culture" in the seventeenth century in France, an era when the creation of textual knowledge in the name of science and reason sat alongside the making of popular musical, theatrical, and hymnal-religious culture.[47] Although a wholesale association of the realm of the "oral" with the "subaltern" should be avoided—in South Asia, orality is as central to Brahminical orthodoxy as to lower caste devotionalism—modern culture, at least, has become conditioned by the dialectic of orality and literacy and in turn categorizes its own members in a way that parallels the later work of historians of capital and social change. Orality and literacy mark class, access to power, and privilege at both the local level and in the context of "world history" and in the theory of social evolution.

In response to Goody and Watt—essentially to Goody—R. W. Niezen tried to untangle the implications for their study in the exploration of sacred writing.[48] Niezen directly engages Claude Lévi-Strauss when he proposes the notion of "hot societies" that possess "restricted literacy" and "cold societies" with "widespread literacy."[49] Niezen compares literacy in the hot society of medieval Christianity in Europe and the cold society of contemporary African Islam among the Wahhabi of West Africa. The author's goal is to prove that scriptural literacy is a particular species of literacy that may engender a "hot" society (as in medieval Christian Europe) but does not lead to the kind of dynamic impulse to history, individuality, and revolution that Goody assumes to exist (in ancient Greece, for example).[50] Niezen asserts that in societies where literacy is tightly controlled by religious institutions, historical consciousness is stifled. Goody himself came to a more nuanced understanding of restrictions placed on literacy through social stratification, hence restrictions to historical consciousness.[51] Yet the dialectic of orality and literacy still holds sway, as highly conditioned as its conclusions may be.

There is perhaps no place where the antagonism between orality and literacy is more apparent than in the modern science of philology, which J. Z. Smith places at the center of the history of religions as a discipline. In particular, the creation of critical editions of certain texts attributed to discrete authors has long occupied an important place in South Asian religious studies. In his influential work *An Introduction to Indian Textual Criticism,* S. M. Katre describes the interference of oral traditions with written ones in Sanskrit manuscript literature as a "pathology of texts," a systemic illness of the body of work, using a term couched in the ultimate science, that of medicine.[52] Orality, for Katre, caused the slow disintegration of the exact literate record; it eroded the written word by its unsystematic oral interpolations. Trained in London as a philologist, Katre, a

Maharashtrian Brahmin, returned to his hometown of Pune to become the director of the Deccan College Postgraduate and Research Institute and a prominent figure in many important critical editions, including that of the *Mahābhārata* under the direction of S. V. Sukthankar (1887–1943). Sukthankar was more tolerant of the influence of orality than was his colleague. Sukthankar believed that the problems of variation stemmed from the condition of oral transmission where the mind is hard-pressed to keep from meddling with an original author's intentions.[53] The mind was prone to the lax transmission standards of orality; writing was a solution to the problem, but was constantly in battle with the undertow of the oral world. When copies of narratives or other texts did not match, the culprit was likely a scribe who allowed the *heard* to infect the *written*.

Several studies centered on South Asia have engaged this "divide" between orality and literacy, viewing the bifurcation with skepticism, but often, it seems, from the perspective of literacy invested with orality. Peter van der Veer has discussed the Orientalist creation of a textual foundation for Sanskrit literature through the composition of critical editions based on manuscripts that reflected the "primarily oral and performative nature" of narratives, such as the Vedas.[54] The transfer of oral traditions into textual, "scientific," arenas is tracked by van der Veer on a continuum between Brahminical and Orientalist philology.[55] Wendy Doniger proposes the juxtaposition of "fluid" and "fixed" written texts that exhibit purposeful and productive relationships with orality.[56] Philip Lutgendorf's extensive study of the performative context of the *Rāmcaritmanas* argues that text and performance are inseparable; the two constitute one strand of praxis.[57] Stuart Blackburn, A. K. Ramanujan, Kirin Narayan, Anne Feldhaus, and Joyce Flueckiger, among other folklorists of South Asia, have all amply demonstrated the deep involvement of orality and literacy, especially in the retelling of epic tales.[58] J. S. Hawley has regularly invested the literary study of *bhakti* with ethnographic context and comment in order to draw out the oral and performative worlds in which *bhakti* exists.[59] In a discussion of the various "textures" of the Telugu *Kumārarāmuni Kathā*, Rao, Shulman, and Subrahmanyam show how a written portion of the narrative is clearly not a "written text" but a "recorded" one, a transcription of an inherently oral discourse.[60] Given the depth and number of these studies, one would be challenged to sustain the argument that South Asia has witnessed the hegemonic ascendancy of literacy over orality.

The British social anthropologist Jonathan Parry conducted an ethnography in Benares, collecting oral data about how literacy and orality mix in the construction of history.[61] Parry took Goody's ideas to task in the context of the "Brahminical tradition" or "traditional Hindu India."[62] Parry investigated the categories of "Brahminical" and "traditional" as they play out in relationship to Sanskrit and the pronouncements of Sanskritic scholars. He interviewed priests, scholars, and "householders," asking them what constitutes authoritative history in their worldview.[63] His project sought to understand what forms of oral knowledge underwrote authority. What Parry found was a consistent reference to Sanskritic sources as preeminent among all literary sources. However, as a literary authority, bound up in Sanskrit texts, Sanskrit served as a kind of *oral* trope of authority among people who never had *read* and never could read Sanskrit. References to Sanskrit texts were a way to establish the authority of a statement, but no actual written text was required; the oral reference alone contained authoritative power. Parry suggests that orality and literacy, at least among Hindus in contemporary Benares, combine effectively to form a gateway between "tradition" and innovation based on Sanskrit literary works as a model for reasoned assessments.[64] The purviews of orality and literacy are not mutually exclusive, and neither is credited with sustaining either "tradition" or "cognitive modernism," supposedly a necessary precondition of historiography.[65]

An alternative way to imagine the relationship between orality and literacy is presented by Michel de Certeau in his study of the practices of "everyday life." He has suggested that the modern idea of writing and authorship occurred because writing had lost its connection to orality.[66] Progressive developments in writing began to refer to earlier written sources, rather than to "original" oral ones, and writing took on a character all its own. The symbiotic connection between orality and literacy was lost. In the modern-day West, writing came to inhabit a kind of elevated structure above orality, a technology thought to maintain greater clarity and precision of communication so long as its referents, its basis for substantiation, remained within the written record. Such an idea is readily apparent in the work of Goody and Watt, for example. Although they clearly state that literacy is always afloat in a sea of orality,[67] the advent of self-referential writing is also the advent of history, a lifeboat on the ocean of information. But this shift to a self-referential writing system can be seen not as a positive, progressive advancement but, rather, as the mark of a loss of cultural integrity and a schism that takes on the shapes of class differences. Brought to the level of global comparison, this division comes to mark civilizations as "premodern" and "modern" or "developing" and "developed." The dialectic of orality and literacy is at the heart of the self-serving judgments of the modern world.

In the Maharashtrian Namdev tradition, no rupture with an oral tradition is marked, and no teleology of development following the line of literacy is upheld. The idea that the social world into which Namdev is inserted ever evinced a "transition" from the oral to the written cannot be sustained, and very few concrete examples exist anywhere in the world of a clear transition from an oral society to a literate one—this distinction is one of the key problems of the orality-literacy debate. Instead, in Namdev's Maharashtrian public memory there is a systematic interweaving of orality and literacy that yet privileges orality at least rhetorically through the biography and autobiographical statements attributed to Namdev. When set alongside the abiding importance of *kirtan* in the Maharashtrian Namdev tradition, the superior position of performance makes good sense. In other contexts, such as those that surround Tukaram or Jnandev, literacy is often ascendant but still in partnership with orality and performance; antagonism is not found between these realms. This chapter demonstrates how orality functions in a system of writing, producing texts that serve and, in some cases, transcribe performance. The Namdev tradition in Maharashtra participates in both spheres of writing and speech. Yet the tradition does invest orality, specifically performance, with an influence over literacy. How can the largely modern dialectic of orality and literacy help explain the Maharashtrian Namdev tradition?

The logic of transmission in the tradition in Maharashtra is clearer if the term "oral" or "orality" is abandoned, for several reasons. First, "orality" has been conditioned by a relationship with "literacy," which is hard to extricate from a teleology that places orality as an early step toward literacy. A tradition that uses the voice and body to communicate over time, rather than paper and ink, should not be seen as a tradition fixed in some premature stage of cognitive or technological development. Second, the idea of orality often invokes a sense of narrative chaos, or at least of the instability of a message, a constant cause of correction for the text critic and philologist. Poststructuralism brought to the forefront the old idea that even written words are never fixed symbolically, but are always interpreted or misinterpreted. In short, orality and literacy are equally incapable of precisely preserving and communicating a message. Third, the term "oral" should be abandoned because it suggests that literacy serves no purpose whatsoever within the context of "the oral" or that literacy is a technology outside the ken of an oral tradition's practitioners. Nothing could be further from the truth in the Maharashtrian Namdev tradition. The past 150 years have seen the prodigious creation of texts regarding Namdev in Marathi, Hindi, Punjabi, and English, among other languages. Namdev's followers regularly use print and writing, and these include famous performers.

For these three reasons primarily, I use the term "performance" to stand for some of the ideas associated with orality, but with the caveats mentioned above and others to come. As to orality's archrival, literacy, I prefer the term "permanence," in the sense of something immutable, to indicate the intentions of those who commit to writing narratives that they wish to make fixed and unchanging.[68] The idea of permanence captures more accurately what I believe is the collective sense of the power of writing and printing in modern society. However, I do not want to suggest that those who choose performance as a means of preservation do not also wish their materials to be eternally available—that is, performance does not exclude the desire to preserve materials. Rather, it assumes that preservation and change are linked; whereas the idea of permanence in this context assumes that preservation and immutability are linked. The conceit here is that literacy has provided the ability to preserve data over time more accurately; to distribute it more widely (especially in modernity, which is always concerned with the reach of the "global"); and to allow for referentiality. This means that some level of permanence is required for progress, and writing has been a vital innovation in human communication to allow progress through various vistas. The essential benefit of literacy, in theory of the modern, has been this sense of permanence, this fight against chaos, decay, and inertia, a place for reason to substantiate and sustain itself against time.

In the terms of the dialectic proposed here—"performance" and "permanence"—the emphasis on the former in the Maharashtrian Namdev tradition is centrally important in understanding what has value within the tradition. The skill of narration and the ability to entertain are vital; the ability to write is not. But the secondary status of writing does not also mean that an idea of authorship, however conditioned by literacy, is not present. Authorship is essential here in ways quite similar to patterns of authorship in modernity. The author organizes and validates subjects; the author focuses critical attention; and the author generates meaning. In performance, the interweaving lines of authorship, from past to present, are apparent, but in the texts examined here the lines of authorship become obscured; in literacy produced by the Maharashtrian Namdev tradition, it is even harder to ascertain who is an "author."

This is ironic from a modern perspective, in which writing essentially created the modern author. Elizabeth Eisenstein has suggested that in early modern Europe, the rise of the printing press produced the idea of the modern author as a single agent, and it is toward this creation that postmodern critics of authorship orient their arguments.[69] But as seen in Lohiya's text, for example, the idea of authorship in the Maharashtrian Namdev tradition has not taken as its central concept the sovereign, creative author. Instead, the tradition has kept at its core a corporate model of authorship. Through the media of writing and print, as well as through the medium of performance, this corporate configuration has shifted and expanded, but has not transformed itself into a mirror image of the modern Western author that Eisenstein sees produced through the world of print. Yet texts, printed and handwritten, exist in the tradition and are important as a temporary archive for performance, as a resource to performers, and, in rare cases, as a fossilization of *kirtan,* a snapshot of the *kirtankar* caught in the act.

In discussing the "historiographical operation" in France, Michel de Certeau proposed viewing writing as "the inverted image of practice."[70] Inverted because it must mirror the subject of its history, but must necessarily do so from the present, backward. In other words, the practice that is the subject of histories moves forward in time, and the historian, in an action necessitated by his or her position later in time, works backward, "prescribing for beginnings what is in reality a point of arrival, and even what would be a vanishing point in research."[71] I would argue that the Namdev tradition in Maharashtra, operating in a historiographic mode, sought to address this very problem by reinventing the past in the present through performance, by blending time within performative space and finding in writing ways of assisting this process. And this mode of performance so conditioned a historical epistemology that literacy could not supplant performance as the dominant technology of historical composition.

The notebook tradition described here is a residue, a literate trace of a more dominant practice of performance. Yet this residue has served as an archive in major pilgrimage and religious centers and is the bedrock of modern printed editions. A line of performance fuses together the lineages of orality and literacy (and print) in the Maharashtrian Namdev tradition. My contention here, however, is that performance remains dominant, held up as a superior medium not just of expression but also of maintenance. Although I would not argue that the resilience of performance in the Maharashtrian Namdev tradition is to be interpreted as a protest or challenge to literacy or the power of writing,[72] the realm of the "oral" seems always to be associated with the "peasant."[73] Here, I do not believe that the association of the Namdev Maharashtrian tradition with performance is to be read as a feature of resistance to the field of power but, rather, as a strategic choice of media, in this case performance and human media, reinforced by Namdev's consistent association with the *kirtan*. The Namdev Maharashtrian tradition has been surrounded by writing and has used writing, but in the service of performance. The permanence sought in the commitment to writing associated with Jnandev or Tukaram is replaced by a desire to preserve a tradition in inherently oral media, to keep it true to its (oral) word.

Part 1 of this book seeks to express the practices associated with Namdev's public memory in Maharashtra. Chapter 1 investigates history and hagiography; chapter 2 studies the centrality of authorship; and chapter 3 explores the interplay of orality and literacy. As sets of practices, these activities constitute what I call the "will to remember" that is evident in *bhakti*. This will is expressed through performative and written media and through both scholarly historical inquiry and popular biographical recollections. Together, these practices form publics as they all require audiences and assume that audiences demand further instantiations of memory. In Part 2, the discussion advances from the practices of public memory to historical moments when *bhakti* has replied to the demands of public memory.

PART II

◈ PUBLICS OF MEMORY ◈

NAMDEV AND THE NAMAS

*He was not a man; he was a continent. He contained whole crowds
of great men, entire landscapes.*
—GUSTAVE FLAUBERT ON SHAKESPEARE

D URING THE course of research for this book, a friendly joke circulated about me among scholars and some people affiliated with the Namdev Maharashtrian tradition in Pune and Pandharpur. I acquired the nickname "Christian Nama," a reference to my studies of Namdev.[1] I asked about the nature of this joke with the person whom I believed to be its source. My friend said it was a reference "to the other Namdevs," that is, those poets whose poetry, because of a proximity of names and styles, had been associated, and sometimes mistaken for, the poetry of Namdev of the fourteenth century. It is a common feature of Indian poetic traditions that authors incorporate their names into a final line of their poetry and that this name is often a *nom de plume* or a pseudonym. The line is referred to in Marathi, Sanskrit, and other Indian languages as *nāmamudra* or *bhaṇitā* and resembles the *takhallus* of Urdu poetry. The word *bhanita* literally references what has been "spoken" but also means "relation" as in relating the essence of a thing, as well as "description."[2] Similarly, *namamudra* indicates the "sign" or "symbol" (*mudra*) of a composer's name (*nama*). It functions as a "signature," but in the much older sense of this word, as a "sign" or a "stamp" of authenticity.[3] In other words, it describes or even symbolizes a genre of authorship, as much as it might suggest a sole author. I refer to this word or phrase as an ideograph in order to convey the way these "signatures" often function as symbols of authorship but are not a direct ascription of authorship to an individual. An ideograph is as likely to convey the *idea* of a Namdev song, to signal its type, as it is to suggest that Namdev actually composed the song.[4] This suggests that there have been many figures over time who have used Namdev's ideograph in some form to signal that they are composing a Namdev-esque song. Thus other composers, such as Vishnudas Nama, Shimpi Nama, Nama Yashvant, and Nama Pathak, not only use "Nama" in their ideographs but compose songs that bear some key similarities to those of the first Namdev. My friend informed me that I was entering into this stream of "Namas" because I was writing a book on Namdev; I was *conveying* Namdev in some sense. Of course, I have not taken "Nama" into my own name, nor do I compose poetry (at least not very well). Nonetheless my friend's point interested me because it hinted at a fascinating notion of authorship at work in the Namdev tradition and how people who participate in that tradition are remembered and marked as participants. It also suggested a system of continuity that rests with processes of approximation and mimesis, diverging from a direct correspondence between name and authorship.

In this context, public memory involves questions of historical and practical authorship in the ways an author is conveyed into the present through a mimetic process signaled by ideographs. The study of Indian devotional traditions has often taken the form of tracing literary remnants by reference to a name, of collecting all "Kabir" or "Surdas" songs together because of the approximation of ideographs or other markers of author-genre. Indeed, as seen in previous chapters, this is one significant way that old manuscripts are organized, by collecting songs by author.[5] The modern scholarly practice of grouping songs according to ideograph follows conventional text-critical methods and has regularly engaged the idea of an original author or the recovering of the author's intentions within a text. Scholars who undertake these text-critical explorations perform a vital service to scholarship, producing critical editions of works that are the foundation of translation, exegesis, and recovering cultural history, but are also deeply historical. By historical I mean that a good critical edition thoroughly notes the approximate age of texts, the location or even genealogy of the documents, the context of their transmission, and the orthographic details that indicate something about the literary and political economies in which they existed.

Almost all text critics of *bhakti* figures encounter the common problem of a multiplicity of authorship. For example, take the figure of Kabir. Linda Hess has written convincingly of "three Kabir collections" that suggest three very different biographically and spiritually marked authors evident through textual and performative practices.[6] These three Kabirs are significantly different in the content and impression of the verses attributed to them. Of course, the various traditions that remember Kabir do not believe that there were three; they do not accept this academic and textual distinction. Likewise, J. S. Hawley has written about the expansion of the corpus of songs associated with Surdas, charting how this number grew after the *sant*'s time. Some of these songs may have been late discoveries or recovered from lost manuscripts, but Hawley is right to suggest that the bulk of these additions can be accounted for only with recourse to the idea that later poets composed in the name and style of Surdas.[7] Winand Callewaert and Mukund Lath, in their work on Namdev's Hindi corpus, suggest that the value of text critical work is historical in nature. It recalls the earliest written layers of a literate tradition but cannot claim to encompass an "original author."[8] What remains is an image of which songs were important enough to be written down, and to survive to this day, thus providing a sense of the general shape of a corpus at the furthest available moment in time. The case of Namdev in Maharashtra displays these same problems to the text critic, and a long tradition in Marathi exists from the nineteenth century onward dedicated to sorting out which songs attributed to Namdev are likely to have been composed by someone who fits the profile of the Namdev of the fourteenth century.

There are at least two views of this "problem of authorship." The first view holds that songs produced in periods and by figures different from that of the original author are "spurious"; they are not authentic because they are clearly not the product of the author whose work is being edited. Text critics working with this perspective try to shape a text that follows logical rules suited to sifting through songs or compositions and judging which ones are the oldest and hence the most likely to be original to the historical author. This view implicitly assumes that the accumulation of songs in an author's name after the death of the author is a problem engendered perhaps by copyists, proto-editors, or performers.

The other view is that the accumulation of songs represents a conscious process that is not necessarily concerned with the kind of authorship outlined as "modern" in chapter 2. From this perspective, it is evident that authorship is a process not tied to faithfully preserving a set of songs created by a single author but, rather, of maintaining a performance tradition that involves several kinds of authors operating at once in a chain of anamnesis, of remembering through imitation with variation. Shifting focus to this more flexible notion of authorship, we might begin to ask how authorship becomes historically construed as a thing that is embodied in a plethora, or even a linked genealogy, of individual creators (the corollary to the modern author) who shared a notion of the architecture of composition in which individuality becomes integrated with transhistorical forms. In other words, could the many Kabirs, Surdases, or Namdevs represent a system of authorship rather than a degradation of authorship? Could there be intention behind the actions of the many individuals who composed songs in the names of *sant*s long gone?

In the case of Namdev, the later poets whose work is interwoven with that of first Namdev took certain steps to ensure this kind of interconnection, and this suggests that a traditional text critical approach used to hew to the intentions of an original author would deny access to the theory and practice of authorship that animates six centuries of performance and textual production around the name of Namdev. The later composers used "Nama" in their names in some way, and they wrote on themes and in styles associated with Namdev.[9] There was no attempt to disguise a distinct identity, yet there was no desire to have an entirely separate identity, either. Marathi literary scholars of the past century and a half have almost unanimously agreed that there are several "Namdevs" at work in Marathi literary history.[10] Mahipati, as early as 1767 in his *Santalīlāmṛta,* gives the biography of the first of these "other" Namdevs, Vishnudas Nama, who is clearly distinct from Namdev of the fourteenth century. These Namdevs are distinguished by specific compositions associated with their names, as well as references made to them by other figures, especially in hagiography. However, these distinctions among authors who use the term "Nama" in their names begins to break down in the song-literature meant to be a part of the *kirtan* tradition, which forms the substance of the many handwritten collections of songs and the modern printed editions of Namdev's attributed work. In this environment of song, performed and written, the compositions of the various Namas are intertwined, and their many ideographs appear interspersed with the signature line associated with Namdev of the fourteenth century, *nāmā mhaṇe.* A complex, multifaceted, and historically interconnected notion of authorship appears to be at work here, what I call anamnetic authorship.

The first signs of anamnetic authorship are evident in manuscripts from the late sixteenth century, such as the copious Dhule manuscript finished in the early seventeenth century, just as the Nizam Shahi Sultanate fell to Aurangzeb and the Mughals. The late sixteenth century in Maharashtra is a period of fascinating intercultural development, as the Portuguese establish themselves along the Konkan coast and the Nizam Shahi Sultanate controlled northern Maharashtra (the location of Dhule), while the Bijapur

Sultanate controlled the southern portion (the location of Pandharpur). In both regions, a historical watershed emerges in textual evidence regarding the songs of devotional figures. One figure in particular, Eknath (c. 1533–1599), one of the five key *sants* of the Varkari tradition, is especially important in inaugurating an explicitly textual tradition of maintaining and archiving the songs of the *sants*.

This period likely set the stage for a tradition of authorship that melded performance and the need for permanence in a way that produced the phenomenon of anamnetic authorship associated with Namdev, taking advantage of associations made between Namdev of the fourteenth century and later composers. A distinction between the first Namdev and later composers who used "Nama" in their ideographs was blurred, but not erased—it held difference and similarity together. Indeed the interplay of difference and similarity became a site of a strategic reapplication of the notions of authorship already present in the performance tradition of *kirtan*. Authorship could be collapsed, articulated, and differentiated in ways that appear purposeful and collectively enacted in the process of constructing a public memory of Namdev sustained by centuries of intervention by other "Namas."

NAMDEV AND THE NAMAS

The period between the first, or "original," Namdev and the first figure to use "Nama" in his own name is an era in Maharashtra often described as a "dark age" spanning from roughly the early fourteenth century to the early eighteenth century. This period is characterized as one of Muslim conquest and the subjugation of Hindus, including the repression of Hindu-inflected art, architecture, and public culture. The last of the Yadava rulers, Ramchandra, ruled from 1271 to 1309, but the Yadava kingdom become a tributary state of the Khalji empire, under the rule of Alauddin Khalji and centered in Delhi, as early as 1294. In 1317, the Yadava kingdom was formally annexed to the Khalji dynasty of the Delhi Sultanate and was almost entirely destroyed by Muhammad bin Tughlaq, of the Tughlaq dynasty of the Delhi Sultanate, in 1327. In 1347, the Bahmani Sultanate ruled over the area of Maharashtra, and when it disintegrated into the Five Sultanates of the Deccan, the region of Maharashtra was dominated by the Nizam Shahi rule and Bijapur rule. By the third quarter of the seventeenth century, Maharashtra was at the center of the decline of the Deccan Sultanates' powers, the encroachment of the Mughal Empire under Aurangzeb, and the reign of

Shivaji, beginning in 1674. Colonial occupation would take hold in the early part of the nineteenth century. The period in between the fall of the Yadava kingdom and the rise of Shivaji's nascent Maratha empire did not witness a total subjugation of a Hindu population to Muslim power but, rather, political alliances across religious boundaries, made among landed, powerful elites. Chapter 5 displays, in part, how it would be wrong to read an undifferentiated Muslim "other" as a political and cultural enemy in Maharashtra from the fourteenth to the eighteenth centuries. Yet the "dark age" still retains, in Maharashtrian historiography, the character of Muslim oppression and conquest.

In Marathi literary history, the boundaries of this Dark Age differ, though they still tend to relate to religious affiliation. From the sixteenth to the seventeenth century, regional literary production increased significantly in northern India under the rubric of *bhakti*, and this efflorescence appeared to be matched in Maharashtra, even though "Muslim" rule still held sway in the region, as was the case in northern India. The remembered birth of Eknath in the mid-sixteenth century signaled at least the literary decline to this period of darkness, but one might assume, rather, that is was the apex of a process begun in the fourteenth and fifteenth centuries, the efflorescence of a centuries-old vital "Hindu" religious history that was only now returning to copious written form. Invariably, the perceived pause of two centuries in literary production is attributed to the advent of Muslim political power in the Deccan region—and sometimes to the complicity of Hindu high, landed castes and families in the political orders of Sultanate India. S. G. Tulpule, for example, writes that "the onslaught of the Muslims . . . reduced the social, religious and cultural life of Maharashtra to a skeleton."[11] Although Islam is generally regarded as having been a deterrent in those tenebrous times, K. M. Panikkar and S. G. Tulpule have also suggested that Sufism, though it rode the "onslaught" of Islam and constituted its own "infiltration," did indeed provide a tonic to the languishing non-Muslim religious literary life by reducing the "monopoly of the learned" and allowing regional literatures to rise.[12] Tulpule also notes the possible impact of the drought and famine of 1396–1408.[13] So the darkness of the so-called Dark Age is likely more a product of elite control of literary production, whether Hindu or Muslim, and the real-world effects of natural disaster and political strife. Eknath, in all these respects, reveals a liminal character, at once at home amid religious elite social structures and yet purporting to speak in the language, and to the concerns, of the subaltern and suffering. For our purposes, an important conjecture made by Tulpule should be noted. He suggests that the

Marathi literary legacy of the twelfth to early fourteenth centuries chiefly had been maintained through the Dark Age by performance traditions, such as *kirtan*.[14] In lieu of written records or state largess, Marathi literary-religious materials survived through oral performance and social systems of transmission. Outside the pale of writing, courts, and chronicles, inside the world of the performing body and voice, the practices of composition in regional languages continued unabated. It is in Eknath's period of the mid-sixteenth century that the first written records of Namdev's Marathi songs appear, such as the autobiographical *Tīrthāvaḷī* in 1581 and at least two voluminous manuscripts—from Dhule (1631) and Pandharpur (seventeenth century)—holding more than a thousand songs attributed to Namdev. The oldest extant written record of the biographical *Tīrthāvaḷī*, as well as portions of the *Ādi* and *Samādhi* attested in manuscripts dated to shortly after Eknath's time, within fifty years of his remembered date of death. The proximity of these written records to the Dark Age of Maharashtra might support Tulpule's thesis that performance, recorded later by these manuscripts, flourished sufficiently in the preceding centuries to merit some representation in written form. However, the immediate presence of so many artifacts of religious performance associated with earlier *sant*s, as well as the rise of a significant new *sant*, Eknath, might also point to an opposite conclusion, that the Dark Age was not so dark, but instead saw the bright light of a performance art tradition, if also the dearth of a written record of that tradition, hence the illusion of absence. One might argue that the new systems of taxation and economic communication of the Bahmani Sultanate, the Deccan Sultanates, and later the Mughals in the Deccan region all inspired, rather than stifled, the production of written records of the songs of Maharashtrian *sant*s. The key figure in this pivotal literary moment is Eknath, and in this *sant*'s period several practices of remembrance are solidified: textual conservation, *kirtan* performance, and an elastic, expansive notion of authorship.

Eknath was a *sant* whose biography in the Marathi public sphere often stands to contest the negative associations of Muslim power in the Deccan as well as the political anti-Brahminism that arose in Maharashtra in the Peshwa period, reaching its apex in the late colonial period. His traditional life span covers the latter three-quarters of the sixteenth century. He is said to have been born into a Brahmin family in the city of Paithan, a center of Brahminical learning and orthodoxy that was within the Ahmednagar or Nizam Shahi Sultanate of the Deccan within his lifespan. This is where Jnandev and his siblings were required to demonstrate their Brahminical status to a committee of Brahmin officials, a story narrated by

Namdev in the *Ādi* (see chapter 1). Legend recalls that Eknath's parents died in his infancy, and he was raised by his grandfather, Bhanudas (late fifteenth to mid-sixteenth century), a devout Varkari and someone credited with having returned the famous image of Vitthal to Pandharpur, after it had been "hidden" (or stolen) by Krishnadevaraya of Vijaynagar in 1521 and brought to Hampi to "protect" the image from Muslims.[15] Thus Eknath entered the stream of Varkari memory as the grandson of a hero of Pandharpur. However, his religious direction reflected the religiocultural pluralism of the Deccan in the sixteenth century. Although he was a Brahmin, his songs aim toward the language of "the people," not erudition, employing the metaphors of labor and popular linguistic registers; he betrays no caste elitism in the songs commonly attributed to him. As mentioned earlier, some scholars believe that Eknath's guru, Janardan, was a member of the Sufi order Sijrā-i-kādrī.[16] This might not be true, but the association between Eknath and Sufism indicates the cultural pluralism of the late sixteenth century in the northern Deccan region. Although some early Marathi scholarship suggests that Eknath disguised his guru's connection to Sufism in his own day, the ideograph found in Eknath's songs is "Eka Janārdana," a hybrid of his name and that of his guru. Marathi scholarly work since the 1970s has clearly shown the connection, through Janardan, that links Eknath, Sufism, and the Varkari tradition, even if Janardan's affiliation as a Sufi is a historically tenuous assertion.[17] Also known as Janardanaswami, he was resident at Daulatabad (Devgiri), holding both secular and religious positions within the political/social matrix of Muslim rule in the region. A modern manifestation of this sort of religious pluralism is visible in the figure of Sai Baba of Shirdi (d. 1918), a Sufi *pir*, a preponderance of whose devotees are Hindus in Maharashtra. Whatever the religious pedigree of Eknath's guru, the interreligious conditions of his biography seem clear.

Eknath was remembered as an exceptional *kirtankar*, and a genre of Marathi *kirtan* emerged, called Eknathi *kirtan*, characterized as invested in worldly metaphor and the plight of the "common man" rather than in mythological story-telling. Yet Eknath's legacy is primarily a literary one. Although he has miracles associated with his life in hagiographical fashion, he is remembered for his literary interventions on behalf of a Maharashtrian Hindu, and principally Varkari, public in the sixteenth century as an editor and preserver of important textual sources. He is perhaps best known for collecting all versions of the *Jñāneśvarī* available to him in the sixteenth century, collating them, and creating a critical edition of this text. A colophon attributes this "corrected" version of the *Jñāneśvarī* to him in 1584.[18] This text-critical endeavor is unique among the Maharashtrian Varkari *sant*s and indeed among *bhakti* figures in general.

In addition to editing the *Jnāneśvarī*, Eknath completed a commentary in Marathi on the eleventh book of the *Bhāgavata Purāṇa* and a shorter poetic composition recalling a story from the tenth book of the *Purāṇa*, the bridegroom-selection or "self-choice" (*svayaṁvara*) of Rukmini. Toward the end of his life, he is remembered as having begun, and almost completed, a retelling in Marathi of the *Rāmāyaṇa*, called the *Bhāvārtha Rāmāyaṇa*. These works bring texts well-known in Sanskrit into the realm of the vernacular, into Marathi. Eknath's hagiography contains many stories of the resistance that he faced from fellow Brahmins in this endeavor. Thus Eknath generated a reputation for being a bridge between an elite public sphere of Sanskrit and the realm of common Marathi. In this regard, his work, especially the story of Rukmini's *svayamvara* and the retelling of the *Rāmāyaṇa*, seem composed for performance.

Eknath is clearly a sort of *sant*-scholar, a conduit of learning for the common Marathi-speaking person of the sixteenth century. Yet his efforts to re-establish the public memory of Jnandev go even further than the critical editing of Jnandev's eponymous text. He is also remembered as having discovered the lost site of Jnandev's entombment or *samadhi*, the story of which is attributed to Namdev. Hagiography recalls that Eknath had a vision of Jnandev in a dream. Here is the song in which he recalls this dream:

Jnaneshwar appeared in a dream
And told me something bewildering.
"Divine One, radiant as the sun,
One who speaks only of the Highest Brahman,
The root of the Ajana tree has ensnared my throat.
Come to Alandi and loosen it."
This was the dream, so I went to Alandi,
Where I found a door submerged in the river.
[Eknath] received his grand reward;
I met the great teacher Jnaneshwar.

The dream prompted Eknath to travel many miles to the home of Jnandev, Alandi, which sits along the Indrayani river. There, in the water, he noticed the top of a temple and, submerged in the water, the door to the forgotten *mandir*, called Siddhabet. Near this submerged temple, higher on the bank of the river, he saw a tree. The word in the song is *ajānavṛkṣa*.

In Marathi, *ajāna* means "not-born" or "sui generis," absolutely unique, one of a kind; *vṛkṣa* means "tree." Thus it is a wholly unique tree that appears in Eknath's dream. When he spotted the tree, he is said to have noticed that its roots encircled a small tombstone on the ground. There he found the site of Jnandev's *samadhi,* which had been lost for almost three centuries. He refurbished the tomb and, by doing so, began the yearly commemoration of Jnandev's *samadhi,* which continues to this day.

As this song demonstrates, Eknath represents a kind of "renaissance" in Marathi literary and religious history in the sixteenth century, but of a very particular kind. This is an initiation of physical site and text as loci of public memory. But we never read of the need for Eknath to refurbish the performance tradition of which he is a part, and so another reason the idea that the fourteenth to sixteenth centuries constitute a period of literary and social deprivation should be viewed skeptically. Regardless of whether Eknath was individually responsible for the new cultural forms that arose around his lifetime, he is emblematic of new practices that came to shape a more robust system of remembrance. This system is exemplified in part by Eknath. Eknath embodies the fulfillment of the patterns set out ostensibly by Namdev centuries before in the context of performance, an interweaving of text and orality under the logic of performance. Given the apparent connection regularly found between textual transmission, literacy, and the idea of singular authorship, how would Namdev's legacy have emerged from the intervening centuries? How might it have appeared in Eknath's period of renewal and refurbishment of text and site, the rejuvenation of a performance tradition? How might this period have lent a model of authorship for subsequent centuries?

The answers to these questions might lie with the emergence of that curious set of composers, the other Namas. The first of these new Namas was said to be Eknath's contemporary, Vishnudas Nama, and subsequent Namas took up Namdev's name as it appears in his ideograph and compose new songs, but on related themes and in congruous ways with the "old" Namdev. These new Namas spanned the sixteenth to the nineteenth centuries. Distinguishing these Namas of the fourteenth and sixteenth centuries is difficult to do within the general body of songs attributed to the first Namdev. One way is open to the literary historian when we find compositions other than discrete songs attributed to one of these other Namas. For example, a composer named Vishnudas Nama is known by a composition attributed to him, a Marathi retelling of portions of the *Mahābhārata,* supposedly composed in 1535. He also appears to be referenced by other composers of the period, such as Mukteshwar, and hence interference by other composers in later periods provides another means of locating later Namas.[19] Living throughout the sixteenth century, Vishnudas Nama is often assumed to have been born a Brahmin, though there is significant dispute on this point.[20] No biography exists of Vishnudas Nama, other than a reference by Mahipati, as mentioned above. Thus, on the one hand, Marathi literary history records a distinct author whose works are organized under the name "Vishnudas Nama;" on the other hand, songs attributed to this author intermixed with those of a figure who lived several centuries earlier, Namdev. This presents the perfect recipe for textual confusion.

Confusion arises primarily with regard to the vast collection of songs attributed to Namdev. Perhaps two-thirds of the corpus contain the ideograph commonly associated with Namdev of the fourteenth century, *nama mhane*, or "Nama says." However, amid those songs attributed to the first Namdev are self-aggrandizing titles, such as "Viṣṇudās Nāmā," or Nama, the servant of Vishnu, as well as "Kṛṣṇadās Nāmā" or Nama, Servant of Krishna, and also simply "Nāmā." These possible "nicknames" that appear for Namdev in songs attributed to Namdev later become the foundation for the names of subsequent Namas. So the songs generally regarded as the product of the first Namdev contain within them multiple possibilities for alternative names, and these possibilities are tapped by the later Namas.

Some scholars have sought to distinguish between the first two Namdevs—Namdev of the fourteenth century and Vishnudas Nama of the sixteenth century—in various ways that were supposedly evident in the songs. Some have suggested that a greater use of archaic or Old Marathi signals the songs of the fourteenth-century Namdev. But if Namdev's songs have been preserved primarily in oral, performative forms, it is likely that the demands of performance would update and modernize language over time. This situation makes the idea of the fossilization of historical language a problematic method for adjudicating authorship. However, one interesting generalization can be made. Songs attributed to Vishnudas Nama appear to employ repetition to a greater degree than do songs attributed to the earlier Namdev or other figures. Although this is a very general observation, it is tempting to imagine that if the notion of repetition appealed to Vishnudas Nama as a poetic device, it may also have appealed to this author as a device of practice, that is, of repeating or even mimicking the work of the earlier Namdev. Rather than signs of distinction maintained in ways internal to songs, there seems to be a play on distinction and similarity throughout the handwritten and printed anthologies. For example, songs attributed to Vishnudas Nama are interspersed with those of Namdev but collectively address the same theme. The collection of songs that has appeared in printed editions for over a century as the *Paṇḍharī Māhātmya*, or "The Glories of Pandharpur," can serve as a representative example. This collection begins with a long song attributed to Vishnudas Nama, followed by songs attributed to the first Namdev, then more attributed to Vishnudas Nama. Of the forty-eight songs under this thematic heading, twenty-six have the ideograph *nama mhane*, nine have the ideograph "Vishnudasa Nama," or a variation, such as "Nāmyācā Swāmi," and thirteen have ideographs not exclusively associated with either or simply marked "Nāmā." The three longest songs in the collection are attributed to Vishnudas Nama; the rest are all generally the same length. Two forms of verse are found: one with three rhyming lines, and a fourth that rhymes with the fourth of all other stanzas; and another of two rhyming lines, by far the more common form. Both forms contain both ideographs. There is no indication of possible distinction according to the age of the language used or to any other characteristic. Thus, despite distinct authorial ascriptions, there is no difference in subject matter, language, or style. We cannot clearly judge whether one author is using two or more names, or two or more authors are purposefully blurring lines of dissimilarity.

Despite these conflations of authorial identity, a particular pattern emerges. The collection begins and ends with songs attributed to Vishnudas Nama, and two of his three long songs appear almost as summaries of the collection as a whole. The earliest manuscript in which some of these songs appear is from Dhule (1631), an archival manuscript that is roughly coterminous with the floruit of Vishnudas Nama, and in this source the long song by Vishnudas Nama leads the collection, which closes with a song attributed to Namdev. The ratio of songs attributed to each composer is otherwise similar. Later manuscripts appeared to build on this pattern, eventually closing the series with a song attributed to Vishnudas Nama.

This pattern of framing and organizing a selection of songs with those attributed to Vishnudas Nama is suggestive. It appears that here Vishnudas Nama (whether a distinct author or alternative *nom de plume*) is a title used to indicate the agent who has collated songs attributed to the earlier Namdev, forming them into a thematic unit that extols the virtues of Pandharpur. This is not explicitly stated, but one can imagine the logic of performance at work here, the collection of songs on a single theme forming an archive for a performance on the glories of Pandharpur, an especially important subject for *kirtan*s surrounding the pilgrimage of the Varkaris and in general, a good repertoire of songs to have on hand when performing before those who revere both the pilgrimage and the pilgrims, the bulk of Varkari devotees. If Vishnudas Nama in the sixteenth century is a performer and a literate connoisseur of texts, in the mode of Eknath, then the act of performance and the project of textual organization meld in the structure of these manuscripts.

If we imagine a historical figure and distinct author, who is both performer and text editor, following the mold of Eknath, it is conceivable that this scholar-performer could take on a variation of the name of Namdev as his performative practice circulates around the famous compositions of this earlier *sant*. Such a course of action would fit with established patterns of recording performative materials and would also account for the ways in which Namdev's songs came to be grouped into themes. Such an editor-performer might, in his capacity as editor, collate songs under themes used regularly in performance, the byproduct of which might be written texts that follow genres within a *sant*'s corpus of songs that have currency in performance. In his capacity as performer, such a figure might include his own songs, relevant to the collated themes, in the same text as an aid for performance.

This theory might also account for the general body of songs attributed to Namdev, which took thematic form over centuries of performance and literary recording, becoming grouped under headings such as the one discussed in chapter 3 pertaining to the "arrival of Uddhav." But what do we do with collections of songs that appear to have been composed, or intended in some way, to represent a single unit on a single theme or story from the very beginning of composition? Who composed the *Ādi*? The two versions of the *Tīrthāvalī*? The *Samādhi*? Or the numerous biographies of other *sant*s? This is a matter of far more contention than the authorship of individual songs because these long compositions represent the kind of creative genius that is the soul of the notion (or one might say the hagiography) of the modern author.

S. B. Kulkarni, following earlier scholars, such as J. R. Ajgaonkar, has suggested that Namdev of the fourteenth century composed the *Ādi*, while it was Vishnudas Nama who composed the biographical *Tīrthāvalī* and the *Samādhi*.[21] Vishnudas Nama's ideograph appears nowhere in the text of the *Ādi*, but neither does it appear in the *Samādhi*. The only ideograph in the autobiographical *Tīrthāvalī* of 1581 reads *nama mahne* (the ideograph associated with the first Namdev) while Vishnudas Nama's ideograph appears in nine out of sixty-one songs in the later biographical *Tīrthāvalī*. However, ideographs do not form the basis of the arguments of Kulkarni and others. Instead, they look to other factors familiar to text editors who search for authorial habits and intentions. For example,

Kulkarni notes that Ajgaonkar believed that the poetic and intellectual strengths of the *Tīrthāvalī* were not reflected in the bulk of songs attributed to Namdev. Given the possible biography of Vishnudas Nama that claims him to have been a Brahmin, or at least a scholar of Sanskrit, references to philosophical issues generally within the purview of Sanskrit literature suggest to these scholars a more educated, and hence they believe a Brahmin, mind. There is also the common practice of the purported author's assuming a role in the stories narrated; thus Namdev becomes a character, like Jnandev or any other figure, in the biographical *Tīrthāvalī* and *Samādhi* texts, which are both recounted in the third person. This raises suspicion for some critics that another author's hand is at work here.

The ascription of these texts to two different "Namdevs" also lends historical viability to hagiographical accounts. Although nowadays flight and rail have made possible a vacation covering all of India, the notion of a man walking the length and breadth of India in a lifetime, much less doing it twice, is astounding. Furthermore, because Namdev is remembered as having come into contact with so many figures who were so far apart in chronological terms, like Jnandev of the thirteenth century and Akbar of the sixteenth century, the idea that more than one person traveled under the name of Namdev has a sensible appeal. Kulkarni, in the persuasively argued "Namdev in Punjab: Vishnudas Nama," suggests that Vishnudas Nama is the Namdev widely remembered and depicted in northern India, especially among Sikhs.[22] He draws on a wide range of evidence—genealogy, architecture, text, and public memory—to suggest that many of the songs and compositions signaled by Vishnudas Nama's ideograph belong to a period inflected heavily by the hybrid Islamic-Hindu (Persian, Hindavi, etc.) literary culture of northern India in the sixteenth century. Kulkarni also uses the little-studied autobiographical *Tīrthāvalī* attributed to 1581, a date that would square with the accepted floruit of Vishnudas Nama, to suggest its authorship—as well as its implied wanderlust—should also go to this later composer. Although the copies of the 1581 *Tīrthāvalī* I have surveyed contain the ideograph *nama mahne*, and hence do not point toward Vishnudas Nama, Kulkarni's work persuasively argues that this text belongs to a period well after Namdev of the fourteenth century.

Yet the question here is not the historical unraveling of identities and facts—nothing conclusive can be inferred from such scant evidence—but the public memory of a figure and the ways in which authorship conditions this memory. If the two *Tīrthāvalīs* are, for example, the overall work of Vishnudas Nama, certainly the biographical version draws its subject from the legend of the first Namdev's travels. Vishnudas Nama, in this scenario, selected a story from the life of Namdev, retold this story, and "signed" his name to the composition, rather than appending Namdev's ideograph. Investing the biographical version with references to Jnandev and his siblings makes the presumed historical context clear: this is a story about the first Namdev, even if the author of the story is the later one. If we accept that Vishnudas Nama is the author of the autobiographical *Tīrthāvaḷī*, and if we understand him to have made explicit associations between himself and the first Namdev, we must view this autobiographical *Tīrthāvaḷī* as likewise supporting itself on the legend of the first Namdev's travels, in essence, on the charade, if you will, of its autobiographical, as opposed to biographical, nature. It is also then something like historical fiction in the first person. This changes the condition of autobiography here. If the text is about the travels of the sixteenth-century Namdev, it is autobiographical in the conventional sense, a tale of his sixteenth-century journey. But if it is written in the sixteenth century to appear to be the autobiography of the fourteenth-century Namdev, then its status as "autobiography" is a strategic fiction, an effort perhaps to use the first-person narrative as some kind of historical proof, to put the narrative of the journey into the voice of the *sant* traveler.

The authorship of Vishnudas Nama, when he enters the streams of remembrance associated with Namdev, is both parasitical and independent. The description "a servant of Vishnu" (*viṣṇudās*) appears to be present in songs not attributed to Vishnudas Nama or any of the other Namas, that is, in songs attributed to Namdev of the fourteenth century, as noted above. This is also true of Namdev's Hindi corpus, where numerous songs would refer to the *sant* (self-reflexively) as *viṣṇudās nāmā*. The songs of the Maharashtrian *sant*s are filled with references to "slaves of Vishnu." In the biographical *Tīrthāvaḷī*, for example, Jnandev refers to Namdev as *viṣṇudās*, as does Mahipati in the *Bhaktavijay*.[23] Thus the title likely taken by this poet in the sixteenth century might be a direct reference to how the first Namdev is said to have described himself in relation to Vishnu/Krishna/Vitthal. Recall that Eknath combined his name with that of his teacher, Janardan, calling himself "Eka Janardana," Janardan's Eknath. Janabai, about whom there is equal controversy regarding dates of life and number of "Janis," is remembered as having used Namdev's name with her own, calling herself "Nāmayācī Dāsī Janī," or "Nāmayācī Janī," or simply "Dāsī Janī," in silent reference to Namdev.

The Marathi retellings of portions of the *Mahābhārata* attributed to Vishnudas Nama bear no relation to Namdev or to Varkari religious practice in particular. But when Vishnudas Nama appears to compose songs about Namdev, about subjects in Namdev's hagiography, taking up themes associated with Namdev, and referencing the public cultural spheres that remember Namdev by tapping a collective store of songs and stories, a more complex kind of authorship is implied. In this case, the way in which the name Vishnudas Nama borrows an epithet that may have been used by the first Namdev, or by his contemporaries to refer to him, is perhaps the least of the ways this later Nama becomes an author by mimesis and innovation simultaneously. This is not a case of simply borrowing a portion of a previously famous author, but a method of tapping a complex cultural system of public memory that uses authorship to maintain a performative genealogy, and interconnection of authors over centuries.

Vishnudas Nama is important in another way in the public memory of Namdev. He appears to have set a precedent that was subsequently followed by at least two more Namas. In the second half of the sixteenth century, a figure named Nama Yashvant appeared. He seems to have been a devotee of Vitthal and a Varkari, who was born in the district of Solapur, according to Khanolkar, but who also retained a great interest in the *pir*s of the region, much like Eknath. Khanolkar mentions that songs attributed to Nama Yashvant reference the Bahmani Sultanate, thus making explicit his historical difference from Namdev of the fourteenth century.[24] Songs attributed to Nama Yashvant occur only twice in the government's anthology of Namdev's songs, apparently in two versions of the same song.[25] Even in these cases, it is unclear whether "Nama Yashvant" is to be read as a title within an ideograph or as part of the entire last line, reading, in both instances, "Thus, Nama became famous [*yaśavanta*] by seeking refuge at Vithoba's feet." Both songs appear in relatively old, and copious, manuscripts, including the Dhule manuscript of the very early seventeenth century and the manuscripts of Pandharpur and Shivala of the seventeenth century.

What this suggests about multiple authorship is uncertain. If these are songs attributed to a figure other than Namdev, this might serve as evidence that would date Nama Yashvant to the period of the Dhule manuscript's composition, thus agreeing with Khanolkar's dates for the poet's life. However, Nama Yashvant is more commonly remembered as the author of a story about Namdev's marriage, called *Nāmāce Lagna*, a popular publication for pilgrims in Pandharpur. My archival research uncovered this song only once in a *bada*, probably from the late eighteenth century.[26] Thus it appears that Nama Yashvant is best known as the author of a single story about Namdev that positions him after the timeframe of the Bahm-

ani Sultanate and indisputably aside from the fourteenth century. It is unclear whether Nama Yashvant took his name from the two verses found in
the government's edition of Namdev's songs or whether the songs found in
this anthology are attributed to Nama Yashvant. However, the connection
between the two figures is apparent: Nama Yashvant expands the memory
of Namdev by interweaving poetic anamnesis, ideograph reference, and
clear biographical composition.

The final Nama, Shimpi Nama, probably lived in the eighteenth century.
According to Khanolkar, he was born into the *shimpi* caste, to parents
named Satavaji Shimpi and Janakibai, around the area of Umbraj in Karad
district of southern Maharashtra during the rise of the Marathas in the
Deccan.[27] Kulkarni suggests that Shimpi Nama relocated to Pandharpur
early in his life, becoming a devotee of the *sant*s.[28] Interestingly, Kulkarni
also suggests that Shimpi Nama even worked to spread the fame of his predecessor, Vishnudas Nama, bringing a new circle into the cycle of anamnetic authorship, a reinforcement of the previous authorship of not one but
two "Namdevs."[29]

Whether or not Shimpi Nama is the given name of this poet is impossible to know. But, as in the case of Vishnudas Nama, there are precedents
for the phrase *śimpī nāmā* in songs attributed to Namdev of the fourteenth
century and his purported contemporaries. For example, Parisa Bhagavata, the late thirteenth-century Brahmin who possessed a touchstone
(encountered in chapter 1), is attributed a song in praise of Namdev as
follows:

> You are a *shimpi*, Nama [*tūṁ śiṁpī nāmā*];
> I am of the highest caste.
> See how I have fallen
> Into the useless trap of the ego.
> Having become devotees of god [*devabhakta*]
> We both are of one form.
> From this point of view,
> It is clear that I am one and the same as you.[30]

Shimpi Nama's presence is minuscule in the Government of Maharashtra's edition of Namdev's songs, where only five songs have his ideograph.
Two appear as part of a thematic group called the *Santa Mahimā*, or "The
Glories of the Sants," which celebrates the virtues of being a *sant*, a text one
would expect from someone devoted to the worship of the *sant*s in particular.[31] One or more songs in this section of fifty-three are also attributed to

Vishnudas Nama; the rest have Namdev's ideograph. A Shimpi Nama song next appears in the middle of the biographical *Tīrthāvaḷī* story, where a few verses are attributed to Vishnudas Nama along with those of Namdev again. The final two occurrences of Shimpi Nama songs in the government edition appear toward the end of the anthology, in a section on the forms and *avatar*s of Vishnu, once again accompanied by the songs of Vishnudas Nama and Namdev. Thus a pattern emerges in which two or three Shimpi Nama songs are inserted in larger thematic sections, as are songs attributed to Vishnudas Nama.

As is the case with all the "other Namdevs," Shimpi Nama has a much more prominent place in the *Sakaḷa Santa Gāthā*, the largest and most frequently reprinted anthology of Namdev's songs, and a text considered authoritative by many Varkaris. Here, in section 6, is a series of biographies (*caritra*) of *sant*s who, in the generally accepted public memory of *bhakti*, lived well after Namdev—Kabir, Mirabai (sixteenth century), Bhanudas (late fifteenth century), and others. These are mixed with biographies generally associated with Namdev of the fourteenth century, detailing the lives of his contemporaries, such as Janabai. Both Khanolkar and Kulkarni attribute these biographical songs of later *sant*s to Shimpi Nama. This suggests that Shimpi Nama, composing in the eighteenth century, imitated the biographical work of Namdev of the fourteenth century. The imitation appears to go even deeper. Tulpule suggests that Shimpi Nama created a series of songs entitled *balkrida*, or "Child's Play," songs, recalling the childhood of Krishna.[32] One of the extensive thematic units attributed to Namdev of the fourteenth century is, likewise, a *balkrida* series, which dominates the earliest written collection of Namdev's work, found in Dhule and dated to the very early seventeenth century; the *balkrida* songs attributed to the first Namdev are also the first stand-alone handwritten text found among the *bada*s, with a colophon placing it at the end of the nineteenth century. These are the most popular songs from Namdev's corpus that *kirtankar*s employ. It seems more than coincidence that Shimpi Nama, in emulating other stylistic and thematic subjects germane to Namdev's memory, would take up this significant and famous topic associated with the first Namdev's legacy.

AUTHORSHIP AND ANAMNESIS

I have already presented my argument about "corporate authorship," how multiple authors participate in investing a performance piece with a unique genealogy of authorship, and how this is done in an embodied, "corporate," way, using the words and biographies of former authors, and embodying gestures and guises that also recall those authors. Thus a modern-day *kirtankar* uses the songs and stories attributed to earlier *sants*, interweaving these materials with his or her own creations, and even dresses in a way that recalls the great *kirtankar*s of the past, of which Namdev is the archetype. I believe that this hybrid notion of authorship is also present in the phenomenon of successive and interconnected "Namas" appearing throughout history from the sixteenth century to the nineteenth century, all making references to the first Namdev, of the fourteenth century, and sometimes to each other. The figures who make up this lineage of Namas participate selectively in the flow of memory about Namdev. They each have work associated with their name that is not confused with that of Namdev of the fourteenth century, yet they also produced songs and biographies that appear to purposefully blend into work attributed to the first Namdev. Thus there are two ideas of authorship. The first is commonly understood: the sole author, who produces a text in his or her name, and whose biography informs the veracity of the text. Without this sense of the author, the other sense of authorship, in the anamnetic mode, is incomprehensible. The second idea of authorship combines the "corporate" with something more, an anamnetic quality, which is socially grounded and historically conscientious, more so perhaps than the sorts of replication and mimesis seen at the moment of performance.

Marathi literary scholarship, like most literary scholarship, was deeply influenced by the power of the sole author to command the meaning and dissemination of a text, to abrogate its interpretation and its recreation in the present. The sole author became the key to a text's unfolding logic. In debates about the intermixing of the songs of Namdev with the other Namas, emphasis has been placed on this condition as a mistake of performers and text editors, as the willful replacement of scholarly rigor with devotional sentimentality. The European and American counterparts of Marathi literary scholars have by and large placed similar emphasis on the historical impossibility that so many songs, in such a linguistic variety, and under a handful of names, could be attributable to one author. The desire to maintain the objective clarity of the principle of the single author has prevented the raising of other questions and the proposition of different answers to the riddles of authorship.

The best studies of the literary and cultural phenomenon of *bhakti* in South Asia look to writing to piece together a picture of the past. They follow routes of literary redaction and anachronistic interpolation as winding and ancient as the back lanes of Benares. These studies take a central figure, or an "author," as the guiding principle of a vast body of work. Foucault eloquently summarized this situation by referring to the modern author as the "principle of thrift" amid the vast array of texts (quoted in the acknowledgments), interpretations, and biographical fragments that make up our ideas of authors and their compositions; the author became the locus of meaning, allowing texts to take shape and aiding in their interpretation by reference to the "intentions" and biography of the author.[33] Textual studies of *bhakti* trace these multiple paths to the author, and the finest among them record the historical messages each twist and turn broadcasts along the road. In terms of empirical methodology, the study of *bhakti* can be characterized as philological in its essence (as J. Z. Smith suggested), though it has often creatively and productively dealt with orality in the context of literacy.[34] Yet the hold of the author, reflected in "modern" terms as sole arbiter of meaning, is tenacious, even when studies demonstrate that the traditions themselves do not hew to the idea of sole authorship.

A recent collection of translations of songs attributed to Kabir by Vinay Dharwadker begins with an introduction that posits two distinct kinds of authorship: the historical, individual author and what Dharwadker variously calls "a community of authors" and "collective authorship," perhaps in reference to similar ideas and terms present in work on biblical textual analysis and postmodern treatments of authorship.[35] Although Dharwadker begins his essay with an elaboration of the "historical" Kabir—demonstrated through that preeminent site of biohistory, lifespan dates—he suggests that after the real death of the author (or perhaps even during the author's life), a community of authorship assumed the voice of Kabir to perpetuate his practice as a kind of biographical motif. In order to "'crack the code' that is 'Kabir,'" Dharwadker urges his reader to see a collective sense of authorship inherent in the principles of "the *bhakti* movement."[36] He writes,

> When [a *bhakta*] begins to produce discourse devoted to God as one of his primary (karmic) means of attaining *mukti* [salvation], the community of *bhakta*s around him serves not only as an audience, but also as a reservoir of textual energy and a pool of potential collaborators.[37]

The liquid metaphors Dharwadker employs here remind one of the great "Ocean of Sur" or *Sūr Sāgar*, the vast collection of songs attributed to the *sant*-poet Surdas (sixteenth century), through which Hawley and Bryant have waded with the help of text critical and historical studies.[38] Hawley argues that the oceans of poetry surrounding figures such as Surdas are accumulations of the compositions of generations of singers who invented verse in the idiom of a famous *sant*-poet and mark their genre with the "name" of the *sant*-poet.[39] Whether this is done as an homage to the *sant*-poet, an investment of a composition with spiritual authorial weight, or an adherence to a literary genre, Hawley makes plain that the collective activity of centuries of authors composing in a single name is beyond doubt. Indeed, as Dharwadker concurs, this kind of collective authorial agency is fundamental to *bhakti* as a literary field.

Dharwadker nicely illustrates how a composition in the name of a famous *sant* takes place with reference to the Sikh *Ādi Granth* of 1606. He notes how the six Gurus who composed *śabad*s signed the name of Guru Nanak, citing the "real" origin of each composition in the marginalia of the text.[40] Guru Arjan famously composed a song with the signature of "Kabir," yet also noted his position as the song's true "author."[41] The "Kabir Code" is plain enough: Kabir is a genre, a motif of textual production, invested with a historical and theological persona. However, Dharwadker's treatment, and the Sikh case, show the community of authorship operating within a literate environment. The Gurus may have composed in the name of Nanak or Kabir, but they *noted* their activity—they left a written record. Hawley and Bryant's work is emblematic of the strain between orality-performance and literacy. The great Ocean of Sur is a flowing body of texts. This "ocean" can be said to form a literal "vortex," a cone-shaped history of transmission of texts that grows ever larger, even while its center of gravity recedes farther from view.[42] The questions posed by the Namdev tradition is less textually oceanic since we have some texts, but nothing like the textual traditions of the Sikh canon or that of Surdas or Kabir. What kind of record can remain when text is deemphasized, leaving few margins for notes, no vortex of recessions, but only a trace of written records, surrounded by the song, the voice, and the performer? What do we do when a tradition rhetorically rejects literacy in the name of its founder yet perpetuates composition and records some of its material in written forms in the name of Namdev over its long history?

The array of Namas present in compendiums of work associated with Namdev does not represent a failure of proper textual method or a breakdown of sole authorship. Rather, it reflects a practice of authorial continuity that is enlivened by, and exists within, the performative world of *kirtan*. This world of performance surrounded Namdev's legacy in Marathi from the earliest point and into the present. If what buoyed Marathi literature along during its "dark" centuries between the death of Namdev and the time of Eknath was *kirtan,* this would explain a few things. First, it would indicate how songs managed to survive this period, from which few other written records remain. Second, it would help clarify the peculiar mix of literacy and orality that is at the heart of why the literary *sant* Eknath, who rescued the text of the *Jñāneśvarī* from obscurity, would remain within both a Varkari lineage and a Maharashtrian public culture that valued, perhaps even demanded, the performance of *kirtan* of written texts. Third, it would reflect what preceded and followed the "Dark Age," suggesting a continuity of practice that has been the rule ever since the fourteenth century, and throughout the periods of colonialism, modernity, and globalization on the subcontinent.

Mimesis and replication, as systems of public memory, have their roots in other practices of repetition and resonance in India. Gestures and words are repeated in acts of worship, such as *ārtī,* the use of *mantra,* continuous circumambulation of a sacred site, and the various vows that people make to do something, some action, a certain number of times. Such activities are all well known in the anthropology of religion in India. Hindus of all sorts often say or write the name of a deity continuously (called *japa*), and this appears as a motif in many legends. Valmiki famously saves himself from a life of sin and crime by accidentally transposing two syllables, *ma* and *rā,* which he chanted continuously for years. He began by dwelling on death, or *marā,* but soon was chanting, unconsciously, one name of God (or *the* Name of God, to some), or *rāma.* The simple, but excessive, repetition negated his sin. Repetition is a recurring path to religious merit in India and offers regular plot devices to stories.

Repetition also bears a relationship to memory as it pertains to texts. Pandits and teachers in India for centuries have established their authority in part on their ability to recall from memory particular sacred texts, such as the Vedas, the *Bhagavad Gītā,* and large sections of the epics. In Maharashtra, for example, the memorization and ability to repeat portions of the *Jñāneśvarī,* or the text in its entirety, is a sign of extreme erudition and religious attainment; this fact perhaps recalls that the original venue for the composition was oral, in the oral song form of the *ovī.* In some cases, a text committed to memory is considered more auspicious or "pure" than one consigned to writing. A Hindu priest or *pūjārī* presiding over a ritual, such as a wedding, would ideally never consult a written text but recite Sanskrit verbal formulae from memory alone. The process of memorization in these cases is rote repetition; only when the text is committed to memory can one begin to understand its meaning. There are parallels here throughout South Asia. A traditional Muslim education at a *madrassa* begins with the memorization of the Qur'an, and Sikhs memorize, in whole or in part, the sacred *Guru Granth Sahib.* In many cases, memorization by rote repetition significantly precedes literacy; the ability to read is secondary, a safeguard against forgetfulness, but not a replacement for memorization. This system of education has endured for thousands of years and well into the present, as several ethnographic studies have shown.[43] The most celebrated story-tellers or commentators of texts would deliver public recitals and lectures without the aid of written materials. In the story of the legendary origins of the *Mahābhārata,* for example, the "author" of the work, Vyasa, recalls the story from memory, a continuous stream of recollection recorded by the elephant-headed deity, Ganesh. Within the epic literature itself, memories are within memories, characters asked to recall episodes from the lives of people, deities, and other creatures, which they have heard or witnessed. Many of these stories are themselves repetitions of other stories, with slight changes, which appear in other literary compendia in India. Thus memory, mnemonics, and repetition existed symbiotically, as they do today.

Within the corpus of songs attributed to Namdev, repetition is common. In songs, lines and phrases are repeated, a device of oral performance common the world over and practiced today in contemporary *kirtan* (not to mention in most popular music worldwide). The same songs appear, in slightly different forms, throughout the body of work attributed to Nam-dev and across languages. One example is provided by two songs attributed to Namdev in two different languages. The first is in Hindi, and the second in Marathi:

I was born into a family of tailors,
But I cared only for Lord Shiva.
I stitched by day; I stitched by night
And my heart was never at peace.
Needle and thread, scissors and measure,
I went to work in Shiva's heart.
Nama says,
I'm stitching a shirt for Vithoba,
And am blessed in this world.[44]

Why should I trouble myself with class or caste?
I work full-time in God's tailor shop.
My imagination is the ruler and my tongue is the scissors—
With the Lord's say-so, I'll cut the knot of death.

Let me adorn my coat with the name of the Lord
And I'll stitch a pattern taming mortality itself.
Wearing a coat like this, how can I but live with God?
The needle of memory, the thread of love—
Nama's mind is woven with the Lord's.[45]

The first version of this song, which is in Marathi, appears in the oldest and largest Marathi manuscript collections, beginning in the very early seventeenth century. The second version of the song, in Hindi, has appeared broadly in the various collections recalling Namdev in northern India, in the Dadu Panth, Kabir Panth, and Sikhism beginning in the seventeenth century.[46] Both songs are attributed to Namdev of the fourteenth century, containing the ideograph that would signal this level of authorship, as opposed to any of the other Namas noted in this chapter. The songs appear to be versions of one another or perhaps recreations based on either an earlier song (in either language or neither) or simply a similar poetic trope. Yet the structural resemblance of the two songs suggests a retelling of some previous version of the song, in some language.

What is particularly interesting is that these two songs in Marathi and Hindi have been preserved together in Maharashtrian archival manuscripts and performers' notebooks for at least three hundred years. Why would the Maharashtrian Namdev tradition preserve two such similar songs, from the very threshold of the written record? I believe the answer to this question is intimately related to the reason why multiple Namas appear over time, recalling Namdev's legacy, yet altering it as well. Namdev becomes the focal point for the creation of a unique public culture that sustains his memory through mimesis.

The two songs are about several things at once, all germane to *bhakti* in theory. They recall Namdev's traditional biography, referencing both his caste occupation as tailor (or cloth printer in northern India) and his rejection of that occupation in favor of a life of devotion and performance. They both address the existential benefits of *bhakti,* the freedom from death, and the blessed peace of proximity with one's deity. Appearing in these two languages in the Marathi record, they might also emphasize Namdev's cosmopolitan, multilingual remembrance, a *sant* of significance in and outside Marathi-speaking spheres. Yet the deeper importance of these two songs is perhaps more subtle. They are repetitions of each other or represent a broader practice of repeating, or imitating, earlier songs both in terms of themes and content. And they infer, therefore, that repetition was important in Namdev's pan-Indian legacy, in expanding his memory.

Repetition and imitation are important concepts in the songs as well. Sewing and stitching, highly repetitive acts, become metaphors for the work of *bhakti*, for the production of devotional songs and stories. Namdev stitches day and night, without rest, in the Marathi song; in the Hindi song, the faculties of performance—the imagination and the voice (metonymically represented by the tongue)—become the tools of a new trade, an imitation of the work of the tailor transposed into the world of the performative *sant.* Inchoate in the first song, a further sentiment of repetition and memory is explicit in the second, contained in the word *surati,* "to hear, repeat, and remember," which I have loosely translated as "memory," and is more correctly a form of anamnesis, the recollection of the past through imitation and repetition.

The Hindi song invokes the "the needle of memory" (*surati kī sūī*) and the "thread of love" (*prem kā dhāgā*). *Surati* is derived from the Sanskrit word *śruti,* "to listen."[47] At first glance, this might imply opposing ideas of textual formation in classical Hinduism, where *shruti* refers to "heard" or divinely received texts, primarily the Vedas, and *smrti* refers to manmade texts, the product of humans. But *surati,* as derived from *shruti,* references not the "hearing" of the text so much as the way *shruti* texts have traditionally been maintained, that is, through memory, not writing, and, in particular, through repetition. Although "memory" is perhaps a more poetic fit for the song, the meaning implied in anamnesis specifies an act of repetition as way of recalling the past, suggesting an active engagement of memory, a reinforced remembrance. Repeated in *bhakti* songs throughout northern India, *surati* connotes speaking the name of God, listening to its enunciation, and actively propagating the sound through time in a way that is exact, ritualized, and disciplined but also unique to the practitioner, part of an individual's religious goals. The word invokes the oral quality of memory, the verbalization of it, and hence the practice of performance. In this song, the word *surati* is indicative of a larger method of recalling the past through practices that constitute an exercise of a collective anamnetic will. Listening and speaking, audiences and authors/performers create a resonance between the past and the present through memory based on speaking and listening.

The two songs above are both attributed to Namdev and about Namdev. In this sense, the songs are instantiations of *surati,* of repetition and memory. They are performance pieces, repeatedly heard by an audience over hundreds of years (their importance is evident in their mutual representation in Marathi manuscripts from an early period), which must have reinforced the function of an oral memory centered on a historical figure. They recall details about Namdev that are more than biographical but imply techniques of recollection as well. In their content they rehearse the life of Namdev and reinforce through their various versions the necessity of repetition for the sake of memory, the practice of anamnesis. Furthermore, as songs meant for performance, they situate this memory within a *bhakti* public. The nature of a *bhakti* public is implied here through the conjoining of the "needle of memory" in the Hindi poem above to the "thread of love." Here the word for love is *prem*, a term often associated with "divine love" and mutual commitment. The thread of love refers to the practice of personalized devotion through *bhakti*, shared with others, knitted through time.

Memory and repetition appear conjoined throughout the songs attributed to Namdev in the Maharashtrian corpus, both in Marathi and in Hindi. The imperative formulation *nāma smarā,* or "remember the Name," as a means of salvation (*uddharaṇa*) is often encountered in Namdev's songs; indeed, in Old Marathi the noun *smaraṇie* indicates "one who is remembered," that is, one's deity.[48] The remembrance of the name is more than recalling to mind—it implies repetition. The repetition of the names of a deity is an old practice in South Asia, common to Hinduism, Buddhism, and Islam, and is especially prevalent in *nirguna bhakti* of northern India. In this that context, Namdev, especially in the *Guru Granth Sahib,* is intimately associated with the practice of repeating "the Name." In the *Guru Granth,* a song attributed to Namdev states:

> Hey tongue [*jihabā*]! Say "Śrī Gobind"
> Or I will slice you into a hundred slivers.
> Hey tongue! Paint yourself in a new shade [*raṅg*]: Hari!
> Hari! Hari! Relish that vibrant color [*suraṅg raṅgīle*].
> Any other use of you is a mere waste.[49]

And later, Namdev is remembered to have asserted:

> I don't chit-chat with anyone.
> My tongue laps up the name "Ram." [50]

Again, in metonymic fashion, the tongue presents not only an oral but a performative command to repeat the name of a deity. Although Namdev's remembrance in Marathi does not portray him as a *nirguna bhakta*, as he is portrayed widely in northern India, the repetition of the Name remains important, as numerous Marathi songs evince.

The call to remember is also significantly present in one of the key collections of songs attributed to Namdev of the fourteenth century, the *balkrida* songs, a title also given to a collection attributed to the last of the Namas, Shimpi Nama, probably of the eighteenth century, as shown above. Here the figure of Uddhav consoles the forlorn *gopi*s with memories of Krishna, and the call to remember the absent deity permeates these songs. This is an episode that represents what might be called the first layer of Krishna hagiography, the first retellings of Krishna's childhood, for the succor of the *gopi*s. A performative practice, embodied by Uddhav, of repetition and memory, in the service of *bhakti,* is within view of the public, as represented by the *gopi*s.

Repetition, memory, and performance recur throughout songs attributed to Namdev, together suggesting a process of anamnesis as a means of preserving and recording. Although no explicit connection is made between the injunction to remember by repeating and the mimesis of Namdev by later Namas, the general will to remember by repetition is an indication of why subsequent Namas appeared within the Maharashtrian Namdev tradition. The songs above suggest that repetition was systemic in the tradition in Marathi, a key part of public memory across languages and times. In Namdev's songs, repetition occurs in explicit relation to orality and public presentation.

As discussed above, the nature of authorship can be plastic, and authorial power is located within the embodied performance, but in "corporate" relationship to other authors, those of songs and of style. Without an explicit pronouncement by any of the Namas about their authorial activities as they entered the stream of Namdev's public memory, we can only infer that the tradition provides space for this kind of mimesis. If mimesis is seen at work in this way, we can understand the larger practices of anamnesis, ranging from performance, to iconography and sartorial replication, to the substance of verses preserved in Namdev's name that suggest repetition as a means for continuity and devotional expression. Rather than view the multiple Namas as features of a disintegrating chain of sole authorship, or as the confusion of nineteenth-century text editors, we can regard this phenomenon within the context of other anamnetic, mimetic acts within the scope of the Maharashtrian Namdev tradition. Principally, this practice of authorship can be viewed within the larger context of performance, the location of both Namdev's abiding memory and the public presentation of that memory. The plethora of Namas can be interpreted as reflecting a purposeful practice of public memory within a *bhakti* tradition governed by its own rules of operation and recollection.

{ 5 }

MEMORIES OF SUFFERING
IN THE EIGHTEENTH CENTURY

Our crime against criminals is that we treat them as villains.
—FRIEDRICH NIETZSCHE

If he is devoted solely to me,
Even a violent criminal
Must be deemed a man of virtue,
For his resolve is right
—KRISHNA'S COUNSEL TO ARJUNA,
BHAGAVAD GITA (9.30)

EVERYONE LOVES a good bandit story, and Indians are no exception. India's best film directors have created a steady stream of films—*Nayakan* (1987), *Parinda* (1989), *Satya* (1998), *Vaastav* (1999), *Company* (2002), and many more—all exploring the social and internal lives of the heroic criminal. Many deal with the "reality" (*vāstav*) or "truth" (*satya*) of Indian urban poverty and the desperate choices that lead to a life of crime. The socially and economically afflicted person who turns to criminality can be a heroic, sympathetic, and even redemptive figure in popular imagination. Many of these films juxtapose the hegemony of the state—embodied in the police and politicians who are increasingly villainous characters in Bollywood cinema—with the rule of law on the streets and in the slums. The celluloid criminal becomes an outlaw of the state and civil society but is fully integrated in microcosms of economic deprivation.

The best of these outlaws are essentially good and noble, qualities preserved in the crush of scarcity. Take, for example, Kathryn Hansen's study of an early twentieth-century play in Hindi called "Sultānā Ḍākū" ("The Sultan-Thief"). The subtitle "garībom kā pyārā," or "one loved by the poor," illustrates the celebrated nature of some thieves.[1] Legendary thieves and thief-characters, especially those with religious affiliations, were often beloved figures as well.[2] By the nineteenth century, and probably earlier, in popular theatrical forms in India the thief had become a glamorous character, rather than a vile one. In Parsi theater—popular throughout the Bombay Presidency and south India in the nineteenth and early twentieth centuries—the bandit was a figure of martial prowess who lived by a moral code of sorts—honor among thieves. A Parsi theater playbill in the collection of Roja Muthiah, in Chennai, provides great detail about the character of the thief.[3] The play, *Parsi Satharam*, was staged on May 13, 1920, in Karaikkudi, Tamil Nadu, and featured a character named Azaku, who was described as a thief (*tiruṭan*). The playbill goes on to compare the character of the thief to other popular sorts of thieves both local and cosmopolitan:

> Thief here refers to a thief of the district, a very dangerous thief, a professional thief, like the incomparable Japanese thief, or Australian thief, or American thief, or Rangoon's Bungalow thief, or a Parsi or Belgian praiseworthy thief, or a thief who roams around groups of soldiers, or a thief who has won a competition in India, a thief of thieves, a dancing thief, perfectly suited for the drama, a thief appropriate for the songs, a prestigious thief, a thief who will be appreciated by all as a righteous thief, a world-admired and kind thief, a thief who is not afraid of his enemies, a thief who shines by his actions, a thief appreciated even by intellectuals.

The thief described in this playbill does not fit the mold of an ordinary purse-snatcher or masked mugger. This advertisement speaks of a thief who is righteous and fearless, dances and sings, and "shines by his actions." The description is of a heroic character, not a nefarious one. He is a "social bandit," as Hobsbawm coined the phrase, a hero to some, usually the subaltern, and a bane to others, most often the elite and powerful.[4] The portrayal and reception of the character of the thief turn on the economic and political position in society of the audience or public. Like the "prose of counterinsurgency" expressed in Ranajit Guha's work in the historiography of moments of subaltern defiance, the bandit narrative might offer a poetics of quotidian resistance for the subaltern, generated not in moments of violent insurrection but, rather, as a composite of the small rebellions of everyday life compressed and exemplified in the biography of a single heroic figure.

This poetics of quotidian resistance can be explored through two sets of narratives about Namdev. The first, from the eighteenth century, exists primarily in Marathi and claims that Namdev resorted to criminality and violence at a time of universal desperation during the fourteenth century. The second illustration, retold over many centuries, involves the purported meetings between Namdev and various figures of temporal, political authority. Although both sets of narratives are cast in the late thirteenth century or early fourteenth century, the rise of their popularity, and their oldest extant iterations in textual form, probably take full form in the eighteenth century in Marathi, and it is in this century that these stories of resistance found their hold on the imagination of an audience. Each story is summarized below, with notes on its sources and likely precursors and the context of the narratives within the eighteenth-century Marathi-speaking Deccan region.

In the context of Namdev's Maharashtrian public memory, the eighteenth century is significant for several reasons. During the period there was tremendous regional literary production amid a cultural milieu composed of Mughal and European colonial influences.[5] The era also witnessed warfare of varying severity. The death of Aurangzeb in 1707 left a century of unstable Mughal governance in its wake. The era marks the rise of Maratha power under the Peshwa office through the campaigns of Bajirao I from 1720 to 1740 and its decline after the Battle of Panipat in 1761. European power was ascending through military struggles such as the Carnatic Wars of 1746 to 1763, the Battle of Plassey in 1757, and the two Anglo-Maratha wars (1774–1783 and 1803–5). Within these political fluctuations, and throughout the subcontinent, records and folktales recall the exploits of various "heroes" and brigands who established small fiefdoms or terrorized trade routes and defenseless townships. Some of these stories can be, and have been, read as small-scale rectifications of the excesses of Mughal-era agrarian taxation and administrative pilfer.[6] Other stories recount the acts of desperately poor men or unpaid roving soldiers. From these and other possible sources, a few legends arose about the righteous but cruel bandit in eighteenth-century India.

NAMDEV AS NE'ER-DO-WELL

The story that Namdev was a robber is just that: a story, without any corroboration in historical documents or sources, which is, of course, common in hagiography. Many of Namdev's contemporary followers, and scholars of Namdev's legacy, stridently deny the legend (as seen in chapter 6 in the context of nationalist historiography), and there is no historical reason to doubt their assertion that this story is apocryphal. However, the story has had a currency over the past three hundred years and remains contentious even today. My interest is in exploring the longevity of this tale, situating it in its context, and reflecting on its possible use in a practice of remembrance. By doing so, *I do not suggest that there is any historical truth to this legend and no one with whom I consulted for this project put any credence in the story of Namdev's robber days.*

As noted above, many aspects of Namdev's biography are repeated in other biographies: ad infinitum, we hear of Namdev turning the temple, causing Vitthal to drink milk from his hand, having Krishna repair his hut, and so on. However, in songs attributed to Namdev's companions—such as Cokhamela, Janabai, and Visoba Khecar—the story of Namdev's robber days is never mentioned. Furthermore, the legend is absent from north Indian biographical traditions; it appears neither in the work of Narsi Mehta nor in the texts of the Dadu Panth, the Kabir Panth, or Sikhism. Although the story is popularly known today in all these traditions and throughout western, central, and northern India, it is not represented in any textual or loosely fixed written or oral tradition; that is, to my knowledge no song or biography outside Marathi sources portrays Namdev as a criminal.[7] Only in Marathi are there clear articulations of this legend of Namdev's robber days, and it is primarily in Marathi that the legend met its greatest critics. However, the narrative of Namdev as a robber did play a prominent role in several Hindi films, and at least one Marathi film, and in other biographical retellings in the twentieth century. The story had sufficient currency in popular culture to be a major subject of discursive intervention for those who wished to position Namdev as a "saint of the nation."

How the story of Namdev as a robber originated in Marathi is difficult to trace, and early instances are not necessarily connected. Quite possibly the oldest record of the story is in a text of the Mahanubhav religious order, mentioned earlier, the *Līlācaritra,* which is a biography of their spiritual leader, Cakradhar. In brief, the story, told through the character of Cakradhar, narrates the exploits of two thieves named Vitthal and "Nemdev" who were killed while attempting to steal cattle.[8] Their fellow villagers erected a "hero stone" to them, and, as the years went by, Vitthal became the deity associated with Krishna, who was also a *gopāl,* that is, a cowherd, literally, a "cow-protector," another name for Krishna. Vitthal's companion, Nemdev, may have no connection with Namdev of the fourteenth century, but this need not obstruct the connective powers of history, and thus the story of Nemdev and Vitthal, told by the Mahanubhavs, might mark the beginning of the association of robbery with the biography of Namdev. Interestingly, the author of a key text of the Mahanubhavs, Nagadev, also known as Bhatobasa, is remembered to have been a "wayward youth" converted by Cakradhar in the thirteenth century.[9] It is unclear whether the *Līlācaritra* or the story mentioned in it that is possibly about Namdev would have been known to those who have told a similar story in later time periods.

The second source, though harder to situate in text or time, is perhaps the epicenter of the narrative about Namdev's wayward days. An autobiographical song in the Marathi corpus attributed to Namdev contains the details of his childhood, early life as a robber, and return to Pandharpur to repent and devote his life to Vitthal. I have not found this song in any of the sixty Marathi manuscripts that I have examined; and because the editorial committee of the Government of Maharashtra's anthology of Namdev's work refused to include the song, we have no record from them on the presence or absence of the verse from the manuscripts that its members consulted.[10] It is, however, well-known and anthologized in many of the editions of Namdev's work available today, most notably in the *Sakaḷa Santa Gāthā*.[11] A second song, present in most editions of Namdev's Marathi work, including the government edition, makes a passing reference to at least two significant aspects of the story: that Namdev bore weapons, as a robber would, and that he cut his own throat at a Shiva temple as atonement for his sins.[12] Both songs are examined below.

Regardless of whether the Mahanubhav biography initiated the story of Namdev as a robber, by the early eighteenth century Namdev's robber legend, in a much different form, had made its way into sacred biographical prose and poetic compositions in Maharashtra. This is evident in our third source, a biography of Namdev attributed to Dattatreya, an eighteenth-century Brahmin hagiographer and *kirtan* performer discussed in chapter 1. Dattatreya is remembered to have lived just after Tukaram's time; the biography of Namdev, succinctly titled *Nāmdevācī Ādi Samādhi*, or "The Beginning [and] the Threnody of Namdev," contains a colophon with the date 1723.[13] Dattatreya is remembered as the son of the Marathi poet and *kirtankar* Shridhar Najharekar (late seventeenth to eighteenth centuries).[14] Toward the conclusion of his biography of Namdev, Dattatreya makes mention of a Shridhar who composed, or at least "recounted" (*varṇilem*), the story of Jnandev's *samadhi* as well.[15]

Dattatreya is said to have grown up in a Deshastha Brahmin family of Pandharpur. His biography of Namdev is composed of almost three hundred *ovi* Marathi verses. Dattatreya's story of Namdev's life, probably in the beginning of the eighteenth century, provides the first biographical record to assert Namdev's purported career as a thief and a murderer, a *bhakta*-turned-despondent clochard-turned-criminal, who eventually renounced a life of plundering for a life of peaceful piety and peregrination.

Essentially, the two biographical sources—Namdev's song and Dattatreya's hagiography—give the same details about Namdev's criminal days. As a young man, faced with grim prospects, he fell in with a gang of thieves, who may also have been roving mercenaries. The biographical song, our second source, is attributed to Namdev, though it is told in the third person,[16] and describes the incident this way:

> Day by day, Namdev grew up,
> And his father had him married.
> The Ocean of Destiny rises and falls,
> And Namdev fell in with a gang of marauders [corāsaṅgeṃ].
> They would strike down even a Brahmin for the sake of the simple and
>   poor.
> They committed many murders.[17]

And this from Dattatreya's eighteenth-century biography:

> It was the Age of Darkness
> And a time of tremendous calamity.
> Everyone was bound for ruin.
> Namdev witnessed the decline as the days went by,
> And this was the fate into which he was born.
> Namdev's father had him married when he was seventeen years old,
> And Namdev began to work,
> Despite being surrounded by a great evil in the land.
> Eventually, he fell in with low-caste miscreants [cāṇḍāḷ]
> Who were highway robbers [mārgaghna].[18]

The narrative by Dattatreya goes on to describe how news of Namdev's plundering spree reached the land's ruler, whom Dattatreya names "Toblakh," a reference to Muhammad bin Tughlaq, the Tughlaq dynastic ruler of the Delhi Sultanate from 1324 to 1351. In a bid to better administer his domain over the Deccan plateau, Tughlaq briefly moved his capital from Delhi to Devgiri, the former capital of the Yadava kings that Tughlaq renamed Daulatabad; the town lies 200 miles north of Pandharpur. It is in this context of Tughlaq's short stay in Maharashtra, around 1327, that Dattatreya situates this story. Upon hearing of the contumacious activities of Namdev, the story goes, the sultan sent a cavalry to end Namdev's mayhem, but Namdev single-handedly defeated the entire regiment. After this victory, Namdev took respite in a small town called Aundhya, near

Pandharpur, and began patronizing the local temple dedicated to Shiva or Naganath and generously contributing to its upkeep.

There Namdev lived anonymously until one day, when, while entering the temple, he noticed a woman begging with her young son just outside. When he asked about their hardship, the woman told him that a terrible criminal named Namdev had killed her husband, a Brahmin, and made her a widow, her son fatherless, and their lives hopeless.[19] They were without sustenance and any means of economic survival, all because of this dastardly Namdev, enemy of the people. Dattatreya recounts what happened next:

> Goose-bumps covered Namdev's skin
> And tears welled up in his eyes.
> He said, "Why didn't I think that among those . . . men I
>   killed there would be one child made helpless?
> How many more cry for their fathers like this boy cries? And I don't even
>   remember killing his father!
> O Lord! Let the God of Death stalk me.
> Then who would see to my salvation?
> Let all the possible horrendous ends come upon me.
> My time of suffering, let it come.
> What if this woman and her son were my family?
> Who were the man's mother and father?"[20]

Namdev drew his weapon, entered the temple, and slit his own throat in an attempt at suicide, spilling pints of blood onto the *linga* of Shiva at the center of the shrine.[21] The temple priest rescued Namdev, bandaged his neck, and set him outside, where Namdev confessed everything to him and others who had gathered. The priest informed him that he had—quite by accident—redeemed himself by offering his own blood to Shiva and that he ought to return to Pandharpur, his hometown, and live the life of the devotee he was meant to be. The remainder of both the autobiographical song and Dattatreya's biography recount the usual details of the rest of Namdev's life as an ardent devotee of Vitthal.

Although this story does not appear in any form in the government's edition of Namdev's songs, there is an oblique reference to it. In this particular song, Namdev's wife, Rajai, is complaining to Vitthal's wife, Rukmini, about the tribulations of being a spouse to such a distracted devotee. She laments:

Our father knew the skill of scissors and thread
Namdev carried arrows and a knife.
Alone he confessed to the wailing wife,
And unsheathed[22] the blade at Naganath.[23]

The song appears in at least two manuscripts consulted by the editorial committee, from the Namdev collection at Pandharpur, and both were likely composed in the eighteenth century. The audience is given the barest hint of the story, sufficient to orient the narrative for any knowing listener. Thus, we might assume that the story was known well enough to make such a scant reference a discernible one. Whatever the history of this legend before the eighteenth century, it seems that in Marathi-speaking regions it was known to the devoted public.[24]

Namdev's days as a robber appear to qualify the *sant* as an example of Eric Hobsbawm's "social bandit," a figure who emerges from the "peasantry," and who is a "criminal" to the powerful and elite but a "hero" to the peasant and common person.[25] There are certainly many differences between Namdev's legend and the numerous stories discussed by Hobsbawm in his study, *Bandits*. But Hobsbawm does provide a close theoretical articulation of the social phenomenon that surrounds figures that represent a kind of political-economic rebellion, unclearly articulated and generally divorced of overt politics, but nonetheless observed, particularly by the disenfranchised, as a heroic counterforce against oppression.[26]

Namdev was not alone on the wayward path of the social bandit in Indian hagiography; several sacred figures had legendary criminal records of their own. The first *ācārya,* or spiritual leader of the Mahanubhav tradition in Maharashtra, Nagadev or Bhatobasa of the thirteenth century, is remembered to have been a roadside waylayer in his youth.[27] The south Indian *vaishnava alvar* Tirumangai/Tirumankai, possibly of the eighth century, is said to have been a member of the *kaḷḷar* caste/community.[28] As Dirks has pointed out, though *kallar*s were generally identified as thieves throughout Tamil-speaking regions, they were nonetheless landowners, chieftains, and—in Pudukkottai—kings.[29] Dirks has demonstrated the role of colonial favor and politics in conferring on the *kallar*s of Pudukkottai the status of kings, while other members of the *kallar* caste/community were labeled thieves via the pronouncements of the Criminal Tribes Act of 1871.[30] Tirumangai is remembered as a "petty chieftain," who commanded a small military—not a king, but not a simple criminal either. Indeed, it is hardly uncommon to find criminals becoming kings.[31]

Tirumangai's popular hagiography recalls an episode when he began stealing from the rich—in true Robin Hood fashion—in order to maintain what was then the nascent Śrī Rangam temple in Tiruchirappalli, Tamil Nadu.[32] Vishnu and Śrī, his "consort," elected to intervene by posing as two gold-bedecked newlyweds. Tirumangai waylaid a couple on the road and, unaware of their divinity, made them surrender their precious goods. Only one item would not part from the groom: a toe ring. In an effort to wiggle the gilded band free, Tirumangai was forced to bow so close to the groom's feet that his forehead laid upon them. At that instant, he realized whose toe ring he held in his hand and repented for his actions.[33] Namdev's story, too, involved a temple and a change of heart in a errant holy man brought on by a realization of whom he was victimizing in his attacks. In Namdev's case, however, it is not God who is the victim but a helpless widow and her child.

The famous sage Valmiki, purported author of the Sanskrit *Rāmāyaṇa*, has a criminal record of his own. The popular story of Valmiki's unruly days recalls that, as a young man, he ambushed travelers and plundered their belongings. One particular day, he chose to burgle the legendary seven sages (*saptarṣi*). Valmiki demanded their goods, but in response the sages asked him a question, "Would your wife and child share the burden of your sins in their future births?" Valmiki insisted that they would, but just to be sure, he told the sages to wait where they stood and said he would soon return. Valmiki went home to confirm that his wife and child were willing to bear his sin. They said that they would not share his sins in their lives to come. The gravity of his crimes struck Valmiki, and he returned to the sages, eager to repent. They suggested that he meditate on all the deaths he had caused as a robber and murderer. He did so, chanting the Sanskrit word *mara*, or "death," as mentioned in chapter 4. This morbid mantra slowly inverted over time into "Rama," the name of the king-hero and deity of the *Rāmāyaṇa*. By the accidental transposition of two syllables, Valmiki redeemed himself.[34]

Sikh *Janam Sākhī* literature about the life of Guru Nanak includes the story of another criminal, one that has clear echoes of Valmiki's story and a sense of continuity with that of Tirumangai. The story recalls that Guru Nanak—like Namdev—traveled much of his life to sites of religious importance to both Hindus and Muslims throughout India and beyond, including Mecca.[35] On the road, a robber named Bhola accosted him and demanded his clothes.[36] Just as in the story of Valmiki and the seven sages, Guru Nanak suggested that Bhola return to his home and ask his family if they would share in the responsibility for his actions in their later lives.

Bhola did so, and, like Valmiki's family, his declined to share the burden of his sins. Bhola returned to Guru Nanak—who had dutifully waited for him along the road. The robber asked to be taught by the Guru. Nanak obliged, making him a Sikh, teaching him a *shabad* that extolled the virtue of singing the divine Name.

The similarities between the stories of Valmiki and Nanak's Bhola are so striking that it appears as if they share an essential theme or "tale-type" as folklorists would call it;[37] we saw other similarities of this kind between Nanak and Namdev.[38] The two stories share the same primary dilemma of providing for one's family through "evil" or criminal deeds, yet discovering that one's family will not share in the repercussions of those deeds.[39] Is it possible that something more than repetition is going on here—a kind of historical communication in a shared vocabulary of biographical images and moments?

A significant difference to note, particularly in relation to Hobsbawm's idea of the social bandit, is that these other stories involve offending one's family (Valmiki and Bhola) or offending God (Tirumangai). For Namdev's legend, however, the implication, while influencing the notion of "family," can be read more as a "public" offense, an offense to social order generally, not to anyone known to him personally (like his family) or to God. Instead there is a public offense that contains within it a critique of both economic distress and the uselessness of economic excess: by his deeds, a widow and her child—two helpless victims—are rendered destitute, even though the temple outside which they beg daily has benefited from a share of the spoils of Namdev's robberies. The juxtaposition of an impoverished widow and fatherless child, with a well-endowed temple, both resulting from the same actions, clearly structures an implied argument in the public realm about economic excess and the spoils of violence, and perhaps the blind eye of religious institutions to these situations. One interesting difference between Namdev's legend and the archetype of the social bandit espoused by Hobsbawm is that Namdev *ceases* his criminal acts for these public socioeconomic reasons, that is, in order not to render further economic misery to any single person, rather than *continuing* his actions in order to increase the economic benefit to nonelites. It is as if Namdev had imbibed Kant's second categorical imperative: he refused to use people as a means to an end. The public good is the target of Namdev's renunciation of violence.

This particular legend about Namdev is discussed here from the point of view of two similar, but often separate contexts. The first is that of the "social bandit" of the eighteenth century in India and a likely social, economic, and political milieu. The second is that of the armed warrior ascetic, a model important in the development of many religious traditions in India.

THE OCEAN OF DESTINY IN THE EIGHTEENTH CENTURY

The eighteenth century in particular records a good number of brigands operating in and around the Deccan during the decline of Mughal power, the expansion and contraction of Maratha might, and the rise of British hegemony.[40] In a discussion of the Telugu regions of the eighteenth century, J. F. Richards and V. N. Rao note:

> The breakdown of state power and public order, and economic distress, touched off by a series of droughts, pushed troops of impoverished men from their normal occupations as peasants or artisans, into various forms of beggary, vagabondage and brigandage. Unpaid, disbanded soldiers also turned to banditry.[41]

Richards and Rao detail the careers of two figures, Riza Khan, an Afghan Muslim officer of some standing who turned himself into a feudal warlord; and Papadu, a low-caste, poor Telugu bandit who built a substantial army of mercenaries. Whereas the former's bid for power repositioned him in the politics of south India in the eighteenth century, the latter, having never had access to this political order, remained "lawless" and a "rebel." However, as Richards and Rao point out, Papadu has received considerable narrative attention through Mughal chronicles, folktales, and a play written in 1972. Through these iterations, Papadu's character and legacy change from that of a ruthless opportunist to a warrior charged with redressing "the grievances of the suffering common people in the hands of rich and cruel lords."[42] Although Richards and Rao attribute the movement of the narrative from chronicle to folktale and Telugu play as a shift from "history to legend," it is clear how the narrative serves its audience and time, using the same set of "facts" in the application of an interpretive strategy for a particular community. What is also clear here is the slide from "history to legend" accompanied by a shift of medium, from written chronicle to oral tale to staged performance. Whatever the sources that record narratives about these figures are called, the profile of the "bandit" in politics, economics, and public culture of the eighteenth century is apparent.

It is also noteworthy that, in the story of Namdev's criminal days, a landlord, who earns a living by his own manner of plunder and extortion, sent the soldiers killed by Namdev. Michael Kennedy, a colonial forensic ethnologist of the early twentieth century in India, recounts several moments, unsettling for the British police forces, when bandits turned into popular folk heroes because they targeted figures of political and economic power. Such folk heroes, or those who capitalized on the fame of heroes, were aided by local villagers and townspeople, thus frustrating attempts to foil their activities.[43] The forces of economics were apparent to many sections of colonial governance charged with maintaining law and order. Christopher Bayly offers a note penned by the superintendent of police of the North Western Provinces in 1815, near Mirzapur, in which a Mewati states, "I was formerly a *ryot* [peasant], but, finding that I was not allowed to reap what I have sown, I became a robber. Under the Company's Government the case is different. I will now therefore become a ryot."[44] Such a direct connection between politics/governance and the fortunes of one person would doubtless spawn a call to action among some, whether through violence, politics, or both. The tragic life of Phoolan Devi (1968–2001), the infamous "Bandit Queen" turned politician,[45] offers only the most recent example of how bandits can come to represent the frustrations and injustices felt by an entire community or several communities, and how this frustration can be translated into local, regional, and even national political prestige.

Stewart Gordon's multiple studies of the history of eighteenth-century Malwa and Maratha power have yielded images of how the "bandit" and "marauder" represented both a political reality and a rhetorical designation of colonial device. His rethinking of groups such as the Thagīs, Bhils, and Piṇḍārīs provides a picture of a period fluctuating between chaotic struggles for power among groups, large and small, and the systematic mechanisms of politics in the Deccan. The Pindaris, for example, were quite prominent in the Maharashtrian Deccan and, as a group, formed a principal constituent of various Maratha armies in the eighteenth and early nineteenth centuries.[46] Small landowners were forced to cull cadres of soldiers at the request of whatever larger ruling power claimed their lands, and thus were many young men, erstwhile agricultural laborers, conscripted and forced to fight.[47] During the campaign season, which usually fell during the cold months of the year, these groups of soldiers would receive as their pay the "right" to plunder any village, town, or enemy that they conquered. However, when the campaign season came to an end and soldiers returned to their nearby fields, some found themselves in foreign lands. In order to make a living, they continued to plunder, often moving from village to village in bands, draining the resources of particularly unfortunate areas completely dry.[48]

Of these conscripted or de facto soldiers, many may have been warrior ascetics. Lorenzen has argued that warrior ascetics had lucrative military occupations open to them: as protectors of extensive lands, both private and temple-owned; as armed guardians of temples; as mercenary soldiers; and even as "independent political adventurers."[49] Militant Hindu groups and armed warrior ascetics likely have long been a part of India's religious landscape.[50] The twin temperaments of Shiva—motionless ascetic and fierce creator/destroyer dancing within a ring of fire—offers an early archetype of the ascetic as warrior, ferocious in battle and resolute in severe meditation meant to generate worldly, superhuman powers (*siddhi*). William Pinch has traced histories of ascetic militarism in northern India since the eighteenth century, noting that Hindu monks (*sadhus*) "were accustomed to bearing arms while on pilgrimage routes through Bengal and in some cases possessed the right to levy contributions from villages" as well.[51] As a more recent example, during the famous Kumbha Mela pilgrimage in 1956, violent rioting occurred between several antagonistic *akhārā*s, or "regiments," of warrior *sadhu*s vying for the position of the first to bathe at the pilgrimage's zenith.[52] Pinch also states that Hindu *sadhu*s would enlist in the armies of landlords and the rulers of small kingdoms;[53] *sadhu*s were simultaneously monks *and* warriors, a hybrid certainly not unusual for Asia and one that recalls the early militant charter of the Jesuit order in Catholic Europe.

The British in India found armed *sadhu*s a troublesome lot. For four decades starting in the 1760s, Hindu *sadhu*s and wandering Muslim *fakīr*s engaged in small-scale sustained rebellious activity against the armies and allies of the East India Company.[54] Naturally, after these encounters the British took a keen interest in monitoring and controlling militant religious organizations. Pinch has pointed out that the British empire had the most trouble managing warrior ascetics and organized militant religious groups along its periphery of power, especially in Punjab, Rajasthan, Bengal, and in the largely autonomous domains of the Marathas of the eighteenth century.[55] Certainly these unruly activities helped justify the expansion of the boundary of colonial power in the service of "protection" from militant religious groups. Some of the fiercest confrontations in the mid- and late eighteenth century occurred in equally "uncolonized" regions, such as in hill countries, impassable mountainous terrain, and forests, which seem also to be the universal home of the "bandit."[56] These are the sorts of areas that the Maratha militias mastered, especially under Shivaji in the late seventeenth century. They are also ideal places for the legendary and real activities of famous bosky brigands, just as in the Robin Hood legend of the English forests.[57] It is interesting to note that the Robin Hood legend and the Namdev robber legend are in many ways coeval. Like Namdev, Robin Hood was said to have been active during the late thirteenth and early fourteenth centuries, but his legend as a robber did not fully form until the eighteenth century, and his legend continues to this day, spanning some seven hundred years of retelling.[58]

The nexus of religious practice and martial prowess is visible in the environment of temples and places of pilgrimage. Scholarship has established that routes and temples associated with pilgrimage centers are more than simple devotional foci; they are also complex sites of commerce, politics, and cultural production.[59] Bayly has discussed the economic role of armed ascetic groups such as Gosains and Banjaras in connection with the maintenance of pilgrimage routes and sacred sites. He has shown that many well-established pilgrimage routes and sites had institutionalized economies of trade. For the Marathas, the early eighteenth century was a high point in their patronage and political prestige in Benares, for example.[60] Inscriptions at Pandharpur make clear that the Vitthal temple received royal patronage from the Yadavas in 1277. That year, the Yadavas sent their minister, Hemadri, with a generous donation to the temple and a copper plate inscribed to commemorate the gift.[61] Around 1324, under Muhammad Tughlaq's reign, the remnant of the Yadavas was defeated. During the war between Tughlaq and the Yadavas, the former destroyed much of Pandharpur, including most of the Vitthal temple, in the process of annihilating the resistance of the Yadavas in the Deccan region. Tughlaq did this because Pandharpur was a focus not just of religious importance but also of political prestige and hence of martial protection. Many studies have pointed out the central importance of temples for the political and economic systems of precolonial India;[62] Pandharpur, as a temple that was a point of political economic importance in the Deccan region, was certainly of this ilk.

Bayly has suggested that mobile pilgrimage units, often a conglomeration of "corporations," some armed and some unarmed, were largely responsible for seeing to interregional trade and communication across politically divided boundaries and were tapped by new political elites as conduits for their goods and services.[63] The notebooks of *kirtankar*s indicate that this profession was tied to pilgrimage places for its audience and longevity; the *kirtankar* was charged with the duty of recording some of the mundane information of the market, including prices, exchange equivalents for goods, and the kinds of environmental factors that would affect agricultural and other kinds of production, such as droughts, floods, and famine. Even today in Pandharpur, the pilgrimage city is home to a thriving business community, where the economic venture of capitalism meets the religious endeavor of pilgrimage. What is more, as is common in other places, such as Tirupati, Benares, and the various homes of the Kumbha Mela, any savvy politician must make an appearance in Pandharpur—usually by helicopter—at the larger of the two yearly pilgrimages in early July. Pilgrimage destinations are, and were, nodal points in networks of communication, trade, political prestige, and record-keeping, all seamlessly interwoven into the "religious" fabric of their existence.

It seems clear that, for hundreds of years, pilgrimages and pilgrimage sites provided a parallel social and cultural structure, alongside other ones, such as agricultural centers, mobile military campaigns, and urban settlements. People moved among these social structures, linking them by their travel as centers of economic, political, and religious capital. The robber story shows that Namdev finds anonymity in one world, as a fugitive in the temple in Aundhya in the heart of the Maharashtrian Deccan, from another, in the countryside of the Maharashtrian Deccan as a robber; geographically, however, they are the same world. He moves between the two in a way that suggests their interconnectedness, but also implies the kind of shifting identity that they afforded—an outlaw in the countryside, a devotee at the temple. Or, to put it another way, he was the kind of figure who could be lawless outside "society" but be reabsorbed into society as well, as a fully participating member, a feature of Hobsbawm's "social bandit."[64] The long tradition of begging and almsgiving outside temples, along pilgrimage routes, and especially during the height of particular pilgrimage seasons is also noteworthy. The Brahmin widow seeks solace outside the temple, and here the two worlds—those of the brigand and of the *bhakta*—meet and transform Namdev's fate or, rather, the meeting forces Namdev to select one of two points that lie along a continuum of nonelite identities. The story registers a shift in his social status from one side of the "law" to the other; he becomes a good citizen, in a sense, a good social *bhakta*. He is, as the etymology of the word *bhakti* implies, "sharing and caring," albeit in a highly selective way and at the point of a knife.

The full explication and dissemination of this story about Namdev may have taken place during the eighteenth century for the reasons enumerated above—the economic plight of many in lands torn by war, crossed by pilgrimage routes, and dotted with temples at the receiving end of patronage or plunder. Namdev's martial character would not have stood out in legends about other devotees with a wayward past, and his "arrow and knife" would not have appeared out of place in the context of holy men who bore arms.

Namdev's north Indian followers recall a popular story that likely originated in the eighteenth century. The story asserts that Namdev's hereditary caste, far from being lowly, was that of a warrior or *kshatriya*, specifically a *tānka kshatriya*, a caste name whose origin can be traced to the mythohistorical time of Parashurama. The story recalls that Vishnu came to Earth as Parashurama in order to check the arrogance of *kshatriyas* and challenged all foolish comers to a duel. Parashurama killed all who accepted his challenge, but some *kshatriyas* refused, perceiving that Parashurama was Vishnu himself. Namdev's ancestors were such "conscientious objectors" and chose to hide (*chipnā*) from Parashurama rather than face his challenge. Those who hid earned the title of *chipī*, "hider" and thus Namdev's caste name, in northern India, is often spelled *chipī*, a "hider," rather than *chīpī*, a "cloth printer."[65] The ethnological argument here mediates two *varṇa* identities, that of *shudra* and that of *kshatriya*, allowing a single *jati* to claim either affiliation. But there may be another argument, a reference to a historical relationship with violence that determined much of the life of communities and individuals in eighteenth-century India.

It is not hard to read into the robber story of Namdev's life and the tales of his confrontation with temporal powers a hero of the subaltern set before the spectacle of power. The narrative of economic suffering and violence is as much a part of popular culture in eighteenth-century Maharashtra as in twenty-first-century Bombay (Mumbai), evident in the films cited at the beginning of this chapter. Hobsbawm's "social bandits," he contends, are always, to some degree, rebels as well, economically and politically counterposed to those who dominate a field of power.[66]

From the point of view provided by Namdev's legacy, a more complex morality was invoked to explain why otherwise good people might turn to bad deeds, why Namdev, who had been a child devotee, would fall in with criminals, and why his story might offer a narrative of socialization for groups and individuals for whom theft, war, and murder were a way of life. The Varkari tradition has made allowances—and even carved out new social spaces—for the full panoply of society. Since the sixteenth century, the Varkari tradition has produced songs and *sant*s that embraced ever-widening groups, a discourse that could accept variety while still endeavoring to deter "antisocial" behaviors by providing narratives of social (and religious) redemption. It is evident through this biographical detail in

Namdev's legacy that disenfranchised soldiers or marginal thieves fell within the purview of the redemptive discourse of the tradition. For centuries Maharashtrian *sant*s (and other religious figures) had invested the language of devotional poetry with the words of the so-called commoner, the language of agriculture, craftwork, and labor.[67] The seventeenth-century Maharashtrian *sant* Ramdas employed the language of martial valor, certainly in recognition that the military life was a common choice—or forced vocation—from the seventeenth century onward, especially for the poor and low caste. The "working class" and conscripted soldiers make up the kinds of people who might be attracted to the cultural structure of annual pilgrimages and pilgrimage sites in the Deccan. Certainly, they would have come into contact with traveling performers who presented Namdev's songs and biography to pilgrimage audiences. Namdev as robber; Namdev as military leader who defeats a sultan with nothing more than his faith in Vitthal—these rhetorical motifs would have drawn an eager audience.

The perspective of political geography shows that throughout the long history from the present stretching back to when Namdev was purported to have lived, Pandharpur was often at the center of war in the Deccan region. Whether between the Yadavas and the Delhi Sultanate in the eleventh through fourteenth centuries or between the British on the western coast and the Marathas on the Deccan Plateau or between the Marathas and the Nizam of Hyderabad's warriors just south and east or Mughal troops to the north in the seventeenth through nineteenth centuries, Pandharpur always straddled tense feudal borders. The legend of Namdev's criminal days seems to have been invoked to speak to people caught between "religious" and "military" worlds, a stratum of war and piety in the eighteenth century. Perhaps the story gave its audience a model with whom they could identify—a young man caught up in turbulent times, who turned from a martial life to a settled, religious one. The Namdev tradition may have been interested in rehabilitating its disenfranchised youth besieged by geographies of power. Perhaps the story reiterated that there was no Rubicon separating its wayward members from the rest. No overt statement to this effect has emerged, but these stories appear consistently in the performance genre of *kirtan* (as well as film), and *kirtan* almost always has a moral, social, or ethical lesson to impart to its listeners. Namdev's robber story has a moral tale of both loss and redemption, perhaps offered to an audience to address their ethical dilemmas, as well as a more general woe of society in the Maharashtrian Deccan in the eighteenth century. The story of the sultan provides another kind of victory, a chance for the "common person" to be cast in the mold of a *sant* who faces down a sultan.

The story would have sat well amid other tales of the ascendancy of Maratha power in the eighteenth century.

Hobsbawm also succinctly describes the impact of the "social bandit" who, regardless of his misdeeds, is still a more amiable force to subaltern sensibilities than are most types of governance. He writes that nonelites "no doubt . . . shared the general feeling . . . that roving bands of armed men were something one knew how to deal with, but the government was both more incalculable and more dangerous."[68] The eighteenth century, especially in Maharashtra and in the second half of the century, is when the colonial city of Bombay rose, European sea power dominated trade along the Konkan coast, and inland military expansion was forcing the Maratha Confederacy to yield to British strength. Namdev's story of social banditry might also be a story of the periphery of power, perhaps as much as that of the Marathas who needed to control their expanding forces in the first half of the eighteenth century and of the British who were troubled by small bands of roving mercenaries. Recall also that in many accounts Namdev kills a Brahmin, and perhaps in no time as much as in the eighteenth century under Maratha Peshwa rule in Maharashtra could the equation between Brahminical authority and the state be drawn as concretely. Although the state appears peripheral in the accounts seen here, something of Hobsbawm's idea that the state looms as an indiscernible force, overcome in the narrative, but lingering as its trace arises in these stories is detectable. However, in the story of Namdev confronting some power of temporal authority, the shape of the state becomes far more defined.

POWER AND DEVOTION

Why does the story of Namdev's criminal activities hold a place in the popular remembrance of him in the Marathi-speaking world despite its almost complete absence from pan-Indian hagiographical networks, the *kirtan* performance tradition, or the Marathi textual remnant of the tradition? Who would want to maintain this story and why? What position does this narrative have in "religious" traditions in India? To answer these questions, I posit that *bhakti* has a well-articulated narrative of its own efficacy, particularly in the face of oppression from temporal authority. Although the historical value of the narrative is suspect—the idea that miracles engendered by a *bhakta*'s ardent devotion can challenge the might of temporal rulers—the social historical message expresses the same anxieties as those articulated in the robber legends.

I discuss the direct connection made between devotional efficacy and temporal power, where the former defeats the latter, by presenting two well-established narrative modes in devotional Indian literature of the seventeenth to nineteenth centuries into which Namdev's legend is inserted that exemplify this atypical alignment of power. Both modes are present in and outside Marathi sources and thus point to a larger motif of remembrance in Namdev's name. The first arises through multiple examples of the "good demon" crystallized in the legend of Prahlad. The second involves an interaction between a temporal authority—a Hindu king or Muslim sultan—and a lowly *bhakti* figure, another common scene in the devotionalism of India.

Jan Gopal, the purported author of Dadu's biography, composed a narrative about the good demon Prahlad around the early seventeenth century; the oldest available manuscript is from 1636, a full century before the first written records of Namdev's bandit legend. The story of Prahlad is also present in the *Viṣṇu Purāṇa* and *Bhāgavata Purāṇa* traditions and thus is widely recalled in both Sanskrit and regional languages. As Gopal narrates it, the son of the demon king Hiranyakashipu resolved to worship Vishnu, a decision that raised the ire of his fiendish father. The father attempted to kill his wayward son, but Vishnu interceded for his demon-devotee in the form of the man-lion (*nārasiṃha*) *avatar*. Vishnu as Narasimha burst forth from a nearby pillar of the palace and ripped out Hiranyakashipu's beating heart in fabled kungfu fashion.[69]

David Lorenzen situates Gopal's retelling of the Prahlad story amid uses of the narrative in other regional sources, most important in relation to Namdev and Kabir. He offers the conjecture that low-caste *nirguna* composers adopted the story by relating themselves to it as "good demons" who worship Vishnu, as citizens of the lowest rungs of society who win God's attentions against all social odds. Lorenzen states that these stories constitute "a metaphor for the downtrodden . . . pious persons who have become the oppressed victims of the rich and powerful."[70] Prahlad's serial tortures at the hands of his demon father, and the tortures inflicted on Kabir and Namdev by temporal authorities, are similar and may have served as a kind of biographical archetype to describe the suffering of Kabir and Namdev when pitted against worldly might. It is important to note that Jan Gopal was a devotee of Dadu, and thus the Prahlad story—and possibly its caste allegations—had an important role in both the Dadu Panth and in early Sikhism, where Namdev is amply represented. Indeed, Namdev seems entwined in the legacy of Prahlad in various regional religioliterary communities, from the Varkaris to the Dadu

Panthis, Kabir Panthis, and Sikhs, where Namdev is regularly associated with Prahlad.

Some of the oldest versions of the Prahlad story in regional literature are found in three songs attributed to Namdev in the *Guru Granth Sahib,* also found in the *Kartārpūr Pothī* collected and assembled by Guru Arjan in 1604.[71] A slightly older, but not significantly different, version of this same song is found in the Fatehpur manuscript dated to 1582 and is one of the eleven songs in that manuscript attributed to Namdev.[72] Kabir retells the story of Prahlad in the *Guru Granth Sahib,* as does Raidas.[73] The story is told by Guru Amar Das (sixteenth century) in three songs in which the narration has been altered in order to highlight the importance of a guru and of reciting the Name.[74] In a fourth song, Guru Amar Das compares Namdev and Kabir to Prahlad, noting that—like Kabir and Namdev—Prahlad needed only the Name, a guru, and his will to survive, obviating the necessity of the "study of karma and dharma."[75] In describing Namdev and Kabir, Guru Amar Das notes that the two were a "tailor" and a "weaver," respectively, and that they "recognized the word of Brahman and lost their egoism and their caste."[76] Songs attributed to the sixteenth-century Marathi *sant* Eknath contain the suggestion that Namdev was earlier incarnated as Prahlad, and, later in the eighteenth century, Mahipati connects Namdev and Prahlad in a passage in which Vitthal speaks to Gonai, Namdev's mother: "Just as in the line of demons, the *bhakta* Pralhad [sic] became an avatār by being born to Kayadhu, so Nama the servant of Vishnu has been born from you for the salvation of the world."[77]

Namdev's Marathi songs regularly mention Prahlad in a variety of contexts. The Government of Maharashtra's edition has fifty songs. The good demon appears in rosters of *avatar*s and the reasons for those incarnations. Prahlad surfaces in sermons on the efficacy of *bhakti* and the power of reciting God's name. The government's edition of Namdev's songs charts at least two separate, though small, collections of songs attributed to Namdev that mention Prahlad as above. The largest *bada* within the Pandharpur archive contained one collection of some five to seven songs about the "good demon."[78] A second collection of three to five songs was found in a much smaller notebook uncovered by the editorial committee.[79] Both collections are probably from the eighteenth century. A handful of songs are found in the oldest manuscript in the collection consulted by the Maharashtra Government's editorial committee, which is attributed to 1631. Songs bearing the names of Namdev's companions, Parisa Bhagavat (late thirteenth century) and Janabai include mention of Namdev as an *avatar* of Prahlad. The government edition also records three

Hindi songs attributed to Namdev and preserved in Marathi *bada*s that mention Prahlad. Callewaert and Lath also record these songs in their critical edition of Namdev's Hindi materials, where they note that all three Hindi songs belong to the Gopaldas *Sarvāṅgī* completed in 1627.[80]

According to hagiography, then, Namdev seems to have been associated with Prahlad throughout the course of the Namdev tradition both in Marathi and outside Marathi sources. Manuscripts suggest that this association was certainly present from the mid-seventeenth century onward. Mahipati's eighteenth-century assertion that Namdev is an *avatar* of Prahlad might have its origin in the pronouncements of Namdev's two companions mentioned above and in the generally steady appearance of Prahlad in Namdev's songs. The idea that this association with a "good demon" hints at a martial or criminal narrative foundation is at least probable, and certainly the concept of Namdev relying on God for spiritual *and* physical salvation is well known. Namdev's "helplessness" is a common motif in songs attributed to him and in hagiography, as is his presumed bravery when facing conflict, especially with figures of power, such as Brahmins, kings, and sultans. Just as Prahlad faces his powerful father and relies on the intercession of Vishnu, Namdev (and many other *sant*s) face temporal authority, placing their fate in divine providence.

In addition to the association between Namdev and the persecuted good demon Prahlad, there is a second prominent example of Namdev representing the disenfranchised or powerless who faces temporal authority and defeats it. This second example involves a meeting between a figure of power and a famous *bhakta*, a narrative plot found throughout Indian devotional literature. In this case, Namdev is summoned to confront a powerful ruler, who in some stories is a Hindu king and in others a Muslim sultan (see Ill. 1.3).[81] The presence of this motif in hagiographical songs about Namdev perhaps begins with Narsi Mehta (fifteenth century), and includes Hariram Vyas (sixteenth century), Anantadas (late sixteenth century), Nabhadas (early seventeenth century), Priyadas (eighteenth century), Caturdas (eighteenth century), and can be found in the *Prem Ambodh Pothī* (c. 1693). In the *Guru Granth Sahib* Namdev is remembered as having been summoned to confront a sultan.[82] Here is a passage from a Hindi song in the *Guru Granth Sahib*, which appears (purposefully, I think) in the text after a story narrated by Namdev about Prahlad:

The Sultan had Nama bound.
[He said,] "Show me your Hari Bithula

By bringing life back into the body of a slaughtered cow.
If you fail, I will cut your throat where you stand."
And this is just what the Pādśāh [sultan] did [to the cow]:
He slaughtered the cow, and no life remained in its body.
[Namdev said to the sultan,] "Whatever I do is but nothing.
Whatever is done, God does it."[83]

The sultan became furious at Namdev's cheeky response and had him thrown down before a mad elephant. But Namdev survived the elephant's advance and even pacified the pachyderm merely by singing a song to God; with this song, the dead cow came back to life. Eventually, the sultan realized that this odd man was indeed invested with some sacred power. The sultan repented and sent a message to Namdev through his retinue of advisors. The message was simple but striking: "Forgive me, Hindu, I am your cow."[84]

The first literary articulation in Marathi of this pervasive legend may be found in the *Mahikāvatīcī Bakhar,* mentioned in chapter 1. The *bakhar,* the reader might recall, is a prose chronicle or history common in Marathi from the fifteenth century to the eighteenth century. The *Mahikāvatīcī Bakhar* is one of the oldest of the genre and is a compilation of at least six *bakhars* edited into this form in Shivaji's court of the seventeenth century. Generally speaking, the six parts are placed in descending chronology, with the most recent first and the oldest last. The story about Namdev's confrontation with a Muslim ruler occurs toward the end of this *bakhar* in a portion whose composition is attributed in a colophon to 1538, though the actual date when the story was transcribed is likely to be earlier, particularly if each of the six *bakhars* in the *Mahikāvatīcī Bakhar* follow a similar pattern of placing the stories last in reverse chronological order.[85] The sixth and last section of the *bakhar* is dated to 1478, and it is likely that the Namdev story was composed sometime between 1478 and 1538. The historical martial narrative spans a period from the early twelfth century to seventeenth century and concerns mostly royal matters. The section preceding the one about Namdev discusses the fall of the Yadavas under Ramchandra in 1297 and subsequent political actions up to the first quarter of the fourteenth century. However, it concludes with the founding of Ramnagar by Ramshah (Kunwar Ramraj) in 1262 in present-day Gujarat. The section regarding Namdev thus does not appear to be directly connected to the two historical narratives that bookend the section, and so we must look to the story itself to get a sense of what time period is being described.

According to the *bakhar,* an unnamed sultan summons Namdev while he is on pilgrimage to Varanasi. Here is a portion of the story:

> Once there was a *bhakta* of Hari, a tailor named Namdev. While he was on a pilgrimage to Varanasi, he was summoned by a Padshah.[86] Slanderous things were being said about Hindus and so Namdev reasoned that the Padshah would most likely kill him. A plate with a small piece of rotten cow meat [*kaṃdurī*][87] was placed before Namdev.[88] He was then forced to eat the rotten meat. Just in time, Lord Vitthal came to the rescue of his devotee. A jasmine [*kuṃdurī*][89] plant flowered where the meat had been. The miracle shocked the Padshah. So the Padshah began asking Namdev questions. "Please, what caste [*jati*] do you belong to?" he [politely] asked Namdev. Namdev replied, "Sir, I am a tailor [*simpā*] by caste." This is what he said. Thus Namdev had the upper hand. The Padshah honored Namdev, even though the Padshah had been at fault. The Padshah had an heir, Sultan Togil. And he had another heir, Sultan Peroj Shah. Thus in seven years, there were three Padshahs.[90]

The Padshah or sultan of the narrative appears to be Giyasuddin Balban of the Slave Dynasty of the Delhi Sultanate, who ruled from 1266 to 1286 from Delhi. Balban had a protégé, Tughril Khan, called Togil in the text, who was the governor of Bengal until he was killed by Balban in the late thirteenth century for claiming his own right to Balban's throne. After Balban's death, and following wars among Balban's remaining generals, Sultan Jallauddin Firozshah ascended the throne in 1290. In the text, he is called "Peroj" Shah. The text thus charts the decline of the Slave Dynasty and the establishment of the Khilji Dynasty, though this happens between the end of Balban's reign and the beginning of Firozshah's reign.[91] The story therefore takes place both in northern India and in a time period that is roughly within the range of the other stories discussed in this section of the *bakhar.* Furthermore, the story was likely narrated and hence recorded here around the late fifteenth or early sixteenth centuries. Stories such as this one become important in later modern constructions of Namdev as a humanist or in Marathi, as someone who espoused *manavatavada,* or "humanism" as a "saint of the nation" (*rashtriya sant*). The humanist cast comes primarily from his perceived efforts to ease Hindu–Muslim animosities—he reaches a détente with the Padshah—and this feeds his position as a protonationalist, the subject of chapter 6.

There are many ways to read this story. I assume that in some rudimentary form, it was present, and perhaps recorded, close to the period of the colophon, that is, in the mid-fifteenth century. The year named in the colophon, 1538, would place the text, and hence the retelling of the story, just after the disintegration of the Bahmani Sultanate, but perhaps it was composed during the Sultanate's final years. In terms of Maharashtrian history Giyasuddin Balban is not particularly important to the regional political and cultural reality of Maharashtra either in Namdev's purported period of life or in the period of the *bakhar*'s composition. Invoking a contest with the Delhi sultan, Giyasuddin Balban, is thus peculiar. But one could imagine that this story, articulated during Bahmani power or the reconfiguration of the five Deccani Sultanates thereafter, in the period between the decline of the Delhi Sultanate and the rise of the Mughal period, does two things: it tells a story in a way that is acceptable within hegemonic structures that monitored public culture in the region, that is, it posed no challenge to the narrative of Deccani Sultanate power; and it contributed to the understanding that Namdev was vital to north Indian public memory too by putting him in the north, specifically in Benares and then Delhi. In other words, it puts Namdev's challenge to temporal, and here Muslim (and specifically Delhi Sultanate), authority, in the north and away from the time and place of Bahmani or Deccani Sultanate rule. It also displays the weakness, in a sense, of the rule from Delhi, an increasing reality under the Lodhis during the mid-fifteenth century. It is a political comment, from the Deccan, about the north, while remaining an unlocalized socioreligious comment about Muslim political power and Hindu social power in the fifteenth century in Maharashtra. This reading shifts emphasis if the period of composition is assumed to be the mid-seventeenth century, perhaps during Shivaji's reign, but the shift is in many ways slight. The same need to display a weakened center of political power in Delhi is felt, but this is in relation to the Mughals, in this case, and not the Delhi Sultanate. But in this latter period, the language of religious difference would have been even more powerful.[92] Whatever the historical context of the story's composition, its referent—the encounter between Namdev and a Padshah or sultan—appears to have had established itself as a core narrative in Namdev's biography, finding repetition in a large field of hagiography, as mentioned above, from Narsi Mehta (fifteenth century) to Hariram Vyas's work of 1580, then later by Anantadas in 1588, then Nabhadas in 1600 and Priyadas in 1712, and Caturdas in 1720—as well as in the *Prem Ambodh Pothi* of around 1693.

In the eighteenth century, Mahipati briefly tells the story of Namdev and the sultan, though he neglects the story of Namdev's robber days. Mahipati's version is curious. It takes as a given the story of Namdev tested by the Muslim king, called an *avindharāja* in the text, an "unpierced king" and hence a Muslim by metonymy. In other words, the point of the story is not the confrontation, but the communication between Namdev and Vitthal. Mahipati relates how a Muslim king hears of Namdev's performances while Namdev is in the north visiting pilgrimage places. He wishes to test Namdev and does so by killing a cow. Namdev says it will take four days to raise the cow. For four days, Namdev prays to Vitthal to no avail, but on the fourth day, Vitthal comes. Namdev scolds him for taking so long, and Vitthal replies that he had no choice because Namdev had told the Muslim king it would take four days. Namdev should have told him that it would happen immediately, Vitthal tells him. Mahipati concludes the story by saying, "Blessings have come upon this Vaishnava hero [*vīra*]; he has made the Bearer of the Bow [Ram, and thus Vitthal] enslaved [*vaśa kelā*]."[93] Mahipati does not invoke the robber story, but bookends his story of the confrontation with the Muslim king with suggestive metaphors. Here, at the end, he refers to Namdev as a hero and suggests a kind of conquest, invoking not an image of Vitthal in Pandharpur or the pastoral Krishna, but Ram, the warrior, with bow in hand. Mahipati also introduces an interesting metaphor when he opens the story by comparing the Muslim king's anger upon hearing of Namdev "the way a thief curses to himself when the moon rises."[94] If Mahipati's own work should be seen as a literal transcription of a *kirtan* performance (as chapter 3 argues), then Mahipati is tapping some public memory about these stories, referencing them skilfully, and as skillfully displacing them from Namdev.

The story then is about a miscommunication between Vitthal and Namdev or, rather, the power the devotee has over the object of devotion, a common theme in Mahipati's work. Although Mahipati does not provide a reference for his source text for this story—and Mahipati is known to be scrupulous at citing his sources—it appears that he follows the *bakhar* account and not the account of Dattatreya, produced thirty years after Dattatreya's version and thus possibly known to Mahipati. The shape of Mahipati's account follows the *bakhar* account in that both are framed by Namdev's travels in the north, in search of pilgrimage places, and the desire to test the *sant*, rather than persecute him. Both versions end with the Muslim ruler bowing to Namdev and a peaceful dénouement. This is not the case with Dattatreya's account.

Dattatreya includes a significantly expanded version of the Padshah episode that effectively combines several themes: Namdev's waywardness; his martial prowess as indexed by a military appellation; the connection to Prahlad, made explicit in pan-Indian hagiography; the confrontation of a lowly, uncultured figure and a powerful temporal authority; and the power of religious conviction over political force.

Dattatreya's version of Namdev's confrontation is situated after a narrative that describes the anguish of Brahmins at the decline of Vedic learning and before the story of Jnandev's voluntary entombment or *samadhi*. A connection is apparent between the story of Vedic demise and Namdev's confrontation: at the beginning of his recollection Dattatreya overhears God lament, "[My people] have all wandered away. I no longer appear in their dreams. Their *karma* is sullied."[95] The protagonist of the narrative then enters the story, someone described as "Sultan Toblakh Padshah," who appears to be the same figure that ordered Namdev's capture in the robber story mentioned above, that is, Muhammad bin Tughlaq, the second sultan of the Tughlaq Dynasty. Tughlaq complains that Namdev has not come to him to pay his respects. The sultan gives an order, "Nama the Tailor, I want that bandit [*puṇḍa*] to demonstrate his religious expertise [*gosāviṃpaṇe*] to me!" The sultan sends this message to Namdev, who in turn asks Vitthal, "Should I take up this challenge? I'm not a religious expert. . . . I'm no good at debating scripture [*lekhi*]." Before an answer is received, the sultan's envoy comes to retrieve the brigand-*bhakta*. At this point, a new title for the sultan is introduced: the word *yavana*, or "foreigner," a Sanskrit term first applied to the Greeks, and later to Muslims. Throughout the remainder of the narrative, *yavana* is a key appellation Dattatreya gives to the sultan.

Namdev arrives at the sultan's assembly in the garb of a Varkari *sant*, wearing a Tulsi-bead necklace and singing the names of Vitthal. The sultan demands, "Show me your Vitthal," to which Namdev replies, "Maharaj, my Vitthal is in your heart. Hindu, Turk, or other races [*varna*]—God is never neglectful of anyone." The sultan is not impressed and orders a baby cow to be brought forth. The calf's head is severed and placed before Namdev, who now receives from Dattatreya the title *nāyak*. In Marathi, this word has a variety of meanings—"hero," "leader," "husband," "master"—all of which carry the connotation of a martial, mighty position. This is the common term used to designate the leader of the various militias that operated around the Deccan throughout the seventeenth, eighteenth, and nineteenth centuries. The term appears regularly in Marathi *povada* and *lavani* literature, where the subject is either martial exploits (*povada*) or a woman yearning for her husband who is often away at battle (*lavani*). It is also a common term for the leader of a band of mercenaries and suggests Dattatreya's earlier story about Namdev's criminal days.

The sultan orders Namdev to reanimate the calf or be trampled on by an enraged elephant. Namdev begins to "remember" (*smaraṇ karaṇe*) Vitthal, but to no avail. A half-hour goes by and the sultan has Namdev bound and set under the feet of the elephant. Namdev is given one last chance: "If you convert to my religion [*yātī*] I'll spare your life, Hero [*nayak*] Nama." Vitthal enters at this point to save his devotee from "immorality" (*adharma*). The elephant goes wild with rage, but then lowers his enormous trunk and gently touches the feet of Namdev. Dattatreya interjects an analogy here: "Panduranga . . . quickly demonstrated a wealth of compassion, just as quickly as the time when Prahlad called to Narasimha [*nṛhari*] for protection. At the very moment of recalling [*smaran*] Hari, he was here." The elephant dies, inexplicably, while the cow returns to life—a symbol of martial power (both Hindu and Muslim) succumbing to a symbol of Hindu devotion.

The assembly is struck with awe, and the sultan sees God's "enormous form" (*viśāl rupa*) with mace, discus, and red eyes. In a panic, the sultan runs to his queens' chambers, but cannot escape the terrifying form. The sultan's queens fall at Namdev's feet and plead not to be made widows. Namdev intercedes on the sultan's behalf requesting mercy for the "foreigner." The sultan is spared and praises Namdev. Dattatreya closes this section of his biography as Namdev returns to his home where all the *sants* have gathered to remember the name of God (*nāmasmaraṇ*) in "play" (*līlā*).

This account from the eighteenth century connects several hagiographical dots. Namdev is referred to as a robber, a military chief, and a *goswāmi* or *gosāvi*—an ascetic with religious expertise. His illiteracy is hinted at as he protests participating in a "debate" on scripture, and his utter reliance on Vitthal is apparent. Dattatreya manages to interlace the legend of Namdev pacifying the elephant and the legend of Namdev either being served cow meat (the head is given to him) or presented with a dead cow. Dattatreya seems to have made the sultan even more despicable by portraying the cow as a calf. What is more, the death of the elephant and the revival of the calf seem to invoke a dialectic between martial power and religious conviction, with the latter bettering the former. Thus, Namdev's character is summarized in this story in a way that takes advantage of the wide range of interplay present in his Maharashtrian and north Indian hagiography, to articulate how religious power betters temporal authority.

As mentioned above, the sultan depicted in this story appears to be Muhammad bin Tughlaq, referred to as "toblakh" here. The second sultan of the Tughlaq Dynasty of the Delhi Sultanate, Tughlaq ruled from 1325 to

1351 and shifted his capital, around 1327, to Devgiri, renaming it Daulata-bad, in north-central Maharashtra. The story is unclear on whether Nam-dev meets Tughlaq in Delhi or in Daulatabad, but the text seems to assume that they meet in Daulatabad.

Among the many strategies for reading this story, one seems to resonate most strongly with the likely context of public memory in the eighteenth century. Dattatreya's colophon places the composition of this text in 1723, the reign of the Peshwa Bajirao I during his expansion of Maratha power northward against the Mughals and southward against the Nizam and Bi-japur. One can imagine a propagandist sentiment in the image of Tughlaq fleeing Vitthal and hiding among his queens, disguising himself as one of them. The emasculation is clear enough, and the image appears to offer a fanciful echo of Tughlaq's decision to move his capital back to Delhi from Daulatabad, which he did for political reasons germane to the metropole of Delhi and not resistance in the Maharashtrian Deccan. But this also sug-gests something of the military adventures of the Maratha armies under Bajirao as they moved northward against the listing Mughal empire.

There may also be a less political, more quotidian point to this story. As mentioned earlier, this time period is remembered as one of tremendous hardship in the Deccan, despite military-political successes of its governing entity, and a general state of forced conscription prevailed through many regions. As Bajirao's armies advanced, they acquired—often by force—more soldiers from the regions around their operations. Furthermore, the era between the death of Shivaji and the rise of Bajirao was a violent period in the history of Maharashtra. The location of Dattatreya in or around Pand-harpur in the early eighteenth century may have been relatively secure, but the memory of past plunder would no doubt have been fresh, in particular, Tughlaq's destruction in Pandharpur.[96] This narrative, expanding as it does on the evil and cowardice of the sultan—and the refusal of a hero-*bhakta* to renounce his faith—may have resonated so as to combine a kind of Maratha martial propaganda with a more conventional *bhakti* narrative. Although the Maratha Confederacy may have been in its ascendance, the narrative portrays "Hindus" as oppressed by *yavana*s. No doubt this narrative was free to be composed and disseminated, as well as preserved, in an environ-ment outside the ambit of Muslim rule. The rhetorical strategy of portray-ing a community in hegemonic power as one oppressed by an "enemy" who lacks power is a tactic readily apparent today in the discourse of modern Hindu nationalism.

The general account of this meeting between Namdev and a sultan is historically highly suspect; there is no record of such a meeting in any non-*bhakti* work, nor is it likely that Tughlaq, or Giyasuddin Balban for that matter, would have entertained an audience with such a lowly figure. But the idea of a *bhakta* or other religious person encountering and better-ing a figure of temporal authority is a very common tale-type in north Indian hagiography. Many *sant*s and *bhakta*s appear to encounter kings and sultans through centuries of hagiography. William Smith records many tale-types involving such encounters in his work *Patterns in North Indian Hagiography*.[97] These types range from fairly benevolent encounters, such as those between the Mughal ruler of the sixteenth century, Akbar, or his clever minister Birbal and a host of *sant*s, who have included Haridas, Surdas, and even (very anachronistically) Namdev. The second kind of en-counter involves the threat of death or punishment, as is the case with Namdev and Kabir, for example.[98]

It is this second type of story that responds to the violence and power relations of a given time. In the case of Namdev's encounter with a sultan, the story introduces a legend of Namdev's encounter with Tughlaq or Bal-ban into Namdev's life story and intermixes it with those of others who have suffered in similar ways, most notably Prahlad. Historically, Pandhar-pur could not be physically saved from the violence of war that Tughlaq and his armies waged in the Deccan, but discursively, Namdev could be positioned by various traditions as the victor of a different conflict with the same conqueror or perhaps with another Sultanate figure, such as Balban. This event reverses the historical reality of Tughlaq's destruction of Pand-harpur, the heart of the Namdev community in Maharashtra, resituating Namdev in the heart of Sultanate territory in the Balban version in the *bakhar* literature. And, indeed, in Dattatreya's account, Vitthal himself is in the heart of the sultan, as Namdev says. Hence, it presents an upturned power relationship, a mighty master who is bettered by a subaltern figure.

The image of the sultan as Namdev's "cow" in the Sikh recollection is striking and carries multiple valences: the cow has been resurrected after being slain by the sultan and in some way signals his own redemption, but the cow is also deified by many Hindus, and this strikes a remarkable equa-tion between the Muslim sultan and a sacred Hindu animal. It might also act metonymically to further the idea that the earlier defeat of a "Hindu" kingdom (the Yadavas) is being reversed—the Hindus (the cow) are fighting back. Dattatreya's account further juxtaposes the death of the general mar-tial animal, the elephant, at the sultan's court, with the presence of the calf, perhaps signaling what is a common motif in *bhakti* literature, particularly in Marathi devotionalism, the separation of a calf from its mother (*vatsalya*). Finally, the recollection of defeat of Maharashtrian-Yadava forces at the hands of Tughlaq centuries earlier might have lent this story some inspirational effect within the ranks of conscripted soldiers fighting to expand the Maratha empire/Confederacy against Muslim and non-Muslim rule at the periphery of its territory. All these possibilities, and many more, would have constituted the public cultural reception of this story in its multiple forms and tapped troves of public memory echoing the sentiments and social conditions of their various contexts of reception.

Two different narratives, reproduced over five centuries and in multiple locations—the story of Namdev as a robber and the story of the confrontation between Namdev and some figure of temporal authority—are surveyed and engaged here. Dattatreya's account brings together both narratives as he retells the two general stories and suggests that their relationship hinges on the "darkness" of the age, the necessity of action in a time of scarcity and suffering. The very fact of the longevity of these narratives should indicate their implicit importance. Furthermore, the reception of these narratives, which reflect an ever-adaptive oral core, may signal a particular kind of historiography, a way of writing the past that hews to the desires of specific audiences—the subaltern in this case, who lived in a time of social upheaval. The structure of this historiography is evident in the multiple sources tapped and audiences targeted in the creation of the various narratives cited in this chapter. I have read these narratives with this historical strategy in mind, suggesting that they are themselves products of a kind of historicism, a reworking of a common narrative determined by the social conditions of a new period, in this case, the eighteenth century primarily. This seems to be a conscious decision by those eighteenth-century figures who relayed these stories into their own time. The stories are retold not because they must be preserved but because they can be retold to convey a new story, the story of the present, cast as a story about the past. All histories are written in the mode and genre of their age, and these stories are no different. But this kind of reading yields a historiographic problem. How can the public memory of Namdev manage to represent him as a figure of the past with historical accuracy and, at the same time, use him strategically in constructing contemporary narratives that use history as a narrative technique to tell the story of their present conditions?

The problem can be approached by assuming that the *historicity of Namdev* should be relinquished in order to understand how he is used throughout the centuries as a *device of history*. Namdev cannot be both at once—historical and historically heuristic, that is, the events described cannot be both true in the historical sense and true in their metaphorical sense simultaneously. At the beginning of this book, I laid out the differences between the pursuit of Namdev as a historical figure and his use as a figure of memory. Here it is my contention that Namdev is used in the service of public memory—the traditions of recollection reviewed here are not historical in their effort to recover Namdev but, rather, history is a literary device employed by the narratives. This is an example of historical memory, of a mode of remembering that accesses history and brings it into the service of its objectives, which are usually social objectives. If these narratives through time have addressed the conditions of life for the likely audiences of these retellings, they are social historical sources for the eighteenth century, but not the fourteenth century, not for Namdev's time.

This proposition raises another question: what is the mode of entry into the fourteenth century through the eighteenth century that is at work here? For the contemporary scholar, it is textual and literary, the materials of preservation. But in the eighteenth century—and in many contexts today—it is performative. The reinvention of the bandit and sultan narratives represent the emphatic reliance on performance as an adaptive historiographic strategy—with one important caveat: history, here, is not modern history. This turn toward modern history is explored in chapter 6, which engages the management of Namdev's legacy through various media, that is the performative space of the "imagined community" of the Indian nation, which is also the preeminent site of modern Indian historiography, and of all modern historiography in general—the nation. Here, in the eighteenth century in Maharashtra, these narratives emerge from nonmodern contexts, from realms of experience outside European social structures, still ensconced in the world of the late medieval Deccan, in the cultural field of the Maratha polity, yet to be absorbed into the colonial world. Namdev's legacy will make this transition, as shown below, but here, at the cusp of this momentous change, nonmodern historical memories, narratives that existed in the ephemera of performance, are now accessed by only their barest traces.

{ 6 }

A SANT FOR THE NATION IN THE NINETEENTH
AND TWENTIETH CENTURIES

The Bhakti *movement rescued our society in the Mediaeval Period
from total subservience to ritual and the rigours of the caste system. In
every part of the country saints arose who preached love and brotherhood,
and proclaimed that everyone, irrespective of birth or wealth, could
earn redemption through faith and service. Sant Namdeo was one
of the foremost of such teachers.*
—INDIRA GANDHI

IN THE mid-twentieth century India won its independence and with
that freedom ostensibly came the liberty for its citizens to write histories of their nation. Many scholars of the postcolonial period have asserted that India was denied the agency to write its national history because
of its late entry into modern nationalism, its long colonial legacy, and the
virtual copyright placed on the idea of the nation by Western modernity.
Yet it is amply apparent to any observer that India writes multiple histories
of its past through the lens of nationalism undeterred.

This chapter does not argue against the position that the idea of the nation and the writing of history are very much a part of the Euro-centric
world. However, what is questioned here is the assertion that all histories,
all products of the disciplined imagination exercised on the past, must be
judged according to the criteria of modernity. Ernest Gellner wrote of the
histories of nations that "the cultural shreds and patches used by nationalism are often arbitrary historical inventions. Any old shred and patch
would have served as well."[1] This chapter holds instead that the shred and
patch of the nation as remembered in the pan-Indian articulation of the
Namdev tradition may be anachronistic, but it is not arbitrary.[2] The Namdev tradition comprises a purposeful endeavor to write a history of the
nation with characters who espouse humanism (*manavatavada*) and a
sense of a cohesive national identity and who lived several hundred years
before freedom was won in India. This chapter takes up a theme begun in

chapter 1, where hagiography evinces a kind of historiography that links multiple linguistic, cultural, and religious communities through commonly told and remembered sacred pasts. It also continues the subject of chapter 5, which showed that one particular sacred biographical narrative is positioned within a political-economic context in order to recuperate the legend of a "social bandit," or a *sant* challenging temporal authority. In chapter 5, however, the historical use of Namdev required an ahistorical deployment of Namdev's public memory where Namdev became a device to tell the history of a new present moment, primarily situated within the eighteenth century. Based on this idea that modes of historiography exist within the "religious" framework of the Namdev tradition, this chapter takes up one of the central subjects of modern Western historiography, the history of the nation, and views it in the context of this tradition.

In the later years of the independence movement and the postcolonial period in India, particularly from the mid-1960s onward, Namdev increasingly entered the Indian public sphere as a national "integrator" or a "saint of the nation" (*rashtriya sant*). Indeed, as Gandhi's quotation above indicates, it is in the nineteenth century that the English word "saint" is prefixed to Namdev's name as a gloss for *sant*. This position as a saint of the nation extended from biographical and ethical features of Namdev's remembrance, especially his legendary travels throughout India of the fourteenth century and the portrayal of social egalitarianism among his community of fellows. His position within a larger pantheon of protonationalist heroes was framed by the ideals of Gandhian pluralism, Nehruvian social democracy, and a kind of Hindu secularism or Hindu modernity. Namdev has not maintained social capital in the world of majoritarian Hindu politics espoused by the Hindu Right under the rubric of "Hindutva," the political thesis that the status of being Indian is coterminous with the status of being socially and religiously a "Hindu." This is important because Namdev's position within one articulation of the Indian nation is "humanistic," not religiously chauvinistic. Discussions of religion, politics, and nationalism in India, and elsewhere in the world, are dominated by a discourse of extremism, fundamentalism, and the forces of the Far Right on the political spectrum. But religion has a strong effect on the politics and nationalist imagination of more center-oriented political actors, an interaction largely ignored by scholars and critics. Instead, when one sees "religion" and "nation" or "politics" together, one often assumes the character of rightist ideology. However, the fields of religion and nation that come to characterize Namdev's legacy in the public sphere of central, western, and northern India from the twentieth century to the present is championed by the same social and political forces that espouse secularism, humanism, and socialism—hallmarks of political centrism in India.

The discussion that follows examines Namdev's position within the "imagined" nation, highlighting three important interventions. First, Namdev's purported criminal life is marked for attention in scholarly and popular print because his stature as a nationalist hero depends on his moral clarity as a person. The robber story is the thorn in the side of a larger story, that of Namdev's egalitarian, democratic ideal of *bhakti,* which he is remembered as spreading throughout India in the fourteenth century, laying the "seeds," as it were, of a free, and even "secular," Indian nation, for a modern Indian public to come. The second area of study is the way Namdev is positioned in the public sphere, inflected through *bhakti,* which sought to represent Namdev in two ways: as a "humanist" and as belonging to the Marathi-speaking region but integrated into "India" as a whole. He therefore also provided a model for multilingual, multicultural Indian civil society. This assertion is substantiated through literary references and through the *lieux de mémoire,* or sites of memory, following Pierre Nora, presented in chapter 1.[3] The third perspective sees Namdev within a history that takes an unmarked, nonsectarian concept of "religion," what I call "Hindu secularism," as a defining feature of the mode of nationalism that dominated Indian political and public life in the first four decades of Independence. Throughout this chapter recur the themes of Namdev's position as a figure of articulation, in this case within the context of a national imagination, and the ways that Namdev becomes integrated into historiographic systems germane to the imagination of the modern Indian nation.

FROM DASTARDLY DACOIT TO APOSTLE OF NATIONAL INTEGRATION

From the end of the nineteenth century until the present, fifteen major publications have anthologized Namdev's work, and the majority of these chose to include the infamous autobiographical song discussed in chapter 5 that recalls Namdev's robber days. The first compendium of Namdev's songs in Marathi, compiled by R. S. Gondhalekar in 1892, did not contain the robber song.[4] In 1894 the Marathi scholar and public intellectual Tukaram "Tatya" Gharat published an anthology that contained the song but offered no rationale for its inclusion. Shortly thereafter, in 1898, V. L. Bhave, a doyen of Marathi literary studies, published the first edition of his massive *Mahārāṣṭra Sārasvat* in which he reiterated the robber story.[5] T. H.

Avate's *Sakaḷa Santa Gāthā,* considered almost canonical to the Varkari faith, has consistently printed the infamous verse from its first run in 1908 to its most recent reprinting in 1999.[6] Gharat's edition, however, had become a standard for scholarly study until the publication of the Government of Maharashtra's own edition of Namdev's songs in 1970. These two editions—by Avate and by Gharat—bolstered by the pronouncements of figures like Bhave, formed a kind of consensus and might have led scholars such as Macauliffe in 1906 to mention the story in his work, followed by Ajgaonkar in 1927[7] and Ranade in 1933.[8] Indeed, the story of Namdev's bandit days is often repeated by contemporary scholars and is one of the first biographical details presented in the most recent edition of the *Encyclopedia Britannica.*[9] The famous *kirtankar* V. Jog published his anthology *Śrī Nāmdevācā Gāthā* in 1925 at Chitrashala Press in Pune, a publishing house renowned for its "religious" publications, and his edition included the robber song. One other famous edition, especially for use by *kirtankar*s, is the *Nāmdevarāyāmcī Sārtha Gāthā,* edited by Pralhad Subandha in six volumes between 1949 and 1962; this compendium includes the song as well. However, in 1970, when the Government of Maharashtra published its critical edition of Namdev's songs, it refused to include the contentious verse on the grounds that it was spurious, even though it likely was present in many of the notebooks consulted for the project. Why would this story of robbery and murder, reiterated for centuries before and consistently printed in modern anthologies, become the target of revision and rejection primarily in the twentieth century?

In 1927, the Marathi scholar J. R. Ajgaonkar wrote a biography of Namdev in which he asserted that Namdev was a robber in his youth.[10] Within eight years, in 1935, at the height of the Indian nationalist movement, the first substantial book-length refutation of the legend of Namdev's robber days appeared. The book, *Śrī Santa Śiromaṇi Bālbhakta Śrī Nāmdev Mahārāj He Daroḍekhor Hote Kāy?* (Was The Great Principal Child Devotee, The Great Master Namdev, A Roadside Robber?), directly contests the scholarship of Ajgaonkar, as the title amply indicates. The author of the study, P. N. Pataskar, argues that the legend of Namdev's dastardly deeds could not be true, in a way that is much like the argument that Shakespeare, the nondescript son of a glove maker, could not have been the master poet of *Hamlet.* Essentially, the argument is a biographical/psychological one in which Pataskar suggests that a child devotee, who had convinced God himself to drink milk from his hand, could not have later used those hands to murder a Brahmin or steal from the rich. Furthermore, if the stories of Namdev's travels are to be believed, Pataskar asks, how could

Namdev have both robbed and plundered, while still traveling to sacred sites all over India with a heart of love?[11] Pataskar bolsters his biographical argument with letters from experts in Marathi literature concurring with his thesis. Luminaries in the field like S. V. Dandekar, G. V. Tulpule, P. D. Kulkarni (alias Panduranga Sharma), and Shridhar Ketkar rally their support around Pataskar's assertion. Important for our point here, Namdev is portrayed as a vital cultural and national hero throughout this text, though, for obvious reasons in 1935, this latter point about nationalism is muted and sublimated; yet the idea that dominates this compendium is the need to salvage the reputation of a national hero, a sentiment that overrides any appeal to scholarly historical adjudication. The collection also demonstrates a clear self-understanding of the public sphere as a space under the influence of public intellectuals and academics who carefully navigate the straits of objective scholarship and religious or cultural conviction and do so with a particular public in mind, in this case, the coalescing Indian public.[12]

Eight years after Independence, the Namdev robber story again became a bone of contention. Despite Pataskar's polemical work and the support of important scholars, the portrayal of Namdev as a robber persisted in various forms. *Patitapāvan*, a feature film made in 1955 by D. K. Films of Bombay, inspired a second round of public defense from Namdev's followers. The film portrayed Namdev as a robber who converts to Islam, but later returns to Hinduism, but of a *niruni* sort. This biographical invention plays on a common scholarly theory that *nirguna* theology was inspired by, and responded to, the monotheism of Islam, a position often expressed in terms of the fulmination of *nirguna bhakti* in Sikhism, which emerges from the religious pluralism of Islam and Hinduism in northern India in the sixteenth to eighteenth centuries to form a uniquely new religious tradition. In any case, the reasons for these moments of conversion and waywardness are portrayed as essentially economic and political, rather than religious or theological. In the film, Namdev is a victim of being in the wrong place and the wrong time, not a figure possessing "criminal intent."

For almost two years, letters were written back and forth between India's Ministry of Information and Broadcasting censor boards and various organizations and individuals representing the Maharashtrian Namdev tradition in the state of Bombay (collectively termed the "Nāmdev Samāj" or "Namdev Community"), including groups like the Namdeo Sneh-Sanvardhak Mandal (Namdev Association for the Fostering of Friendship) in Pune, the Namdeo Shikshan Sahayyak Sahakari Mandal (Namdev Organization for Cooperative Educational Collaboration) in Bombay, and the newly formed

Patitapavan Nishedha Samiti (Committee for the Prohibition of [the film] *Patitapavan*) in Bombay. The outcry came almost exclusively from Maharashtrian followers of Namdev, in the form of editorials in Marathi-language papers, and magazines and essays in scholarly and popular journals. At first the Board of Censors asserted that the film's producers had provided ample historical evidence that Namdev had indeed been a robber, a fact verified by the many biographies of Namdev, the scholars who cited this story in their work, and supposedly by Namdev himself in the autobiographical song attributed to him (discussed in chapter 5). Curiously, relatively few premodern sources, and almost none outside Marathi, suggest Namdev was a robber, though the modern sources are clear on the subject. The Board of Censors may have simply relied on "common knowledge" and popular stories, which were themselves often replicated in scholarly work. However, in May 1956, at the request of the legislators of both houses of the state of Bombay, the makers of *Patitapāvan* lost their license to exhibit the film in the state until they removed all depictions that were offensive to followers of Namdev. Rather than reshoot or edit the film, the producers simply took *Patitapāvan* out of circulation and considered the matter closed. Importantly, the legislature cites its reason for taking this action as based on the idea that the film defiled the memory of a hero of the Indian nation.[13]

This particular battle over Namdev's historical legacy, fought as it was primarily in the Marathi public sphere, and in opposition to a Hindi film, should be seen in the context of the political climate of the region in the 1950s. As early as the mid-1930s, as the British Raj began to foresee its full disintegration in India, Marathi speakers in what was the multilingual Bombay Presidency were calling for a sovereign political and monolingual region to be called Maharashtra. In less than a decade after Independence, when the Bombay Presidency became Bombay State, comprised primarily of Marathi- and Gujarati-speaking regions cobbled from the northern areas of the former Deccan Sultanates, a movement began to form around the idea of a separate Marathi-speaking state, containing Bombay, a call for statehood in line with the state's Reorganization Act of 1956. Proposals for a Gujarati-speaking state, to be called Gujarat, also demanded to include the city of Bombay. In 1956, the Samyukta Maharashtra Samiti, the "United Maharashtra Committee" began political agitations for the formation of Maharashtra and the inclusion of Bombay in the new state's domain. On May 1, 1960, the movement saw its demands fully realized.[14]

In this climate, which began in the preindependence period as a "literary" movement in the name of Marathi, political, economic, and social battles were waged in the name of language. In the Samyukta Maharashtra

Movement lie the seeds of regional politics in Maharashtra, especially in the growth of the Communist Party and of the Shiv Sena and the consolidation of the Congress Party's Maratha/Kunbi caste base—three adversaries who still define Maharashtrian politics to this day. The battle over the exhibition of *Patitapāvan* serves as one of many preludes to the full-fledged struggle for the Marathi linguistic identity of Maharashtra, an identity tied closely to the remembrance of famous figures of Maharashtrian religion, literature, history, and politics. The Maharashtra state education minister, M. D. Chaudhari, made this clear in 1970 when he wrote in the preface to the Maharashtra government's critical edition of Namdev's songs that "Wherever the songs of the *sant*s has not entered, that place is not a Maharashtrian home."[15] The minister's statement expresses the culmination of the language-state struggles of the 1950s that resulted in the reorganization of states and the creation of Maharashtra.

Thus the environment of protest against the film in 1955–56 was one of a brew of simmering linguistic regionalism that would naturally boil over in reaction to a non-Marathi film portraying a "Marathi" *sant* in what was perceived to be a negative and degrading way. Furthermore, the effort to tarnish the legend of Namdev by painting him as a robber in this film or other media is not simply in defense of a Marathi literary figure of great repute but also reflects the conscientious positioning of him within the broad expanse of the "heroes" of the Indian nation, each exhibiting a regional contribution to a national cause. In this way, the projected incorporation of a Marathi-speaking state, purified of non-Marathi influences, can also be read into the Indian nation, just as a Maharashtrian *sant*, his hagiography purified of taint, is integrated into India's nationalist protohistory.

Despite the best efforts of those who opposed the veracity of the robber story, another incident seemed inevitable. After what had, by the mid-1960s, become a veritable campaign to eliminate this aspect of Namdev's legacy from religion, art, and history texts, a challenge arose yet again in 1966 during a program on All India Radio (AIR) on the occasion of Tukaram Beej, a holiday celebrating the Maharashtrian *sant* Tukaram held in March. As in the case of *Patitapāvan*, the narrator of the AIR program, Vasant Bapat, described Namdev as a "plunderer" and "dacoit." Under the leadership of R. M. Bongale, the Namdeo Samajonnati Parishad (Society for the Advancement of the Namdev Community) raised a protest against the AIR script used in the Tukaram Beej broadcast. In an exchange of letters sometimes absurd in its portrayal of government bureaucracy, AIR argued that characterizing Namdev as a dacoit, like the characterization of

Valmiki, was a compliment: it glorified the *sant*'s ability to repent and overcome his vices. Thus the broadcast was not intended to be insulting; rather, it should have been taken as flattery of Namdev, so argued AIR. Bongale responded that the issue was not one of flattery or insult, simply historical inaccuracy, and the supposedly "long-standing" legend of Namdev as a dacoit was a recent development by scholars conducting faulty research and thus the story was false. Bongale sent post-haste a copy of Pataskar's 1935 treatise on the subject so as to "enlighten" the staff of AIR. They replied with the same statement, that it was flattery not offense that they intended, hence the "robber" reference would remain in the script. After five such exchanges, the matter was left unresolved, but Vasant Bapat's program was not broadcast again on AIR nor was I able to trace any copy of it in any archive.[16]

In an attempt to forever disprove the story of Namdev's criminal days, many Maharashtrian followers and admirers of Namdev came together to produce another collection of essay and letters in the hope that the question of Namdev's criminal past would finally be put to rest. The need to quell any further iterations of the robber story seemed all the more acute following regional and national celebrations of the seven hundredth anniversary of Namdev's birth in 1970. In 1980, several prominent Marathi scholars—G. V. Kavitkar, R. M. Bongale, R. C. Dhere, A. Kamat, and V. M. Bachal—edited a volume of essays intended to debunk the persistent legend of Namdev as a robber. The collection opens with a portion of Pataskar's first salvo from his 1935 book written in response to Ajgaonkar's 1927 biography of Namdev. Almost twenty other essays appear in the work, all arguing various facets of the defense of Namdev's character. An appendix provides letters from devotees and scholars to government and other officials written to protest various public depictions of Namdev as a former robber, especially the film of 1955. They also opposed the inclusion of Namdev's robber days in *Sāhitya Prabhā*, a government-issued ninth-grade history textbook in Marathi. The reference was eventually deleted.

Among the scholars who contributed to this volume, most had written other works that argued for Namdev's presence in the pantheon of nationalist heroes, perhaps just as Namdev had been written into the pantheon of *sant* heroes in western, central, and northern hagiography in preceding centuries. Ashok Kamat, who currently holds the chair of Namdev studies at Pune University, is a premier scholar of Namdev in Marathi and Hindi. He is especially important in portraying Namdev as integral to the history of the Indian nation. *Ek Vijay Yātrā*, or "A Victorious Journey," which he wrote with R. C. Dhere and published in 1970, eloquently constructs a narrative plot that centers on the metaphor of Namdev's journey throughout India with a scholarly retelling of that journey as it is popularly received, while simultaneously treating Namdev's songs and his interrelationships with other religious traditions. As Kamat and Dhere state in their introduction, "After seven hundred years, the imprint of Namdev's pervasiveness among the people of India is immeasurable."[17] The text serves to intertwine Namdev with the popular religious culture of central, western, and northern India.

The edited volume by Kavitkar et al. that seeks to fully discredit the robber story reveals a self-conscious management of Namdev's identity in print, self-conscious in its understanding that belief and the science of historiography meet in debunking the dacoit myth of Namdev, just as they meet to establish the protohistory of the Indian nation through his legacy. Many of the essays in the volume state implicitly and explicitly that an early figure of Indian nationalism could not also have been a robber and a murderer. Such a statement represents an illogical, ethical contradiction, they argue, taking recourse to higher criticism, adjudicating text based on authorship and historicity. But the overall impetus of the text is to align Namdev's biographical and discursive production with the idea that he articulated at least one vision of a unified land. Through their essays and correspondence reproduced by Kavitkar et al., scholars respected in their fields of literary studies, history, and social science led the protest against public depictions of Namdev as a robber.[18] This concerted reaction cannot be characterized as merely the project of devotees or members of Namdev's caste community, though certainly people with these identities or affiliations comprised the members of the campaign against the story. Rather than framing it simply as an insult to a public ethnic memory felt by members of Namdev's general community, scholars raised the protest to the plane of public intellectual debate, a reaction sadly absent from more recent debates about famous figures of history in Maharashtra.[19]

Throughout November 1970, various programs were held to honor Namdev, all featuring a mix of political figures, government officials, and religious leaders—and each assembly began and concluded with a rendition of the Indian national anthem. The attendees included the then-president of India, V. V. Giri; the finance minister; and the chief ministers of Maharashtra and Rajasthan.[20] Several souvenir volumes contained letters of praise for Namdev as a figure of the nation from lofty government officials, including Prime Minister Indira Gandhi, who wrote a letter containing the panegyric that opens this chapter.[21] The committee established in New Delhi to oversee celebrations was composed of members of both Sikh and Varkari communities, from Maharashtra, Rajasthan, Uttar Pradesh, and Punjab. Jagan Nath, of the Namdev Mission Trust in New Delhi, produced a retrospective of those celebrations and others that followed in 1975, 1978, and 1980, along with a collection of letters of praise and special interest stories under the title *Namdev: The Saint-Poet*.[22] In an interesting remark in connection with a fund-raising drive to build a new center for the Namdev Bhavan in Delhi, Jagan Nath writes, "Happily, the followers of Sant Namdev are spread all over the world and some of them are affluent."[23] This is the first reference to Namdev in the context of "economic globalization" that I have encountered. In any case, this and the many other souvenir volumes that record copious correspondence from Indian political leaders all speak of Namdev's profile as an early nationalist figure in the Hindu secularist, that is, post-Nehruvian centrist mode.

In 1991, Ajay Phutane produced the film *Sant Nāmdev*, the most recent of three films about Namdev made in the past fifty years. This film is half in Marathi and half in Hindi. The first portion of the film describes Namdev's early life in the Maharashtrian Deccan and draws from his Marathi hagiography; this portion is in Marathi. When the plot shifts to Namdev's days as a traveler and Maharashtrian expatriate in Rajasthan, north-central India, and Punjab, the language changes to Hindi. The film was created in conjunction with a larger social network forged among those who revere Namdev in Punjab, Uttar Pradesh, and Maharashtra, and the language usage clearly reveals this regional mix. Not only does the film harmonize Namdev's pan-Indian hagiography and the sometimes-conflicting details of his life in these different areas, but it also serves to exhibit the cross-cultural and cross-religious appeal of Namdev followers, which is at the root of Namdev's inclusion in the history of the modern Indian nation. In this film, Namdev is abducted by thieves, but refuses to participate in their marauding. Instead, he sings his *kirtan*s and eventually converts half the group to the worship of Vitthal. The other half, all incorrigible criminals, are eventually hunted down by the local ruler and taken away. This film is examined in detail in chapter 7.

In 1998, Sridhar Ranganath Kulkarni of Hyderabad wrote *Sāhitya Setu* (A Bridge of Literature), suggesting that Namdev figured in the genesis of Hindi and the spread of *nirguni* devotionalism in northern India, providing some of the first religious utterances that would later form Sikhism, an argument made well before by Kamat and others. Kulkarni asserts that Namdev understood the potential for wide social currency in Hindi as a national language almost six hundred years before the idea become law, and—by most accounts—well before the idea of an Indian nation was on anyone's mind.[24] Certainly Namdev makes regular appearances in the public sphere of Hindi in the twentieth century. Namdev surfaces in the work of Ramchandra Shukla, Shyamsunder Das, Ramkumar Verma, Parashuram Caturvedi, V. Mohan Sharma, Balwant Rai, Bhagirath Mishra, Rajnarain Maurya, Hazariprasad Dwivedi, and many others. In Marathi and English, Namdev is traced in the work of V. K. Rajwade, S. V. Dandekar, R. D. Ranade, R. G. Bhandarkar, R. C. Dhere, and S. G. Tulpule. Kulkarni's thesis rests in part on Namdev's pervasive presence in the public spheres of Hindi and Marathi, not just in scholarly works but in theatrical performances, radio broadcasts, popular publications, films, and, of course, in the *kirtan* performances and other media for the songs of the centuries of *sant*s that remember Namdev.

Yet this agenda of integration, as seen in the struggle over Namdev's twentieth-century identity, is based not on a wholesale appropriation of Namdev by a general nationalist discourse but, rather, a careful control of Namdev's historical profile by various parties. In the service of a pan-Indian nationalist sentiment, Namdev's status as a former robber plays into the recuperative promise of a secular, humanistic nation, protecting and stewarding the culturally upward swing of its "less fortunate" others. But from the point of view of Namdev's direct followers, such a recuperation of their figure may translate into a cultural position of inferiority. This situation is similar to the struggle of some scholars of Kabir to reformulate the *sant*'s history in a subaltern mold, devoid of affiliation with *vaishnava* sectarian figures such as Ramanand.[25]

Kulkarni's work anticipated the nationwide commemoration of the 650th anniversary of Namdev's death or Samadhi Anniversary in 2000, when the *sant* was invoked in pamphlets, lectures, and publications as a figure of national integration. At a conference on Namdev in Pune in July, almost half the papers presented were directly or indirectly about Namdev and the nation. All India Radio invited N. N. Relekar—a prominent authority on, and devotee of, Namdev, as well as someone who traces his genealogy to Namdev—to compose the script of a multipart program on Namdev's songs and legacy, thus obviating the kinds of protest incited in earlier decades.[26]

Over the past eighty years, those who preserve Namdev's legacy have struggled in the public sphere with these twin representations—Namdev as a nationalist figure and Namdev as a robber. To observe this struggle is to see how various sources, often coded as "religious," such as hagiographies, are used in writing modern public history drawn from a larger and older store of public memory, itself a kind of cultural historiography where the past and present, the here and the away, meet in a single discursive space.[27] It is also to witness a deep interlacing of religious and ethnic identity mapped onto the cultural and linguistic geography of India. Juggling regional and pan-Indian identities is one of the definitive features of Indian nationalist historiography. Far from posing a challenge to national integration, the presence and participation of figures rooted firmly in regional terrain (and linguistic spheres) became the building blocks of Indian nationalist sentiment well into the 1980s. Making no claim to hegemony, the dominant voice of Indian nationalism has always pronounced a narrative of regional hybridity. Namdev represents an ideal locus for explicating this hybridity because of the agreements struck among various regional systems of remembrance that invoke Namdev and that allow their native legends to flourish while also articulating those narratives with the pan-Indian vision of Namdev as an "apostle of national integration."

NAMDEV AND THE OLD MAP
OF THE NEW INDIAN NATION

In 1964 the government of India commissioned a series of lectures on issues of national cultural cohesion, which were later aired on AIR and published by the Ministry of Information and Broadcasting. These lectures commemorated the legacy of Sardar Vallabhbhai Patel (1875–1950), a freedom fighter, nationalist leader, and chief architect of India's postindependence integration of princely states into the new state union of India. One of those published lectures, delivered by V. Raghavan, a professor of Sanskrit at the University of Madras, concerned a pan-Indian hagiography that reflected the activities of "great integrators" among the "saint-singers of India."[28] Namdev appears in Raghavan's roster of integrators, which includes Tukaram, Ramdas, and Jnandev from Maharashtra, and other *sants* and holy figures drawn from the entirety of regions of the modern Indian state.[29] Namdev's position as a cosmopolitan Maharashtrian person in the national imagination is due to several facets of his legacy, but of all these aspects, the core explanation for his inclusion in a nationalist discourse on integration must rest on the legend of his travels, which is also the root of his position as an "integrator" of literary-devotionalism in central, western, and northern India over the past seven centuries. The story of Namdev's travels throughout India is preserved and maintained in a variety of creative works.

As noted in chapter 1, the *Tīrthāvaḷī* narratives, whether the biographical version or the autobiographical one, are not about integration at all. The biographical version is primarily a story of Namdev suffering the arrogance of Brahmins in Pandharpur, where Vitthal comes to his aid. In many ways it appears to be an anti-Brahmin treatise. Whatever travel is narrated in this version finds its completion within the first third of the story and takes the protagonists (Namdev and Jnandev) no further than Dwarka before they return to Pandharpur. In all, the biographical *Tīrthāvaḷī* is a cautionary tale *against* pilgrimage to any place other than Pandharpur and, as such, is difficult to read as a story that presents a "united" India in any fashion.

The autobiographical version, much less commonly known, impresses the reader with a narrator far from home, suffering separation from his deity in Pandharpur, and bewildered by the differences that he observes in other pilgrimage places. In this version Namdev does literally chart out the contours of the modern Indian nation, going no farther to the northwest than Rajasthan and no farther east than Puri, while voyaging from as far north as the Tibetan plateau and to the southernmost town of Kanyakumari. Furthermore, his travels do enact a *pradakṣiṇā* of the "heart" of India, that is, Namdev ventures in a counterclockwise fashion consistent with ritual practice at temples and other holy sites, and this pattern has been read by some scholars and popular writers as a prognostic benediction of the Indian nation. Writing the preface for the Maharashtra publication of the *Śrī Nāmdev Gāthā* in 1970, Minister of Education M. D. Chaudhari asserted that Namdev had circumscribed the territory of "the heart of India" (*āntara bhāratī*) through his travels.[30] One Maharashtrian yogi and *kirtankar,* K. G. Wankhade, embarked on a journey to retrace Namdev's footsteps throughout India, performing *kirtan*s along the way, as a living symbol of Namdev's nationalist proclivities.

Yet the instantiation of the "truth" of this story is not invested in the *Tīrthāvaḷī*. Instead, what gives credence to this idea of Namdev's ability to integrate the Indian nation is the distribution of his legend throughout the field of Hindu hagiography in central, western, and northern India; the inclusion of his songs in various regional literatures; and the physical presence of sites of remembrance, Pierre Nora's *lieux de mémoire,* throughout India. These features of public memory make up the historiographic cairns of Namdev's legacy in modern India.

Namdev's ubiquity in central, western, and northern India is evident in a network of memorials (*smritisthala*) and shrines (*mandir*) throughout these regions. Memorials and shrines to Namdev exist in most major cities in Maharashtra—Solapur, Kolhapur, Pune, Bombay, Nagpur, and Nasik, for instance—and in numerous smaller towns, like Alandi, Dehu, Narsi Bahmani, Aundhya Naganath, and, of course, Pandharpur.[31] Punjab is perhaps second in hosting sites of Namdev's remembrance, with *gurudvār*s dedicated to Namdev throughout the region, in cities such as Amritsar, Bassi Pathana, Gurdaspur, Marad, Bhattival, Duniyapur, and especially Ghuman.[32] In Himachal Pradesh, Namdev shrines can be found at Manjara and Sunvali.[33] In Rajasthan are shrines in various places including Pushkar, Ajmer, Jaipur (home to three shrines), Gangapur, Kota, Dholpur, Khilchipur, Sitamandi, Narasimhagad, and Khanpur.[34] In Uttar Pradesh, five are within the vicinity of Haridwar alone, including a "monastery" (*maṭh*), and another six elsewhere in the state.[35] Madhya Pradesh and Haryana have three more memorials to the *sant*.[36] The age of these various shrines spans the sixteenth century to the early twentieth century, suggesting a sustained, variegated physical remembrance.

Along with these shrines, many cities are home to organizations devoted to Namdev's legacy. In Delhi, there is the Namdev Mission Trust on Lodhi Road, and the Namdev Bhavan nearby. In Pune are Namdev Ram Mandir in the cantonment area, which is also home to the Shri Namdeo Snehsamvardhak Mandal, and at least two Namdev *mandir*s in the Old City. At the University of Pune, there is a Namdev Studies Department, adjacent to the Marathi Studies Department. In Bombay are the Namdeo Shikshan Sahayyak Sahakari Mandal near Shivaji Park and the Patitapavan Nishedha Committee, also called "Patitapāvan"—an organization formed to oppose the 1955 film about Namdev's life, as mentioned above. Also in Bombay, there is the Namdeo Samajonnati Parishad, organized in 1967, in response to the other "misrepresentation" of Namdev in the AIR broadcast in commemoration of Tukaram's birthday. These organizations appear not to have expired with the end of their campaigns, as if to guard against future perceived disparagements. In Pandharpur, of course, is the Namdev Mandir within feet of the Vitthal temple; the two comprise the spiritual and social center of the Namdev community in Maharashtra.

Pierre Nora, with characteristic French concision, notes that "memory attaches itself to sites, whereas history attaches itself to events."[37] Nora's point here is one of distance: when the location of a thing is transformed into an objectified narrative of its "event," then memory has become history. Nora sees "cemeteries, museums, and anniversaries" as sites of memory and notes "topographical" examples, "which owe everything to the specificity of their location and to being rooted in the ground."[38] Although Nora's concern is with the creation of a hegemonic modern history of the

French nation, at the expense of what he sees as a sacred, memory-centered counterhistory that has been overrun in modern France, his idea is that such sites that were once "proof" in a historical sense have now become "memory" in a modern sense, an archive for the past that has "little or no historical capital."[39] Nora's romantic views of "peasant culture" notwithstanding, he does observe interestingly that these "sites of memory" provide a kind of historiography in everyday life, a text written in places and objects that bypass the gaze of professional historians. Nora invokes memory as the "secret of so-called primitive or archaic societies" that are reminiscent of Partha Chatterjee's idea of the "secret history" of the Indian nation, secret, perhaps, from elite historians, but available to be read in certain sites associated with the experience of subalterns, in the space of gender and especially religion.[40]

The map of the future Indian nation drawn by Namdev's travels and maintained by text and memorial site works as a kind of physical nationalist history. This process is not, however, modern. As seen throughout this book, when Namdev appears outside Maharashtra, he is summed up as an articulative figure connecting languages, religions, and times. Here, as in chapter 5, Namdev becomes a device of history, but in this case, those who see him as such—historians, intellectuals, devotees, and scholars with nationalist proclivities—require he be rigorously historical while also maintaining a metaphorical use. I posited that one cannot have both a historical Namdev and Namdev as a device of history, but I have made this assertion in the context of premodern historical memory. However, in the context of modern historiography and the nation-concept, which is so reliant on modern historiography, the two divergent ideals—Namdev as historical figure and Namdev as device of history—instead must be held together. This is clearly shown in the efforts to divest Namdev's Maharashtrian legacy of the perceived taint of criminality, an appeal made to the adjudication of history explicitly and implicitly to the need for a nationalist figure. The narrative of Namdev's travels, while they pose significant problems to the modern historian, nonetheless acquire the sanction of history, "proven" by the ubiquity of Namdev's public memory, in song and in hagiography, throughout central, western, and northern India. The appeal, then, is made not to the truth of Namdev's journey, but to the fact of its historical record. Regardless of whether Namdev traveled in the places the autobiographical *Tīrthāvaḷī* of 1581 recalls or whether one Namdev or many comprise the composite "Namdev" of the field of *bhakti* hagiography, the textual, memorial, and performative traces of this figure are what constitute his position as a "national integrator." It is, in some sense, a historiographic argument, not a historical one. It is an argument based on the very fact that evidence remains, not on the final adjudication of that evidence. This marks the difference between a religious belief in the protohistory of the Indian nation as outlined by Namdev's travels and the secular assertion that Namdev, as a device of history, causes a linguistic and geographical diversity to cohere into a modern nation. A religious appeal would assert a belief in the historical truth of Namdev *a priori*. But a Hindu secularist, centrist-nationalist view would require only the trace of the possibly historical figure. These things are deeply invested with historicity: they are the archives of historians, they are historically defensible. This is how Namdev, a feature of religious traditions and religious biography, can become a figure integrated into a self-consciously secular project, the building of the modern Indian national historical character in the second half of the twentieth century. The point of mediation at this nexus of religion and secular history is the way Namdev becomes a figure of humanism.

POSTCOLONIAL NATIONS AND RELIGIONS

Amid numerous celebrations and symposia held across the country in 1970, a number of publications heralded Namdev's importance in the history of the Indian nation, phrased in vaguely religious terms. The Maharashtra Information Center and the Government Central Press of Maharashtra produced a short essay in English on Namdev by the Marathi scholar M. A. Karandikar.[41] The preface to the essay sums up the contents of its thirty pages:

> National integration is the need of the hour and Saint Namdev by virtue
> of his crossing the linguistic and geographical barriers to enlighten the
> people in areas far away from Maharashtra can truly be called Apostle of
> National Integration.[42]

Intertwined in this simple description is a unified idea of religion, secularism, and nationalism that came to characterize the post-Nehruvian period of Congress rule at the center and in many states. This policy of social governance can be described as Hindu secularism, a perspective that appears similar to the secularism of the United States, which remains deeply characterized by Christianity, heard in common mottos such as "One Nation Under God" and "In God We Trust," yet set at a safe distance from actual Christian practice—the latter would be characterized as "the Religious

Right" or Christian fundamentalism. In Karandikar's text, interestingly, terms reference Christianity, such as "saint" and "apostle," yet these religious appellations are gained through "national integration" across boundaries of language and geography, the secular map of a nation. This statement was made almost two decades before the full rise of the Hindu Right in Indian national politics, when political discourse indulging in religious metaphors was replaced by the explicit use of religion, particularly Hinduism, in the public and political spheres of India in ways far removed from the impulse of "national integration."

Namdev's influence on the trajectory of the Indian nation certainly might appear as a form of "religious nationalism." However, the kind of religious nationalism associated with Namdev is not that of the so-called Hindu Right, as pointed out above. Instead, Namdev's legacy constitutes one of many "secret histories" of the Indian nation embedded in a field often identified by Western scholars and others as "spiritual" or "religious," but by reference to sentiment rather than doctrinal content. In this case, Namdev's religious contribution to the nation suggests one of the key features of Hindu secularism in general, a reference to the ethics of humanism, a notion in Western history that has its own long and complicated relationship to Christian religious thought.

Several key elements of Namdev's hagiography appear to have become seamlessly enmeshed in the eighteenth century and carried into the twentieth century. What is worthy of preservation from this earlier hagiographical tradition is the general character of Namdev as a figure who represents the downtrodden, helpless, landless, and powerless—a position designated in contemporary scholarship as "subaltern." Yet this designation in the Marathi public sphere, when associated with *bhakti* figures, is also conditioned by a sense that humanism (*manavatavada*) is the purview of the subaltern, not the elite; to be a humanist, in this sense, is to suffer the pains of human life without the mediation or comforts afforded by wealth and power.

Namdev's *manavatavada* is expressed in two ways: through the ascription to him of a sentiment that opposes caste, class, or gender discrimination; and through a motif, which borrows in part from Kabir because it is in some ways difficult to detect in songs and biographies associated with Namdev, that is, that Namdev assuaged the rivalries of Hindus and Muslims. In a volume of essays published in 1970 by the government of Maharashtra and intended as a companion to the edition of Namdev's songs that it had commissioned, Dhananjay Kir writes of the "Humanist Namdev" that his travels throughout India served to "spread the light of wisdom," a reference to an oft-quoted verse attributed to Namdev in which he proclaims "let's dance with passion in the *kirtan*, and spread the light of wisdom in the world."[43] Kir cites Marathi and Hindi songs that reiterate Namdev's lowly status; his opposition to Brahminical orthodoxy and orthopraxis; his rejection of caste and class; and his inclusive social politics. Namdev is quoted in Hindi, "My caste is low and debased, Lord of Pandhari. Why did you make Nama the tailor this way?"[44] A Marathi verse, in manuscripts from the eighteenth century, reads, "These [Hindu] Gods, they are broken by the Turks, drowned in water [by Hindus], yet they never utter a single complaint."[45] Although this song, also present in the Marathi corpus, is clearly of the *nirguni* variety, it is often used to express Namdev's "balanced" assessment of orthodox religious culture, where he is neither dogmatically Hindu nor sympathetic to dogmatic Islam.[46] Similarly, Kamat and Dhere quote a Hindi song attributed to Namdev: "Hindus worship in the temple and Muslims in the mosque. Namdev happily serves the lord, neither in the temple nor in the mosque."[47] The demonstration of Namdev's "nondenominational" position, entwined with the biographical persona of Kabir, is implied by the authors in another quotation: "Hindus are blind and Turks can't see straight. A smart man is better than both."[48] Namdev here is carefully construed as someone who worships humanity and does so in ways that circumvent sectarian rivalries. But songs such as these are very few and far between in either Namdev's Marathi or Hindi corpus; the presence of Islam does not form a major theme in Namdev's received corpus of songs in Marathi or Hindi. Indeed, if materials regarding Namdev's confrontation with a sultan, discussed in chapter 5, are considered, it would be easy to suggest that Namdev's legacy is of Hindu-Muslim animosity, not détente. But this, of course, would be to read monolithic messages into the specifics of the stories, that is, to misread those stories and songs as participating in a world more of the device of the "clash of civilizations" or Orientalism than of the worlds in which these various narratives were constructed as contextualized here. Yet this did not prevent Hindu secularism from permeating Namdev's nationalist historiography or selecting those few, albeit evocative, lines from the vast body of Namdev's pan-Indian literary corpus that addressed Hindu-Muslim unity, one of the key issues of Indian nationalist humanism.

In the copious collection of essays edited by N. N. Relekar, H V. Inamdar, and N D. Mirajkar, called *Śrī Nāmdev Darśan*, D. K. Sant wrote an essay on "Namdev's Humanism."[49] Sant attributes to Namdev a sentiment of temporality or worldliness (*aihikatā*) that participated in the development of a sense of the historical (*aitihāsik*) in India. The author insists that Namdev helped Maharashtra become part of the nation of India by balancing cosmopolitism and regionalism in his own biography and corpus of verses, a balance made with the assistance of a historical impulse. Sant also draws a striking analogy when he asserts that Namdev was the Erasmus of Maharashtra, thus making the connection with humanism unmistakable.[50] Yet what sort of *manavatavada* did Namdev espouse? One that sometimes rejected orthodox Muslim and Hindu practice, perhaps, but one surely invested with religious language and actions well within the ken of Hinduism. What kind of nation is imagined through the eyes of Namdev?

The nation is often configured as a byproduct of modernism, as Ernest Gellner and Benedict Anderson contend was the case in Europe and elsewhere,[51] or a modular epistemology brought to colonial societies, as Anderson, Partha Chatterjee, and others suggest.[52] Rarely, however, do Western scholars situate the nation outside modernity, and with good reason. Hobsbawm, among many others, has argued that the idea of the nation is a specifically modern Euro-American one that has been adapted, by hook or crook, to the rest of the world's nations, most of which are former colonies of a European power.[53] India shows the strong presence of the British—both directly through British colonial officials and through the Western education of India's premier nationalists—in the mechanics of the construction and division of South Asia into modern nations. Also heard is the language of modern nationalism, secularism, humanism, capitalism, and democracy. Attempts have been made to bypass the dominance of colonial historiography in Indian nationalist histories, but these investigations tend to rely on modernist categories of historical periods, such as golden ages, feudal ages, and medieval and dark ages, or, as in the case of postcolonial studies, to take colonial India, the rise of capitalism, and British history as the central lens of analysis. Moreover, India demonstrates a strong reliance on modern concepts of governance that draw on democratic sentiment, liberty, the rights of individuals, or Marxist class consciousness. Nehru, for example, in *The Discovery of India*, regards Ashoka (third century B.C.E.) and Akbar (sixteenth century) as progenitors of Golden Ages and forefathers of the secular nation.[54] A second example is Radhakumud Mookerji, who, writing at the beginning of the twentieth century, created a popular history of the Indian nation from the myths and stories commonly labeled religious.[55]

Current political organizations of the so-called Hindu Right promote histories that undercut the influence of colonialism and recall examples of a (often ironically) tolerant universalist Hinduism easing the conflicts of language, religion, and ethnicity in a precolonial era, such as the Gupta period of the fifth and sixth centuries. Although Namdev might seem a likely hero for Hindutva, he never appears in the rhetoric of the Hindu Right. In response to various "Indian" histories of the nation, Western scholars writing in English have regularly countered this apparent "neo-Hinduism" as a nationalist construction. Wilhelm Halbfass, for example, wrote of nineteenth-century "nationalist" figures like Bankim Candra Chatterjee (1838–94) and Rammohan Roy (1774–1833) that:

> [T]hey could not have been Neo-Hindu [nationalists] in the complete sense of the term because the nationalism which Europe was bringing to India had not yet attained its full bloom in their day; Neo-Hindu nationalism in turn is inseparable from modernization and Westernization.[56]

Although Halbfass does not bring this out, Roy is particularly interesting because he seemed to believe that the British and their packaged modernity were as essential to India as the development of a kind of native nonmodern history of the nation. Roy saw the need to implement modern nationalism modeled on the West, while accounting for its history with the indigenous materials of the Indian past independent of colonialism.

Nicholas Dirks has suggested that history is a sign of the modern and, furthermore, that we can see the link between history and the nation as equally evocative of modernity.[57] Indeed, conceptions of nation and history have come in the larger parcel of modernity in Europe, but here a second equation could be added to the parsimonious one given by Dirks: namely, that religion is also a sign of the modern. Where nations and history are found, so is religion in its particular modern form, buttresses and defined with reference to secular or nonsecular states; and the same Enlightenment epistemologies that gave rise to the stalwart ideas of modernity—history, nation, science, Man, etc.—have also provided "religion" as a category distinct from "secular" or "scientific," for example. Talal Asad has essentially made this point in his work *Genealogies of Religion:*

> Historians of seventeenth- and eighteenth-century Europe have begun to recount how the constitution of the modern state required the forcible redefinition of religion as belief, and of religious belief, sentiment, and identity as personal matters that belong to the newly emerging space of private (as opposed to public) life.[58]

Concepts of the nation, history, and religion wrap themselves together in the fabric of modernity in Europe and North America. The political historian Carlton Hayes, after living through two world wars, expressed the idea that nationalism itself was a religion, replete with "interior devotion," "worship," "belief," the icon of the flag, "universal liturgical forms," "pilgrimages and processions," and "temples" and other sacred structures.[59] He concluded:

> Moderns may regard their medieval ancestors' veneration of images, icons, and relics as savoring of "superstition," but let them replace, say, a statue of St. Joseph with a graven image of Abraham Lincoln, an icon of the Blessed Virgin with a lithograph of Martha Washington or of the somewhat mythical Molly Pitcher, and a relic of the Holy Cross with a tattered battle flag, and they display a fitting reverence.[60]

Does the Namdev tradition represent an alternative history of the nation outside the scope of modernity, one that invests a national teleology with the "spirit," perhaps in a Hegelian sense, of a religious impetus driving toward "freedom," toward the modern secular democratic nation-state? As seen with Kabir in the Hindi public sphere, as well as other figures of a culture often expressed in the language of religious sentiment, Namdev is used to articulate a diverse national history, a religious character who is made to bolster a secular worldview, but one that appears to embrace the "religion of man," a form of humanism, here called Hindu secularism in one of its uniquely Indian forms.

Namdev's pan-Indian legacy appears alongside the stream of theorizing about the nation and the development of nationalism, running downstream in support of some theories and upstream counter to others. In Anderson's formulation of the nation as a delimited and imagined community, Namdev's perambulations are portrayed as a boundary; the areas through which he is said to have traveled thus circumscribe the boundaries of the modern Indian nation—drawing, his followers believe, a map of the India to come.[61] Pierre Bourdieu presents an interesting metaphor for culture in *Outline of a Theory of Practice* that seems harmonious to this old map of the new Indian nation traced presciently by Namdev centuries earlier:

> It is significant that "culture" is sometimes described as a *map*; it is the analogy which occurs to an outsider who has to find his way around in a

foreign landscape and who compensates for his lack of practical mastery, the prerogative of the native, by the use of a model of all possible routes.[62]

In Bourdieu's assessment, a text, the map, exists between the "outsider" and "insider," that is, between the traveler and the residents of the land; what is more, the map is a cooperative creation though, naturally, the balance of power in the creation of real maps was not always equal. Namdev, in his pan-Indian legacy, is both native and outsider, he is both one who employs the map as a figure with a regional designation within the ambit of "Marathi," but also someone who becomes a key to the map, if the geography of devotionalism or the discourse of the Indian nation is viewed in the context of public culture. Invoked in the first half-century following Indian independence, Namdev serves to help plot the route of the new Indian nation set against ancient, and even sacred, terrain.

In contradistinction to Anderson's ideas about the imagined nation, I do not see Namdev's legacy in regard to the nation as having been predicated on undoing the literary hegemony of a universal sacred language.[63] Instead I see a cosmopolitan, universalizing language formed from the symbols of a shared hagiographical tradition that constitute a common historiographic vocabulary. However, at one and the same time a restatement of Namdev's regional significance is expressed through his legendary travels and through his printed anthologies. This is vital to his function as a nationalist figure: like the Indian nation, his pan-Indian biography seems composed of distinct regions—Maharashtra, Rajasthan, and Punjab, for instance—that are brought together to help form a unitary perspective—the *sant* or northern *bhakti* tradition, writ large.

In *Nations and Nationalism*, Ernest Gellner, writing as the "most radical of the modernists" as one critic put it,[64] effectively rejected any premodern antecedent to the nation; that is, he argued that the nation and modernity are synchronic.[65] However, Gellner did assert that nationalism and its narratives should endeavor to see that ethnicities do not compete with polities, a principle institutionalized in India's constitution, where states are proscribed from being formed along ethnic lines but can be created along linguistic ones (among other criteria), though, of course, language is regularly invoked as a sign of an ethnos.[66] This constitutional provision imposes an artificial division that does not accord with Anderson's theory of an imagined community; here, the structure of the Indian federal polity restricts the imagination, as it were, with respect to ethnicity or religion. However, Namdev is a figure of productive and positive ethnic—and linguistic—interaction, an agent of the imagination of a community, to be sure. He functions to integrate various possible national imaginaries.

Eric Hobsbawm famously characterized nationalism and its narratives as the "civic religion" of modernity, arguing that the nation is the narrative that sacralizes what is held to be secular in the modern world.[67] Although Hobsbawm is generally not convinced of the truth of any narrative that asserts the antiquity of the nation, he does seem to believe that the narrative and the very existence of the nation must have an antecedent in "evolved" protohistories of the nation.[68] Furthermore, Hobsbawm finds in religion "a paradoxical cement" for national narratives.[69] Namdev's nationalist legacy resembles a creature that moves like a religion but sounds like secular history, much like Hobsbawm's civic religion. However a relationship between religion and history is construed, it is certain that national histories are always elaborated along the lines of relative morality and ethics; the nation is a moral community, no matter how unstable that morality might be in any given observer's estimation. A mark of the modern, that is, history is construed in the context of another emblem of modernity, the nation. And finally religion is unabashedly represented and carefully utilized through sacred biography negotiated in a modern public sphere in India that exalts humanism as a sign of a *sant*.

Namdev, as he is portrayed in the context of the Indian nation, becomes an emblem of Hindu secularism. This requires that he embody a host of characteristics that are also required in Hindu secularism. Namdev is regionally distinguished as Maharashtrian, yet he is cosmopolitan in his reach, as shown by his travels and by the many sites of memory associated with him. Namdev is multilingual and shifts among at least three religious spheres: Sikhism, *nirguni bhakti,* and *saguni bhakti*; at times, he is also made to mediate Hindu and Muslim polarities. He is critical of all dogmatic, elitist religious practices, whether Hindu or Muslim, and abides by a personal devotion—he thus interiorizes his religious proclivities and does not translate them into violence (in the twentieth-century context, anyway) or oppression. Namdev's perceived mediation between Hindus and Muslims in this nationalist context is probably the reason for the absence of another narrative—the confrontation between Namdev and a Muslim ruler—recuperated in the nationalist project. Namdev practices modern religion in this way, where religion inflects his morality toward pluralism and acceptance and away from antisocial deviation. Yet this devotion reflects the hegemony of Hinduism in India in that Namdev remains Hindu in essence, while open to all religions. He is portrayed as a humanist, someone who rejects all unjust divisions of caste, class, gender, race, and religion. It is in this context that he must not take the shape of a robber or murderer, yet his challenges to oppressive authority can remain. Namdev as historical figure, national "apostle," or humanist visionary can thus personify the nation in a way that appeals to its Hindu majority without claiming Hindu chauvinism and to the diversity of its regional landscape without claiming a Maharashtrian nativism. The *sant* can become abstract yet historical, an idea to suit the equally abstract yet historical notion of the modern nation itself.

[7]

THE IDEA OF NAMDEV IN TWO FILMS IN
THE TWENTIETH CENTURY

Lincoln isn't a man with ingrown toenails; he's an idea.
—MARIO CUOMO

I N THE summer of 2000 I attended many events in Maharashtra to mark
the 650th anniversary of Namdev's death—performances, speeches, con-
ferences, and dedications. On one cool night in July I sat with three hundred other people in one of the larger Vitthal temples in the Old City of
Pune. We arrayed ourselves as if for a *kirtan,* facing the front of the temple,
seated in the wide vestibule in two blocks separated by an aisle, more or less
segregated by gender. Rather than a *kirtankar,* we sat facing a projection
screen, with a reel-to-reel projector behind us, humming and alight, ready to
show a film made nine years earlier called *Sant Namdev.*

The film we were about to see had been directed by Yeshwant Pethkar
and produced by a prominent Ayurvedic doctor in Pune, Dr Ajay Phutane,
who was in attendance that night. He had produced the film with the help of
Namdev organizations in Maharashtra, Delhi, and Punjab, among Hindus
and Sikhs. In the course of making this film, a new fellowship emerged between Namdev devotees throughout India, particularly between Maharashtrian Hindus and Punjabi Sikhs. A chartered bus had carried a contingent of
Sikh admirers of Namdev from Punjab, many from Ghuman, where Sikhs
believe Namdev passed away, and these guests from northern India were
present at the screening. People had also come from Pandharpur and other
cities to attend this screening and celebrations, and the flow moved toward
Pandharpur as well, where Maharashtrian Varkaris believe that Namdev
died on the steps of the Vitthal temple. As chapter 1 suggested, there are

many issues of contention among the numerous communities and religious traditions that remember Namdev, and I was curious to see how these various differences would be resolved in the film. Would Namdev be Maharashtrian or Punjabi? What language would he speak? How would the filmmakers depict Namdev's life? Would they illustrate the persistent story of his days as a robber or the confrontation with the sultan? Where would Namdev "take *samadhi*" in this film? In Ghuman or at the Vitthal temple in Pandharpur? Would the film highlight Namdev's importance in the secular nationalistic public sphere or his currency in Marathi public culture specifically? How would the filmmakers manage the vast public memory in India that surrounds this *bhakti* figure from Pandharpur to Punjab?

On my most recent visit to India, in the summer of 2005, I had another opportunity to view a film based on the life of Namdev, displayed through an old 16mm projector. We were viewing the only extant copy of this particular film, also called *Sant Namdev*, which had been made in 1949 by Keshav Talpade, better known for his 1948 film *Tigress*. The latter film starred the Anglo-Greek actress Mary Evans, known in India as "Fearless Nadia," famous for performing her own stunts on camera. Although an odd companion to *Tigress*, Talpade's *Sant Namdev*, shot in black and white in Marathi, became well known in the Marathi-speaking regions of Bombay State following independence. The film is long out of circulation, and the last known copy of it, the one we viewed, was missing its final reel. The quality was poor, and both sound and image had worn away, but the delight and devotion inspired by this film transcended the badly deteriorated celluloid.

Films are preeminent sites of public memory, and since the inception of filmmaking in India, *bhakti* has held a consistent position on the silver screen. The Maharashtrian filmmaker Dhundiraj Govind Phalke (1870–1944), considered the "father" of Indian cinema, is said to have been inspired by a viewing of the silent French film *La Vie du Christ* (1906, dir. A. Guy and V. H. Jasset), in 1911 in Bombay. This led him to resolve that Indian films should be made to represent the figures of Hindu devotion. In silent, black-and-white films he famously recorded the stories of Krishna, Rama, and Prahlad, as well as Mirabai, Eknath, and Namdev, among many others.[1] Although the production of such "devotionals" shot for movie theaters waned in the 1980s, notwithstanding the enormous success of Ramanand Sagar's *Ramayana* television series, films on the gods, goddesses, and "saintly" figures of Indian religious life continue to be made today, as discussed below.[2]

At least five films have been made on the life of Namdev. Phalke produced a silent, black-and-white film called *Sant Namdev* in 1921, the first film made on any Maharashtrian *sant*. Phalke's Namdev film has since

ILLUSTRATION 7.1 Still of Namdev and Gonai from Apte's film.
SOURCE: USED BY PERMISSION OF THE NATIONAL FILM ARCHIVE OF INDIA.

been lost, perhaps a victim of the fire at the Film and Television Institute of India's archives in January 2003. In 1937 Bapurao Apte directed a black and white Marathi film entitled *Namace Mahima* (The Glorious Story of Nama), but this film too is no longer available. The National Film Archive of India has only two black-and-white stills from the film, perhaps depicting Namdev as a child with his mother (Ill. 7.1) and as a young man bearing cloth for his father (Ill. 7.2). Chapter 6 mentioned the ill-fated Hindi color film *Patitapavan,* made in 1955 by D. K. Films; it is no longer in distribution, and I was unable to locate a copy in Bombay, Delhi, or Pune. Thus only two films that directly detail the life of Namdev are available: Keshav Talpade's black-and-white 1949 *Sant Namdev* in Marathi and Yeshwant Pethkar's 1991 color film of the same title, with dialogue in both Marathi and Hindi.[3] Namdev is thus part of a public memory of Maharashtrian *sant*s enacted in film, in at least two languages, over the course of the history of cinema in India, and the fate of the films made about him is similar to that of films made about his famous compeers.[4]

Separately, the two films reveal different understandings of Namdev's legacy as they negotiated the received Maharashtrian (and non-Maharashtrian) memory of Namdev discussed throughout this book.

ILLUSTRATION 7.2 Still of Namdev from Apte's film.

SOURCE: USED BY PERMISSION OF THE NATIONAL FILM ARCHIVE OF INDIA.

Together, the films help uncover the complexity of public memory that surrounds Namdev and in a way that frames significant concerns of the past
half-century of independence as they filter through the prism of Namdev's
life. The films, made forty-two years apart, serve as tentative summaries of
a famous biography at two important junctures in Indian history: the first
just after Indian independence and the second just before a veritable revolution in India's economy, politics, and public culture through the full application of neoliberal reforms begun in the 1980s. Situated in these contexts,
both films survey a sacred past invested with religious and historical importance to Namdev's followers and to the imagination of India's progression from diverse cultural landscape to modern nation. In this endeavor,
the films make explicit the role of *bhakti* in creating publics and the process
by which memory through media sustains the legacy of a *sant*.

SANT NAMDEV, 1949

The poster for Keshav Talpade's *Sant Namdev* depicts the *sant* in vibrant
saffron with a lamp lit behind him, the smoke of which merges with an im-

ILLUSTRATION 7.3 Poster of Talpade's film.

SOURCE: USED BY PERMISSION OF THE NATIONAL FILM ARCHIVE OF INDIA.

age of Vitthal over his right shoulder (Ill. 7.3). The image appears to be painted from a publicity still of the actor Jayaram Shiledar in his role of Namdev taken for the film. In addition, several other stills were circulated, including a still from a scene depicting the debate between Parisa and Namdev; a still of Lalita Pawar in the role of Rajai; and a still showing Namdev atop a horse, curiously an image with a narrative match in hagiography only in the context of Namdev's robber story (Ill. 7.4)—nowhere else in any reference to Namdev have I encountered the portrayal of Namdev on a horse, deeply martial semiotic assertion. This interesting mode of referencing the martial aspects of the robber story, without giving it credence, is apparent in Talpade's film. And the reference is all the more striking when

ILLUSTRATION 7.4 Publicity still of Namdev atop a horse beside Rajai, Talpade.

SOURCE: USED BY PERMISSION OF THE NATIONAL FILM ARCHIVE OF INDIA.

one considers that this still appears to have been the chief one in circulation as an advertisement for the film.

The film begins in an undisclosed narrative time in the context of a *kirtan,* a highly appropriate frame narrative for a story about Namdev. A *kirtankar* performs before an audience, which is told that it will hear the stories of Namdev's life. Throughout the film, the *kirtankar*-narrator interjects commentary, offering transition between episodes in the life of the *sant.* As the sequence of episodes that track Namdev's life and compose the film largely emulate Mahipati's account of Namdev's biography, the viewer might be led to conclude that it is Mahipati who is depicted in the role of the narrating *kirtankar.* In any case, the *kirtankar* stands in the usual pose

THE IDEA OF NAMDEV IN TWO FILMS [223]

of the Naradiya performer, with his audience seated around him, and as his *kirtan* begins the viewer enters the memory of his exposition through a scene segue to Namdev's time in late thirteenth-century Pandharpur. Thus *bhakti* and public memory, through the performance of *kirtan,* provide the narrative frame for Talpade's film.

The viewer is given a depiction of Namdev as a child *bhakta*. First he leads a *kirtan* as a child with an audience of children, including Janabai. The difference between this *kirtan* led by Namdev and the *kirtan* that frames the film as a whole appears to purposely elaborate the distinction discussed in chapter 2 between Naradiya and Varkari *kirtan,* a distinction made regularly in Namdev's songs and biography as well. Namdev's audience of children moves, dances, and repeats refrains, generally emulating the form of Varkari *kirtan;* the narrative frame *kirtan,* by contrast, is performed before a seated, subdued audience. Importantly, both periods of reference—the timeless frame narrative and the historicized period of Namdev—begin with *kirtan*s, as if to emphasize that both Namdev's life and the retelling of it are meant for performance.

The film almost immediately invokes memory and *bhakti* as interrelated. Namdev and Janabai stand together as children before an idol of Vitthal and they sing: "Vitthal makes our lives blissful; the memory of Vitthal is like mother's milk," verses perhaps appropriate for child-*bhakta*s for whom mother's milk is a more immediate memory.[5] As the song continues, the children transform into adults on the screen, yet the song remains the same, a link between past and present is coded in the transition. Namdev as an adult appears to carry out his labor as a tailor joylessly. He sets bags of cloth atop his horse and rides from the house.[6] But he is soon distracted by a wandering group of *bhakti* singers and carelessly abandons his horse to follow the singers. The scene elucidates Namdev's detachment from worldly affairs, especially those of occupation and domestic life. In addition, the scene serves another function. This is the moment captured in the main publicity still for the film, Namdev and his horse, obliquely referencing the robber legend. Here the film perhaps offers a reasonable explanation for why Namdev would ride a horse and why this fact would later be misconstrued or elaborated on as the skill of a warrior-brigand.

When Namdev arrives with the singers at the Vitthal temple, he and the others are denied entry by a group of Brahmins, who are in the process of counting bags of money. They lock the door to the temple to ensure that the *shudra* stays out. Namdev stands forlornly at the door and sings to Vitthal a song about how the deity saves the fallen and most wretched of the world, "Hearing the name of the One Who Saves the Fallen [*patitapāvan*],

I have come to the door [of the temple]. But because He is not there I have turned back again."[7] Abandonment by one's deity is a perennial theme in *bhakti* throughout India, and Namdev voices this anxiety here. At the song's conclusion, to the amazement of all, including the Brahmin priests, the doors open.

This episode involving denial of entry to the temple does not appear in Namdev's received biography.[8] Instead it seems to invoke debates about temple entry for low caste and "untouchable" or Dalit Hindus that were vital points of caste conflict in late colonial and newly independent India, especially in south India in the 1930s, and persist to this day. In Maharashtra, throughout the early part of 1947, one particular political and social leader, Panduranga Sadashiv Sane (1899–1950) or Sane Guruji, publicly campaigned to have the doors to the Vitthal temple in Pandharpur opened to Dalits. His efforts culminated in a ten-day fast that gathered sufficient force of public opinion in Maharashtra and throughout India against the recalcitrant Brahminical authority of the temple that the doors were opened, at least officially if not fully in practice, to Dalit devotees. In early 1950 the Indian constitution was ratified, including Article 25, which mandates allowing Hindus of all castes free access to temples, but the letter of the law has not been followed consistently. Although Namdev is not a member of a Dalit caste, his low status in the traditional Brahminical *varna* hierarchy as a *shudra* allows Talpade to connect Namdev to contemporary issues of public concern. Talpade appears to directly engage, through invention, this vital moment in Marathi and Indian public culture. Indeed, this film reinvents many aspects of Namdev's Maharashtrian remembrance in order to address issues that pertain to the film's present.

While these events unfold around the temple, in Namdev's home his elderly father has grown ill and Namdev's wife comes to find the *sant*, who is evading his domestic duties. Namdev relents under Rajai's chastisement, and he is next seen seated in a small, makeshift shop, where he is stitching clothing for sale (Ill. 7.5). The Marathi song he sings here is discussed in chapter 4: "I was born into a family of tailors, but I cared only for Lord Shiva."[9] As he begins to give away clothing to the poor, it is clear that he is incapable of participating in the economies of daily life. Soon his stock of clothing is depleted, and he must approach the local money-lender to finance his business at the risk of mortgaging his house. The money-lender is understood to be a Brahmin, and the mounting non-Brahmin critique is apparent.

Namdev returns to the temple and performs a *kirtan* in which he argues against distinctions in the world between people—if one believes in

ILLUSTRATION 7.5 Namdev sitting in his makeshift tailor shop, Talpade.
SOURCE: USED BY PERMISSION OF THE NATIONAL FILM ARCHIVE OF INDIA.

Vitthal, everything is a manifestation of him. The song against social difference occasions a challenge from a Brahmin in attendance, who is Namdev's rival and later devotee, Parisa Bhagavat (see chapter 1). This scene dramatizes the famous *samvad* between Parisa and Namdev, though without an amicable resolution—Namdev betters the Brahmin, who hurriedly leaves the temple humiliated. In this exchange, Namdev is portrayed as aggressive and commanding, facing the challenge of caste-based abuse with a certain degree of machismo. He is not meek, relying merely on the grace of Vitthal.

This particular encounter solidifies the non-Brahmin character of this film. Following the assassination of Mohandas K. Gandhi in January 1948 by a Maharashtrian Brahmin, Nathuram Godse, India experienced riots and violence directed at Brahmins, especially in cities like Bombay and Pune. Although Maharashtrian anti-Brahmin sentiment has a long history, including such social luminaries as Jyotirao Phule (1827–1890) and Bhimrao Ramji Ambedkar (1891–1956) and drawing much of its anger from Maratha resentment over the Brahmin-dominated Peshwa rule of the Maratha Confederacy, the events of 1948 refocused attention on non-Brahmin sentiment. Made one year after Gandhi's assassination, this film was no doubt viewed in light of these events and an aggressive anti-Brahminism in the Marathi-speaking regions of India, already signaled by the reference to struggles over temple entry, over the denial of entry to Dalits by Brahmin temple administrators. Consistently, Talpade engages caste as a central concern of Namdev's biography.

A series of loosely connected hagiographical scenes follow the episodes with Parsi, including the story of Namdev's damaged hut and Vitthal's intervention. When Namdev is next seen, his father and mother have died and his family is in dire economic straits. His wife has met Parisa's wife, and the two have exchanged the touchstones that turn iron to gold. Rajai shows Namdev the miraculous stones, which he tosses into the river, where they are indistinguishable from normal river stones. Parisa is furious as he confronts Namdev along the riverbank in a visualization of an episode well known in Maharashtrian public memory. Namdev reaches into the water and pulls out stones randomly. Each is revealed to be a touchstone in the hands of the truly devoted, and Parisa becomes Namdev's devotee; the hierarchy of caste is reversed as the Brahmin touches the feet of the *shudra*. The dénouement here appears to be twofold: a resolution of both domestic-economic suffering and caste-based conflict. But for Namdev's wife, the domestic issue is yet to be resolved.

Although Parisa has been converted to the way of *bhakti*, Namdev's wife is still unconvinced, concerned as she is with mundane affairs—a gendered motif found in many *sant* stories, particularly those about Tukaram and his wife. In the next scene Rajai is seen at home surrounded by empty pots, unable to feed her two children. In desperation she finds a deep well and plunges into the water with her two children. This act of *jalasamadhi*, suicide by drowning, is not present in Mahipati's account of Namdev's life or most biographical accounts in India in general, though it is present in Dattatreya's biography of Namdev (see chapter 1). In Dattatreya's version, the entire family dies together. Here, however, Vitthal appears as a stranger and saves Rajai and her children from their watery deaths. When the family returns home, they find all their pots overflowing with grain. Rajai is finally convinced of the power of *bhakti* and touches Namdev's feet, asking for forgiveness for her doubt. Thus the twin concerns of economics and family strife appear at last to be resolved.

Namdev's tribulations seem to place him at the cusp of a spiritual transformation. Jnandev and his siblings arrive from Pandharpur and the testing of Namdev by the handless potter, Gora Kumbhar, is depicted (Ill. 7.6). Namdev is, of course, found to be *kaccā*, an unfinished "pot." Humiliated, he turns to Visoba Khecar, whom he discovers supine with his feet upon

ILLUSTRATION 7.6 Gora Kumbhar tests the saints, Talpade.
SOURCE: USED BY PERMISSION OF THE NATIONAL FILM ARCHIVE OF INDIA.

the *linga* (Ill. 7.7). The viewer is treated to the special effect of *linga*'s appearing ad infinitum as Namdev tries to move Khecar's feet off the aniconic symbol. The lessons of nondualism are imparted, and Namdev's attention shifts from his inner world of Pandharpur, temple, home, and family, to the outer world of India at large. This is a turning point in the film that couples Namdev's spiritual awakening with his peregrinations that lead him northward, all suggesting the different theological messages of his songs, broadly speaking, between his Marathi corpus and his Hindi one, a difference between *saguna* and *nirguna bhakti.*

The *sant* walks and performs songs while what appears to be a clay or mud topographical map of India, in its pre-independence form (including the areas of Pakistan, Bangladesh, and Sri Lanka), is superimposed on him. The *kirtankar*-narrator appears, also in superimposition, and recounts how Namdev spread the teachings of *bhakti* during his voyage, thus uniting the land. This collage of images interweaves post-independence India with Namdev and the *kirtankar* who is providing the framing narrative for this remembrance of Namdev. In a curious visual cue, the single image of Namdev is split into five identical images spread out over the area of India—perhaps a suggestion that the one Namdev inspired mimesis or multiplication of other "Namdevs," as argued in chapter 4 (Ill. 7.8). Other than this play of image, no

ILLUSTRATION 7.7 Visoba Khecar with his feet on Shiva's *linga*, Talpade.
SOURCE: USED BY PERMISSION OF THE NATIONAL FILM ARCHIVE OF INDIA.

information is given about Namdev's travels throughout India. It is a gesture, and nothing more—a footnote to the film's primary preoccupation, Namdev's Maharashtrian public memory, shaded by caste conflict, domestic strife, and spiritual struggle. Namdev is never shown actually in any locale in northern India, and the depiction of the subcontinent in its entirety makes no suggestion about where, indeed, Namdev went. As mentioned, the two versions of the *Tīrthāvaḷī* differ significantly on this point. In the biographical version, first recorded in 1636, Namdev goes only to northern India, but in the older version, the autobiographical one recorded in 1581, Namdev travels to India's farthest southern tip. Talpade's gesure here implies the latter legend of a pan-Indian voyage.

Because the last reel of the film is lost, the narrative prematurely ends with Namdev's return to Maharashtra. His return is followed by the story of the turning of the Shiva temple in Aundhya. One of the early scenes of the film had shown Namdev denied entry to the Vitthal temple until the doors, under the power of Vitthal himself the viewer is to presume, are flung open. Now toward the end of the film, Namdev again is denied entry to a temple. Namdev performs his *kirtan* at the back of the temple, true to the legend so well-represented in his various Indian biographies, and the

ILLUSTRATION 7.8 Five images of Namdev superimposed on a likeness of India, Talpade.

SOURCE: USED BY PERMISSION OF THE NATIONAL FILM ARCHIVE OF INDIA.

temple turns toward him; he is granted entry by the temple's deity while denied entry by the temple's Brahmin caretakers. The moral imperative of egalitarian temple access defeats the politics of caste discrimination. The scene is also evocative of mystical ecstasy and yogic power, as the temple does not so much turn as rapidly and dizzyingly spin in place. The backdrop of the *kirtan* that has sparked the frenetic gyration is a design of two intertwined snakes at the rear of the temple—a motif that suggests yogic power and perhaps the Natha cult as well, of which Namdev is remembered to have entered with his initiation by the Natha *yogi* Khecar. Thus many religious worlds unite in this penultimate moment: *shaiva* and *vaishnava*, yogic and *bhakti*, public and inner, outside Maharashtra and within. Yet the recurrence of the issue of temple entry seems the primary subject of public address in this moment, and indeed forms a kind of framing motif for the film as a whole that suggests Talpade's overriding concerns with issues of caste discrimination, particularly in Maharashtra, in the late 1940s.

Sadly, the fifth reel ends here, leaving unanswered how Namdev is depicted in his last moments of life. Given the way the film hews to the story broadly as Mahipati has told it, it seems plausible to assume that Namdev does not travel northward again. Perhaps he is shown attending to Jnandev's *samadhi* or perhaps he is represented as taking *samadhi* on the second step of the Vitthal temple. However, Talpade has allowed himself significant moments of invention, portraying Namdev as a *kirtankar* in his childhood, for example, or placing Namdev atop a horse, or situating Namdev in conflict with the Brahmin officials of the Vitthal temple and denied entry by them. He has intermingled the miraculous and the mundane, much as Namdev's previous biographies and autobiographical songs have done. It is perhaps fitting that the unintentional end to this film leaves conclusions to the imagination of the audience.

Talpade's *Sant Namdev* emphasizes several key points in Namdev's public memory in Maharashtra, told as a sometimes disconnected series of episodes, what Gayatri Chatterjee has called the "discursive" rather than "narrative" mode of Marathi *bhakti* cinema.[10] The discourse of the film has focused on Namdev as a low-caste devotee and Marathi-speaking, a Maharashtrian indeed, almost to the exclusion of his pan-Indian character. Instead of Namdev's role as a national force of unification, the film presents a collection of episodes revolving around the conjoined polemics of Brahminical casteism, economic oppression, and mundane strife. This is a Maharashtrian Namdev called into a Maharashtrian present, the mid-twentieth century, and made to address the concerns of a *bhakti* public, in this case an audience grappling with the transition from colonialism to postcolonial independence and non-Brahmin sentiment in the public sphere. Two issues are therefore clearly addressed by the film: how does Namdev continue to represent Maharashtrian and Marathi-speaking culture in an Indian world? And how can Namdev's legacy help adjudicate the difficulties of caste in the new democracy?

Viewing a film produced so close to the end of British colonialism in India, a contemporary viewer might be dismayed to see no trace of "nationalism" or a critique of the departing colonialists. But the need for those who might identify with Namdev is perhaps to search for continuity at a time of upheaval rather than celebrate its antecedent of change. The end of colonialism did not also mean the end of caste strife or economic oppression. Hence these issues appear more important than the changing political order. The anxieties of the late colonial period were far less about British colonialism per se as about what would fill its vacuum. The most pressing issues were, of course, the potential (and later actual) partition of India and the politics of religious-communal representation in the future states and at the center. In the Bombay Presidency before 1947, and in Bombay State afterward, the context for the production of this film would be the public memory of issues that both preceded and integrated with colonial rule. Talpade's film seems to engage two primarily: the enduring animosity between Brahmins and dominant or low castes, which was not ubiquitous but was apparent; and, related, the gray area between caste and class as it would manifest itself in a postcolonial, social democratic, capitalistic India. Namdev in this film becomes a metaphor for the weight of these issues.

Namdev is retained and reinforced here as Marathi-speaking, low caste, and poor, yet heroic as well, especially when facing the challenges of mundane life and spiritual debate. These seem to be his enduring characteristics over and above specific, though momentous, circumstances. In this way, Talpade's *Sant Namdev* is a document recording a Maharashtrian public memory, couched in terms of *bhakti*, but projected for a contemporary audience, depicting for it in uncertain political times the enduring hardships of life for the subaltern.

SANT NAMDEV, 1991

Sant Namdev was made in 1991 and released in 1995. The film was directed by Yashvant Pethkar, whose career began in 1947 with Hindi films of a nonreligious nature. In 1951, Pethkar made his first Marathi film, *Vitthal Rakhumai*, about the deities of Pandharpur. His best-received film was *Keechaka Vadha* (The Slaying of Keechaka, 1959), a retelling of a popular vignette from the *Mahabharata*. He continued to make Marathi and Hindi films, both widely commercial and devotional, until the mid-1970s. *Sant Namdev* was his first film in almost two decades. Sadly, Pethkar died before the film's release. The film was screened for the first time in Israel in 1995 at an event hosted by an Israeli Maharashtrian cultural organization most likely composed of Marathi-speaking Indian (Bene Israel) Jews who had settled there.

Whereas Talpade's film was couched within the discourse of a *kirtankar* performing for an audience, Pethkar's film opens and closes under the gaze of Janabai, Namdev's ever-faithful disciple. The film commences with her entry into Namdev's family and ends with her gazing at the deceased *sant* on the steps of Vitthal's temple in Pandharpur. She represents our historical witness to events. In this sense, we are positioned, as an audience, with a public memory sustained within the ambit of Maharashtrian *bhakti*, but also as a memory, perhaps, of one of Namdev's key companions. Talpade framed his film as a performance, but Pethkar's film provides a more anamnesic kind of observation that bookends the narrative. Songs in the name of Janabai represent Namdev's first, and perhaps most devoted, biographies, and Pethkar taps this double sense of witness and devotion through this innovative framing gaze. This film is Janabai's memory, the stories she knows and has told through songs attributed to her.

The first several scenes of Pethkar's film establish a number of biographical points of reference. First, Damashet, Namdev's father, is seen wearing a sacred thread, thus rejecting any perception of his status as a *shudra*. However, at several points in the film, Namdev (who also wears the thread) is called a *shudra* (always by Brahmins), hence the film is self-consciously addressing this contentious issue of Namdev's caste status and that of all *shimpis*. It is quickly evident that Namdev is not interested in the family tailor business, only in worshipping Vitthal. And an early encounter with a benevolent if gruff Muslim customer, Khan Saheb, in Damashet's house, imputes to Namdev and his family a kind of civil secularism; the scene is also a product of poetic license—nothing like it exists in Namdev's received biography up to this point. In this scene, Damashet speaks Hindi with Khan Saheb, and the customer holds the child Namdev lovingly in his arms. Religious harmony is immediately displayed. This scene with Khan Saheb, partially in Hindi, foreshadows later scenes, as Namdev in Pethkar's film, far more than in the film by Talpade, is situated in Hindi-speaking northern India. The movie-goer is meant to know already that Namdev was also a native speaker of Hindi, in addition to his Marathi mother-tongue. Furthermore, it is inferred that Namdev lived at a time of Muslim influence and, perhaps, power, in the Deccan, but power exercised in such a way as to lead to the ideal secularist moment portrayed here—two men of different faiths amiably exchanging goods and services for currency inside the inviolate inner space of the home.

Pethkar returns to convention in the next several scenes, where Namdev feeds milk to Vitthal and grows into a man who is an accomplished *kirtankar*. His fame spreads throughout Pandharpur, and this raises the ire of Parisa Bhagavata. When Parisa confronts the *bhakta*, telling him that as a *shudra* he should serve Brahmins, not sing Vitthal's praises, a much more meek and deferential Namdev is seen here than in Talpade's film. Namdev offers no retort, but merely touches Parisa's feet. Yet the audience, aware of the ultimate outcome of their interactions, might see strength in humility in Namdev's restraint. This scene also invokes caste conflict, especially that which is associated with Brahmins, but without antagonism. This is the second such scene to do so; the first opened the film, as Brahmins bathing in the Bhima River ridiculed Damashet for sheltering a *shudra* (Janabai) and stitching clothes for Muslims.

Namdev soon meets Jnandev and his siblings and is tested by Gora Kumbhar (Ill. 7.9), following which he meets Visoba Khecar. As in Talpade's film, the spiritual transformation Namdev undergoes is highlighted, but it appears quite explicitly to be a reconciliation of two modes of *bhakti, nirguna* and *saguna,* thus reflecting the status that Namdev has long held in Hindi and Marathi literary-religious criticism. Whereas this encounter with Khecar in Talpade's film prepares Namdev to travel throughout India, in Pethkar's film the lessons of Khecar supply Namdev with rhetorical muscle to confront his archrival, Parisa. Cokhamela is toiling away at building a wall for Parisa when Namdev and his troupe pass by singing songs to Vitthal. Cokhamela entreats his employer, Parisa, to let him quickly have sight (*darshan*) of Namdev, whom he calls simply *deva,* or God. Parisa tells him that if wants to see a *deva,* he can do so from afar by looking into the temple that Parisa maintains; he cannot actually enter that temple because he is a *mahar,* or "untouchable." Namdev intercedes in

ILLUSTRATION 7.9 Gora Kumbhar tests Namdev, Pethkar.

this exchange, and a recreation follows of the famous debate between Namdev and Parisa on caste, nondualism, and spirituality. Namdev persuades Parisa that God is present in all people, regardless of caste, and in all things. This impresses Parisa, and he is convinced, a fact he signals by touching the feet of both the *shudra*, Namdev, and the *mahar*, Cokhamela.

As this détente is reached between high caste and low, two other problems rise to the surface. First, Namdev is confronted by his wife regarding his absence from their domestic life. In the midst of this dialogue, a favorite in performance and biography, Namdev learns that in the center of Pandharpur *shaivas* and *vaishnavas* have taken up arms against each other. He rushes to the town square and quells the battle with the same appeal to nondualism. This moment is the invention of Pethkar, but stands as an illustration of Namdev's general character as a mediator of *shaiva* and *vaishnava* difference. Just as this succeeds, he is again called to his domestic life. Back at home, Namdev is scolded by his mother for his continued neglect of the duties of a householder. He insists that his mother should never come between him and Vitthal and that he has given up all labor to serve God. The mother leaves in disgust to level her complaint against Vitthal, a scene often repeated in *kirtan* and present in Mahipati's biography. This transpires off-screen, however. On-screen, a humorous exchange follows between Namdev and his wife, Rajai—the quarrels and resolutions of domestic couples have a long-cherished position in Maharashtrian public entertainment. These moments of "comic relief" indicate the film's indebtedness to traditional performance arts, such as *tamāśā* (folk theater) and *kirtan*, where such asides and scenes are common, perhaps revealing the desire to open the scope of public consumption.

Soon Jnandev and his siblings arrive to see Namdev, and Jnandev proposes that they travel together. However, the voyage is simply to the outskirts of the city, where three groups of devotees converge. This convergence appears to mimic the meeting of *diṇḍī*s, or groups of pilgrims who travel together during the *vari*, or biannual pilgrimage, at the outskirts of Pandharpur. Namdev suggests that this procession should take place twice a year, in the months of Karttik and Ashadh, and the viewer is to understand that the film is offering a portrayal of the initiation of the *vari* pilgrimage itself. Namdev here also sings one of his most famous verses: "Let's dance joyously in the *kirtan*. Let's light a lamp of knowledge in the world."[11] This verse has become a motto to modern practitioners of *kirtan*, despite the fact that the *Śrī Nāmdev Gāthā* committee did not find it in any manuscripts they consulted, so it does not appear in their edition. The connection between the performance of *kirtan* and the enactment of the *vari* is made explicit in this moment, and both are attributed to Namdev in this film.

The scene ends with quotations, in part, from a pivotal moment in the biographical *Tīrthāvaḷī* when Jnandev has asked Namdev to reveal his practice of *bhakti* (highlighted in the introduction to this book). This interaction takes place as a kind of sanctioning of Namdev's spiritual development. Namdev, though he intellectually understands *advaita* as Visoba Khecar has taught him, states plainly that "without dualism there is no *bhakti*." This is his argument against the aggressive nondualism of Jnandev—the common public (*loka*) needs *bhakti*, hence they need to understand God and devotee as separate entities, but capable of intimacy.[12] This moment is important for the film, which is highlighted in several ways. It occurs at the apex of a round of songs, by several characters, all extolling the virtues of *bhakti*, performance, and the vision of Vitthal. It crowns a discursive event that situates Namdev at the center of both *kirtan* practice and the pilgrimage to Pandharpur, metaphorically at the very center of the Varkari religion. Prompted by Jnandev, Namdev expounds on his idea of *bhakti* as he stands at the central meeting place of the three lines of pilgrims who come from different directions. Finally, with this assertion of duality, Namdev implies the needs of a public who either do not know, or do not accept, abstract theological ontology in lieu of personal, experiential devotion.

The scene in which these plateaus are reached takes place before an audience, the streams of people who gather around and stand as witnesses, through whose eyes ostensibly the moviegoer sees this vision of the inauguration of a religious tradition. This moment, coming at almost the midpoint of the film, also marks a turn toward a darker investigation of human nature and the ability of people to bear suffering. Namdev has matured as a theological thinker and *kirtan* performer, but he lacks experience of the world. The film now tracks a series of events that give Namdev depth and test his faith in perilous circumstances.

The mood shifts first with the depiction of Jnandev's voluntary entombment, or *samadhi*. Although Namdev tearfully pleads with his friend to remain among the living, Jnandev enters his tomb undeterred. When Namdev asks Vitthal to explain why Jnandev did what he did, Vitthal responds that Namdev is still a "child" and that his "pilgrimage" (*yātra*) is not yet finished, a metaphor for his spiritual development. Thus Namdev sets out for northern India. The camera tracks Namdev across verdant hills, beside rivers, through fields—all the while singing a song in Marathi about the beauty of the land, that is, India. At times he pauses to look back at the land he is leaving (Ill. 7.10). His hair grows long, a beard forms on his

ILLUSTRATION 7.10 Namdev traveling to the north, Pethkar.

SOURCE: USED BY PERMISSION OF THE NATIONAL FILM ARCHIVE OF INDIA.

face, and he slowly turns into a figure suggestive of Sikh practices and appearance (cf. Ill. 1.2). Although this song is in Marathi, almost the entire second half of the film is in Hindi. When he happens upon a village, everyone speaks in Hindi, and Namdev's displacement is apparent by the linguistic difficulties that he encounters.

In this new context, a set of issues arise with which the film must grapple. The most important one that Pethkar undertakes is the contentious association of Namdev with robbery. Namdev is accosted by thieves as he is traveling in the woods (Ill. 7.11). When the thieves find that he carries nothing with him, they question him and notice that his language is Marathi. One thief speaks Gujarati and converses briefly with Namdev in this language, thus further expanding Namdev's linguistic reach and insinuating a connection to the latter fourteenth-century *sant* Narsi Mehta, who traces his genealogy in part to Namdev.[13] Namdev asks the thieves, in his innocence, what it is that they do, and they say they are robbers (*dākū*). Namdev tells them that they are blessed because they are of Valmiki's ilk. None knows of the *Rāmāyaṇa*, however, of which Valmiki is the purported

ILLUSTRATION 7.11 Namdev accosted by thieves, Pethkar.
SOURCE: USED BY PERMISSION OF THE NATIONAL FILM ARCHIVE OF INDIA.

first author. This is a skillful hagiographical device used by the filmmakers to both assert that Namdev was not a robber yet may have associated with robbers, yet nullify the negative connotations of being a robber, with reference to Valmiki. This also foreshadows the redemption of at least some of the thieves, just as Valmiki was redeemed, through the repetition of God's name and the "good works" associated with the social aspects of *bhakti*.

This scene, which culminates in a series of episodes involving this band of criminals, appears to address the legend of Namdev's criminality, important in the eighteenth century and negotiated in the twentieth century. Here, the film allows the viewer to make a series of connections, presenting the idea that Namdev became associated with criminals because of his desire to propagate the worship of Vitthal, as Hari, Krishna, or by other names. At this point the film has Namdev meet a widow and interjects a scene of him worshiping a *linga,* a non sequitur that makes sense only in the context of the larger legend in public memory of a "criminal" Namdev meeting a widow outside a *shaiva* temple; Pethkar is clearly managing the robber legend in Indian public memory at this point. The sequence presents the idea of redemption and a change of heart exemplified in the contrite criminals, rather than in Namdev, who is blameless in this retelling of the story. Thus the legend of Namdev as a robber is displaced, explained as a confusion or conflation of history. This is an important intervention that appears to recognize the strength of public memory and the need to engage even those aspects of it one might wish away. As noted in several chapters, the story of Namdev as a robber is in one song attributed to Namdev (but apparently not present in old manuscripts) and in one obscure biography, by Dattatreya; it may also have some purchase in an old Mahanubhav hagiography. It is not present in northern biographies of Namdev or in the songs of other *sants* throughout India who invoke Namdev. Yet the story is persistently present and as well-known today as it was from at least the eighteenth century. This persistence is a feature of Namdev's public memory, and it is to this public that the film addresses itself, aware that such issues are in the minds of audiences and cannot be ignored.

The film continues through a series of events that serve to demonstrate the rise of Namdev's fame in the region, which the viewer is to understand is Punjab, specifically the area of Ghuman, where Sikhs believe Namdev lived the latter portion of his life and where he died. In the key scene of this section Namdev convinces a Muslim landowner's administrator not to punish a poor criminal who stole grain to feed his starving family. Although the story does not appear in any hagiography, to my knowledge, it extends the question of criminality and redemption, but connects it to a theme that has run throughout the film thus far: the subaltern's condition of economic poverty and the hardship of labor. In exchange for the release of the man, Namdev offers grain, which he produces, without explanation, from a bag he carries over his shoulder. The Muslim landowner's administrator is amazed, as are the others gathered around (Ill. 7.12). The portrayal of this episode in the film echoes Namdev's encounter with the Muslim ruler in other hagiographical sources (see Ill. 1.3). Shortly thereafter, the Muslim landowner himself hears of Namdev's deeds and of the nature of his songs and recalls that when he was stationed in Pandharpur he once knew a very devout Hindu boy, who sang of Vitthal rather than Ram, the name Namdev now uses for God in north India. Thus Namdev and Khan Saheb are reunited, and the union of Muslims and Hindus foreshadows, purposefully, the development of Sikhism, of which Namdev is an important canonical part. This story thus resonates with the legend that Namdev confronted various Muslim figures of power and sought the resolution of religious differences. The key elements of public display, punishment, and miraculous salvation, in relation to the power of *bhakti*, are present.

ILLUSTRATION 7.12 Namdev confronts local landowner's administrator, Pethkar.

SOURCE: USED BY PERMISSION OF THE NATIONAL FILM ARCHIVE OF INDIA.

In the final scenes of the film, Namdev has reached an advanced age. He tells his now-copious crew of followers that they should no longer serve him but, rather, "serve the poor, humble, and suffering," again an invocation of *bhakti*'s usual public. Namdev says that Vitthal is calling him for *darshan.* One follower delivers a short speech:

> Since you came to Ghuman, there has been no violence between Hindus and Muslims. Brahmins, Kshatriyas and Jats—they all eat together. All the Muslims worship Ram and all the Hindus perform Muslim prayers. Because of your *kirtan*s, everyone has forgotten their caste and has become one community [*jati*].

This is a key summation of the film, occurring before the very last scenes and enunciated by a devotee of Namdev, who is also one of the former criminals brought back to lawfulness by Namdev. He speaks of *bhakti*, but not of a particular deity or even practice. Instead, he tells of social cohesion,

ILLUSTRATION 7.13 Final *kirtan* of Namdev in Ghuman, Pethkar.
SOURCE: USED BY PERMISSION OF THE NATIONAL FILM ARCHIVE OF INDIA.

of peace among castes and religions, instigated by Namdev's principal means of propounding *bhakti,* his performances of *kirtan.* What this character praises is the creation of a new public, a *bhakti* public, where ideals of sharing, mutual respect, and even religiously interwoven practice are hallmarks, furthered in performance.

Namdev performs one last *kirtan* (Ill. 7.13) before his followers exit the frame, and Namdev is laid down to sleep by his two closest attendants, who leave to find water for their master. When the attendants return a few moments later, Namdev is gone. He is next seen in Pandharpur—to which he has traveled by miraculous means. The aged Namdev arrives at the steps of the Vitthal temple but is too weary to mount them. Vitthal descends the steps to comfort his devotee in his last moments of life (Ill. 7.14). Namdev says that he had intended to compose a million songs, but was not able to do so. He asks Vitthal to appoint this task to someone else in the future—the audience knows the recipient of this charge will be Tukaram in the seventeenth century, and a genealogy is marked, from one *sant* to another. Namdev dies, and the scene fades to an image of the bust of Namdev on the steps of the Vitthal temple.

ILLUSTRATION 7.14 Namdev dies at the Vitthal temple in Pandharpur, Pethkar.

SOURCE: USED BY PERMISSION OF THE NATIONAL FILM ARCHIVE OF INDIA.

These final sequences of scenes seek to unite the contending claims of Sikhs and Varkaris about where Namdev died and resolve this dispute through a miracle, a common feature of hagiography. The use of this miracle is startling in several ways. This miracle is entirely the invention of the filmmakers and is thus revealing about the ways in which legends continue to be invented, or interpreted, in order to maintain Namdev's public memory. It also goes against the grain of the "realism" of the film, which has in other ways sought to balance the miraculous with plausible scenarios, to explain why something that was at the moment rather ordinary might later be construed as a miracle. Thus Namdev does not meet a Muslim ruler but, rather, a minor landowner, suggesting that legend inflated the story to its current proportions. He is not a robber who kills thousands of soldiers with his own hands, but a simple wanderer who is harassed by robbers and through his personal charisma manages to change their hearts. The film is rife with engagements with real-life issues, particularly those relating to domesticity, caste conflict, economics, and labor. The addition of new miracles to Namdev's Maharashtrian public memory, something found in the films of both Pethkar and Talpade, should be indicative of a long-standing tradition of intertwining mundane concerns with miraculous events in the retelling of the life story of a "holy" figure. Yet the invention of this particular miracle must rely on the prevalent public memory of Namdev that recalls that he died in two places at once—again, public memory strongly influences the film.

This final scene also features the image of Janabai, advanced in years, peering from behind the columns of the temple to watch Namdev's final moments with Vitthal unfold. Just as a *kirtan* set in an undefined present framed Talpade's film, the presence of Janabai frames Pethkar's film. The film closes with a verse, "God has become Nama; Nama has become God." Interestingly, this song does not appear in any printed anthology or in any manuscripts that I consulted in my research—the act of composing songs anew for devotional films and having characters sing them as if they were their own compositions is common, found in Damle and Fattelal's *Sant Tukaram* (1936) and many other films. This particular song sung by Janabai appears to be inspired, however, by at least two songs that express the essential oneness of *sant* and deity. In two songs in the *Śrī Nāmdev Gāthā*, Janabai asserts, "God and *sant, sant* and God, Jani says, I believe these are one," and in another, "The *sant* belongs to God, and God belongs to the *sant*, Jani says, in this important matter, there is no separation."[14] As in the final miracle of Namdev's appearance in Pandharpur, Janabai's song is an invention, but one that draws from a pool of public memory, in this case, preserved in these two songs. This evinces the extension of public memory through mimesis.

This final song also reinforces the broad spectrum of belief associated with Namdev throughout India, as someone who accepted the doctrine of nondualism but practiced a strategic *bhakti* dualism. But perhaps most important it signals the significance of the audience. The film could simply have ended with Namdev's death on the steps of the temple. Why did the filmmakers find it necessary to include this final witness, to insert Janabai into this scene, and to have her sing a song, ostensibly a medium through which this event can be remembered? Namdev's final moments are viewed through the eyes of Janabai, who is perhaps his first biographer, and stands in as the filmgoer's witness to these events. Even in his final moments, a connection to a public, hence to a chain of memory, must be maintained. Janabai will remember, and therefore so will we.

Namdev's journey through celluloid has revealed several things. His public memory remains important enough to attract primarily Maharashtrian filmmakers to retell his life story and to do so in ways that respond to the desires of a viewing public. The makers of both films drew on Namdev's memory because he was well-known by the Maharashtrian public at large and his memory brought association with a sense of *bhakti* that had political and social implications. In the case of Talpade's film, the narrative inscribes the subtexts of the pressing issues of caste conflict, anti-Brahminical sentiment, temple entry, the economic future of India's newly postcolonial poor, and the ways in which the stories of a "medieval" Indian *sant* can reflect on these conditions.

Anxieties about this time of uncertainty and upheaval are balanced against a will to remember Namdev in particular, iconic ways: as a child *bhakta*, as a simple and low-caste man, as someone who suffered economic hardship, and as someone who always retained a personal relationship with God. Pethkar's film suggests similar sets of concerns. Namdev here is also someone who suffers caste oppression and economic hardship, but these features are regularly relieved by miracles and divine intervention. Instead, it offers a portrayal of spiritual development that appears linked to national progression. Unlike Talpade, Pethkar depicts in detail Namdev's life outside Maharashtra and implies the *sant*'s importance to the development of the literary and cultural spheres that are rooted in the north.

Namdev is far more a figure of national integration in Pethkar's film; Talpade's concerns were perhaps more local. In Talpade's time, the reality of a newly unified Indian nation sometimes threatened the sovereignty of a Maharashtrian public culture within which Namdev was a key character. Pethkar, who embraced the idea that Namdev's travels unified India, made his film at a time when India was moving toward neoliberal reforms and embracing the transnational economies of "globalization." Recall that the film was first screened not in India, but in Israel at the behest of a Maharashtrian organization. Thus the first audience for this film was neither in India nor predominantly Hindu. In this context, perhaps a reminder of the sovereign nation, as defined by the peregrinations of this historical figure, was deemed important, both to Indians in India and abroad. The modern media of film is as deeply responsive to the public culture of its time as eighteenth-century hagiography was responsive to its historical context. I have read these films as I have read the performance tradition of *kirtan*, the manuscripts that preserve Namdev's literary legacy, the physical sites of memory associated with Namdev, and the multiple contexts for retellings of Namdev's life as all responding in similar ways to a vibrant public culture stretched over centuries, with its own systems of memory, in which Namdev remains both device of recollection and social critique, as well as an object of reverence in his own right.

CONCLUSION

Different cultures. Different histories.
—MARSHALL SAHLINS

THIS BOOK was written in two parts that are mutually dependent and sequentially logical. The first part, "Practices of Memory," was largely the result of ethnohistorical study, and it aimed to set out the systems and enactments that form the practical core of the public memory of Namdev in Maharashtra. Chapter 1 differentiated "history" from "memory" in heuristic terms and pointed out that those who remember Namdev do so in ways that are not necessarily concerned with historical accuracy or the science of the past. Rather, they attempt to faithfully represent a different vision of the past, not as static and bygone, but as dynamic and in constant contact with the present. Chapters 2 and 3 presented the core of the logic of memorial practice in Namdev's Maharashtrian public memory. I approached the logic of these practices of memory in Namdev's Maharashtrian cultural field by noting how all of them revolve around the *kirtan.* These two chapters are built on the observations of ethnography, from my time spent among Namdev's admirers in Maharashtra and throughout India. I sought to understand what Namdev means in these contexts, what shapes his public memory and why. In this environment, especially in Maharashtra, performance is preeminent. This is not necessarily the case for all other *sant*s, or for Namdev in all his articulations outside Maharashtra, but it is indisputably the case for Namdev in Maharashtrian public memory.

Chapter 2 provided an ethnographic and textual account of the dynamics of *kirtan* and the kind of authorship it requires, which I describe as "corporate" in order to communicate the central position of embodiment, of the living intervention of the *kirtankar,* and of its multiple nature that involves several nodes of authorship at once. I began chapters 2 and 3 on this point, at the site of ethnographic encounter rather than literary-textual encounter, in order to allow my study of Namdev's Maharashtrian public memory to unfold according to the logic with which it has sustained itself and continues to flourish, the logic of performance. If I had approached this public memory from the point of view of texts, of the literary traces and records of manuscripts and notebooks, I would not have captured the conceptual concerns sustained over centuries in Namdev's name that led to the production of these archived materials. This would have been, from an ethnographic point of view, ahistorical as it would have disregarded the historical motivation for the activities that have led to the textual record, scant as it is. Certainly there are *sants* for whom the ideal point of entry into their public memory is textual. This is the case for Jnandev and Tukaram, both of whom are intimately associated with very particular texts, attributed to their own device (that is, quite literally written by their hands), as chapter 2 made plain. Namdev's exception here must also suggest a rule of practice in his public memory, and this is why an ethnography of performance, coupled with its textual reflections, is where I began.

The practice of performance may be preeminent here, but by its very nature of emodiment, it is not permanent and alone cannot sustain a stable archive of memory. Instead the archive of Namdev's songs, preserved in writing as much as in oral memory, is inherently unstable and malleable. Surrounding Namdev there is no mnemonic discipline like the *ars memoriae* of classical or medieval Europe or the traditions of memorizing Vedic or other literature that has a long history in South Asia. In other words, there are no "palaces of memory" that serve to recall the text *as text,* as a fixed form to be interpreted by others, as if written, from memory. Instead, chapter 3 displayed how manuscripts and notebooks that recalled Namdev's songs in Marathi clearly followed the logic of performance, not permanence, and hence made productive use of uncertainty, ambiguity, and lacunae. This was not a question of an oral culture encountering or transforming into a written one (in the mode of Goody and Watt, for example), but a question of practice, of the mnemonic goals attained in texts, a purposeful mode of perpetuation that emphasized performance over permanence. I argued that the structure of the textual record of Namdev's songs conforms to performative practice, not to permanent preservation—the most common mode of the textual archive. In order to make this point, I carefully distinguished between the kinds of records that exist of Namdev's songs—the distinction between *bada* and *pothi*, or notebook and manuscript.

By far, the majority of materials that record Namdev's Marathi songs come from the *bada*s, the use of which is historically confined to itinerant performers. The manuscript set in a place (such as Dehu or Pandharpur) that would slowly accumulate the materials garnered from *bada*s, gathered as performers passed through certain regions on their regular routes, is a secondary record for Namdev's songs. The first layer of the archive, the *bada,* was the tool of performance, though not necessarily of an "oral" culture—clearly the *kirtankar*s who kept their records in *bada*s were literate. Yet the goal of the notebooks is to aid performance, not to record songs for posterity or fix them in a permanent state. To account for this important distinction, I proposed in chapter 3 that the textual records of Namdev's songs in Marathi do not illustrate an interaction between orality and literacy but, rather, intentions along a continuum between performance and permanence. Chapter 3 represents my attempt to remain faithful to the contours of *kirtan* practice laid out in chapter 2 while taking seriously the project of the written archive.

In chapters 4 through 7, the second part of the book, "Publics of Memory," the logic of practice laid out in the previous three chapters is brought to bear on historical moments when Namdev's public memory underwent some important change or engaged some vital social issue. At these moments, Namdev's memory interacts with a receptive public. The first instance, examined in chapter 4, involves the phenomenon of mutliple "Namdevs" emerging at different historical periods, each distinct and consciously enfolded within the field of biographical and thematic authorship shaped by the earliest Namdev, of the fourteenth century—these Namdevs are the same and not the same simultaneously. This chapter on "Namdev and the Namas" is pivotal because it contains both the character of the practices outlined in the first part of the book, especially questions of authorship, and the attention to historical detail in the second part of the book. In this case, I explained the occurrence of multiple Namas by invoking modes of practice laid out in the first part of the book. I associated with memory, rather than history, the preoccupation with practices that reflect the conditions relevant to the context of performance, that is, the need for Namdev's public memory to be ever current, while still recalling the character of the past. This same impetus to reinvent the past in the present in response to public concerns helps explain why multiple Namas emerge at particular times. But the fact that they emerge as both unique authors and as authors whose compositions are conflated with the first Namdev is a process that is germane to the notion of corporate authorship presented in chapter 2. If one projects the ethnographic context of contemporary performance back in time to the sixteenth centuries and later, it becomes plausible that the multiple Namas of history proliferated in performative contexts where authorship was momentary and conditional. The elasticity of authorship in *kirtan* conveys its flexibility to these mutliple Namas. Much of the consternation over these mimetic interlopers into Namdev's authorial timeline comes from a desire to read the textual archive that contains Namdev's songs as adherent upon a sole notion of authorship. As I demonstrated in chapter 3, here too performance dominates permanence in recording the songs of all the Namas as interwoven. Particularly with Vishnudas Nama of the sixteenth century, a careful reading of the sequence and arrangement of songs in manuscripts and notebooks suggests that this Nama and the earlier Namdev are interwoven based on principles of performance in the *kirtan* without regard for maintaining authorial distinction reliant on a sole author.

Thus the practices laid out in the first three chapters enter the analysis of this and other later chapters as a whole. Chapter 5 marked the further movement from Namdev's assumed historical context, the fourteenth century, and toward the way publics of later centuries would use his memory as a device of history. In this chapter I presented the argument that Namdev could not be both a historical figure and a figure utilized in public memory as a device of history. I do not suggest that Namdev's followers at this point deny Namdev's historicity, but that they understand the uses of Namdev vis-à-vis history to be multiple. In this way, I wished to reference the subject of chapter 1 and see that objects of social history, of faithfully recording the social conditions of a particular time and place, were accomplished in the eighteenth century only when Namdev could become a vehicle for commenting on the present. The stories of banditry and confrontations with temporal authority served social historical purposes, but they also displayed Namdev's position in public memory as a metaphor as much as a historical character. The social suffering likely experienced by those who participated in Namdev's public memory of the eighteenth century can be read in the innovations introduced into his legacy in Maharashtra in this period. If the link to public memory was performance, and performance relied on an ever-present link to the contemporary concerns of audiences, then it makes sense that Namdev's public memory would adhere to the needs of its audiences.

When Namdev's public memory is emended and recalled in the context of the Indian nation in the nineteenth and twentieth centuries, this interaction of historical truth and the demands of public memory in contemporary contexts becomes plain. Here, fully within the realms of modernity, of the invocation of positivist historiography and the mythography of the nation, Namdev emerges as a public figure. His legacy of performance is subdued, as are the dynamics of his multiple streams of public memory in the preceding centuries. In its place, a discourse about the "real" Namdev emerges and is linked to questions of public character and historical actions. His legacy as a bandit is historically challenged, while the memory of his peregrinations throughout India is historically accepted, buttressed by references to the wide dissemination of his verses in the Hindi public sphere in particular. The concerns of modernity alter, but do not fully obliterate, Namdev's nonmodern public memory. Here, more than at any other time, Namdev's public character undergoes discipline at the hands of modern methods of scholarly inquiry and the needs of the modern cultural form of the nation.

This "modernization" is both resisted and engaged in film, the subject of chapter 7. It is engaged when filmmakers like Pethkar in 1991 answer the same historical questions of banditry, confrontation with temporal figures of authority, and even the issue of Namdev's panregional status, in the context of a nationalist, secularist narrative. Talpade in 1949 likewise engages with a "modern" Namdev when he uses Namdev's public memory to respond to the anxieties of a Marathi-speaking public just after independence, the same public that will come to communicate its anxieties during the reorganization of states in the 1950s and the multiple public mediations of caste and class in modern India, which grow ever more vital as the twenty-first century proceeds. These two films return us to the practices of addressing the needs of publics displayed in chapters 4 and 5. In these cases, Namdev's public memory is viewed in the context of post-independence linguistic regionalism and in late-modern nationalism in the midst of globalization. The times and concerns are far from the sixteenth or eighteenth centuries, but the process is strikingly similar—the media are modern, but the practices are equally nonmodern. The interaction between publics and Namdev's memory evinces equal force. Observing these two films also allows a return to those nonmodern aspects of Namdev's memory that have endured. In both cases, Namdev is still quintessentially a performer. And when these filmmakers produce new stories for Namdev's public memory in their films, even including new songs, they make all the more evident in this new, modern media of film the practices discussed in chapters 2 and 3.

Throughout the book, then, I pinpointed moments when the functions of public memory serve *bhakti* or when acts of *bhakti* are also acts of public memory. From the earliest period of hagiography or history, the remembrance of Namdev has relied on the observer, whether the fellow *bhakta*, the hagiographer, the performer, the receptive audience, or the modern scholar. Each of these figures is created within a distinct public and draws Namdev into this public for reasons germane to each particular sphere; hence scholars with a nationalist concern in the twentieth century are writing for a public that shares this concern with the cohesion of the nation, whereas a hagiographer of the eighteenth century might extract from a core of memories about Namdev a tale of suffering to deliver to a public that has endured similar circumstances.

I have tried to supply the reader with two sets of tools: a conceptual map of the practices that produce and maintain memory, the content of the first three chapters, and the most significant moments in Indian history when Namdev has been summoned to address the needs of some particular public, the subject of the last four chapters. I have also hoped to demonstrate how the practices of memory account for the means of accessing publics in the historical settings surveyed here. Publics are the product of particular techniques, of practices, and those practices become integrated back into the self-imagining of various publics.

This has been a process of understanding the way memory is inscribed into cultural forms, a process one might call mnemonography, as opposed to historiography. Bringing these two activities together, the mnemonographic and the historiographic, leads to something like what Jan Assmann has called "mnemo-history" or "the history of cultural memory."[1] I have sought to portray the mnemonic convictions of the various publics that have revered Namdev rather than adjudicate the historical veracity of any particular assertion. But to do this, I first had to understand the mode of inscription, which, in the case of Namdev, is primarily performative. I could then ask about the content of memory and the creation of historical publics because I had the means of understanding the systems internal to Namdev's public memory, at least in Maharashtra. However, this is not a common mode of studying Indian *sant*s. A far more dominant mode retains a commitment to the historiography of philology, the investigation of the historical veracity of verse, its links to a purported original author, and its shape as a logical corpus. Although I have not pursued this mode, I could not have written this book without such work, such as the innovative scholarship of Winand Callewaert on Namdev's Hindi corpus or the long labors of the Government of Maharashtra's editorial board for the *Nāmdev Gāthā*. Many of the best studies of *sant*s have inspired this book, such as John Stratton Hawley's work.[2] These studies open up the world of *sant* literature, and they are deeply invested in understanding author and text in the philological and text-critical mode, usually supplying translations based on reliable texts, in the scholarly sense, as the key of access. Such studies ask: When did the *sant* live? What did he or she compose? What did he or she not compose? What did the compositions communicate? What is the cultural context of that communication?

I have tried in this book to ask variations on these questions: Why is the *sant* said to have lived in so many different times and contexts? Why does the tradition maintain a heterogenous body of songs attributed to a *sant* that are internally inconsistent and historically dubious? What systems of memory keep all this intact over seven centuries? How do modern and nonmodern concerns manage to coexist seamlessly in the present? My conviction in this book is that we should also produce studies that are motivated, at their core, by the practices that have produced the literary archives used in understanding any particular sacred figure. This is not to argue for an ethnosociology or adherence to "native concepts," but to read the literary record in light of its logic of production, the shape of its cultural field, or to take seriously the idea that sacred figures have traceable "lives" well outside their historical floruits or biographical contours. They go on living in public memory, reflecting the concerns of historical cultural moments, and hence recording social sentiments, often of the subaltern undisclosed in conventional historical archives.

I hope that this book will provide an example, however flawed, of one way to access the intricate past of sacred figures in South Asia in ways that are ethnohistorical, that seek to see sacred figures at the center of what Dirks has called an "indigenous discourse about the past,"[3] but that still hew to a religious studies conviction that sees religion, as Hawley has argued in the context of *bhakti*, as a viable category of ethnographic, textual, and historical knowledge.[4] Public memory often functions at the expense of historical accuracy, even while both desires are at work in the long tradition that surrounds Namdev in Maharashtra. But whether called "history" or "memory," it still has distinguishable sets of practices and lines of historical plot that can be traced. Philologists know this well, and this is why the science of texts pursues both biography and textuality in its recovery of the past through text. In the Namdev tradition, the site of "text" is the site of the body, of the performer, and not the archive or the manuscript. This

is not true of all *sants*, surely, but because it is true of this one *sant,* it requires a different kind of study to get at the "indigenous discourse about
the past" that operates here.

Indeed, the relationship between history and religion remains in the
shadow of this book's explicit interests, but it was very much front and
center in the early work out of which this book grew.[5] I hope from the
discussions of memory and history in the introduction and chapter 1 that
the reader will see why I characterized the ways people have used Namdev in recalling the past as acts of public memory rather than history. In
essence, the modern edifice of "history" as a discipline and a narrative is
far too massive to be embodied by the exact and narrow tool of the mono-
graph. It will take much more to alter the conceits of modern historiography, as both Chakrabarty and Prakash have admitted in their proposals
for the provincialization of modern historiography or the construction of
"post-foundational" histories.[6] And the problems faced here, with regard
to the legacy of a "saint," are more than the postcolonial predicament outlined by these scholars and others, but reach into the long dialectic between religion and history within modern thought in general.[7] Still, one
might ask: why not enact a radical ethnohistory that considers all the
ways of recalling the past associated with Namdev as history proper?
Some facets the answer to this question, I hope, will form the basis for
future work on religious narrative practices about the past in South Asia
and will involve more than unraveling old Orientalist conceits about
non-Western culture. Instead, the answer to this question lies at the heart
of how the very development of historiography and the philosophy of history in the modern West has conditioned, and brought into being, the
modern idea of "religion." Although historians of anthropology and ritual
have investigated this genealogy for the construction of "religion" in anthropological discourse,[8] the same has not yet been accomplished for
historiographical discourse. The reason for this is two pronged: on the
one hand, scholarship continues to concentrate on the perceived antagonism between history and religion in modernity and the way historical
narrative came to replace religious narrative in the modern secular West.[9]
On the other hand, studies involving postcolonial societies and histories
work against the colonial or the "Orientalist" rather than directly toward
modernity, which holds us all (unevenly to be sure) in thrall. But without
some engagement with the common dispensation of modernity, we cannot see "history" as the totalizing force it has been. The answer to the
question posed above must come from an archaeology of modern historiography since the eighteenth century coupled with the "post-foundational"

challenges that emerge when we study "indigenous" historical discourse outside the modern West.[10]

As much as this book has been about the way the past is recorded and enacted around the name and sign of Namdev, this book has not provided a definitive account of the legacies that surround Namdev in Marathi sources or in Maharashtra. I did not aim to settle the historical or textual questions that have animated 150 years of scholarship in Indian and European languages. These are fascinating questions, but they begin from a premise that imposes a certain discipline on the material that is not always relevant within the structures of the material's productive fields. In other words, much scholarship tends to ask questions that the material not only does not answer but of which it often seems unaware or indifferent. This does not mean that we should not ask such questions. Indeed, historians should and must ask such questions. In this book, however, I sought to understand what questions seem to be of concern in the public memory of Namdev over multiple time periods. Since the nineteenth century, Namdev's followers and admirers began to engage historical veracity, questions of authenticity, and issues of literary attribution, but this did not seem to disrupt the much longer practices of performing Namdev's songs, adapted to cultural and historical contexts, and constructed around principles of elasticity and adaptation.

This has been my attempt in any case, but I am well aware that this book, by its very existence, enters into a discursive terrain that Namdev did not travel on his mythopoetic tour of the Indian subcontinent or of the human soul in relation to its divine objects. And as hopeful as I am that I have captured some of the mechanisms and convictions internal to Namdev's public memory in Maharashtra, I have also participated in applying terms and conditions all my own. Ideas about "publics" and "memory" are present in the materials that I covered in this book, but not in the explicit ways I use them. By addressing *bhakti* as public memory I seek to use contemporary theoretical language to understand multiple "presents" that have now past in the social life of communities that have remembered Namdev in Maharashtra. By the nature of the scholarly project, I have circumscribed Namdev's public memory and packaged it for a twenty-first century English-reading audience. This work is deeply invested with my own disciplinary proclivities and intellectual influences spread between ethnography, historiography, and literary studies. But I endeavored to make these lenses as transparent as possible, or at least translucent, to allow some of the Elysian light of Namdev, a fascinating figure in any time period, to shine through.

NOTES

PREFACE

1. Assmann 1997:15.
2. See Hobsbawm 2000 [1969].
3. See Lorenzen 1996.

INTRODUCTION

1. Note that the term *sant* is used in Marathi not to indicate *nirguna,* or "unqualified" theology, but simply as a designation for a "good" and "sacred" person. Indeed, the Marathi Namdev is a *saguna* figure, while his Hindi songs often took on the character of *nirguna* devotionalism, particularly in relation to Sikhism and Kabir, as shown below.
2. Throughout the book, I refer to the region that is the present-day state of Maharashtra in order to avoid cumbersome geographical and historical qualifications. However, the state of Maharashtra has existed only since 1960, though the term as a designation of place is much older, certainly was used in the seventeenth century, and was likely used as early as the seventh century. Therefore, "Maharashtra" in this book indicates the core Marathi-speaking regions of central-western India that are roughly coterminous with the boundaries of the present-day state. In addition to geography, the term *Maharashtrian* sometimes indicates Marathi public culture not limited to the modern period.
3. Crooke 1896:299.
4. Saussure 1983:166. See also Derrida (1998 [1976]) whose neologism *différance* was inspired by such ideas of Saussure.
5. In this section I draw on Hawley and Novetzke in Doniger 1999.

6. See Jacobsohn 2005 for an excellent study of Indian secularism. Jacobsohn refers to Indian secularism as "ameliorative," suggesting that its form takes a more purposeful approach to allowing religious expression of many sorts, particularly to minority religious communities. See also Madan 1998. My comparison here of American and Indian secularisms is not meant to be judgmental. Indeed, with the rise of the Hindu Right in India since 1996 and the rise of the Christian Right in the United States since 2000, neither system of secularism appears to succeed at keeping fundamentalist religion and politics in separate spheres.

7. See Prentiss 1999:17–41 and Sharma 1987.

8. See Monier-Williams 1993 [1851]:743; Sharma 1987:40–41.

9. See Pollock 1998, where he argues that royal and courtly discourse in regional languages for the most part preceded religious discourse.

10. NG: 346 [song 916.11].

11. NG:346–347 [song 917.1–9, 17]. This exchange figures prominently in the 1995 film *Sant Namdev*, discussed in chapter 7.

12. NG:347 [song 918.1–2].

13. "What Is Enlightenment?" [1784] in Gay 1973.

14. Dewey 1927.

15. Habermas 1991 [1962].

16. See Assmann 2006:85; Bodnar 1992:13–20.

17. See Hardgrove 2004; Haynes 1991; Yandell and Paul 2000.

18. See Orsini 2002; Wakankar 2003.

19. See Breckenridge 1995.

20. See Habermas 1991 [1962].

21. Cutler 1987:19.

22. See, for example, Brass 1974, 2003; and Varshney 2002.

23. Cohn 1996.

24. Dirks has explored the relationship between caste, colonialism, and public displays of status in *The Hollow Crown*, and more recently of the reinscription of caste in Indian public culture through the hegemonic ordering of social in the colonial period (Dirks 1993). Appadurai has explored publics or public culture in a number of venues, for example, Appadurai 1981, 1996. For Breckenridge, see Breckenridge 1995.

25. Freitag 1989; Hardgrove 2004; Haynes 1991. See also Yandell and Paul 2000.

26. Orsini 2002; Wakankar 2003.

27. In addition to their numerous publications, Appadurai and Breckenridge founded the journal *Public Culture* in 1988.

28. What one might call a competing tradition of the study of public culture exists in Australian cultural studies, inaugurated by the work of Donald Horne (Horne 1986).

29. Warner 2005:11–12.

30. Geertz 1973.

31. Berger 1967,

32. Bourdieu 1993.

33. Warner 2005:15.

34. This is almost universally true, even in influential work on publics, especially public culture and the public sphere, in South Asia, such as those conducted by Appadurai and Breckenridge, Orsini, Freitag, Hardgrove, and Haynes. Warner, while not discussing South Asia, is equivocal on the historical emergence of publics, where sometimes he attributes them to modernity and at other times begs ignorance

about the issue in non-Western, nonmodern contexts. In my reading, there is nothing about "a public" in Warner's formulation that fixes the phenomenon in modernity nor of public culture as it is used by the authors above. The public sphere, if one follows Habermas, is by definition a modern phenomenon, bounded by the same conditions as the idea of the nation or of history, for example.

35. Warner 2005:67–124.
36. Prentiss 1999:24.
37. Monier-Williams 1993 [1851]:743.
38. Ibid.
39. Ibid.
40. See Prentiss 1999; Sharma 1987.
41. See Borofsky 1987; Comaroff and Comaroff 1987; Farriss 1987; Fogelson 1974, 1989; Gewertz and Schieffelin 1985; Hill 1988; Ortner 1989; Taussig 1984. For the need to guard against the forced placement of different understandings of time and history in the "othering" of anthropological subjects, see Fabian 1983.
42. One example, where memory is important, is in the work of the Annales school historian Jacques le Goff (1992).
43. Chakrabarty 2000.
44. Prakash 1990, 2000.
45. See Wolf 1982.
46. Vansina 1960:53. See also Brunschwig 1965.
47. See Novetzke 2006.
48. For opposing views, see, for example, two works: Lal 2003 and Rao et al. 2003.
49. See, for example, Blake 1866.
50. See Braudel 1958.
51. See le Goff 1992:51–100.
52. Assmann 2006:87–88.
53. See Halbwachs 1980 [1925].
54. See LaCapra 1998; Nora 1989; Ricœur 2004.
55. See Castelli 2004; Wyschogrod 1998; Yerushalmi 1982.
56. Klein 2000.
57. Halbwachs 1980 [1925].
58. Assmann 2006; Sturkin 1997.
59. On Aby Warburg, see Fentress and Wickham 1992; Rampley 2000.
60. Bellah et al 1985.
61. Johnson et al. 1982.
62. Assmann 2006.
63. Davis and Starn 1989; Foucault 1977.
64. Certeau 1988; Collingwood 1994 [1946]; le Goff 1992; Nora 1989.
65. Assmann 1997:14–15.
66. Anderson 1983; Cressy 1989; Duara 1995; Hobsbawm and Ranger 1983.
67. Castelli 2004; Certeau 1988 [1975]; Hervieu-Léger 2000 [1993]; Nora 1989.
68. Hayes 1960; Smith 1986;.
69. Carruthers 1990; Coleman 1992; Hutton 1993; Matsuda 1996; Nora 1992; Terdiman 1993.
70. Halbwachs was a Catholic man who married a Jewish woman; politically, Halbwachs was a communist. His personal sentiments about religion are not speculated on here.
71. For a superior study in the tradition of this line of investigation, see Castelli 2004.

72. Nora wrote the entry for "collective memory" in le Goff et al. 1978:398.
73. Nora in Nora and Kritzman 1996:xvii.
74. Nora 1989: 9.
75. Ibid.:13–14.
76. Ibid.:7.
77. See Assmann 2006; Butler 1989; Connerton 1989; Fentress and Wickham 1992; and the special issue in 1986 "Memory and History," *History and Anthropology* 2:2. For the fountainhead of debates about orality and literacy, and their impact on history and memory, see the work of Goody and Watt, especially Goody 1968, 1986; Goody and Watt 1963.
78. In particular is the work of Jan and Aleida Assmann.
79. Derrida 1998 [1967].
80. For a lucid survey of history, orality, and memory through the works of Lévi-Strauss, Lyotard, and Clifford, see Klein 1995.
81. See Bourdieu 1984 [1979]; Lang and Lang 1990; Taylor 1996
82. See Coombes 2003; Filene 2000; Phelan 1997; Phillips 2004; Toews 2004.
83. Perhaps the finest among these is Callewaert and Lath 1989.

1. A SANT BETWEEN MEMORY AND HISTORY

1. See Ashley and Sheingorn 1999; Ashton 2000; Bynum 1987, 1991; Castelli 2004; Coon 1997; and Mooney 1999.
2. Hervieu-Léger 2000 [1993].
3. Hegel 1956 [1837]:2.
4. Ibid.:162.
5. For example, see ibid.: 139, 140, 141, 148, 155, 162, 166, and 167. Ironically, it is the dream, in Halbwachs's work, that is where memory is not social.
6. For example, see Collingwood 1994 [1946]:56, 221–225, 293–294.
7. Ibid.:365–367.
8. Assmann 2006:179.
9. Le Goff 1992:xvii.
10. Ibid.:xi.
11. Ibid.:xviii; Certeau 1988. For an interesting, but woefully underinformed, view of India's lack of "the historical mentality," see le Goff's comments on India as a place of "no significant evolution" for long periods of time and of "a resistance to change" based on the work of Louis Dumont on caste (ibid.:132–133).
12. Rao et al. 2003.
13. See Ali in Inden et al. 2000:166, 225.
14. White 1975.
15. Halbwachs 1980 [1925].
16. It was first published in 1908 and has been republished every decade or so ever since.
17. For more on Jnandev, see Kiehnle 1997a and 1997b.
18. See one of the three opening quotations in Inamdar 1999.
19. Interconnected with the always-contentious subject of a figure's floruit, the debate over whether Namdev and Jnandev were contemporaries also invokes the idea that multiple authors signed works using the names "Namdev" and "Jnandev." Many studies exist in Marathi, Hindi, and English on these subjects. For the most recent works on Jnandev in English, see Kiehnle 1997a and 1997b.
20. Tulpule 1979:316.

21. For more on *pañcakṛṣṇa* and the Mahanubhavs see Feldhaus 1983, 1984; Feldhaus and Tulpule 1992; Raeside 1989; and Feldhaus in Thiel-Horstmann 1983:120–142.

22. Tulpule 1979:318. The oldest manuscripts of the *Līlācaritra* date from the early seventeenth century.

23. Ibid.:317. In the case of Namdev, the legend of his early life as a waylayer has been hotly disputed for over 150 years. On the controversy surrounding Namdev's life as a robber, see chapter 5.

24. Ibid.:316.

25. Deleury 1960:181.

26. Ibid.

27. For more information, see the critical edition of the text produced by V. B. Kolte in 1986.

28. Kulkarni 1992c:23–25. See Feldhaus and Tulpule 1992. Interesting, the title of the work literally means "memorial" and, as a work of *bhakti*, might offer some broad corroboration to my contention that *bhakti* and public memory are intimately linked.

29. Tulpule 1979:320–321.

30. Deshpande 1968:74. The appearance of the ideograph "Vishudas Nama" invites the usual contest over whether the name indicates Namdev of the fourteenth century or Vishnudas Nama of the seventeenth century. In this case, it is likely a reference to the former. See Kulkarni 1992c:23.

31. Ibid.:24–25; see also Kulkarni 1992b:2.

32. See Deshpande 2002, 2007; Guha 2004.

33. Tulpule 1979:443.

34. Kulkarni 1992b. See also Kavitkar in Relekar et al. 1970:705.

35. Kulkarni 1992b.

36. See R. N. Relekar in N. N. Relekar et al. 1970: 863–900, and Kulkarni 1995.

37. The text literally reads something like: "My mother caused me to come forth [into the world] through the dirty, urine-defiled [place]" (*malamutrim*).

38. NG:513 (song 1240).

39. NG:i.

40. Vyas 1940:149.

41. NG:vii–xi.

42. Bharadvaj 1931 [1898].

43. For example, for date of death Bhagat Ram (1936) gives 1370; Puranadas (1888) gives 1364; William Crooke (1896) gives 1443, as does Farquhar (1920), and Adkar (1972) lists a number of possibilities, including 1423 and 1363.

44. Ranade (1933), Hari (1953) and Singh (1981) believe that Namdev died in Pandharpur, having returned from his travels in northern India for this purpose alone. Macauliffe (1906) and Mishra and Maurya (1964) place Namdev's final days in Ghuman, Punjab. Koratkar (1926) puts Namdev's burial place in Narsi Bahmani in Marathwada.

45. The entire image can be viewed in Binyon 1921:plate XVIII.

46. Mahipati 1890 [1762]: preface, verses 8–9. The rest of the chapter draws from Mahipati's account. I cite only direct references.

47. Ibid.:37–39.

48. See Garg 1960:193–248. Another biography may belong to this period. A manuscript attributed to Krishnananda (1600?) containing a *Nāmdev kī Paracaī* is said to be housed in the Nagari Pracarini Sabha archive in Varanasi (Mishra and Maurya 1964; Singh 1981) and was reprinted by K. G. Vanakhande in 1970. However, I have

not had a chance to read over this biography and cannot comment on its contents, but only point to its possible historical situation.

49. Callewaert and Lath 1989:37.

50. Lorenzen 1991:78.

51. Callewaert and Lath 1989:38 [chap. 1, verse 5].

52. Avate 1908:2–37.

53. Unfortunately Avate did not give any editorial information about the selection of songs nor has any subsequent editor of the *Sakaḷa Santa Gāthā.*

54. Despite this story, Mahipati also reports that Gonai, Namdev's mother, carried Namdev in her womb for nine months. See Mahipati 1919:chap. 4, verses 149, 170.

55. Mahipati 1890:chap. 4, verses 13–37.

56. See Barthval 1936; Dikshit 1970; Joshi 1940; Koratkar 1926; Pangarkar 1933; and Sharma 1957.

57. Mahipati 1890:chap. 4, verses 38.

58. Ibid.:chap. 4, verse 202.

59. Although it is possible that Mahipati had access to the *bakhar* literary reference to a similar encounter, his own explicit invocation of Nabhadas, and the wide popularity of this story in northern India, indicate Nabhadas as the more likely root of Mahipati's authoritative stance on this story. Furthermore, Nabhadas would carry more "hagiographical capital" than a *bakhar* within the realm of sacred biography.

60. See Lorenzen 1996:15 and Vaudeville 1993 for more on Namdev's position in relationship to Kabir and the Kabīr Panth.

61. As Hawley has shown, Kabir may be a figure of *nirguna bhakti,* but his songs still contain echoes of the sentiment of *saguna,* through the relating of miracles, encounters with deities (of other *sant*s), and descriptive terms of God. See Hawley 2005, chap. 15.

62. Vaudeville 1993:233.

63. Hawley 2005:270. See also Dharwadker 2003; Hess in Schomer and McLeod 1987:111–142.

64. For example, see Kabir in Callewaert and Op de Beeck 1991:309–310, verse 45; 310, verse 48 [from the Kabīr Granthāvalī]; 367, verse 86; 367–368, verse 92 [from the Kabīr Bījak]. In songs attributed to Kabir, Namdev's ideograph usually appears as *nāmāṃ.* This is also the case for Ravidas, Surdas, and Haridas. Dadu refers to Namdev as *nāmmdev.*

65. B. N. Mundi mentions some similarities between the biographies and "philosophies" of the two figures. See Mundi in Relekar et al. 1970:809–828.

66. See Machwe 1968.

67. Ravidas in Callewaert and Op de Beeck 1991:445 [verse 84]. See also Vaudeville 1993:233n55 on the link between Namdev and Kabir.

68. *Śrī Gurū Granth Sāhab* 1952. The songs are Rag Maru, Ravidas verse 1, line 2 [p. 1106]; Rag Asa, Ravidas verse 5 [p. 487]; Rag Asa, Ravidas verse 2 [p. 487–488].

69. See Lorenzen 1991; Vaudeville 1974.

70. For more on *sant*s as national integrators, see Hawley in Babb and Wadley 1995:107–136; Raghavan 1966.

71. See the assessment of Namdev's position in north Indian religious literary traditions by Lorenzen 1996:11 and in the Marathi tradition by Vaudeville 1996:218. Namdev shares this position with Ramanand (c. 1350).

72. Hawley 2005:14–15.

73. Sharma (1987) is right to point out that *jnana* should be construed as the pursuit not of knowledge but, rather, of a particular kind of knowledge.
74. My thanks to J. S. Hawley for this observation.
75. Mahipati 1890:XII, 173–174.
76. In NG:563–571 [songs 1346–1383].
77. See Novetzke in Beck 2005: 113–138.
78. See Lorenzen 1996:157 for a translation of a verse by Hariram Vyas about Namdev, "to whom even Kanhai submitted"; see also Joshi in Relekar et al. 1970:802–807; Pauwels 1996. In Anantadas, the story receives only a short reference, among others, perhaps indicating its fame already at the time of the composition of Anantadas's biography of Namdev.
79. See Mahipati XXI:61 [p. 343].
80. Interestingly, in this particular story, Mahipati refers to Namdev as a "Vishnudas" (XXI:177 [p. 353]).
81. NG: Appendix A, *Jānābāīce Abhaṅga* section (p. 983, song 408).
82. Callewaert and Lath 1989:41–44.
83. The presence of the song in manuscripts consulted by the *Śrī Namdev Gāthā* government committee is not mentioned, as it rejects the song as apocryphal for other reasons discussed in chapter 5. It has been printed and reprinted for almost a century in the *Sakaḷa Santa Gāthā*, a text almost canonical for the Varkaris. There it appears as song number 7.

2. PUBLIC PERFORMANCE AND CORPORATE AUTHORSHIP

1. Katre 1954:20.
2. Tulpule 1979:353. Note that this is disputed by many of Eknath's admirers.
3. NG: songs 507, 1304, 1570, 1719, 1916; song 441 by Jani; song 1 by Visoba Khecar.
4. There is at least one mention of Namdev having written a *granth*, which in old Marathi can mean either a "poetical composition" or a "scripture." The reference appears at the end of the biographical *Tīrthāvaḷī* (NG: song 961:16). However, in the oldest version of this text, the *granth* is attributed to Jnandev, who indeed is associated with physical books or scriptures. The ideograph seemed to have been changed later. As I argue elsewhere, the biographical *Tīrthāvaḷī* seems to be a compilation of songs by various *sant*s, perhaps organized by Namdev (or *a* Namdev), and variously attributed to Namdev or Jnandev. In any case, the Varkari tradition remembers Namdev as the author of the biographical *Tīrthāvaḷī*, as well as the autobiographical one.
5. Ibid., song 2218, in the Hindi section. See Callewaert and Lath 1989:323 (song 112), where it is contained in manuscripts from the early seventeenth century.
6. According to Molesworth (1991 [1831]:720), this verb means, "to write; to draw, delineate, or trace." In modern spoken Marathi, the word means "to physically write something" and "to trace something," but it also indicates the act of composing literature. Thus one often hears in Marathi that Namdev "wrote" songs, though the meaning is not literally that he physically wrote down his songs. According to Tulpule and Feldhaus (1999), in Old Marathi the meaning was the same as Molesworth asserts (p. 610). Though the editors give the gloss "to record," the sense of the usage is to record a written text, that is, to copy a text, not to record in general. As the verb appears in Old Marathi that I have read—and in particular, in colophons to old manuscripts—the verb *lihiṇe* means to physically write something down. In

contradistinction, Namdev (like many other *sants*, though they may also physically write their songs) is said to "speak," referring to the verb *mhaṇaṇe,* as in *nāma mhaṇe,* or "Namdev says."

7. NG: Janabai section, song 419, verses 1–3.
8. Muktabai.
9. NG:Appendix A, *Jānābāīce Abhaṅga* section (p. 983, song 408). The apparatus in this section indicates that the song appears in a manuscript from Pandharpur and another from Shiraval, both with no date given. The Pandharpur manuscript is one of several others, and one of those manuscripts bears a colophon that gives the date *shaka* 1657, or 1735 C.E. However, the editors of the anthology estimate the age of most of the manuscripts from Pandharpur at around 250 years old or from around 1700 C.E. I would press the date back another fifty years, but not earlier than 1635 C.E. That the same song—word for word—appears in two separate manuscripts suggests the song in oral form is at least fifty years older than its earliest written record.
10. NG:1023, song 516, verses 2 and 3. The song, previously unpublished according to the editors of the NG, was found in one of the oldest collections, contained in Dhule. Another version, most likely a later version, can be found in NG:701, song 1810.
11. Benjamin 1968 [1936].
12. NG:song 1240, verses 4 and 6.
13. Most of these figures were also performers, but their performance abilities are not highlighted as essential to their remembered characteristics, as is the case with Namdev.
14. Mahipati tells another story, in the context of Tukaram's biography, in which Vitthal does become a scribe for Namdev (205–207 [chap. 48, verses 55–75]). However, this song is obviously set within a constructed frame story to provide a context for a song by Tukaram, in which he recalls how Namdev appeared in a dream to him and requested that he continue the work of composing songs to Vitthal. See Sakhare 1990b:571, verses 3597 and 3598. It is interesting to note that only after this dream, according to Mahipati, did Tukaram begin *kirtans* in which "he uttered words full of pathos and love" (ibid.:verse 79]).
15. See Slawek 1996.
16. Mansukhani 1982.
17. Lord 1960; Parry 1971. See the challenge posed to Lord's theory in Smith 1977.
18. For the differences marked out between ritual and performance—and the congruities—see especially Turner 1974, 1986a, and 1986b.
19. Reception theory is different from late modern theories of authorship in that the former invokes a particular hermeneutics in uncovering textual meaning, while the latter involves the ontology of the text itself and the power structures that buffet authorship and readership. However, the two are certainly related and profit from one another's investigations.
20. Tulpule and Feldhaus 1999:160. Tulpule and Feldhaus list four inscriptions as evidence dated 1146, 1164, 1248, and 1289. Of the locations of these inscriptions—Bhandak, Savargav, Manur, and Rohilagadh, respectively—the closest to Pandharpur is Savargav (Savargao), and the reference is to an Amba Devi temple, not to the Vitthal temple in Pandharpur. No inscriptions have been in found in Pandharpur that use the word *kirtan.*

21. See Dagens's essay "Le temple corps du dieu," in Balbir, Pinault, and Fezas 1996.
22. Cf. Ramanujan's explication of *jangama* among early Virashaivas (Ramanujan 1973).
23. Neither Molesworth 1991 [1831] nor Deshpande 1997 [1967] glosses *kirtan* as "temple."
24. See Koparkar 1997:21 [appendix 4]. See Abbott and Godbole 1996 [1931]:70 [chap. 4, verse 172]. See also ibid.:355 [chap. 21, verse 199]: "Dnyaneshwar said to Jani, 'Namdev has assumed four *avatara*s: Pralhad [*sic*], Angad, and Uddhav, and made Krishna subservient to him.'"
25. See the NG:song 923, verses 8–12 [p. 350], and Appendix "Ka" [pp. 1035–40].
26. Ibid.:song 1074, verses 3–5.
27. Ibid.:song 1046, verse 4.
28. Ibid.:song 423, verse 5.
29. Ibid.:song 1466, verse 1–2.
30. Ibid.:song 369, verse 3.
31. Ibid.:song 408, verse 4.
32. This connection is also perhaps indicative of the *shaiva* artifacts present in the Varkari tradition, particularly at its earliest stages, with figures like Namdev and Jnandev.
33. Narada is intimately associated with *bhakti*, especially in primary Sanskrit texts such as the *Bhakti Sūtra* compositions and in the *Bhāgavata Purāṇa*.
34. The most popular *sant* for selection in a Naradiya *kirtan* is Tukaram (seventeenth century).
35. Personal communication with Graham Ajit Bond, August 2001.
36. NG:song 1783, verses 3–4.
37. For more on the Varkari tradition, see Deleury 1960; Karve 1962; Mokashi 1987; and Youngblood 2003.
38. See NG:songs 1140 [p. 478] or 1187 [p. 496], for examples.
39. See NG:song 108 [p. 908] by Gonda or song 311 [p. 960] by Jani.
40. Ranade 1984:122.
41. Tukaram is equally famous as a skilled *kirtankar*, evinced by the fact that a professional *kirtankar* (Vishnupant Pagnis), rather than a professional actor, was cast in the role of the *sant* in the famous V. Damle and S. Fattelal film *Sant Tukaram* (1936).
42. Bourdieu 1993:76. For Bourdieu, the artistic field and the religious field are intimately linked. See Bourdieu in Bourdieu and Wacquant 1992:86.
43. See also Prentiss (1999) on the idea of "embodiment" of *bhakti* as metaphor in text and theology of praxis.
44. Narayanan 2003:501.
45. Assmann 2006:83.
46. Minnis 1984:11–12.
47. Ibid.
48. See William of Wheteley's commentary on the *De Disciplina Scolarium* attributed to Boethius in Sebastian 1970.
49. Quoted in Minnis 1984:12.
50. See Masters 1991.
51. See Grier 1996.
52. Colas 1999.
53. Pollock 2001:7; 1985, 1989, 1990.

54. Jones 1796.
55. Katre 1954:30.
56. Ibid.:30.
57. Barthes 1977 [1968]:143.
58. See Shillingsburg 1996. Shillingsburg also discusses alternatives to the dominance of authorial intention in the editing of texts. See also Fisher 1992. Fisher portrays the development of the scholarly editing profession as well.
59. Latour 1993 [1991]; Trainor 1998.
60. Foucault 1984 [1969]:118.
61. Hawley 1988:287.
62. Hawley does not use "corporate authorship" to describe his perspective on the status of the author. I have employed it here and below in the sense of "combining or uniting into one body" and "collective."
63. The latter symbolic connection is evident in the story of Namdev being tested by Gora the potter to see if he was "sound," which he was not, and thus required a guru, Visoba Khecar, to complete his spiritual awakening.
64. Zelliot and Berntsen 1988.
65. The Marathi Namdev tradition claims that Janabai and Namdev died on the same day. A handful of influential Marathi scholars, such as S. B. Kulkarni, have argued ·that Janabai is a contemporary of the sixteenth-century Brahmin poet Vishnudas Nama (see chapter 4), and hence she is writing about the fourteenth-century Namdev some centuries after he lived. One might explain this verse in the context of the traditional Marathi view that Janabai and Namdev were contemporaries by suggesting that Janabai is remembering Namdev as he is off traveling the Indian subcontinent, the subject of the *Tīrthāvaḷi* tale.
66. See Lutgendorf 1991.
67. Hawley 1981:xii.
68. These two forms of authorship are similarly outlined by Hawley (1988).
69. Prentiss 1999:7.
70. See Hervieu-Léger 2000 [1993].

3. ORALITY AND LITERACY/PERFORMANCE AND PERMANENCE

1. Smith 2001.
2. Ibid.:140.
3. For history in anthropology, see, for example, Faubion 1993:46–50.
4. See Mann 1996:1–50.
5. Ibid.
6. See Kiehnle 1997a:21.
7. See Date and Karve 1995 [1936]:5:2243–2244.
8. One exception to this use of *vahi* in modern Marathi is in reference to Tukaram's *bījakī vahī*.
9. NG:570 [verse 1381].
10. Kiehnle points out this interesting feature of the song in her work on Jnandev (1997a:20).
11. See Gordon 1993.
12. Ranade 1984:132. For more on the connection between patronage and written historical narratives, see Brown 1988:323, 325. See also Goswamy 1966. For instance, many famous performers of the erotic Marathi *lavani* genre, such as Ram Joshi and

Honaji (eighteenth century) became equally famous for their performances of the nonerotic *kirtan*.

13. See Callewaert and Op de Beeck 1991.

14. Callewaert and Lath (1989) would disagree with this assessment. See their chapter "Musicians and Scribes."

15. Ibid.:4.

16. Ibid.:ii–v.

17. NG:i.

18. NG:v.

19. Personal communication, Pandharpur, July 1998. Furthermore, in 2001, Nikte completed a new anthology of Namdev's songs using the Pandharpur manuscripts, and other manuscripts, as a primary resource.

20. The lines read: "utdhavāgamanaprārambha."

21. The popularity of the Uddhav story with Krishna mythology and within the work of *sant* singers has been explored in Hawley 1984. It is also interesting to note that Mahipati considered Namdev an *avatar* of Udho, Utdhav or Uddhav (Abbott and Godbole 1996 [1931]:chap. 9, verses 7–12).

22. Anna Schultz, oral information, July 2000.

23. This is song 201 in the *Śrī Nāmdev Gāthā*.

24. Manuscript accession number 7761 in the collection of Deccan College, Pune, measuring 7.1′ x 6.8′, with 54 folios.

25. The full text of this portion is printed in the appendix.

26. Lohiya 1997.

27. See Woodmansee and Jaszi 1994.

28. We might also notice, as an interesting aside, that at the conclusion of the first *kirtan*, as it is transcribed, is an illustration of two decidedly Christian angels, one playing a trumpet and the other playing a violin!

29. Mahipati in Abbott and Godbole 1996 [1931]:58 [chap. IV:12].

30. Mahipati's tradition floruit is 1716–90. See Khanolkar 1977:237.

31. See colophon in the text, chap. 56, verse 215, and Khanolkar 1977:237.

32. Khanolka:xxvi.

33. From the *Santalīlāmṛta* (1.67–69), quoted and translated in Abbott's introduction to the *Bhaktavijaya* (Abbott and Godbole 1996 [1931]:xxvi).

34. Ibid.:xxvii.

35. According to the *Śrī Nāmdev Gāthā*, the *Ādi* and biographical *Tīrthāvaḷī* appear, with variations, in ten manuscripts out of thirty consulted for the editorial project. Two of these have colophons: from Dhule, dated "1631–1634" for its composition and 1769 for its final shape; and Pandharpur "H" dated 1735. The *Ādi* is also found in Jaganade's manuscript, dated for its final shape to 1731, but attributed to "Jaganade's hand," presumably in the latter part of the seventeenth century. All three sources probably predate the composition of the *Bhaktavijay*.

36. Mahipati 1890 [1762]: chap. 57, verses 220–21.

37. The verb *varṇe* is also glossed by Molesworth as "to sing the excellencies of" (1991 [1831]:735), and in the *Mahārāṣṭra Śabda Kośc* as *guṇa-kathan karaṇe* or "to speak the qualities [of someone or God]" (Date and Karve 1995 [1936]:2757).

38. Mahipati 1890 [1762]: chap. 57, verse 212.

39. Ibid.: verse 223.

40. I have a printed copy of the *Bhaktavijay* from 1890, which is a reprint of an earlier copy, but I do not know the date of that copy. To my knowledge, the first mention

of Mahipati in a Western scholarly publication is in Tassy 1968 [1839]. The first mention in modern Marathi scholarship appears in Janardan 1860. There are apparently earlier mentions of Mahipati in scholarship, but I am unaware of them.

41. Goody 1977; Goody and Watt 1963; McLuhan 1962, 1964; Ong 1982.

42. Goody and Watt 1963:310, 345. Goody and Watt have proposed a fascinating, and troubling, paradigm of scholarship wherein the sociologist should study literate, developed societies, which are those that have history; whereas the job of the anthropologist should be to study oral, illiterate and undeveloped societies, that have no sense of history but merely of present culture (343). They independently moved away from this position in their later work, but the idea that they identify is still prominent in Euro-American thought.

43. Halbwachs 1980 [1925].

44. Other studies examine literacy and orality in the context of cognitive development, such as Luria 1976 and Vygotsky 1962.

45. Stocking 1968. See also Chomsky 1975.

46. Certeau 1988:183.

47. Ibid.:184.

48. Niezen 1991.

49. Ibid.:229. See Lévi-Strauss 1966.

50. Ibid.:253.

51. See Goody 1986, 1987.

52. Katre 1954:20.

53. Sukthankar 1933:lxviii.

54. In Ali 1999:136. See also van der Veer 2001.

55. Van der Veer:143.

56. Doniger 1995.

57. Lutgendorf 1991.

58. Blackburn 1996; Feldhaus 1995, 2003; Flueckiger 1996; Narayan 1989; Ramanujan 1991.

59. See Hawley 1981, 1983, and 1984.

60. Rao et al. 2003:10.

61. Parry in Overing 1985:200–225.

62. Ibid.:200.

63. Ibid.:203–204.

64. Ibid.:221.

65. Ibid.:217.

66. Certeau 1988:137.

67. "We must reckon with the fact that in our civilization, writing is clearly an addition, not an alternative, to oral transmission" (Goody and Watt 1963:345)

68. I use this term without reference to the way in which Eliade and others have used it in the context of "myth" and its functions vis-à-vis history.

69. Eisenstein 1979.

70. Certeau 1988:87.

71. Ibid.:86.

72. Cf. Skaria in Amin and Chakrabarty 1996:13–58, a brilliant essay in which Skaria critiques Derrida through an analysis of writing in the context of the Dangs region of western India in the nineteenth-century encounter with colonialism and suggests that nonphonocentric writing may pose a direct and purposeful chal-

lenge to other technologies of literacy, especially the "logocentrism" identified by Derrida.

73. For example, see Guha 1983:54; Nora 1989:7.

4. NAMDEV AND THE NAMAS

1. My first name is Christian, and, though I am not a practicing Christian, I believe the joke also resonated in a religious way.
2. Monier-Williams 1993 [1851]:745.
3. See Hawley 1988.
4. Ibid.
5. In addition, as seen above, songs are collected by theme, by performance context, by melody or *rag*, etc.
6. Hess in Schomer and McLeod 1987:111–142.
7. Hawley 1979 and 1984.
8. Callewaert and Lath 1989.
9. Although *nama* as an appellation can simply mean "name" thus invoking the Name of God or can suggest "celebrated" or serve as a similar honorific, one does not find this association in Marathi, that is, one does not find Tukaram referred to as "Tuka Nama" for example, as a sign of respect. The prominent place Namdev holds in Marathi hagiography in general suggests that any reference to "Nama" would be a reference to "Namdev."
10. V. L. Bhave (1963 [1898]) distinguishes the first Namdev from Vishnudas Nama, Namdev Shimpi, Nama Pathak, and Nama Yashvant; R. D. Ranade (1933) distinguishes only Namdev and Vishnudas Nama; G. D. Khanolkar (1977) distinguishes Namdev, Vishnudas Nama, Nama Pathak, Nama Yashvant, and Shimpi Nama; S. G. Tulpule (1979) distinguishes Namdev, Vishnudas Nama, Nama Pathak, and Shimpi Nama; S. B. Kulkarni (1992a) distinguishes Namdev, Vishnudas Nama, Shimpi Nama, and Nama Yashvant. I do not include Nama Pathak in this chapter because no songs attributed to him enter the *Śrī Nāmdev Gāthā,* and he is otherwise extremely marginal in the less critically edited *Sakaḷa Santa Gāthā.*
11. Tulpule 1979:344.
12. Ibid.:345; see also Panikkar 1985:163.
13. Ibid.
14. Tulpule 1979:345. See also Skyhawk in McGregor 1992:67–79.
15. See Davis 1993.
16. Tulpule 1979:353.
17. Ibid.:n227.
18. See Dandekar 1953. See also the "pre-Eknath" version of the *Jnāneśvarī* edited by V. K. Rajwade.
19. Tulpule 1979:366.
20. Ranade, Tulpule and Khanolkar, for example, assume he was a Brahmin, but Bhave, Kulkarni, and others, believe he was, like his predecessor—Namdev, born a *shimpi.*
21. Kulkarni 1992a:7.
22. Kulkarni 1993a.
23. NG:344 [song 913.1]. In Mahipati 1890 [1762], throughout.
24. Khanolkar 1977:165.

25. See NG:279 [song 765] and 595 [song 1466].

26. Bhandarkar Oriental Research Institute *bada* number 53.

27. Khanolkar 1977:367.

28. Kulkarni 1992a:7.

29. Ibid.

30. NG:882 [song 14.4–5].

31. NG:309–321.

32. Tulpule 1979:385.

33. Foucault 1984 [1969]:118.

34. See, for example, the innovative text critical work of Winand Callewaert, who, with various collaborators, at a superhuman rate of production, has examined the literary remnant of numerous devotional traditions in northern India, including that which surrounds Namdev.

35. Dharwadker 2003:60. In the case of textual studies of Christianity, see Culpepper 1975. For postmodern formulations similar to Dharwadker's ideas, see Barthes 1977 [1968].

36. Dharwadker 2003:61.

37. Ibid.:61–62.

38. Bryant 1979; Hawley 1979, 1984, 1988.

39. Hawley 1988:274.

40. Dharwadker 2003:61.

41. Ibid.

42. Hawley 1988:274.

43. See Fuller 2001; Parry in Overing 1985: 200–225; Knipe in van der Meij 1997:306–332.

44. NG:511 [song 1232], Marathi. Here, the poet uses the name of Shiva (*śiva*), whom he also worships, in order to make a pun with the word "to sew," *śiva* (with a long middle vowel rather than a short one).

45. NG:810, song 2124, Hindi. See also Callewaert and Lath 1989, where it is song 18 in their critical edition. The song also appears in the *Guru Granth Sahib* in Rag Asa.

46. See ibid.:129 [song 18].

47. Varma 1993: 5:411.

48. Tulpule and Feldhaus 1999:783.

49. Rāg Bhairav, song 1, lines 1 and 2 [p. 1163]; my translation. This song uses synesthesia to mix color and taste, perhaps implying the confounding nature of God's many forms, which is explicit in the latter two verses of the song, where Namdev addresses the complexity of God's "endless forms" (*ananta rup*). My thanks to Jack Hawley for discussing this translation and its mixed metaphors.

50. Rag Bhairav, song 4, line 2 [p. 1164]; my translation.

5. MEMORIES OF SUFFERING IN THE EIGHTEENTH CENTURY

1. Hansen 1983:319–320.

2. This fact is amply demonstrated in a predominantly European context by Hobsbawm 2000 [1969].

3. The reference is to playbill 32 in the collection of the Roja Muthiah Research Library, Chennai, Tamil Nadu. I am grateful to Kathryn Hansen for bringing this playbill to my attention and sharing with me this product of her own research. I am also grateful to Sankaran Radhakrishnan who translated this playbill from Tamil

into English. All translations of the playbill here are his. For more on the Roja Muthiah collection, see Harms 1995.

4. Hobsbawm 2000 [1969].
5. Pollock 1998.
6. For example, see Rana 1981.
7. The story has been cited by several studies in English, including those of Macauliffe 1906; Ranade 1933; and Tulpule 1979.
8. Deleury 1960:181; Sontheimer 1989. However, R. C. Dhere (1984) has suggested that this Vitthal and Nemdev, rather than thieves, were themselves trying to stop cattle thieves, and were killed in the effort.
9. Tulpule 1979:320–321.
10. NG:xv.
11. Sakhare 1990a: 3, song 7.
12. NG:539, song 1305.
13. Kulkarni 1993b:52–68.
14. Khanolkar 1977:384–388.
15. Kulkarni 1993b:68 [verse 180]. Shridhar's biography of Jnandev, *Jñāneśvarcaritra*, composed in the latter part of the seventeenth century, appears to have been a minor composition within his prolific body of work.
16. The use of the third-person perspective by the purported author of a song to describe him- or herself is common in devotional verse in South Asia and does not necessarily indicate a misapprehension of authorship. However, given the possible plethora of Namas before the eighteenth century, this may be the work of one of these other composers. There is no way to know for certain.
17. Sakhare 1990a:3–5 [song 7, lines 16–18].
18. Kulkarni 1993b:60 [verses 31–33].
19. This is not the first time Namdev causes the death of a Brahmin. In a popular story, God comes to test Namdev's resolve in fasting. God disguises himself as a Brahmin who begs for food, and when Namdev refuses because of his vow, the Brahmin dies of starvation. Namdev carries the body to the funeral pyre, performs the rights, and jumps into the flames along with the body. Vitthal shows himself and both God and devotee are saved from the flames. The story is widely told as, for example, by Anantadas, Priyadas, Mahipati, in the *Prem Ambodh Pothī*.
20. Kulkarni 1993b:60 [verses 46–47].
21. There may be elements of ascetic ritualized suicide by decapitation here, as well as echoes of Tantric practice of the "left-hand" variety. Namdev is remembered to have been initiated by a Natha yogi, Visoba Khecar, though his songs are undoubtedly of the *vaishnava* variety.
22. The verb is *vāhaṇe* carries here perhaps three of its several meanings: (1) "to bear" and "to use," (2) "to dedicate, devote, offer in worship"; and (3) "to let flow," as in the flow of blood, when Namdev bleeds from his wound on the Shiva *linga*.
23. In the *Śrī Nāmdev Gāthā* edited by Babar et al (1970), this is attributed to a report by Namdev of a conversation between Rajai (his wife) and Rukmini.
24. As mentioned in the introduction, multiple Namdevs exist in the history of Marathi literature. S. B. Kulkarni argues that the Namdev of this legend is Vishnudas Nama, who is remembered to have lived in the seventeenth century. See Kulkarni 1993b:58.
25. Hobsbawm 2000 [1969]:20.
26. Ibid.:168.

27. Tulpule 1979:321.

28. Varadachari 1966:109.

29. Dirks 1993:5.

30. Ibid.:203–205.

31. Ibid.:10–11.

32. Varadachari 1966:109.

33. This is a popular story with many different retellings. All the versions that I have heard, however, share the detail that Tirumangai was a thief who stole in order to fill the coffers of the Shri Rangam temple.

34. Mani 1998:822–823.

35. I refer to the edition of the *Janam Sākhī* literature edited in McLeod 1980. McLeod observes that the text he consulted, preserved in the India Office Library in London, bears a colophon that gives a date equivalent to 1733, and the name of the text's compiler as Daya Ram Abrol.

36. Ibid.:42–45 [41b–43b].

37. See Aarne and Thompson 1961; Azzolino 1987.

38. Nanak and Namdev share (a) a wanderlust for pilgrimage places; (b) a story of turning a sacred object/place—in Namdev's case a *shaiva* temple, and in Nanak's case, the *mihrāb* in a mosque in Mecca; (c) a tale in which feet must be moved to some place where God is not—in Namdev's case, he moves the feet of his guru, Visoba Khecar, and in Nanak's case, his feet are moved by the mullah of the mosque in Mecca.

39. Nanak met with yet another thief during his travels—it was a hard road indeed! See McLeod 1980:204–206 [193b–196b].

40. See Gordon 1994.

41. Richards and Rao 1980.

42. Ibid.:119.

43. Kennedy 1985 [1907]:95.

44. Bayly 1983:220.

45. Phoolan Devi has been the subject of numerous media accounts. See, for example, the 1994 Hindi film *Bandit Queen* or her autobiography, *I, Phoolan* (1996).

46. Gordon 1994:114.

47. Ibid.:20.

48. Ibid.:114.

49. Lorenzen 1978:71.

50. Ibid.

51. See "Subaltern Sadhus" in Pinch 1996, especially p. 25.

52. Lorenzen 1978:62.

53. Pinch 1996:25.

54. Ibid.:24. See also Shahid Amin's discussion of the Ghazi Miyan in Chatterjee and Ghosh 2002:19–32.

55. Ibid.

56. Hobsbawm 2000 [1969]:16.

57. Lorenzen 1978:68.

58. Hobsbawm 2000 [1969]:139, 157.

59. See Gold 1988; Sax 1991; Urban 2001; van der Veer 1988, 1994:106–137. Conversely, marketplaces are religious sites as well. See Sen 1996 and Yang 1998.

60. Ibid.:137.

61. See Deleury 1960:36.
62. See Appadurai 1977; Breckenridge in Khare and Rao 1986:21–53; Appadurai and Breckenridge 1976; and Talbot 1991. In addition, see discussions of the role of temples in the work of Dirks 1993, Sax 1991, and van der Veer 1988, among many other studies in South Asia.
63. Bayly 1983:29, 128.
64. Hobsbawm 2000 [1969]:53.
65. Oral information from Sham Lal Purwah, Joint Secretary, Namdev Mission Trust, New Delhi, November 14, 2002.
66. Hobsbawm 2000 [1969]:107, 153.
67. For a contemporary study of economic and labor metaphors in religious songs, see Urban 2001.
68. Ibid.:101.
69. Lorenzen 1996:11.
70. Ibid.:25.
71. See ibid.:16 and Mann 2001:51. For the reference for this song and the two others, see Lorenzen 1996:272n2.
72. See Callewaert and Lath 1989:213, 327 [verse 118].
73. Lorenzen 1996:16–18.
74. Ibid.
75. Ibid.:19.
76. Ibid.
77. Sakhare 1990c:670 (song 3554) and Abbott and Godbole 1996 [1931]:70 [chap. 4, verse 172]. See also ibid.:355 [chap. 21, verse 199].
78. Noted as manuscript "Ā" in NG.
79. Noted as manuscript "Pā" in NG.
80. Callewaert and Lath 1989:128–129.
81. I have examined one *bada* in the collection of the Bhandarkar Oriental Research Institute, which the Institute collected from the Shrigonda Jain Mandir in Ahmednagar district, that relates a *samvad* or conversation between Namdev and Mughal emperor Akbar (1556–1605).
82. The sultan in question is not named. Callewaert and Lath suppose that it is Firoz Shah Bahmani, but the text, to my reading, does not make this clear.
83. *Guru Granth Sahib*, Rag Bhairav, song 10 [pp. 1165–1166], verses 1–4, my translation.
84. Ibid.: verse 22: *bakhasī hindū mai terī gāi.*
85. Kulkarni 1992b. See also Kavitkar in Relekar et al. 1970:705; Tulpule 1979:443.
86. *pādśāh=pātasyā*
87. *khāne sānaka kaṃdurī (kaṃdurī=kadurī).* A Marathi word for meat is *kadurī.*
88. No particular word for "cow meat" is used here, but the Persian derivative, *khānā*, in older Marathi implies food eaten by Muslims, and, by extension, beef. The legend retold orally and in other sources also makes a point of the meat being beef. However, in other tales, it is merely a dead cow before Namdev, and not a plate of rotting beef. See Mahipati's account, for example, in Abbott and Godbole 1996 [1931]:171–176.
89. One Marathi word for jasmine is *kuṃdurī.* The author is creating a pun between the word for meat, *kaṃdurī*, and the word for jasmine, *kuṃdurī.*
90. Rajwade 1924:103.

91. See Kulkarni 1992b:2–3.
92. See Laine 2001.
93. Mahipati 1890 [1762]:10.221.
94. Ibid.:10.170.
95. Kulkarni 1993b:67 [verse 55]. The summary to follow is taken from pp. 67–68, verses 54–78.
96. It should be noted here that plundering Pandharpur was not an activity solely undertaken by Muslims. Krishnadevaraya looted the Vitthal temple in 1521 as well, taking the image of Vitthal into the Vijayanagar kingdom. See Davis 1993:30.
97. Smith 2000.
98. A third type involves a king or sultan seeking advice from a *sant,* as one finds, for example, with Madhukar Shah and Hariram Vyas (sixteenth century), Prataparudra and Caitanya (sixteenth century), or Shivaji and Ramdas (seventeenth century).

6. A SANT FOR THE NATION IN THE NINETEENTH AND TWENTIETH CENTURIES

1. Gellner 1983:56.
2. Hobsbawm and Ranger (1983) have noted something similar to Gellner about the process of nations constructing the history of their being and becoming. See especially the introduction.
3. Nora 1989.
4. In 1849 Gondhalekar edited and published a stand-alone edition of the *Samādhi* attributed to Namdev.
5. Bhave 1963 [1898]:126–127.
6. Dilip Chitre, a scholar of Varkari and Marathi literature and a premier poet of Marathi and English, in a personal communication (Pune, India, May 21, 1998) described the *Sakaḷa Santa Gāthā* as being "at the heart of the Varkari tradition."
7. An aside in the *Śrī Nāmdev Gāthā*'s introduction states that Ajgaonkar changed his position in later editions of his publication.
8. Ajgaonkar 1927:21–24; Macauliffe 1906:20; Ranade 1933:186; and Tulpule 1979:334 and 334n129.
9. "Namdev," in *Encyclopedia Britannica,* Encyclopedia Britannica Online.
10. Ajgaonkar 1927:21–24.
11. One might note that pilgrimages are ideal operating grounds for thieves. During the yearly Pandharpur pilgrimage in July, the newspapers regularly report the number of robberies that take place among the Varkaris.
12. In the conceptualization of Habermas, this would be the "political public sphere" of an earlier period in European history when public intellectuals sought to affect political change through collective discursive action. See Habermas 1991 [1962]. However, I use the term "public sphere" in a way that borrows from Bourdieu's critique of Habermas and his own use of the term, which does not see "reason" and "rationalization" as unchanging characteristics of the public sphere, as Habermas did. In this way, Bourdieu more fully investigates those fields often imagined to be outside "rationalized" action: the spaces of art, belief, and literature, for example. See Bourdieu 1993.
13. Kavitkar et al. 1980:36 [appendix].
14. For more on the literary and political aspects of this history, see Palshikar 2007.

15. *NG*: preface, first page.
16. Kavitkar et al. 1980:9–37 [appendix].
17. Kamat and Dhere 1970:1.
18. Yet they couched their scholarship in terms of needing to be sensitive to the religious sentiments of Namdev's followers, and the importance of respecting *bhagavata dharma*, as they so often asserted. Despite the use of such religious language and imagery, the followers of Namdev in Maharashtra, and in particular the *shimpi* community there, are generally aligned with the Congress party, not with the Hindu Right, who also invoke *bhagavata dharma* as their *raison d'être*. I gathered this perspective from interviews with Namdev followers in various conversations during 1998–2002.
19. For example, see a discussion of the controversy in Maharashtra surrounding James Laine's book *Shivaji: Hindu King in Islamic India* (Laine 2001) in Novetzke 2004.
20. *Sant Namdev: 700th Birth Anniversary Souvenir* 1970.
21. Ibid.:n.p.
22. Nath 1983.
23. Ibid.:7.
24. Kulkarni 1998.
25. See Dharmvir 1997 and 2000. See also Wakankar 2003, especially chap. 4.
26. From conversations with N. N. Relekar, Pune, July 2000. The AIR programs, which aired from New Delhi, ran through July 2000.
27. Kemper, for example, describes the interaction between Sinhala nationalism and the text of the *Mahāvaṃsa* as "creating a phenomenon that is both local and foreign, ancient and modern" (1991:10).
28. Raghavan 1966:15.
29. Ibid.:123–128.
30. NG : "nivedan" (preface), 1.
31. Kavitkar in Kavitkar et al. 1970:127–129.
32. Ibid.:119, 122–123. Kavitkar lists sixteen others, including Lahore and Ludhiana.
33. Ibid.:124–125.
34. Ibid.:126–127. Kavitkar lists over twenty sites in Rajasthan.
35. Ibid.:127.
36. Ibid.
37. Nora 1989:22.
38. Ibid.
39. Ibid.:7.
40. See Chatterjee 1993.
41. Karandikar 1970.
42. Ibid.:i–ii.
43. Kavitkar et al. 1970:111. The quotation from Namdev songs is: *nācū kīrtanāce raṁ gīṁ jñānadīpa lāvū jagīṁ*.
44. Ibid.:112.
45. Ibid. See also NG:640, song 1630, verse 2.
46. See Nemade in Lele 1981:113–123.
47. Kamat and Dhere 1970:105. I could not find this song attributed to Namdev or Kabir, but did find an almost identical song attributed to Gorakhnath among his *sakhi* literature (see Callewaert and Op de Beeck 1991:1:491 [song 58]).
48. Kamat and Dhere 1970:105.
49. Relekar et al. 1970:712–726.

50. Ibid.:715–716.
51. Anderson 1983 and Gellner 1983.
52. Chatterjee 1986.
53. Hobsbawm 1990.
54. Nehru 1946.
55. Mookerji 1914, 1921.
56. Halbfass 1990:221.
57. Dirks asserts that there is an "irrevocable link between History and the Nation-State" in modernity (1990:25).
58. Asad 1993:205.
59. Hayes 1960:164, 166–168. Notice, however, that Carleton Hayes also thought that Christian missions in Africa and Asia would curb the "rising obsessive nationalism in those continents" and render them less "belligerent" to "international cooperation and peace," which sounds like a critique of Indian nonalignment policies of the period (1960:182). Obviously, "religion" for Hayes also meant "Christian" in many situations.
60. Ibid.:167–168.
61. See Anderson 1983:15–16.
62. Bourdieu 1971:2.
63. Anderson 1983:78.
64. Hutchinson 1994:19.
65. Gellner 1983:124–125.
66. Ibid.:7.
67. Hobsbawm in Hobsbawm and Ranger 1983:269, 303.
68. Ibid.:4.
69. Hobsbawm 1990:68–73.

7. THE IDEA OF NAMDEV IN TWO FILMS IN THE TWENTIETH CENTURY

1. For example, *Lanka Dahan* (1917); *Shri Krishna Janam* (1918); *Kaliya Mardan* (1919); *Sant Namdev* (1921); *Buddha Dev* (1923); *Satyabhama* (1925); *Bhakt Prahlad* (1926); *Sant Eknath* (1926); *Bhakta Sudama* (1927); *Rukmini Haran* (1927); *Bhakta Damaji* (1928); *Sant Mirabai* (1929).
2. See Dwyer 2006.
3. Namdev does appear as a character in other *sant* films, such as *Sant Dnyaneshwar* (Marathi and Hindi 1940, dir. V. G. Damle and S. Fattelal), but these are the only two films specifically about Namdev.
4. By comparison, Tukaram has had at least six films made about his life, mostly in Marathi, of which two are generally available. At least two films have been made about Eknath, though neither can be located, and about Jnandev there are at least five, three of which are available. For Jnandev: *Shri Dnyaneshwar* (1924, silent, dir. Shrinath Patankar); *Sant Dnyaneshwar* (Marathi and Hindi 1940, dir. V. G. Damle and S. Fattelal); *Sant Nivrutti Dnyandev* (1964, dir. Madhukar Pathak, in Marathi); *Sant Gyaneshwar* (1964, dir. Manibhai Vyas, in Hindi); *Sant Gyaneshwar* (1982, dir. unknown, in Hindi). For Eknath: *Sant Eknath* (1926, silent, dir. D. G. Phalke); *Eknath* (1938, dir. Harshadrai Sakerlal Mehta, in Tamil). For Tukaram: *Sant Tukaram* (1921, silent, dir. D. G. Phalke); *Jai Vitthal* (1931, silent, dir. unknown); *Sant*

Tukaram (1936, dir. Damle and Fattelal, in Marathi and Hindi); *Tukaram* (1937, dir. M. L. Tandon, in Hindi); *Tukaram* (1938, dir. B. Narayan Rao, in Tamil and Telugu); *Sant Tukaram* (1963, dir. Sundarrao Nadkarni, in Hindi and Marathi); *Bhakta Tukaram* (1973, dir. Madhusudan Rao, in Telugu).

5. NG:604 [song 1499.1].

6. Cf. Ill. 7.2 from Apte's 1937 film. It seems that in all films on Namdev, unlike hagiographies about the *sant,* Namdev is shown engaging in his traditional occupation as a tailor, though always in a lackluster, distracted way.

7. NG:659 [song 1691.1].

8. The story is similar to the legend of Namdev causing a Shaiva temple to turn toward him, but, as shown below, this story is already a part of the later narrative of Talpade's film.

9. NG:511 [song 1232.1].

10. Lecture to Penn-in-India students at the Film and Television Archives of India, Pune, July 11, 2005.

11. SSG:54, song 156, verse 1.

12. This is an old idea in Indian philosophical theology, especially in the theories of Madhva (thirteenth c.) and Ramanuja (eleventh c.).

13. See Desai 1969 [1912] and Shukla-Bhatt 2003, as well as Vaudeville in Schomer and McLeod 1987:21–40.

14. NG:976–7 [songs 381.6 and 383.7].

CONCLUSION

1. Assmann 1997:15. See also the introduction.

2. See Hawley 2005:2–9.

3. Dirks 1993:58.

4. See Hawley 2005:318–336.

5. Novetzke 2003.

6. Chakrabarty 2000; Prakash 2000.

7. See Ali in Inden et al. 2000:218–219, 225; see also Novetzke 2003:307–313 and Novetzke 2006. For the idea that history replaces religion in modernity, see Certeau 1988.

8. For example, Asad 1993.

9. Certeau (1988) is the most prominent critic here, but for a recent treatment see *History and Theory* (vol. 45, December 2006).

10. Of the latter, the two best recent studies are by Ali in Inden et al. 2000:165–229 and Rao et al. 2003.

GLOSSARY

Note that most spellings of Sanskrit words conform to common pronunciation practices in Marathi, which means in some cases, for example, "a" is retained at the end of words, and in some cases it is dropped. Since much of the vocabulary of Marathi in the context of *sant* materials draws from Sanskrit, Sanskrit is listed as the source language for many definitions. However, in almost all cases the words are common features of Marathi vocabulary.

Abhang (abhaṅg): Marathi, lit. "unbroken"; a verse form used for devotional songs in Marathi from the earliest period onward. Several types are enumerated in songs attributed to Namdev, including the small (*lahān*) *abhang*, which is of two lines and similar to the *pad* in northern India, with rhymes in the middle and end of each line; a second type called a big (*moṭhā*) *abhang* consists of a series of 3½ line units (six syllables in the first three, four in the last line) where the first, second, and third lines often rhyme. The *abhang* is often considered a form of the *ovi* (see below).

Advaita: Sanskrit [Skt.], lit. "nondual"; in Sanskritic philosophy, one of the most influential schools of thought that argues there is no distinction between God and human souls.

Ajanavriksha (ajānavr̥kṣa): Skt., lit. "unborn" [*ajāna*] + "tree" [*vr̥kṣa*]; a sui generic tree, associated with Jnandev's memorial site in Alandi.

Akhaṇḍa kirtan (kīrtan): Skt., lit. "endless *kirtan*"; a type of performance of *kirtan* that can last hours or days without a break.

Alvar (ālvār): Tamil, lit. "one immersed in God"; a title given to devotional singers in Tamil from the seventh to the tenth centuries in south India.

Anath (anāth): Skt., lit. "lordless"; a term used by Marathi devotional composers, particularly of low caste, to describe their existential anguish; often translated as "orphan."

Arya (ārya): Skt., lit. "excellent," "noble"; the word has many meanings, but in this context, indicates a two-line verse form used in many Indian languages.

Avatar (avatār): Skt., lit. "descended"; a term used to describe incarnations of Vishnu, such as Krishna, but also incarnations of other figures, such as Prahlad.

Bada (bāḍa): Marathi, lit. "notebook"; a term for the notebooks carried by *kirtankars*, usually considered a lower form of "the book" than manuscripts or *pothi*s in Marathi.

Bakhar: Marathi, lit. "chronicle"; an offical, state record-keeping form in prose used in Marathi from the fifteenth century onward.

Balkrida (bālkrīḍā): Skt, lit. "child's play"; a genre of song in many Indian languages that recall the childhood exploits of Krishna.

Bhagat; Skt, Hindi, etc., lit. "a devotee"; the title given to *sants*, *pirs*, and other religious figures whose songs appear in the *Guru Granth Sahib.*

Bhagavata dharma (Bhāgavata dharma): Skt., lit. "the way [*dharma*] of the Lord [*bhagavata*]"; a reference, in general, to *vaishnava* religious practices and beliefs.

Bhaj: Skt. verbal root, lit. "divide, share, bestow, enjoy," etc.; the root of the words *bhakti*, *bhakta*, and *bhajan*.

Bhajan: Skt. lit. "a thing enjoyed or shared"; a public, collective performance, usually in the form of singing one or more names of God repetitively.

Bhakta: Skt. usually lit. "one who exemplifies *bhakti*" but also lit. "distributed, divided, loved" as well as "cooked" as in food or a meal; a term that generally denotes someone who is devoted to something in ways that conform to the general idea of *bhakti*.

Bhaktakaṁsa: Skt. lit. "a plate [*kamsa*] of food [*bhakta*]."

Bhakti: Skt. lit. "distribution, division, belonging to, attachment, devotion"; usually glossed as "devotion"; implies both a devotion to one's deity and a devotion to a community or public.

Bhakti mārg: Skt. lit. "the way [*mārg*] of *bhakti*"; usually juxtaposed to the way of action [*karma*] and learning-meditation [*jñāna*].

Bhaktiras: Skt. lit. "the flavor [*ras*] of *bhakti*"; an aesthetic category for some literary or performative cultural production adjudicated as communicating the essence of *bhakti*.

Bhanita (bhaṇitā): Skt. lit. "spoken" but also "relation" and "description"; the name of the line in Indian (Sanskrit and regional languages) poetry and song, usually ultimate or penultimate, that signifies the purported author's name.

Bhava (bhāva): Skt. lit. "becoming, appearance" and "emotion, affection"; a technical term in classical aesthetic theory, correlated to "sentiments" or *rasa*s generated in performance or literature.

Caritra: Skt. lit. "comportment, exploits"; usually glossed as "biography."

Chipi (chīpī): Hindi, from *chīpnā* or *chāpnā*, "to print," lit. "printer"; a caste name in northern India for cloth printers, sometimes associated with the *shudra varna* and sometimes with the *kshatriya varna;* Namdev's purported caste.

Chipi (chipī): Hindi, from *chipnā* "to hide," lit. "one who hid"; a play on words used by some of Namdev's north Indian followers to relate their caste name, *chīpī* (see above), to the story of Parashuram, an *avatar* of Vishnu who killed all the *kshatriya*s except those that hid (*chipī*), thus implying that Namdev's caste is *kshatriya* because they hid.

Dadu Panth (Dādū Panth): Hindi. lit. "the way [*panth*] of Dadu"; a religious community centered on Dadu Dayal (1544–1603), a Rajasthani *sant;* followers are called Dādū Panthīs.

Darshan (darśan): Skt., lit. "view"; two key meanings are indicated by this term; (1) viewing a diety, sacred person, or sacred object in Hinduism; (2) a term used in the sense of a "school of thought" or "point of view" differentiating the six classical Indian philosophical systems.

Das (dās): Skt. lit. "devotee, servant, disciple"; feminine form is *dāsī*.

Deshbhakti (deśbhakti): Skt. lit. "*bhakti* felt toward the nation/land [*desh*]"; often glossed as nationalism, but carrying explicitly Hindu (though not necessarily Hindu chauvinistic) connotations.

Dharma: Skt. lit. "that which is held together, maintained, made firm"; a key concept in Hinduism, Buddhism, Jainism, and Sikhism that is variously translated by terms ranging from "law, practice, duty, justice" to "way" and "religion," the latter particularly since the nineteenth century. Its antonym is *adharma*.

Dhrupad (dhṛpad): Skt. lit. "refrain"; the refrain line of a song; and also a classical form of Indian vocal music.

Dohra (dohrā): Hindi lit. "couplet"; a meter of rhyming couplets common in old Hindi and *sant* songs. Also spelled *dohā*.

Fakir (faqīr): Arabic, Urdu, lit. "poor"; a Muslim ascetic.

Gopal (Gopāl): Skt. lit. "a male cow-herder"; another term for Krishna, usually in reference to his association with the *gopi*s.

Gopi (gopī): Skt. lit. "a female cow-herder"; from the mythology of Krishna's youth, these are the young women associated, often amorously, with Krishna.

Granth: Skt. lit. "tying together"; refers both to a book and a composition.

Guna (guṇa): Skt. lit. "a quality or characteristic." See *saguna* and *nirguna*.

Gurudvar (gurudvār): Skt., Punjabi, lit. "the door [*dvara*] to the Guru"; a temple sacred to Sikhs that serves as a social nexus and holds the *Guru Granth Sahib*. Also sometimes written as *gurdwara, gurdwar, gurdvara*, etc.

Harikatha (harikathā): Marathi, Hindi, etc., lit. "stories [*katha*] about Vishnu/Krishna [*hari*]"; a devotional performance art known throughout India in which stories about Krishna, *avatar*s of Vishnu, the lives of *vaishnava sant*s, and other subjects are explored in public performance with a mix of song, dance, and exposition. *Harikatha* closely resembles Marathi *kirtan*, and *harikatha* is sometimes interchanged with the word *kirtan* in the songs attributed to the Marathi Varkari *sant*s. An emphasis is placed on linear narrative in *harikatha* as opposed to the two-part structure of exposition contained in Marathi *kirtan*.

Harikirtan (harikīrtan): Marathi, Hindi, etc., lit. "repeating the glories [*kirtan*] of Vishnu/Krishna [*hari*]"; a public devotional form that usually consists of repeating one or more of the names of Vishnu, such as "Hari Krishna," with a group, sometimes with musical accompaniment, and usually to an ever-increasing tempo. This is rarely a narrative, expository, or complex form.

Itihasa (itihāsa): Sk. lit. "thus indeed it was"; a term for a genre of Sanskrit literature that encompasses the epics and *purana* and other materials that are considered accounts of real events from the past; sometimes glossed as "history" and often a translation for the word "history" in Hindi and Marathi, as in the *Bharat Itihasa Samshodak Mandal*, or "The Indian History Research Association."

Janmapatra: Skt., Marathi, etc. lit. "birth [*janma*] document [*patra*]"; an astrological or horoscopic calculation made about an individual, often a famous one, such as a *sant*, based on details regarding the moment of his or her birth (such as time, date, place, arrangement of celestial bodies, etc.). Commonly in Marathi also *janmapatrikā* and in Hindi *janmapatrī*.

Jati (jāti): Skt. lit. "birth"; refers to the cross-religious divisions of Indian society that name any of thousands of "castes" usually associated with a particular form of labor, region, or other charateristic idiosyncratically related to an ethnos, e.g., *shimpi* as the *jati* title for the Maharashtrian tailor caste. Not to be confused with *varna*, another term often glossed as "caste." See *varna*.

Jnana yoga (jñāna yoga): Skt. lit. "the discipline [*yoga*] of knowledge [*jnana*]"; one of the three *yoga*s of the *Bhagavad Gita*, juxtaposed with the disciplines of action (*karma*) and devotion (*bhakti*).

Kabir Panth (Kabīr Panth): Hindi lit. "the way [*panth*] of Kabir"; a religious community primarily in northern India that reveres and centers on the songs and legacy of *sant* Kabir of the fifteenth century. A member of this community is called a Kabīr Panthī.

Kalakshepam (kalākṣepam): Skt., south Indian languages; a narrative public performance art similar to *harikatha*.

Kallar (Kaḷḷar, also Kaḷḷan): Tamil; the caste or *jati* name of a dominant, and in some cases royal, caste in several regions of Tamil Nadu, especially Pudukkotai, Madurai, and Tanjavar. In some areas, Kallars had the reputation of thieves.

Karma: Skt. lit. "action"; used in multiple ways primarily in Hinduism, Buddhism, and Jainism; sometimes indicates a kind of accumulated record of activities in one's life; sometimes indicates "destiny"; sometimes juxtaposed to other modes of soteriology, the other *yoga*s of the *Bhagavad Gita*.

Katav (kaṭāv): Marathi, lit. "ostentatious"; an entertaining poetic metrical form in Marathi.

Kirtan (kīrtan): Skt., Marathi, Hindi, etc., lit. "to recite, to glorify"; a public performance genre in India among Hindus and Sikhs primarily, *kirtan* takes multiple forms in different regions (see, for example, *harikirtan*). In Marathi, *kirtan* is a mixed form of song, dance, theater, exposition, music, and so on, in a fairly structured format. A performer of *kirtan* is called a *kīrtankār*. In Maharashtra, Namdev is considered the first *kirtankar*.

Krishnakatha (kṛṣṇakathā): Skt. lit. "stories [*katha*] about Krishna"; a more specific form of *harikatha*.

Krishnakirtan (kṛṣṇakīrtan): Skt. lit. "repeating the glories [*kirtan*] of Krishna"; a more specific form of *harikirtan*.

Krishnalila (kṛṣṇalīlā): Skt. lit. "the play [*lila*] of Krishna"; a genre of composition and public performance that retells legends from Krishna's life in a theatrical and musical form. The public performance of the *krishnalila*, like the *rāmalīlā* ("the play of Ram"), can take many days or weeks to complete and can travel to various locations.

Kshatriya (kṣatriya): Skt. lit. "ruler"; the second of the four castes in the *varna* hierarchy, usually glossed as "warrior."

Lavani (lāvaṇī): Marathi, Hindi, lit. "beautiful, charming"; a genre of love song, primarily in Marathi.

Lila (līlā): Skt. lit. "play"; refers to both the "playful" actions of Krishna and Ram, that is, their life stories, and the telling of those stories in the context of a "play"; see *krishnalila* above.

Linga (liṅga): Skt. lit. "a mark or sign"; a metonymic representation of Shiva, sometimes resembling or in the form of a phallus and often coupled with a *yoni*, lit. "womb, uterus, vagina, source." A central feature of *shaiva* worship.

Loka: Skt. lit. "the world"; can indicate both the world as in the physical Earth (and other worlds) as well as a (or the) community of humans in the world, i.e., "mankind." In Marathi and Hindi, the word often refers to the public at large.

Mahānubhāv: Marathi; the name of a religious community centered around forms of Krishna that arose in the thirteenth century in Maharashtra.

Manavatavada (mānavatāvāda): Marathi, Hindi, etc., lit. "a vow (*vada*) on behalf of humanity (*manavata*)"; the Indic translation of the modern idea of the humanism. The translation for "humanist" then is *mānavatāvādī*.

Mandir: Skt. lit. "home"; usually indicates a Hindu or Jain temple.

Marg (mārg): Skt. lit. "search, path, custom"; usually indicates a mode of something, as in *bhaktimarg* as the "way of *bhakti*."

Math (maṭh): Skt. lit. "a dwelling"; usually glossed as a type of Hindu monastery.

Maya (māyā): Skt. lit. "illusion"; an epistemological idea in several Indic philosophies and religions that posits the phenomenal world is an illusion.

Mela (meḷā): Skt. lit. "a meeting"; refers to a gathering of any kind; in the context of Hinduism, usually indicates a public gathering at a holy or pilgrimage site at a particularly auspicious time.

Nama mhane (nāma mhaṇe): Marathi, lit. "Namdev [Nama] says [*mhane*]"; the most common *bhanita* or ideograph associated with Namdev's authorial function.

Namakirtan (nāmakirtan): Skt, Hindi, Marathi, Punjabi, etc., lit. "the glorious repetition [*kirtan*] of the name(s) of God [*nama*]"; a simple, repetitive public performance, usually by a group, consisting of the repetition of the name or names of a deity. Not substantially different from *nāmasaṁkīrtan.*

Namamudra (nāmamudrā): Marathi, Hindi, lit. "the symbol [*mudra*] of the name [*nama*]"; a reference to the ideograph of a poem or song. One also finds ideograph referred to as the *mudrikā*, the "little symbol."

Naradiya kirtan (Nāradīya kīrtan): Marathi lit. "*kirtan* in the tradition of Narada"; a type of Marathi *kirtan* genealogically related to the mode of story-telling associated with the ancient Hindu sage Narada.

Natha (Nātha): Skt.; the general designation for a variety of *shaiva* religious communities throughout India who practice various forms of *yoga* and meditation in an attempt to generate superhuman powers and immortality.

Nayak (nāyak): Skt., Marathi, Hindi, etc., lit. "a leader, a hero"; a term for the male protagonist of a drama; also, in Marathi, a designation for the leader of a militia.

Nayannar (Nāyaṇmār): Tamil lit. "leader, exemplar"; poet-singers of Tamil around the seventh to ninth centuries devoted to the worship of Shiva.

Nirguna (nirguṇa): Skt. lit. "having no [*nir*] characteristics [*guna*]"; in the context of *bhakti* and its performative and devotional practices, refers to the worship of a non-anthropomorphic deity, often associated with monotheism, nondualism (*advaita*), and antagonism toward the depiction of deities, pilgrimage, external worship, etc.; often associated with meditative disciplines and especially with *mantra* practices and association with a guru.

Ovi [ovī]: Marathi, possibly lit. "strung together"; a poetic metrical form, the two most common of which are the *grānthik*, or "literary," form, usually recited rather than sung, made of three lines of equal length and one of half the length of the previous three, the form preserved in the *Jñāneśvarī*; and the *kaṇṭhastha*, or "voice" ("oral"), form, usually song, which conforms to the meter of the *abhang* in general (see above).

Padshah (Pādśāh): Persian derivative, lit. "Lord [*shah*] of kings [*pati* or *pad*]"; a term used in the second millennium C.E. in South Asia to refer to a Muslim ruler; also interchangeable with Bādśāh and Sultān.

Palkhi (pālkhī): Marathi, lit. "bed"; the palanquin on which icons associated with Varkari *sant*s are carried from the *sant*'s hometown to Pandharpur or to other locations, as part of pilgrimage, principally of the Varkari pilgrimage to Pandharpur in the month of Ashadh.

Parivar (parivār): Skt., Marathi, Hindi, etc., lit. "family." The term can also have a metaphorical meaning, indicating a group of like-minded individuals, as in the *sant parivar*, the "family" of "saints," that does not suggest biological kinship, but spiritual kinship.

Payri (pāyrī): Marathi, lit. "step"; can refer in Marathi to the second step of the old entrance to the Vitthal temple in Pandharpur that contains a memorial or *samadhi* to Namdev, said to be the site of his death. See Illustration 1.1.

Pir (pīr): Persian lit. "elder"; the title in Persian and Urdu for a holy person, usually a Muslim; common in Sufism.

Pothi (pothī): Marathi lit. "manuscript."

Povada (povāḍā): Marathi lit. "a panegyric"; a Marathi poetic form popular from the seventeenth century onward, usually recounting heroic military campaigns and the lives of famous warriors or kings.

Pradakshina (pradakṣiṇā): Skt. lit. "to the right"; the process of circumambulating a sacred site or object by keeping the site or object on one's right-hand side.

Prasad (prasād): Skt. lit. "favor, grace"; refers to an item given to a deity or holy person (dead or alive) that is returned to the giver and usually distributed.

Prem: Skt. lit. "love"; usually refers to nonsexual love, in the sense of "tenderness" and "affection," as well as "devotion" and "friendship."

Puja (pūjā): Skt. lit. "worship"; the ritual actions and implements invovled in Hindu veneration of a deity or divine figure.

Qawwali (qawwālī): Persian lit. "utterance"; in Sufism, a devotional public vocal and musical performance meant to instill spiritual ecstasy in listeners.

Rag (rāg): Skt. Hindi, etc., lit. "color, melody"; a fixed set of notes, sometimes also fixed in terms of melody and tempo, meant to evoke a particular mood in classical, devotional, and some popular musical forms, both instrumental and vocal. *Rag* also is a means of categorizing devotional songs in northern India in handwritten manuscripts, the exemplar being the *Guru Granth Sahib*.

Rang (raṅg): Skt. Hindi, etc., lit. "color, hue."

Rashtriya sant (rāṣṭrīya sant): Hindi, Marathi, etc., lit. "a national [*rashtriya*] *sant*."

Raslila (rāslīlā): Skt. Hindi, etc., lit. "the play [*lila*] of the dance [*ras*]"; a public dance-play that recalls moments from Krishna's amorous play with the *gopi*s.

Sadhu (sādhū): Skt. lit. "one who is unimpeded"; a Hindu holy renunciate.

Saguna (saguṇa): Skt. lit. "with [*sa*] characteristics [*guna*]"; in the context of *bhakti* and its performative and devotional practices, refers to the worship of a describable, often anthropomorphic deity. Regularly embraces the depiction, in physical and literary form, of deities, their mythology, modes of worshipping them, etc. Often involves described relationships between devotees and deities in human ways, i.e., the love of a mother for a child, of a lover for another lover, etc.

Sakhi (sākhī): Hindi lit. "a witness, testimony"; a rhyming verse form closely associated with *nirguna bhakti* in northern India.

Samadhi (samādhi): Skt. lit. "put together, union"; several meanings, including (1) a state of deep meditation; (2) a tomb or other memorial containing a holy person, usually a *yogi*; and (3) a text that tells the story of the last days of life of a particular figure, usually a holy figure.

Samaj (samāj): Skt. lit. "a meeting, society"; often used to designate ethnic, religious, caste, or other communities.

Samkirtan (saṁkīrtan): Skt., Marathi, etc.; a collective public form of repetitive *kirtan* similar to *namakirtan*, usually singing the names of a deity.

Sampraday (sampradāy): Skt. lit. "transmission"; usually refers to a tradition of some kind, as in a tradition of ritual, thought, etc., also to a genealogy of practice.

Samsara (saṁsāra): Skt. lit. "going around"; the state and conditions of metempsychosis or transmigration in Hinduism, Buddhism, and Jainism. Often synonymous with "mundane life," the everyday toil of life, but also simply of the conditions of human existence.

Samvad (samvād): Skt. lit. "speaking together"; conversation; debate.

Sanga (Saṅga): Skt., Marathi, Hindi, lit. "association"; a social, political, or religious organization or community.

Sant: Skt. lit. "a good person"; in north Indian *bhakti* usually a designation of a religiously accomplished person, often a composer of songs, and commonly affiliated with *nirguna bhakti*; in Maharashtra, the term indicates any of the religiously accomplished figures associated with the Varkari lineage and does not pertain to *nirguna bhakti* especially; often glossed as "saint" or "saint-poet."

Santmat: Hindi, lit. "the thought [*mata*] of the *sants*"; in north India the general term for the broad array of *sant* figures from the fifteenth century onward and usually those associated with *nirguna bhakti*.

Sant paramparā: Marathi, Hindi, lit. "a genealogy [*parampara*] of *sants*."

Shabad (śabad): Punjabi (*śabda* in Skt., Marathi, Hindi, etc.) lit. "a word"; in Sikhism, the compositions of the Sikh Gurus or Sikh Bhagats, that is, any section of the *Guru Granth Sahib*.

Shaiva (śaiva): Skt. lit. "belonging to Shiva"; a designation for a person, place, or thing associated with Shiva, especially related to the worship of Shiva; often used to refer to those individuals and communities that worship Shiva in some form.

Shaka (śaka): Skt., one of two main ways of measuring the passing of years in India associated with Hinduism; the second is the Vikram year. The *shaka* year begins its count in 78 C.E. *Shaka* is sometimes referred to as the *śālivāhan* year after the king Shalivahan, and the year begins its count from Shalivahan's defeat of the king Vikramaditya (after whom the Vikram year is named).

Shastra (śāstra): Skt. lit. "command, instruction"; generally a "science" or knowledge system or a text that details a knowledge system.

Shimpi (śiṃpī): Marathi, lit. "tailor"; a caste (*jati*) name in Maharashtra; Namdev's caste in Maharashtra.

Shloka (śloka): Skt.; a type of verse, usually a couplet with sixteen syllables; most often in Sanskrit, but also in Marathi, Hindi, and other languages.

Shri (Śrī): Skt. lit. "light, luster, auspiciousness"; one name for Lakshmi, the consort of Vishnu, and in particular Lakshmi as depicted in the Shri Rangam temple in Tiruchirappalli, Tamil Nadu.

Shruti (śruti): Skt. lit. "that which is heard"; a classification of texts in Hinduism received divinely by ancient sages, especially the Vedas; usually juxtaposed with *smriti*, humanly devised texts.

Shudra (śūdra): Skt. the fourth and lowest of the fourfold *varna* hierarchy, often referred to as "caste" (see also *jati*).

Smaraṇ: Skt. lit. "remembering, memory."

Smriti (smṛti): Skt. lit. "memory"; the word's two primary meanings are (1) memory and (2) a classification of texts in Hinduism passed down from memory, that is, of human rather than divine origin (see *shruti*); in the latter category are texts such as commentary on the epics and legal texts.

Smritisthala (smṛtisthaḻa): Skt. lit. "the place [*sthala*] of memory [*smriti*]"; a memorial.

Takhallus (takhallus): Arabic lit. "ending"; the signature or ideograph of a poet composing in Persian, Urdu, etc.

Vahi (vahī): Skt., Marathi, Hindi, etc., lit. "diary"; in Marathi, refers to "notebook" used as a memory aid, similar to the *bada* (see above), and not necessary as a written document for archival preservation; cf. *pothi*.

Vaishnava (vaiṣṇava): Skt. lit. "belonging to Vishnu"; a designation for a person, place, or thing associated with Vishnu, especially related to the worship of Vishnu or associationed forms and deities, such as Krishna and Ram; often used to refer to those individuals and communities that worship Vishnu in some form.

Varkari (Vārkarī): Marathi lit. "the ones who do [*karī*] the pilgrimage [*vārī*]"; the title of the pilgrims who go to Pandharpur to visit the temple of Vitthal once or twice a year.

Varna (varṇa): Skt. lit. "appearance, color"; the theoretical socioreligious heirarchy of classes or "castes" enumerated in the Vedas and legal texts, consisting of four ranked parts: Brahmins, Kshatriyas, Vaishyas, and Shudras.

Vishnukirtan (viṣṇukīrtan): Marathi, Hindi, etc. lit. "repeating the glories [*kirtan*] of Vishnu"; a public devotional form that usually consists of repeating one or more of the names of Vishnu. See *harikirtan*.

Vitthal (viṭhṭhal): Marathi; the deity who is the principal object of devotion in Pandharpur and to Varkaris; also commonly called Viṭhobā and Pāṇḍuraṇga.

Yuga: Skt. lit. "a yoke"; refers to an age in mythic world time in Hinduism, usually associated with *vaishnavism*.

REFERENCES

Aarne, A., and S. Thompson. 1961. *The Types of the Folktale: A Classification and Bibliography*. Helsinki: Suomalainen Tiedeakatemia.

Abbott, J., and N. Godbole, trans. 1996 [1931]. *Stories of Indian Saints [Bhaktavijaya]*. Delhi: Motilal Banarsidass.

Adkar, S. K. 1972. *Hindī Nirguṇa-kāvya kā Prārambha aur Nāmdev kī Hindī Kavitā*. Allahabad, n.p.

Ajgaonkar, J. R. 1927. *Sant śiromaṇi Nāmdev Mahārāj āṇi tyānce Saṃkālīn Sant*. Baroda: Purushottama Atmarama Chitre.

Ali, D., ed. 1999. *Invoking the Past: The Uses of History in South Asia*. New York: Oxford University Press.

Amin, S., and D. Chakrabarty, ed. 1996. *Subaltern Studies IX: Writings on South Asian History and Society*. Delhi: Oxford University Press.

Anderson, B. 1983. *Imagined Communities*. London: Verso.

Appadurai, A. 1977. "Kings, Sect, and Temples in South India, 1350–1700 A.D." *Indian Economic and Social History Review* 14:1:47–73.

———. 1981. *Worship and Conflict Under Colonial Rule*. New York: Cambridge University Press.

———. 1996. *Modernity at Large*. Minneapolis: University of Minnesota Press.

Appadurai, A., and C. Breckenridge. 1976. "The South Indian Temple: Authority, Honor, and Redistribution." *Contributions to Indian Sociology* 10:2:187–211.

Asad, T. 1993. *Genealogies of Religion*. Baltimore: Johns Hopkins University Press.

Ashley, K., and P. Sheingorn. 1999. *Writing Faith: Text, Sign, and History in the Miracles of Sainte Foy*. Chicago: University of Chicago Press.

Ashton, G. 2000. *The Generation of Identity in Late Medieval Hagiography*. New York: Routledge.

Assmann, J. 1997. *Moses the Egyptian: The Memory of Egypt in Western Monotheism*. Cambridge: Harvard University Press.

——. 2006. *Religion and Cultural Memory: Ten Studies.* R. Livingstone, trans. Stanford: Stanford University Press.

Avate, T. H. 1908. *Sakaḷa Santa Gāthā.* Pune: Vijayādaśamī Prakāśan. [cited as SSG; for the edition used in this book see Sakhare, below.]

Azzolino, D. 1987. *Tale Type and Motif Indexes: An Annotated Bibliography.* New York: Garland.

Babar, S., et al. 1970. *Śrī Nāmdev Gāthā.* Bombay: Maharashtra State Government Printing Press. [cited as *NG*]

Babb, L., and S. Wadley, ed. 1995. *Media and the Transformation of Religion in South Asia.* Philadelphia: University of Pennsylvania Press.

Balbir, N., G. Pinault, and J. Fezas. 1996. *Langue, style, et structure dans le monde indien.* Paris: Université de Paris III/CNRS.

Barthes, R. 1977 [1968]. *Image, Music, Text.* S. Heath, trans. New York: Hill.

Barthval, P. D. 1936. *Traditions of Indian Mysticism Based upon Nirguna School of Hindi Poetry.* New Delhi: Heritage.

Bayly, C. 1983. *Rulers, Townsmen, and Bazaars: North Indian Society in the Age of British Expansion, 1770–1870.* New York: Cambridge University Press.

Beck, G., ed. 2005. *Alternative Krishnas.* Albany: State University of New York Press.

Bellah, R. N., R. Madsen, W. Sullivan, A. Swidler, and S. M. Tipton. 1985. *Habits of the Heart: Individualism and Commitment in American Life.* Berkeley: University of California Press.

Benjamin, W. 1968 [1936]. *Illuminations.* Hannah Arendt, ed. New York: Harcourt, Brace, and World.

Berger, P. 1967. *The Sacred Canopy.* New York: Doubleday.

Bhagat Ram, B. 1936. *śrī Svāmī Nāmdev.* Ghuman, n.p.

Bharadvaj, R. 1931 [1898]. "Jñāndev va Nāmdev Saṃkālīn Hote Kāy?" *Sudhārak,* December 5.

Bhave, V. L. 1963 [1898]. *Mahārāṣṭra Sārasvat.* Bombay: Popular Prakashan.

Binyon, L. 1921. *The Court Painters of the Grand Moguls.* London: Oxford University Press.

Blackburn, S. 1996. *Inside the Drama-House: Rama Stories and Shadow Puppets in South India.* Berkeley: University of California Press.

Blake, C. 1866. "On the Historical Anthropology of Western Europe." *Anthropological Review* 4:13 (April):158–165.

Bodnar, J. 1992. *Remaking America.* Princeton: Princeton University Press.

Borofsky, R. 1987. *Making History: Pukapukan and Anthropological Constructions of Knowledge.* Cambridge: Cambridge University Press.

Bourdieu, P. 1971. *Outline of a Theory of Practice.* R. Nice, trans. New York: Cambridge University Press.

——. 1984 [1979]. *Distinction.* R. Nice, trans. Cambridge: Harvard University Press.

——. 1993. *The Field of Cultural Production.* R. Johnson, ed. New York: Columbia University Press.

Bourdieu, P., and L. J. D. Wacquant. 1992. *An Invitation to Reflexive Sociology.* Chicago: University of Chicago Press.

Brass, P. 1974. *Language, Religion, and Politics in North India.* Cambridge: Cambridge University Press.

——. 2003. *The Production of Hindu-Muslim Violence in Contemporary India.* Seattle: University of Washington Press.

Braudel, F. 1958. "Histoire et sciences sociales: la longue durée." *Annales* 4: 725–753.

Breckenridge, C. 1995. *Consuming Modernity: Public Culture in a South Asian World.* Minneapolis: University of Minnesota Press.

Brown, D. 1988. *Hierarchy, History, and Human Nature: The Social Origins of Historical Consciousness.* Tucson: University of Arizona Press.

Brunschwig, H. 1965. "Un faux problème: l'ethno-histoire." *Annales* 20:2 (May):291–300.

Bryant, K. 1979. *Poems to the Child-God: Structures and Strategies in the Poetry of Surdas.* Berkeley: University of California Press.

Butler, T., ed. 1989. *Memory: History, Culture and the Mind.* New York: Oxford University Press.

Bynum, C. 1987. *Holy Feast and Holy Fast.* Berkeley: University of California Press.

——. 1991. *Fragmentation and Redemption.* New York: Zone Books.

Callewaert, W., and M. Lath. 1989. *The Hindi Padāvalī of Nāmdev.* Leuven: Departement Orientalistiek.

Callewaert, W., and B. Op de Beeck. 1991. *Devotional Hindi Literature, Vol. I.* Delhi: Manohar.

Carruthers, M. 1990. *The Book of Memory: A Study of Memory in Medieval Culture.* Cambridge: Cambridge University Press.

Castelli, E. 2004. *Martyrdom and Memory: Early Christian Culture-Making.* New York: Columbia University Press.

Certeau, M. de. 1988. *The Writing of History.* T. Conley, trans. New York: Columbia University Press.

Chakrabarty, D. 2000. *Provincializing Europe.* Princeton: Princeton University Press.

Chatterjee, P. 1986. *Nationalist Thought and the Colonial World: A Derivative Discourse?* London: Zed Books for the United Nations University.

——. 1993. *The Nation and Its Fragments.* Delhi: Oxford University Press.

Chatterjee, P., and A. Ghosh, ed. 2002. *History and the Present.* Delhi: Permanent Black.

Chomsky, N. 1975. *Reflections on Language.* New York: Pantheon Press.

Cohn, B. 1996. *Colonialism and Its Forms of Knowledge.* Princeton: Princeton University Press.

Colas, G. 1999. "The Criticism and Transmission of Texts in Classical India." *Diogenes* 47:2: 30–44.

Coleman, J. 1992. *Ancient and Medieval Memories: Studies in the Reconstruction of the Past.* Cambridge: Cambridge University Press.

Collingwood, R. G. 1994 [1946]. *The Writing of History.* New York: Oxford University Press.

Comaroff, J., and J. L. Comaroff. 1987. "The Madman and the Migrant: Work and Labor in the Historical Consciousness of a South African People." *American Ethnologist* 14: 2: 191–209.

Connerton, P. 1989. *How Societies Remember.* New York: Cambridge University Press.

Coombes, A. E. 2003. *History After Apartheid: Visual Culture and Public Memory in a Democratic South Africa.* Durham: Duke University Press.

Coon, L. 1997. *Sacred Fictions.* Philadelphia: University of Pennsylvania Press.

Cressy, D. 1989. *Bonfires and Bells: National Memory and the Protestant Calendar in Elizabethan and Stuart England.* Berkeley: University of California Press.

Crooke, W. 1896. *The Tribes and Castes of the North-Western Provinces and Oudh.* Calcutta: Office of the Superintendent of Printing.

Cutler, N. 1987. *Songs of Experience: The Poetics of Tamil Devotionalism.* Bloomington: Indiana University Press.

Dandekar, S. V., ed. 1953. *Śrī Jñāneśvarī.* n.p., n.p.

Date, Y., and C. Karve, ed. 1995 [1936]. *Mahārāṣṭra Śabda Koś.* Pune: Varada Books.

Davis, N. Z., and R. Starn, ed. 1989. *Representations* no. 26 (Spring):1–6.

Davis, R. 1993. "Indian Art Objects as Loot." *Journal of Asian Studies* 52:1 (February):22–48.

Deleury, G. A. 1960. *The Cult of Vithoba.* Pune: Deccan College.

Derrida, J. 1998 [1967]. *Of Grammatology.* G. Spivak, trans. Baltimore: Johns Hopkins University Press.

Desai, I., ed. 1969 [1912]. *Narasiṃha Mehta Kṛta Kāvya Saṃgraha.* Bombay: Gujarati Printing Press.

Deshpande, M. 1997 [1967]. *Marathi-English Dictionary.* Pune: Suvichar Prakashan Mandal.

Deshpande, P. 2002. "Narratives of Pride: History and Regional Identity in Maharashtra, India c. 1870–1960." Ph.D. dissertation, Tufts University.

———. 2007. *Creative Pasts: Historical Memory and Identity in Western India, 1700–1960.* New York: Columbia University Press.

Deshpande, V., ed. 1968. *Smṛtisthaḷa.* Pune, n.p.

Devi, P. 1996. *I, Phoolan: The Autobiography of India's Bandit Queen.* London: Little, Brown.

Dewey, J. 1927. *The Public and Its Problems.* New York: H. Holt.

Dharmvir. 1997. *Kabīr ke Ālocak.* New Delhi: Vani Prakashan.

———. 2000. *Kabīr: Naī Sadī Meṃ.* 3 vols. New Delhi: Vani Prakashan.

Dharwadker, V. 2003. *Kabir: The Weaver's Songs.* Delhi: Penguin Books India.

Dhere, R. C. 1984. *Śrī Viṭhṭhaḷa Eka Mahāsamanvay.* Pune: Shrividya Prakashan.

Dikshit, A. P. 1970. "Nāmdev kā Kṛtitva." *Rāṣtravāṇī: Santa Nāmdev Viśeṣāṅka* (October–November).

Dirks, N. 1990. "History as a Sign of the Modern." *Public Culture* 2:2:25–32.

———. 1993. *The Hollow Crown: Ethnohistory of an Indian Kingdom.* 2d ed. Ann Arbor: University of Michigan Press.

Doniger [O'Flaherty], W. 1995. *Other Peoples' Myths: The Cave of Echoes.* Chicago: University of Chicago Press.

Doniger, W., ed. 1999. *Encyclopedia of World Religions.* Springfield, MA: Merriam-Webster.

Duara, P. 1995. *Rescuing History from the Nation: Questioning Narratives of Modern China.* Chicago: University of Chicago Press.

Dwyer, R. 2006 *Filming the Gods: Religion and Indian Cinema.* London and New York: Routledge.

Eisenstein, E. 1979. *The Printing Press as an Agent of Social Change: Communications and Cultural Transformations in Early Modern Europe.* 2 vols. New York: Cambridge University Press.

Fabian, J. 1983. *Time and the Other: How Anthropology Makes Its Object.* New York: Columbia University Press.

Farquhar, J. N. 1920. *An Outline of the Religious Literature of India.* London: Oxford University Press.

Farriss, N. M. 1987. "Remembering the Future, Anticipating the Past: History, Time, and Cosmology Among the Maya of Yucatan." *Comparative Studies in Society and History* 29:3:566–93.

Faubion, J. 1993. "History in Anthropology." *Annual Review of Anthropology* 22:35–54.

Feldhaus, A., trans. and ed. 1983. *The Religious System of the Mahanubhav Sect: The Mahanubhav Sutrapatha.* New Delhi: Manohar.

———. 1984. *The Deeds of God in Rddhipur.* New York: Oxford University Press.

———. 1995. *Water & Womanhood.* New York: Oxford University Press.

———. 2003. *Connected Places: Religion, Pilgrimage, and Geographical Imagination in India*. New York: Palgrave Macmillan.

Feldhaus, A., and S. Tulpule. 1992. *In the Absence of God: The Early Years of an Indian Sect*. Honolulu: University of Hawaii Press.

Fentress, J., and C. Wickham. 1992. *Social Memory*. Oxford: Blackwell.

Filene, B. 2000. *Romancing the Folk: Public Memory and American Roots Music (Cultural Studies of the United States)*. Chapel Hill: University of North Carolina Press.

Fisher, J. 1992. "Scholarly Editing, Textual Criticism, and Aesthetic Value: The Garland Thackcray Edition Project, A Case Study." *Studies in the Novel* 24:3:309–321.

Flueckiger, J. 1996. *Gender and Genre in the Folklore of Middle India*. Ithaca: Cornell University Press.

Fogelson, R. D. 1974. "On the Varieties of Indian History: Sequoyah and Traveler Bird." *Journal of Ethnic Studies* 2:1:105–12.

———. 1989. "The Ethnohistory of Events and Nonevents." *Ethnohistory* 36:2: 133–47.

Foucault, M. 1977. *Language, Counter-Memory, Practice*. D. F. Bouchard and S. Simon, trans. Ithaca: Cornell University Press.

———. 1984 [1969]. "What Is an Author?" In *The Foucault Reader*. J. Harari, trans., and P. Rabinow, ed. New York: Pantheon Books.

Freitag, S. 1989. *Collective Action and Community*. Berkeley: University of California Press.

Fuller, C. J. 2001. "Orality, Literacy and Memorization: Priestly Education in Contemporary South India." *Modern Asian Studies* 35:1:1–31.

Garg, R., ed. 1960. *Bhaktamāl*. Vrindavan: Sri Vrindavan Dam.

Gay, P., ed. 1973. *The Enlightenment: A Comprehensive Anthology*. New York: Simon and Schuster.

Geertz, C. 1973. *The Interpretation of Cultures*. New York: Basic Books.

Gellner, E. 1983. *Nations and Nationalism*. Ithaca: Cornell University Press.

Gewertz, D. B., and E. Schieffelin, ed. 1985. *History and Ethnohistory in Papua New Guinea*. Sydney: University of Sydney.

Gharat, T. 1894. *Nāmdevāṃcyā āṇi Tyāṃcyā Kuṭumbātīl va Samakālīnasādhūṃcyā Abhaṅgāṃcī Gāthā*. Bombay: Tattvaviṣayaka Chāpakhānā.

Gold, A. 1988. *Fruitful Journeys: The Ways of Rajasthani Pilgrims*. Berkeley: University of California Press.

———. 2002. *In the Time of Trees and Sorrows*. Durham: Duke University Press.

Gondhalekar, R. S., ed. 1849. *Nāmadevakṛta Jnānadevācyā Samādhice Abhaṅga*. Pune: Jagadahitecchu Press.

———. 1892. *Nāmdevācī Gāthā*. Pune: Jagadahitecchu Press.

Goody, J. 1977. *The Domestication of the Savage Mind*. Cambridge: Cambridge University Press.

———. 1986. *The Logic of Writing and the Organization of Society*. Cambridge: Cambridge University Press.

———. 1987. *The Interface Between the Written and the Oral*. Cambridge: Cambridge University Press.

Goody, J., ed. 1968. *Literacy in Traditional Societies*. New York: Cambridge University Press.

Goody, J., and I. Watt. 1963. "The Consequences of Literacy." *Comparative Studies in Society and History* 5:3 (April):304–345.

Gordon, S. 1993. *The New Cambridge History of India: The Marathas 1600–1818*. Cambridge: Cambridge University Press.

———. 1994. *Marathas, Marauders, and State Formation in Eighteenth-Century India.* Delhi: Oxford University Press.

Goswamy, B. 1966. "The Records Kept by Priests at Centres of Pilgrimage as a Source of Social and Economic History." *Indian Social and Economic History Review* 3:2:174–184.

Grier, J. 1996. *The Critical Editing of Music: History, Method, and Practice.* New York: Cambridge University Press.

Guha, R. 1983. *Elementary Aspects of Peasant Insurgency.* Delhi: Oxford University Press.

Guha, S. 2004. "Speaking Historically: The Changing Voices of Historical Narration in Western India, 1400–1900." *American Historical Review* 109:4 (October):1084–1103.

Habermas, J. 1991 [1962]. *The Structural Transformation of the Public Sphere: An Inquiry into a Category of Bourgeois Society.* T. Burger, trans., with F. Lawrence. Cambridge: Massachusetts Institute of Technology Press.

Halbfass, W. 1990. *India and Europe: An Essay in Philosophical Understanding.* Delhi: Motilal Banarsidass.

Halbwachs, M. 1980 [1925]. *On Collective Memory.* Louis A. Coser, trans. New York: Harper and Row.

Hansen, K. 1983. "Sultānā the Dacoit and Harishcandra: Two Popular Dramas of the Nauṭankī Tradition of North India." *Modern Asian Studies* 17:2:313–331.

Hardgrove, A. 2004. *Community and Public Culture: The Marwaris in Calcutta.* New York: Columbia University Press.

Hari, V, ed. 1953. *Santasudhāsara.* New Delhi: Sasta Sahitya Mandala.

Harms, W. 1995. "Magnificent Obsession." *University of Chicago Magazine* 88:2 (December).

Hawley, J. S. 1979. "The Early Sur Sagar and the Growth of the Sur Tradition." *Journal of the American Oriental Society* 99:1 (January–March):64–72.

———. 1981. *At Play with Krishna: Pilgrimage Dramas from Brindavan.* Princeton: Princeton University Press.

———. 1983. *Krishna, The Butter Thief.* Princeton: Princeton University Press.

———. 1984. *Sur Das: Poet, Singer, Saint.* Delhi: Oxford University Press.

———. 1988. "Author and Authority in the *Bhakti* Poetry of North India." *Journal of Asian Studies* 47:2 (May): 269–90.

———. 2005. *Three Bhakti Voices.* New York: Oxford University Press.

Hayes, C. 1960. *Nationalism: A Religion.* New York: Macmillan.

Haynes, D. E. 1991. *Rhetoric and Ritual in Colonial India.* Berkeley: University of California Press.

Hegel, G. 1956 [1837]. *The Philosophy of History.* J. Sibree, trans. New York: Dover.

Hervieu-Léger, D. 2000 [1993]. *Religion as a Chain of Memory.* Simon Lee, trans. New Brunswick: Rutgers University Press.

Hess, L., and S. Singh. 1986. *The Bījak of Kabir.* Delhi: Motilal Banarsidass.

Hill, J., ed. 1988. *Rethinking History and Myth: Indigenous South American Perspectives on the Past.* Urbana: University of Illinois Press.

Hobsbawm, E. 1990. *Nations and Nationalism Since 1780: Programme, Myth, Reality.* Cambridge: Cambridge University Press.

———. 2000 [1969]. *Bandits.* London: Abacus.

Hobsbawm, E., and T. Ranger, ed. 1983. *The Invention of Tradition.* Cambridge: Cambridge University Press.

Horne, D. 1986. *The Public Culture.* London: Pluto Press.

Hutchinson, J. 1994. *Modern Nationalism*. London: Fontana.

Hutton, P. 1993. *History as an Art of Memory*. Hanover, NH: University Press of New England.

Inamdar, H. V. 1999. *Nāmā Mhaṇe*. Pune: Snehal Prakashan.

Inden, R., J. Walters, and D. Ali, ed. 2000. *Querying the Medieval: Texts and the History of Practices in South Asia*. Oxford: Oxford University Press.

Jacobsohn, G. J. 2005. *The Wheel of Law: India's Secularism in Comparative Constitutional Context*. Princeton: Princeton University Press.

Janardan, R. 1860. *Kavi Caritra*. Bombay, n.p.

Jog, V. H. 1925. *Śrī Nāmdevācā Gāthā*. Pune: Chitrashala Press.

Johnson, R., G. McLennan, B. Schwarz, and D. Sutton, ed. 1982. *Making Histories: Studies in History-Writing and Politics*. London: Centre for Contemporary Cultural Studies.

Jones, W., trans. and ed. 1796. *Institutes of Hindu Law or, The Ordinances of Menu, According to the Gloss of Culluca Comprising the Indian System of Duties, Religious and Civil*. London: Sewell and J. Debret.

Joshi, S. P. 1940. *Panjābāṁtīl Nāmdev*. Bombay, n.p.

Kamat, A., and R. C. Dhere. 1970. *Eka Vijay Yātrā*. Pune: Varda Books.

Karandikar, M. 1970. *Namdev*. New Delhi: Maharashtra Information Centre.

Karve, I. 1962. "On the Road: A Maharashtrian Pilgrimage." *Journal of Asian Studies* 22:1: 13–29.

Katre, S. M. 1954. *Introduction to Indian Textual Criticism*. Poona: Deccan College.

Kavitkar, G. V., R. M. Bongale, R. C. Dhere, A. Kamat, and V. M. Bachal., ed. 1980. *Caṃ dramā Jo Alāṃchana*. Pune: Namdev Samajonnati Parishad Prakashan.

Kavitkar, G. V., D. Kir, H. Inamdar, N. Relekar, and N. Mirajkar. 1970. *Śrī Nāmdev: Caritra, Kāvya āṇi Kārya*. Bombay: Government of Bombay Press.

Kemper, S. 1991. *The Presence of the Past: Chronicles, Politics, and Culture in Sinhala Life*. Ithaca: Cornell University Press.

Kennedy, M. 1985 [1907]. *The Criminal Classes of India*. Delhi: Mittal.

Khanolkar, G. D., ed. 1977. *Marathi Vagmaya Kosh*. Mumbai: Maharashtra Rajya Sahitya Samskriti Mandal.

Khare, R., and M. Rao, ed. 1986. *Food, Society, and Culture*. Durham: Carolina Academic Press.

Kiehnle, C. 1997a. *Songs on Yoga: Texts and Teachings of the Maharashtrian Naths*. Stuttgart: Franz Steiner Verlag.

———. 1997b. *The Conservative Vaisnava: Anonymous Songs of the Jnandev Gatha*. Stuttgart: Franz Steiner Verlag.

Klein, K. 1995. "In Search of Narrative Mastery: Postmodernism and the People Without History." *History and Theory* 34:4 (December):275–298.

———. 2000. "On the Emergence of Memory in Historical Discourse." *Representations* 69 (Winter):127–150.

Kolte, V. B., ed. 1986. *Śrī Cakradhara Līlācaritra*. Attributed to Mhaibhata. Mumbāī: Mahārāṣṭa Rājya Sāhitya-Sāṃskṛti Mandal.

Koparkar, G. 1997. *Pāyīk Nāradāṃce*. n.p., n.p.

Koratkar, K. R. 1926. "Nāmdevācī Narsī." *Bhārat Itihāsa Saṁśodhak Mandal* 7: 1–4.

Kulkarni, S. B. 1992a. "Sant Nāmdevgāthyātīl Cār Nāmdev." *Yugavani* 46 (July–August): 6–10.

———. 1992b. "Sant Nāmdevāṃcī Kāśīyātrā āṇi Mahikāvatīcī Bakhar." *Maharashtra Times* (Bombay), July 5.

———. 1992c. "Smṛtisthaḷātīl Nāmdev." *Yugavāṇī* 46 (May–June): 23–25.

———. 1993a. "Punjābātīl Nāmdev: Viṣṇudās Nāmā." *Nav Bhārat* (January–March): 44–57.

———. 1993b. "Santa Nāmdevāce Eka Āparanparik Pracinā Caritra." *Yugavāṇī* 47 (March–April):52–68.

———. 1995. "Sant Nāmdevāṃcī Assal Vaṃśāvaḷī." *Lokmat Sahitya*, July 9:2.

Kulkarni, S. R. 1998. *Sāhitya Setu*. Mumbai: Rajya Marathi Vikas Samstha.

LaCapra, D. 1998. *Writing History, Writing Trauma*. Baltimore: Johns Hopkins University Press.

Laine, J. 2001. *Shivaji: Hindu King in Islamic India*. Oxford: Oxford University Press.

Lal, V. 2003. *The History of History: Politics and Scholarship in Modern India*. New Delhi: Oxford University Press.

Lang, G. E., and K. L. Lang. 1990. *Etched in Memory*. Chapel Hill: University of North Carolina Press.

Latour, B. 1993 [1991]. *We Have Never Been Modern*. Cambridge: Simon and Schuster.

Le Goff, J. 1992. *History and Memory*. New York: Columbia University Press.

Lele, J., ed. 1981. *Tradition and Modernity in Bhakti Movements*. Leiden: Brill.

Lévi-Strauss, C. 1966. *The Savage Mind*. Chicago: University of Chicago Press.

Lohiya, K. 1997. *Kīrtan Mārgadarśikā*. Pune: Sharada Sahitya.

Lord, A. 1960. *The Singer of Tales*. Cambridge: Harvard University Press.

Lorenzen, D. 1978. "Warrior Ascetics in Indian History." *Journal of the American Oriental Society* 98:1:61–75.

———. 1991. *Kabir Legends and Ananta-Das's* Kabir Parachai. Albany: State University of New York Press.

———. 1996. *Praises to a Formless God: Nirguni Texts from North India*. Albany: State University of New York Press.

Luria, A. 1976. *Cognitive Development: Its Cultural and Social Foundations*. Cambridge: Harvard University Press.

Lutgendorf, P. 1991. *The Life of a Text: Rāmcaritmānas of Tulsidās*. Berkeley: University of California Press.

Macauliffe, M. 1906. *The Sikh Religion, Its Gurus, Sacred Writings, and Authors*. Oxford: Clarendon Press.

Machwe, P. 1968. *Namdev: Life & Philosophy*. Patiala: Pujabi University.

Madan, T. N. 1998. *Modern Myths, Locked Minds: Secularism and Fundamentalism in India*. Delhi: Oxford University Press.

Mahipati. 1890 [1762]. *Bhaktavijay*. Bombay: Nirnaya Sagar Press.

Mann, G. S. 1996. *The Goindval Pothis*. Cambridge: Harvard University Press.

———. 2001. *The Making of Sikh Scripture*. New York: Oxford University Press.

Mansukhani, G. 1982. *Indian Classical Music and Sikh Kīrtan*. New Delhi: Oxford University Press.

Masters, B. 1991. "The Distribution, Destruction and Dislocation of Authority in Medieval Literature and Its Modern Derivatives." *Romantic Review* 82:3 (May):270–285.

Matsuda, M. K. 1996. *The Memory of the Modern*. New York: Oxford University Press.

McGregor, R., ed. 1992. *Devotional Literature in South Asia: Current Research, 1985–1988*. Cambridge: Cambridge University Press.

McLeod, W., ed. 1980. *The B40 Janam-Sakhi*. Amritsar: Guru Nanak Dev University Press.

McLuhan, M. 1962. *The Gutenberg Galaxy: The Making of Typographic Man*. Toronto: New American Library of Canada.

———. 1964. *Understanding Media: The Extensions of Man*. New York: New American Library.

Miller, B., trans. 1986. *The Bhagavad-Gita: Krishna's Counsel in Time of War*. New York: Bantam Classic.

Minnis, A. 1984. *Medieval Theory of Authorship*. London: Scholar Press.

Mishra, B., and R. N. Maurya. 1964. *Sant Nāmdev kī Hindī Padāvalī*. Poona: Poona Vishvavidyalay.

Mokashi, D. 1987. *Palkhi: An Indian Pilgrimage*. P. Englbom, trans. Albany: State University of New York Press.

Molesworth, J. 1991 [1831]. *Marathi-English Dictionary*. 4th reprint. Pune: Shubhada-Saraswat Prakashan.

Monier-Williams, M. 1993 [1851]. *A Dictionary, English and Sanskrit*. London: W. H. Allen.

Mookerji, R. 1914. *The Fundamental Unity of India (From Hindu Sources)*. London: Longmans, Green.

———. 1921. *Nationalism in Hindu Culture*. London: Theosophical Publishing House.

Mooney, C. 1999. *Gendered Voices: Medieval Saints and Their Interpreters*. Philadelphia: University of Pennsylvania Press.

Narayan, K. 1989. *Storytellers, Saints, and Scoundrels: Folk Narrative in Hindu Religious Teaching*. Philadelphia: University of Pennsylvania Press.

Narayanan, V. 2003. "Embodied Cosmologies: Sights of Piety, Sites of Power." *Journal of the American Academy of Religion* 71:3:495–520.

Nath, J. 1983. *Namdev the Saint-Poet*. New Delhi: Namdev Mission Trust.

Nehru, J. 1946. *The Discovery of India*. New York: John Day.

Niezen, R. 1991. "Hot Literacy in Cold Societies: A Comparative Study of the Sacred Value of Writing." *Comparative Studies in Society and History* 3:2:225–254.

Nora, P. 1989. "Between Memory and History: Les lieux de mémoire." *Representations* 26 (Spring):7–24.

Nora, P., ed. 1992. *Les lieux de mémoire*. 7 vols. Paris: Les Frances, La République, Le Nation.

Nora, P., and L. D. Kritzman, ed. 1996. *Realms of Memory: Rethinking the French Past. Vol. 1: Conflicts and Divisions*. New York: Columbia University Press.

Novetzke, C. L. 2003. "The Tongue Makes a Good Book: History, Religion, and Performance in the Namdev Tradition of Maharashtra." Ph.D. dissertation, Columbia University.

———. 2004. "The Laine Controversy and the Study of Hinduism." *International Journal of Hindu Studies* 8:1–3:183–201.

———. 2006. "The Subaltern Numen: Making History in the Name of God." *History of Religions* 46:2 (November):99–126.

Ong, W. 1982. *Orality and Literacy: The Technologizing of the Word*. New York: Methuen.

Ortner, S. 1989. *High Religion: A Cultural and Political History of Sherpa Buddhism*. Princeton: Princeton University Press.

Orsini, F. 2002. *The Hindi Public Sphere 1920–1940: Language and Literature in the Age of Nationalism*. New York: Oxford University Press.

Overing, J., ed. 1985. *Reason and Morality*. New York: Tavistock.

Palshikar, Shreeyash S. 2007. "Breaking Bombay, Making Maharashtra: The Samyukta Maharashtra Movement 1950–60." Ph.D. dissertation, University of Chicago.

Pangarkar, L. R. 1933. *Śrī Dyānēśvar Caritra*. Gorakhpur, n.p.

Panikkar, K. M. 1985. *A Survey of Indian History.* Delhi: Discovery Publishing House.

Parry, M. 1971. *The Making of Homeric Verse.* Adam Parry, ed. Oxford: Oxford University Press.

Pataskar, P. N. 1935. *Śrī Santa Śiromaṇi Bālbhakta Śrī Nāmdev Mahārāj He Daroḍekhor Hote Kāy?* Pune, n.p.

Pauwels, H. 1996. *Krishna's Round Dance Reconsidered: Hariram Vyas's Hindi Ras-pancadhyani.* Richmond, Surrey, UK: Curzon.

Phelan, P. 1997. *Mourning Sex: Performing Public Memories.* New York: Routledge.

Phillips, K. 2004. *Framing Public Memory.* Tuscaloosa: University of Alabama Press.

Pinch, W. 1996. *Peasants and Monks in British India.* Berkeley: University of California Press.

Pollock, S. 1985. "The Theory of Practice and the Practice of Theory in Indian Intellectual History." *Journal of the American Oriental Society* 105:3 (July–September):499–519.

———. 1989. "Mimamsa and the Problem of History in Traditional India." *Journal of the American Oriental Society* 109:4 (October—December):603–610.

———. 1990. "From Discourse of Ritual to Discourse of Power in Sanskrit Culture." *Journal of Ritual Studies* 4:2:315–45.

———. 1998. "The Cosmopolitan Vernacular." *Journal of Asian Studies* 57:1 (February): 6–37.

———. 2001. "New Intellectuals in Seventeenth-Century India." *Indian Economic and Social History Review* 38:1: 3–31.

Prakash, G. 1990. "Writing Post-Orientalist Histories in the Third World: Perspectives from Indian Historiography." *Comparative Studies in Society and History* 32:2 (April):383–408.

———. 2000. "The Impossibility of Subaltern History." *Nepantla: Views from South* 1:2:287–294.

Prentiss, K. 1999. *The Embodiment of Bhakti.* New York: Oxford University Press.

Puranadas. 1888. *Janam Sākhī Śrī Svāmī Nāmdevjī kī.* n.p., n.p.

Raeside, I. 1989. *Gadyaraja: A Fourteenth Century Marathi Version of the Krsna Legend.* London: School of Oriental and African Studies, University of London.

Raghavan, V. 1966. *The Great Integrators: The Saint-Singers of India.* Delhi: Government of India's Ministry of Information and Broadcasting.

Rajwade, V. K., ed. 1924. *Mahikāvatīcī Bakhar.* Pune: Chitrashala Press.

Ramanujan, A. K. 1973. *Speaking of Shiva.* Baltimore: Penguin.

———. 1991. *Folktales from India.* New York: Pantheon.

Rampley, M. 2000. *The Remembrance of Things Past: On Aby M. Warburg and Walter Benjamin.* Weisbaden: Harrassowitz.

Rana, R. 1981. "Agrarian Revolts in Northern India During the Late Seventeenth and Early Eighteenth Century." *Indian Economic and Social History Review* 18:3 and 4:287–326.

Ranade, A. 1984. *On Music and Musicians of Hindoostan.* New Delhi: Promilla Press.

Ranade, R. D. 1933. *Mysticism in Maharashtra.* Pune: Aryabhushan Press.

Rao, V.N., D. Shulman, and S. Subrahmanyam. 2003. *Textures of Time: Writing History in South India 1600–1800.* New York: Other Press.

Relekar, N. N., H. Inamdar, and N. Mirajkar, ed. 1970. *Śrī Nāmdev Darśan.* Kolhapur: Namdev Samajonnati Parishad.

Richards, J. F., and V. N. Rao. 1980. "Banditry in Mughal India: Historical and Folk Perceptions." *Indian Economic and Social History Review* 17:1:95–120.

Ricœur, P. 2004. *Memory, History, Forgetting.* Chicago: University of Chicago Press.

Sakaḷa Santa Gāthā, see Sakhare, below.

Sakhare, N., ed. 1990a. *Śrī Nāmdev Gāthā [Sakaḷa Santa Gāthā]*. Pune: Varda Books.

——. 1990b. *Śrī Tukārām Gāthā [Sakaḷa Santa Gāthā]*. Pune: Varda Books.

——. 1990c. *Śrī Eknāth Gāthā [Sakaḷa Santa Gāthā]*. Pune: Varda Books.

Sant Namdev: 700th Birth Anniversary Souvenir. 1970. Delhi: New India Press.

Saussure, F. de. 1983. *Course in General Linguistics*. W. Baskin, trans. New York: McGraw-Hill.

Sax, W. 1991. *Mountain Goddess*. New York: Oxford University Press.

Schomer, K., and W. McLeod, ed. 1987. *The Sants*. Berkeley: University of California Press.

Sebastian, H. 1970. "William of Wheteley's (fl. 1309–1316) Commentary on the Pseudo-Boethius' Tractate *De disciplina scolarium* and Medieval Grammar School Education." Ph.D. dissertation, Columbia University.

Sen, S. 1996. "Passages of Authority: Rulers, Traders, and Marketplaces in Bengal and Benaras, 1700–1750." *Calcutta Historical Journal* 17: 1:1–39.

Sharma, K. 1987. *Bhakti and the Bhakti Movement*. Delhi: Munshriram Manoharlal Publishers.

Sharma, V. M. 1957. *Hindī ko Marāṭhī Santoṁ kī Din*. Patna, n.p.

Shillingsburg, P. 1996. "Editions Half Perceived, Half Created." *Studies in the Literary Imagination* 29:2 (Fall):75–88.

Shukla-Bhatt, N. 2003. "Nectar of Devotion: Bhakti-rasa in the Tradition of Gujarati Saint-Poet Narasinha Mehta (India)." Ph.D. dissertation, Harvard University.

Singh, M. 1949. *Bhakta Śiromaṇi Nāmdev kī Nāyī Jīvanī, Nāyī Padāvālī*. Ambala, n.p.

Singh, N. 1981. *Bhagat Namdev in the Guru Grantha*. Patiala: Panjabi University.

Slawek, S. 1996. "The Definition of Kīrtan: An Historical and Geographical Perspective." *Journal of Vaisnava Studies* 4:2:57–113.

Smith, A. D. 1986. *The Ethnic Origins of Nations*. Oxford: Blackwell.

Smith, J. D. 1977. "The Singer or the Song? A Reassessment of Lord's 'Oral Theory.'" *Man* 12:1 (April):141–153.

Smith, J. Z. 2001. "A Twice-Told Tale: The History of the History of Religions' History." *Numen* 48:2:131–146.

Smith, W. 2000. *Patterns in North Indian Hagiography*. Stockholm: University of Stockholm, Department of Indology.

Sontheimer, G. 1989. *Pastoral Deities in Western India*. Delhi: Oxford University Press.

Śrī Gurū Granth Sāhab. 1952. Amritsar: Shiromani Gurudvara Prabandhak Samiti.

Stocking, G. 1968. *Race, Culture, and Evolution: Essays in the History of Anthropology*. New York: Free Press.

Subandha, P. 1960. *Nāmdevarāyāṁcī Sārtha Gāthā*. Poona: Namdev Ram Mandir.

Sukthankar, V. 1933. *The Mahabharata*. Poona: Bhankarkar Oriental Research Institute.

Sturkin, M. 1997. *Tangled Memories: The Vietnam War, the AIDS Epidemic, and the Politics of Remembering*. Berkeley: University of California Press.

Talbot, C. 1991. "Temples, Donors, and Gifts: Patterns of Patronage in Thirteenth Century South India." *Journal of Asian Studies* 50:2:308–340.

Tassy, G. de. 1968 [1839]. *Histoire de la littérature hindoue et hindoustani*. 2d ed. New York: Burt Franklin.

Taussig, M. 1984. "History as Sorcery." *Representations* 7 (Summer):87–109.

Taylor, G. 1996. *Cultural Selection*. New York: Basic Books.

Terdiman, R. 1993. *Present Past: Modernity and the Memory Crisis*. Ithaca: Cornell University Press.

Thiel-Horstmann, M., ed. 1983. *Bhakti in Current Research, 1979–1982.* Berlin: Dietrich Reimer Verlag.

———. 1991. *Ramayana and Ramayanas.* Wiesbaden: Harrassowitz.

Toews, J. E. 2004. *Becoming Historical: Cultural Reformation and Public Memory in Early Nineteenth-Century Berlin.* Cambridge: Cambridge University Press.

Trainor, B. 1998. "The Origin and End of Modernity." *Journal of Applied Philosophy* (Oxford) 15: 2:133–144.

Tulupe, S. G. 1979. *Classical Marathi Literature: From the Beginning to AD 1818.* Wiesbaden: Otto Harrassowitz.

Tulpule, S. G., and A. Feldhaus. 1999. *A Dictionary of Old Marathi.* Mumbai: Popular Prakashan.

Turner, V. 1974. *Dramas, Fields and Metaphors.* Ithaca: Cornell University Press.

———. 1986a. *From Ritual to Theatre and Back.* New York: Performing Arts Journal Publications.

———. 1986b. *The Anthropology of Performance.* New York: Performing Arts Journal Publications.

Urban, H. 2001. "The Marketplace and the Temple: Economic Metaphors and Religious Meanings in the Folk Songs of Colonial Bengal." *Journal of Asian Studies* 60:4 (November):1085–1114.

van der Meij, D., ed. 1997. *India and Beyond: Aspects of Literature, Meaning, Ritual and Thought (Essays in Honour of Frits Staal).* London: Kegan Paul; Leiden: International Institute for Asian Studies.

van der Veer, P. 1988. *Gods on Earth.* Atlantic Highlands, NJ: Athlone Press.

———. 1994. *Religious Nationalism.* Berkeley: University of California Press.

———. 1995. "The Modernity of Religion." *Social History* 20:3 (October):365–371.

———. 2001. *Imperial Encounters: Religion and Modernity in India and Britain.* Princeton: Princeton University Press.

Varadachari, K. 1966. *Alvars of South India.* Bombay: Bharatiya Vidya Bhavan.

Varma, R. C., ed. 1993. *Mānaka Hindī Koś.* Ilahabad: Hindi Sahitya Sammelan.

Vaudeville, C. 1974. *Kabir.* Oxford: Claredon Press.

———. 1993. *A Weaver Named Kabir.* Delhi: Oxford University Press.

———. 1996. *Myths, Saints and Legends in Medieval India.* Vasudha Dalmia, ed. Delhi: Oxford University Press.

Vansina. J. 1960. "Recording the Oral History of the Bakuba—I. Methods." *Journal of African History* 1:1:43–53.

Varshney, Ashutosh. 2002. *Ethnic Conflict and Civic Life: Hindus and Muslims in India.* New Haven: Yale University Press.

Vyas, S. 1940. *Kuṁḍalī Samgraha.* Ujjain, n.p.

Vygotsky, L. 1962. *Thought and Language.* Cambridge: MIT Press.

Wakankar, M. 2003. "The Prehistory of the Popular: Caste and Canonicity in Indian Modernity." Ph.D. dissertation, Columbia University.

Warner, M. 2005. *Publics and Counterpublics.* New York: Zone Books.

White, H. 1975. *Metahistory.* Baltimore: Johns Hopkins University Press.

Wolf, E. 1982. *Europe and the People Without History.* Berkeley: University of California Press.

Woodmansee, M., and P. Jaszi, ed. 1994. *The Construction of Authorship: Textual Appropriation in Law and Literature.* Durham: Duke University Press.

Wyschogrod, E. 1998. *The Ethics of Remembering.* Chicago: University of Chicago Press.

Yandell, K., and J. J. Paul, ed. 2000. *Religion and Public Culture.* Surrey, UK: Curzon Press.

Yang, A., ed. 1985. *Crime and Criminality in British India.* Tucson: University of Arizona Press, for the Association for Asian Studies .

——. 1998. *Bazaar India: Markets, Society, and the Colonial State in Gangetic Bihar.* Berkeley: University of California Press.

Yerushalmi, Y. H. 1982. *Zakhor: Jewish History and Jewish Memory.* Seattle: University of Washington Press.

Youngblood, M. 2003. "The Varkaris: Following the March of Tradition in Western India." *Critical Asian Studies* 35:2:287–300.

Zelliot, E., and M. Berntsen. 1988. *The Experience of Hinduism: Essays on Religion in Maharashtra.* Albany: State University of New York.

INDEX

Italics numerals indicate illustrations

Carnatic Wars, 164

Caruth, Cathy, 40

caste, xv, xvi, 1, 4, 5, 6, 9, 10, 15, 19, 20, 23, 42, 43, 51, 55, 59, 60, 63, 67, 70, 76, 82, 87, 88, 89, 95, 125, 142, 151, 157, 158, 169, 177, 180, 181, 184, 193, 199, 201, 209, 210, 224–226, 228–232, 234, 239, 243, 254n24. *See also jati; varna*

Castelli, Elizabeth, 40

Caturdas, 56, 57, 182, 185

Caturvedi, Parashuram, 203

Chakrabarty, Dipesh, 23, 251

Chatterjee, Bankim Candra, 212

Chatterjee, Gayatri, 230

Chatterjee, Partha, 207, 211

Chaudhari, M.D., 199, 205

Chitrashala Press, Pune, 109, 196

Chitre, Dilip, 270n6

Christianity, xii, 8, 28, 125, 208, 209; Catholics and Jesuits, 174

Cidananda Baba, 78

Cohn, Bernard, 16

Cokhamela, 43, 54, 78, 79, 83, 120, 165, 233, 234

Colas, Gerard, 93

Collingwood, R.G., 37, 38

Colonial scholars. *See* "Orientalist" (colonial) history and thought

Communist Party, 199

Congress Party, 199, 208, 271n18

Criminal Tribes Act 1871, 169

Croce, Benedetto, 37

Crooke, William, 6

Cuomo, Mario, 217

Cutler, Norman, 15

Dadu/Dadu Panthis, 2, 60, 107, 158, 165, 180, 181, 258n64

Dagens, Bruno, 82

Dalit/"untouchable"/*mahar*, 43, 224, 226, 233, 234

Damashet (father of Namdev), 54, 232, 233

Damle, V.G., and S. Fattelal, 15, 242, 261n41, 272n3

Damodar Pandit, 45

Dandekar, G.N., 95

Dandekar, S.V., 197, 203

darshan, 9, 11, 86, 117, 233, 239

Das, Shyamsunder, 203

Dattatreya (*Namdevaci Adi Samadhi*), 55, 71, 72, 113, 166–168, 186–191, 226, 238

Daulatabad (Devgiri), Maharashtra, 142, 167, 189

Deccan College Pune: Library, 106; Postgraduate and Research Institute, 126

Deccan Sultanates, 139–141, 185, 198

de Certeau, Michel, 38, 124, 127, 130

Dehu, Maharashtra, 76, 106, 124, 206

Delhi, 46, 57, 71, 167, 184, 185, 189, 201, 202, 206; Sultanate, 45, 139, 167, 178, 184, 185

Derrida, J., 29, 94

de Sausarre, F., 7

Devaki, 113

Devanagari script, 105

devotionalism. *See bhakti*

Dewey, John, 13

Dhana, 53

dharma, 8, 10

Dharwadker, Vinay, 154, 155

Dhere, R.C., 200, 201, 203; and Ashok Kamat, 210

Dholpur, Rajasthan, 206

Dhule, Maharashtra, manuscripts, 51, 108, 113, 138, 141, 146, 150, 152, 260n10, 263n35

Dilthey, Wilhelm, 37

Dirks, Nicholas B., 16, 23, 169, 212, 250

D.K. Films, Bombay (*Patitapavan*), 197, 219

Dnyaneshvar. *See* Jnandev

Doniger, Wendy, 126

Duniyapur, Punjab, 206

Durkeim, Emile, 26, 28

Dwarka, Gujarat, 205

Dwivedi, Hazariprasad, 203

Eisenstein, Elizabeth, 129, 130

Eknath, 7, 76, 77, 79, 85, 89, 91, 111, 113, 117, 118, 123, 139–144, 147, 149, 150, 156, 181, 259n2, 272n4

English (language), xv, 5, 52, 92, 102, 106, 203, 208, 211, 252

ethnology/ethnography, 6, 30, 51, 52, 74, 84, 96, 244, 245, 252; ethnohistory/